PENGUIN BOOKS

GUY GIBSON

Richard Morris was born in 1947 and worked as a writer and lecturer in archaeology and history, prior to his appointment as Director of the Council for British Archaeology in 1991. He has also been made an Honorary Visiting Professor in the Department of Archaeology at the University of York. *Guy Gibson* is his fourth book; his first earned an award from the *Yorkshire Post* and in 1992 he was a Frend Medallist of the Society of Antiquaries of London. He lives with his wife and three children in Harrogate.

D0034107

Richard Morris

WITH COLIN DOBINSON

GUY GIBSON

PENGUIN BOOKS

PENGUIN BOOKS

Published by the Penguin Group
Penguin Books Ltd, 27 Wrights Lane, London W8 5TZ, England
Penguin Books USA Inc., 375 Hudson Street, New York, New York 10014, USA
Penguin Books Australia Ltd, Ringwood, Victoria, Australia
Penguin Books Canada Ltd, 10 Alcorn Avenue, Toronto, Ontario, Canada M4V 3B2
Penguin Books (NZ) Ltd, 182–190 Wairau Road, Auckland 10, New Zealand

Penguin Books Ltd, Registered Offices: Harmondsworth, Middlesex, England

First published by Viking 1994
Published in Penguin Books 1995
1 3 5 7 9 10 8 6 4 2

For permission to quote from published works the author and publishers
are indebted to Routledge (RKP) for extracts from *The Collected Poems of
Sidney Keyes*, edited by Michael Meyer; to Faber & Faber Ltd for
the excerpt from *The Collected Poems of Louis Macneice*, edited by
E. R. Dobbs; and to Michael Joseph Ltd for extracts
from Guy Gibson, *Enemy Coast Ahead*

Printed in England by Clays Ltd, St Ives plc

For Henry, Eva and Edward

We are no cowards, we are pictures
Of ordinary people, as you once were.
Blame us not nor pity us; we are the people
Who laugh in dreams before the ramping boar
Appears, before the loved one's death.
We are your hope.

Sydney Keyes, 'Neutrality', 16 July 1941

CONTENTS

LIST OF ILLUSTRATIONS

LIST OF MAPS

ABBREVIATIONS AND CODEWORDS

ABBREVIATIONS

AA	Anti-aircraft
AAF	Auxiliary Air Force
AC	Aircraftman
a/c	aircraft
ACM	Air Chief Marshal
ADC	Aide-de-camp
AFC	Air Force Cross
AGGTS	Air Ground Gunnery Training School
AI	Airborne Interception: nightfighter radar
Air Cdre	Air Commodore
AOC	Air Officer Commanding
AOC-in-C	Air Officer Commanding-in-Chief
AOS	Air Observer School
A/P	Aiming-point
ATC	Air Training Corps
ATS	Auxiliary Territorial Service
AVM	Air Vice-Marshal
Avro	A.V. Roe & Co. Ltd
B/A	Bomb-aimer
BASO	Base Air Staff Officer
BCATP	British Commonwealth Air Training Plan
BG Flt	Bombing Gunnery Flight
Capt.	Captain
CB	Companion of the Most Honourable Order of the Bath
CD	Canadian Forces Decoration
CFI	Chief Flying Instructor

C-in-C	Commander-in-Chief
CO	Commanding Officer
Cpl	Corporal
CR42	Italian biplane fighters, otherwise known as the Falco, named after Fiat's chief engineer Celestino Rosatelli
DCAS	Deputy Chief of Air Staff
DFC	Distinguished Flying Cross
DFM	Distinguished Flying Medal
DI	Daily Inspection
Do	Dornier
DR	Navigation by Dead Reckoning
DSO	Distinguished Service Order
e/a	enemy aircraft
E boat	German high-speed torpedo boat
EFTS	Elementary Flying Training School
F.541	The part of the ORB which details daily activities, listing aircraft, crews, bomb-loads, etc.
FG	Front Gunner
Fg Off.	Flying Officer
Flak	*Fliegerabwehrkanonen*: anti-aircraft artillery
FLO	Flak Liaison Officer
Flt Lt	Flight Lieutenant
Flt Sgt	Flight Sergeant
FTS	Flying Training School
GCI	Ground-controlled Interception
GP	General Purpose (bomb)
Gp Capt.	Group Captain
HC	High Capacity (bomb)
HCU	Heavy Conversion Unit
He	Heinkel
IAS	Indicated Air Speed
ICS	Indian Civil Service
IFF	Identification Friend or Foe
IFS	Indian Forest Service

Ju	Junkers
KG	*Kampfgeschwader*: Bomber wing
LAC	Leading Aircraftman
Lt	*Leutnant*
2 Lt	Second Lieutenant
Maj.	Major
MAP	Ministry of Aircraft Production
MEW	Ministry of Economic Warfare
MO	Medical Officer
MoI	Ministry of Information
MP	Military Police
NCO	Non-commissioned Officer
NFT	Night Flying Test
NSB	Dutch National Socialist movement; extreme right-wing party of neo-Nazi persuasion
OC	Officer Commanding
ORB	Operations Record Book
OSE	Old St Edwardian
OTC	Officers' Training Corps
OTU	Operational Training Unit
PFF	Pathfinder Force
Plt Off.	Pilot Officer
PPC	Prospective Parliamentary Candidate
RAAF	Royal Australian Air Force
RCAF	Royal Canadian Air Force
RDX	Research Department Explosive
RNAS	Royal Naval Air Service
R/T	Radio-telephony
SABS	Stabilized Automatic Bomb-sight
SASO	Senior Air Staff Officer
SBC	Small Bomb Carrier, for incendiaries
Sec. Off.	Section Officer
SFTS	Service Flying Training School
Sgt	Sergeant

SHAEF	Supreme Headquarters Allied Expeditionary Force
S/L	Searchlight
Sqn Ldr	Squadron Leader
SSQ	Station Sick Quarters
Sub-Lt	Sub-Lieutenant
TI	Target Indicator
Uffz	*Unteroffizier*: Luftwaffe equivalent of Corporal
u/s	unserviceable
USAAF	United States Army Air Force
VAD	Voluntary Aid Detachment
VHF	Very High Frequency
V-weapon	*Vergeltungswaffe*: reprisal weapon
WAAF	Women's Auxiliary Air Force
Wg-Cdr	Wing-Commander
W/T	Wireless-telegraphy

CODEWORDS

ABC	'Airborne Cigar': radio transmitter and German-speaking crew-member carried by Lancasters of 101 Squadron for jamming Luftwaffe fighter control frequencies
Asparagus	Southern sector of the Store Baelt ('Great Belt') between Danish islands of Fyn and Zealand
Broccoli	Northern sector of the Store Baelt between Danish islands of Fyn and Zealand
Carrot	Northern sector of Lille Baelt ('Little Belt') between Jutland and the Danish island of Fyn
Chastise	Operation using bouncing mine to breach German dams
Crossbow	Aerial operation against V-weapon site
Daffodil	Northern sector of Oresund ('The Sound') between Zealand and Sweden

Dinghy	Code for announcement of successful bombing of Eder dam
Forget-me-not	Area outside Kiel harbour
Freya	German early-warning radar
Gardening	Mine-laying by bombers
Gee	Radio-based navigational aid
Highball	Bouncing mine to be used against capital ships
H-hour	Opening time of attack
H2S	Ground-scanning radar used as bombing aid
Jack	Mönchengladbach and Rheydt
Jostle	Airborne transmitter designed to jam Luftwaffe VHF radio-telephone communications; introduced August 1944
Lettuce	Kiel canal
L1	Code for RAF Wellingore in 1940 and early 1941
Market-Garden	Allied airborne landings in Netherlands (Operation Market) combined with thrust by ground forces (Operation Garden), 17–25 September 1944
Millennium	Attack on Cologne by 1,000+ aircraft of Bomber Command, 30 May 1942
Moling	Daylight bombing sortie making use of Gee in conjunction with 8/10–10/10 cloud
Nasturtium training	Mine-laying sortie, often allocated to inexperienced crews
Nigger	Code for breaching the Möhne dam
Oboe	Radio-based navigational aid
Overlord	Invasion of northern France, June 1944
Pampa	Meteorological reconnaissance sortie
Ploughing	Bombing
Pointblank	Directive to Bomber Command and Eighth Air Force in June 1943 calling for a combined bomber offensive against the means of production of enemy fighters

QDM	Magnetic course to steer for base, assuming zero wind
QFE	Barometric pressure at airfield level
Quadrant	Summit conference in Quebec, August 1943
Salmon	Bremen
Serrate	Radar receiver to assist British nightfighters to home in on Luftwaffe airborne radar transmissions
Skate	Brunswick
Tallboy	12,000-lb medium-capacity bomb designed for deep penetration of the ground and subterranean detonation following release from high altitude and spin-stabilized fall
Tube Alloys	Atomic bomb research project
Undergo	Operation (September 1944) to remove Calais pocket
Upkeep	Bouncing mine used against German dams
V1	*Vergeltungswaffe 1*: Reprisal Weapon No. 1, the Fieseler 103 flying bomb ('doodle-bug')
V2	*Vergeltungswaffe 2*: Reprisal Weapon No. 2, the A-4 ground-to-ground rocket
Vegetable	Mine, delivered by bomber
Wanganui	Aerial flare, attached to parachute; 'skymarker'
WC1	Code for RAF Wellingore
Whitebait	Berlin
Window	Metal foil dropped to interfere with reception of German ground-based radar
X-Gerat	German radio-guided bombing aid
X-raid	[Operation against] Luftwaffe intrusion into British airspace

FOREWORD

by Noble Frankland

This book powerfully recalls to my mind the shock which I felt when I heard that Wing-Commander Gibson was missing, that he had failed to return from operations. The news tore across the airfields of England and I think my feeling was shared by almost all of those who, like myself, had been, or were, flying on operations in Bomber Command. He was the personification of all that we had wished to be and when we heard soon afterwards that missing meant dead, it seemed unbelievable and rumour became rife.

It was odd that this was so because we in Bomber Command were more than used to the loss of our comrades. Gibson, however, was special. Already for sixteen months, a long time in Bomber Command, he had been more than a comrade; he was a legend. We had virtually forgotten, or perhaps we never knew, that he was also a man.

Confronted with the Gibson legend, Richard Morris has set himself the task of deciding and explaining what he really was. Many aspirant biographers in their various fields have sought such objectives before, but there can be few who have faced a more difficult problem. A life which was over in twenty-six years is not an easy prospect; one which was distinguished by service in Bomber Command is still less so, for that was a very specialized way of living and is now not even thought of as admirable. A life which became a legend in its own time tends to harbour the myth and to resist the reality. I confess that, when he first told me of his intention, I wondered how Richard Morris would fare and even if his project would survive.

In the outcome, Richard Morris has not only succeeded; he has done so brilliantly, triumphantly and conclusively. He has taken the legend to pieces and reconstructed the man. In doing so, he shows us that Gibson, so far from being among the elect, gifted with all the virtues and skills, was, in fact, rather ordinary and not even endowed with average health. His achievements, therefore, now reappear as all the more remarkable. Gibson the real man is, indeed, a more heroic figure than Gibson the legend and Richard Morris emerges as an historical biographer of the first order, who has definitively set Guy Gibson in an abiding place, which legend and rumour might otherwise ultimately have denied him.

PROLOGUE

Guy Gibson was born about fourteen weeks before the end of the First World War and died a little less than eight months before the end of the Second. For most of the twenty-six years between he attracted little attention. At school he tried at much but excelled at nothing. His early career in the Royal Air Force was undistinguished, and was expected to end in 1939. Only after the coming of war did signs of special calibre begin to emerge, and then but gradually. His main achievement during the first year of war was to survive. Thereafter his combat experience became an accumulating asset, and for a time his resolution – an unusual strong-mindedness which was his main natural gift – had something definite at which to aim. This phase of success culminated in his leadership of the attack on the Ruhr dams in May 1943. Within days he found himself lionized and the most highly decorated airman in Britain's Empire. Between August 1943 and D-Day he became a celebrity in the United States, a protégé of Churchill, a Conservative Party candidate, a mass-media personality and the author of what has become one of the best-selling books to emerge from the Second World War. He was also unhappy. Forbidden to rejoin the war, he was as Samson shorn of his hair. Against their better judgement, his superiors succumbed to his pleading and allowed him to fly on occasional operations. Ill-prepared and over-confident, he was killed within weeks.

So much is well known. Yet until very recently surprisingly little was understood about Gibson as an individual. Apotheosized by the Air Ministry's publicity machine and Richard Todd's portrayal in Michael Anderson's film, he emerges from Paul Brickhill's book *The Dam Busters* as little more than a *Boy's Own* stereotype, and from his own as courageous, buoyant, irreverent and – at times – disarmingly naïve. *Enemy Coast Ahead* is an adventure story in which the writer is cast as a sometimes reluctant hero. It might almost be read as a statement of what Gibson had been told he was supposed to be. The problem lies in deciding what he really was.

Reconstructing a lost life from glimpses and echoes is difficult work, the more so when its adulthood had scarcely been reached. 'Good gracious – what are you going to find to write *about*?' asked a novelist friend. It was a fair question. The action has often been documented, but memories of the intense yet in many ways perfunctory relationships that characterized the wartime society of Bomber Command seldom take us close to Gibson as an individual. Writing to the father of a pilot who did not return from the Dams Raid, Gibson described him as 'a great personal friend'. He was, but they had only been acquainted for six weeks. Relationships measured in such snatches of time are remembered more for what men did than for what they were – or might have become. After half a century it is unsurprising that the most that may be recalled of a comrade is that he was a 'grand type', 'very press-on' or 'a charmer'.

Only those who knew Gibson well take us closer, and even then not always far. Susan Ottaway's account of his family background, written with the assistance of his sister, promises new detail about the tragic circumstances of his upbringing. In 1978 Gibson's wife Eve produced a short memoir which was incorporated in Jan van den Driesschen's book *De dammen brekers*, hitherto published only in Dutch. Eve's typescript, made available after her death, contains informative anecdotes but skirts crucial issues and is chronologically jumbled. Her portrait reveals surprisingly little about the man her husband was. Or is it surprising? They lived together under one roof for scarcely more than a year, and Eve herself later reflected that she never really knew him.

Ground crew recollections of 'Gibbo' are often vivid – a bustling, demanding figure, generally fair-minded, not above cracking a joke, but essentially despotic – yet seldom take us any distance into his hinterland. This is not their fault; as a rule Gibson did not mix closely with those whose duties did not expose them to danger. Or, as Air Vice-Marshal Cochrane carefully put it, 'his relations with his aircrews had a special intimacy which he was never quite able to achieve with his ground crews'. No indeed, and such were the distinctions of class and rank that much the same applied to many aircrew NCOs.

The private opinions of other senior commanders are even harder to ascertain. Coryton, Cochrane and Harris are dead, and perhaps only one of them might have explained why despite his achievements Gibson did not advance beyond the rank he held in April 1942, at the start of his first command. Publicly, Harris considered Gibson 'as great a warrior as these Islands ever bred' and noted his 'natural aptitude for Leadership, his outstanding skill and his extraordinary valour' which 'marked him early for command'. But these words occur in an encomium that introduces *Enemy Coast Ahead*. Next to them let us place the judgement of one of Gibson's former squadron commanders, who was impressed by his 'gutsy' temperament but denies that he was outstandingly gifted. In his opinion Gibson was 'fairly ordinary'. What was unusual about him was that he lived long enough for his staying power and experience to combine in the exercise of single-minded professionalism.

If perspectives from below and from above are elusive, there are others to be sought from the men with whom he flew, and the women to whom he opened his heart. Here is Gibson summoned back in the mind's eye of his great friend David Shannon:

The stance is aggressive – legs apart, knees and calves well braced, hands in trouser pockets or folded across the chest. The facial expression appears mildly pugnacious, with the lower jaw pushed forward and teeth clamped; but the clear eyes are a give-away, ever ready to break into a grin.[1]

The eyes are blue. Yet behind their remembered sparkle and promise of action or mischief lay a more complicated, contradictory and vulnerable figure. Gibson is remembered by all for his verve, by many as thrustingly opinionated and by others – generally his superiors, who knew him only slightly – as disarmingly modest. In fact, for much of the time he needed to impress, a tendency to which colleagues reacted in different ways, but seldom with indifference. As a leader he was both admired and feared. Impulsive, sometimes volcanic, he may have attracted more companions than friends. The real glow of his friendship, which could be unexpectedly tolerant, was reserved for a select group of comrades who shared his passion for operational flying. For them he was (in Shannon's phrase) a Pied Piper, whistling a tune they would – and often did – follow to the world's end.

Some of the contradictions can be resolved by his strongest traits: an ingenuousness which enabled him to confront people, relationships and tasks with unblinking directness; and versatility. This simplicity lent wholeheartedness to his friendships and frankness to his opinions, allowing him to enchant or antagonize with equal ease. We should also remember that features of personality can be modified by surroundings, circumstances, company kept and lessons learned – and that behaviour and responses change, particularly in early manhood, and very particularly under the stresses of war. The Gibson who dropped bombs, flew fighters and rallied, inspired or bullied hundreds of men and women, was forced to mature at an unnatural rate.

Gibson's unrelenting enthusiasm for operations fed rumours that he was unacquainted with fear, or driven by a desire for glory. However, he was not immune from the condition known to Bomber Command's medical analysts as 'flying stress'. Towards the end of his second tour of bomber operations, companions began to notice its symptoms of 'restlessness, irritability, or truculence'.[2] Among his men he remained outwardly steadfast; off-duty, in the arms of a girl-friend, gnawing an empty pipe which he 'used like a dummy', he broke down and wept. It was to women that he seems most often to have confessed his real feelings. Many of the most revealing insights into Guy Gibson come not from the men who shared his aircraft but from the women who shared his bed.

The question, then, is not whether Gibson knew anxiety, but how his fear was annulled. Once again, his childlike ingenuousness provides the key. When asked if he was frightened of dying, Gibson replied, 'No, not really. All my friends are up there waiting for me. When the time comes I shall be quite pleased to see them.' Until then his method was to live by the day, channelling his energy into whatever task was in hand – an operation, a party, a seduction. He awaited death with fatalistic equanimity, but dealt with it as an abstract, preparing for each mission as it came and never conceding his jeopardy in the given moment. This helps to explain why Gibson was least at ease with himself after he had been ordered to stop fighting. The truth is that war suited him. This is not to suggest that he enjoyed it, rather that safety threatened to rob him of the condition which had temporarily made him whole. The last operation was flown at his own insistence. From the outbreak of war he had been convinced that he would not live to see its end. Having survived almost long enough to prove himself wrong, he deliberately re-embraced the threat of death as one might some murderous seductress. He had done it before. On past occasions she had ignored him or fumbled. But on 19 September 1944 he caught her eye, and this time she made no mistake. Guy Gibson's death was unnecessary, and a self-fulfilling prophecy.

Just as Gibson's valour has been over-simplified, so the facts of his physical health belie the picture of robust well-being depicted in books and film. A migraine sufferer in his teens, at least once the victim of a severe infection of the inner ear, he also suffered intermittently from an arthritic condition of his feet which caused him considerable discomfort when walking. On the morning of the Dams Raid a doctor told him that he was unfit to fly. Disregarding pain and doctor alike, he flew anyway and, overnight, became a legend.

Gibson's selection to lead the Dams Raid was the culmination of a distinguished operational career which he had been exceptionally lucky to survive. The international fame which followed was less the end of a steady climb than a sudden lurch aloft, like an aircraft caught in a column of hot air. The Allies, Bomber Command and the British public all needed a resounding success at that point in the war. Churchill was in Washington and needed a diplomatic coup in that very week. Gibson's propaganda role was initially unwelcome to him, but the Ministry of Information triumphed and to a large extent succeeded in turning a complex human being into a stereotype.

So it is that in the half century since his death Gibson has assumed an iconic status. On the fiftieth anniversary of Operation Chastise, newspapers carried advertisements marketing a curious selection of mementoes. Statuettes of Gibson, cast models of Chastise aircraft and commemorative plates were offered at prices which anticipated buoyant sales. Books, articles and essays appeared, products of a Gibson industry which endlessly recycles familiar material about an individual who, like any icon, has become a simple symbol.

In attempting to look beyond the symbol, we find that biography is less a life reviewed than aspects of a life reinvented. Of course, biography relies upon sources which exist independently of the biographer, and to that extent it has a claim to reality. Only in a limited sense, however, can these materials be regarded as objective. Even mundane records are often partial and incomplete, their contents shaped by agendas, decisions or failures which may never be known. As for the testimony of those who were there, we must recognize the tendency for memories to be arbitrary and subversive in what they recall and withhold. Witnesses may dwell on particular episodes and images, bleach out others, or be self-censoring or revisionist for private reasons which never emerge. Eyewitnesses offer seductive insights, but can be as fallible as they are rewarding. Even some of Gibson's closest friends have reported details they have subsequently read about him, in the belief that this is what they observed.

Not everyone welcomes the biographer's work. There are some who would like the stereotype to remain untouched, and others for whom the past is out of bounds. 'Warts and all have no place in the history of a well-proved war hero,' wrote one of Gibson's contemporaries, who gently but firmly declined to talk about him. 'I do not live in the past,' was the message of another. Such reactions are understandable, but misapprehend the nature of history. Good historians do not fish the waters of time, hauling in truths like old boots, nor are they driven by escapist nostalgia. Nothing is achieved by turning our backs on the past, still less by seeking to reduce it to a series of incantatory statements, or a sacred text that may never be questioned. The practice of history is a natural and proper human compulsion. Fears that Gibson's heroic persona would be damaged are unfounded, for historians tamper with legends at their peril. Guy Gibson's image has a resilience which no mere biographer is likely to disturb. And it was never our aim to deconstruct the Gibson legend, only to discover why it is important, and why it works so well.

We can question the false atmosphere in which mundane and sometimes tragic reality is often dissembled. Most people are familiar with Gibson through the film *The Dam Busters*. Readers might be persuaded that the Dams Raid was not flown in romantic monochrome, nor was it led by a polished, calm and entirely clean-cut commander. Little credit was done to those involved in the Dams Raid by presenting their achievement as a triumph over largely technical problems. Gibson's resistance in the run-up to Chastise was so weakened by heavy responsibility, hazard and exhaustion that he developed a disfiguring carbuncle on the side of his face. In the midst of final preparations, knowing that he might not come back, he snatched a few hours to visit a girl he loved dearly. She had recently married another man in frustration at his own unavailability. Like the gouty feet, these are lines from a more vivid, messily human story.

This is a telling irony, for above all the public imagination holds Gibson as a 'clean' figure: a modern, handsome superhero whose reputation has never been challenged by controversy or the slide into doddery old age. In May 1943 the Dams Raid marked the beginning of a period in which the RAF found itself able to kill more and more civilians. In turn, the bomber offensive began to attract open criticism. It was also the point at which Gibson largely dropped out of the war. So in the post-war public mind he wasn't associated with the great firestorm raids, or any of the controversial operations flown by Bomber Command towards the close of hostilities. Gibson died before anyone, apart from the occasional American reporter, could try to engage him over the ethics or efficacy of strategic bombing. His view of the ethics was uncompromising. His opinion of the military effectiveness of the bomber offensive, on the other hand, was more complicated. By late 1943 Gibson had ceased to share (if he ever had) the certitude of his commander-in-chief about the war-winning capacity of Bomber Command, and he began to make potentially controversial speeches in which he said so.

Our purpose in raising these matters is not to urge a revision in anyone's moral judgement of Gibson as an individual, still less to criticize the unavoidable campaign in which he played a distinguished part. It is simply to draw a contrast between perception and reality. The wartime RAF contained a number of individuals who would have been outstanding in almost any field of life. Gibson, arguably, was not among them. In the opinion of a good number who knew him well, he was not a born leader. Guy Gibson was a fairly ordinary, high-spirited, aircrew officer who survived long enough to be given unusual opportunities. He achieved greatness because his combat experience was backed by a practical application of rules of leadership which he had learned: the need to unify his squadrons behind clear aims, to communicate those aims with confidence and to balance discipline with the enlistment of hearts. The disservice done him by popular imagination has simply been to present him as something he was not. We shall find plenty to revere in what he was.

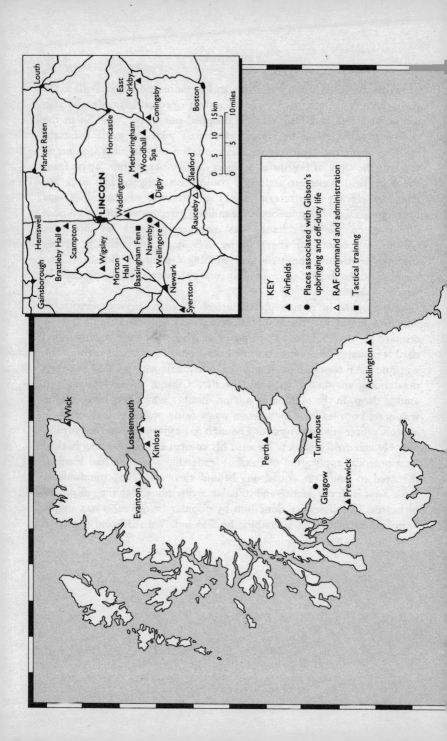

KEY

▲ Airfields

● Places associated with Gibson's upbringing and off-duty life

△ RAF command and administration

■ Tactical training

Louth

East Kirkby ▲

Coningsby ▲

Boston ●

Market Rasen

Horncastle

Metheringham ▲
Woodhall Spa ▲

LINCOLN ●

Waddington ▲

Digby ▲

Sleaford

Rauceby △

15 km

10

5

0

10 miles

5

0

Gainsborough

Hemswell ▲

Bratleby Hall ●

Scampton ▲

Wigsley ▲

Morton Hall △

Bassingham Fen ■

Navenby ●

Wellingore ▲

Newark

Syerston ▲

Wick ▲

Lossiemouth ▲

Kinloss ▲

Evanton ▲

Glasgow ●

Perth ▲

Turnhouse ▲

Prestwick ▲

Acklington ▲

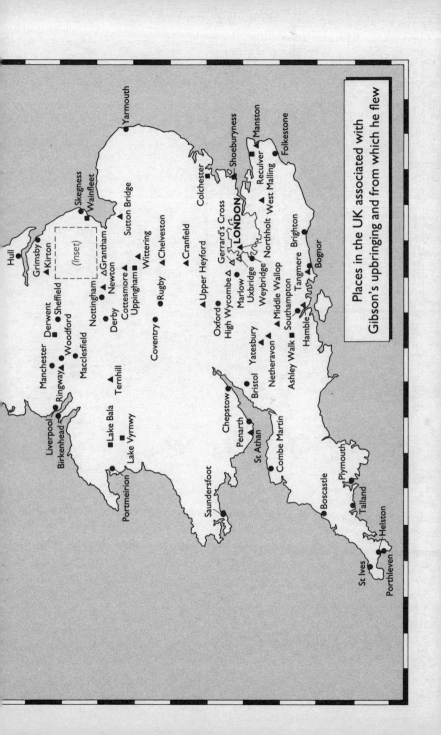

Places in the UK associated with Gibson's upbringing and from which he flew

Part One

BOYHOOD

1918–1937

There is a history in all men's lives
Figuring the natures of the times deceased,
The which observed, a man may prophesy,
With a near aim, of the main chance of things
As yet not come to life, which in their seeds
And weak beginnings lie intreasuréd.

Henry IV, Part 2, III.i

Families

In 1913 Leonora Mary Strike completed her education in a Belgian convent and returned to her prosperous seafaring family in the Cornish fishing port of Porthleven. Nora's father, Edward Carter Strike, was a master mariner; her grandfather had commanded clippers. Captain Strike and his wife Emily lived in a new house poised on the cliffs of Breage Side. One of several daughters, Nora had a lively temperament, artistic abilities and fine looks. Men were drawn to her.

One of them was Alexander James Gibson, a 37-year-old officer of the Imperial Indian Forest Service who was introduced to Nora that year while in England on furlough. Charles Allen might have had Alexander in mind when he observed that,

The British penetration of India in the eighteenth century had provided '. . . a vast system of outdoor relief for Britain's upper classes', chiefly for the younger sons of the country gentry – sons of the manse from Scotland and Ulster, in particular – who found in India a means of restoring their family fortunes without losing their status. In time this aristocracy of working gentlemen formed itself into 'official' India, and was made up of civil and military officers.

Within this dynastic tradition

sons followed their fathers for as many as five or six generations, the eldest son trying for the Indian Civil Service, the second for the Indian Army or the police and so on. Some families tended to specialize, concentrating on one particular occupation . . .[1]

It was so with Alexander's commission in the Indian Forest Service. One of his ancestors had founded it.*

---

* This was another Alexander Gibson, born at Laurencekirk, Kincardineshire, in 1800. His first career was in medicine. In 1825 he joined the East India Company, exchanging his medical career in 1838 for that of Superintendent of the botanical gardens at Dapuri. In 1843 he became the first conservator of the newly founded Forest Service. Alexander died in 1867. An appreciation of his life in the *Proceedings* of the Linnaean Society (of which he was a Fellow) for 1866–67 described him as a man of tough constitution, extreme energy and zeal: qualities which resemble those credited to Guy nearly eighty years later.

Alexander, however, had been born in Russia, to which the Gibson enthusiasm for overseas service had been temporarily transferred in the 1860s, a time when British and German engineers, scientists and business-men found growing opportunities in the east. Charles John Gibson, Alexander's father, appears to have worked first in St Petersburg. In about 1870, after the early death of an English wife with whom he may have had three children, he moved to Moscow and remarried. His second wife was Russian, and with her Charles had two more children: a girl, Vera, and a boy, Alexander James, who was born on 15 May 1876.

Alexander – known within the family as A.J. – returned to Edinburgh to complete his education, but his Moscow childhood gave him a fluent command of Russian. At school A.J. was a serious-minded student with a strong interest in mathematics, and a month after his eighteenth birthday he resumed the family tradition by preparing for entry to the Indian Forest Service.

Probationary foresters were educated at the Royal Indian Engineering College at Cooper's Hill, near Staines. The entrance examination gave prominence to English and maths, natural sciences and languages, none of which appear to have given A.J. any difficulty when he sat the examination in June 1895. He passed the medical board at the India Office and met the further test of being unmarried.

A.J. was one of seven students who went to Cooper's Hill to read Forestry that September. The IFS was a senior government service, socially superior to the army, and the intensive training it demanded left no time for undergraduate indolence. A.J.'s studies included geometrical drawing, forest engineering, accountancy, mechanics, organic chemistry, geology and mineralogy, as well as botany and entomology. In addition there were compulsory drill, gymnastics and riding to prepare for a life on the move. Last but not least, there was instruction in social deport-ment to ready him for the intricate formalities of Anglo-Indian society.

A.J. did well, and in November 1898 he was duly rewarded with a contract as assistant conservator of forests at a salary of 350 rupees per month. His first assignment was to the Kangra division of the Punjab, where the IFS controlled some 9,000 square miles of forest. In 1905 he became an instructor at the Imperial Forest School at Dehra Dun in the Himalayan foothills, being promoted to deputy conservator in the following year.

A.J. was encouraged to investigate the exploitation of resin, a product of *chir* pine from which turpentine could be extracted. He established an experimental distillery, and in 1908 he travelled to France and the United States to study distillation technology. On his return he was appointed assistant to the superintendent of Simla Hill States, and set up two new distilleries near Lahore.

And now he was back in England. Whether he was actively looking for a wife or simply smitten by Nora, his courtship of the handsome teenager followed a well-understood social pattern. The masculine world of the Indian Civil Service and army created a large demand for potential brides, and it was common for members of the ICS and IFS to look for wives at Home between tours of duty. Such matches were often marked by large differences of age. Early marriage for fledgling IFS officers was strongly discouraged, and their low salaries usually ruled it out. It was only when IFS staff gained seniority in their later twenties that they began to consider marriage. Older still, A.J. was outstandingly eligible, the more so for being fit and good-looking.

Whether for love or pragmatism, therefore, and whatever reservations may have existed in Nora's family, in October 1913, about a month after Nora's nineteenth birthday, A.J. asked Edward Strike for his daughter's hand. The engagement was announced on 1 November and the wedding took place at Porthleven's Wesleyan Chapel a month later. The town had seen nothing like it for years. A few weeks later the couple were bound for India. Catapulted from Cornwall to the Punjab, Nora had only the sketchiest idea of what awaited her.

India

British governance was represented more impressively in Lahore than Truro, but away from the Mall, the public architecture and tidy civil lines, India was a shock; her contrasts of wealth and poverty, raucousness and subtlety, the distances, landscapes, smells, diseases, customs, veiled resentments, heat, insects – everything was new. Strange too was Nora's role as mistress of a household attended by servants whose language she did not understand. Beyond this, the wife of a burra sahib had standards and loyalties to uphold and a complicated web of social conventions with which she was expected to comply.

Nora had joined an élite circle. Postings to the Punjab were envied, and A.J.'s ascent of the IFS order had taken him to a senior position in the provincial capital. In Lahore Nora enjoyed considerable luxury and a concentrated social life. During the Cold Weather a suite of rooms was at the Gibsons' disposal in Nedou's Hotel, a large establishment on the Mall. With the onset of the Hot Weather in May the Gibsons withdrew from the plains to their rented bungalow in the cooler air of the hill-station at Simla. Set within its own compound, the bungalow was of superior type, with lofty whitewashed rooms, a broad arcaded veranda and a porch.

They gave it a Cornish name – Talland – and were waited upon by a staff that included a cook, head bearer, bearers, liveried orderlies and, in due course, an ayah. Unlike wives who languished in boredom when their husbands went up-country, Nora was venturesome. She accompanied A.J. on his tours, their expeditions assisted by a retinue of bearers and sometimes an elephant or two which bore items of drawing-room furniture for their camps in the forest.

News of war reached Simla a few months after Nora's arrival. The Punjab IFS staff of nine officers, inadequate even for peacetime purposes, was now further depleted by the departure of three members into the Indian Army Reserve. The six who remained, A.J. among them, laboured to satisfy the greed of the Indian Munitions Board for war materials. From the province came firewood, timber for railway sleepers, tent-poles, lance-staves, bamboo for hutting and, following A.J.'s enterprise, turpentine. Nora, by contrast, had little to do. Surrounded by servants, her first months offered ample leisure to cultivate pastimes, to explore Simla and become acquainted with Alexander's friends.

Simla was glamorous. Spread along a curving ridge in the Himalayan foothills, overlooked by the viceregal palace on its knoll, this was the summer capital of government. Even in wartime its social life was unparalleled. The Mall, denied to Indians and motor vehicles alike, was the exclusive arena of the British pedestrian who could promenade between the dignified mansions that lined it. There were receptions, regimental balls, garden parties, amateur dramatics and events in fancy dress. A.J.'s status ensured invitations to dinners preceded by champagne and liberal measures of spirits. Round about there were shady walks and spectacular waterfalls which made good venues for leisurely picnics. At Talland admiring callers abounded, and photographs of handsome officers begin to appear in Nora's album. After Porthleven, it was thrilling.

Nora was soon pregnant. The Gibsons' first child, a boy, was born at Talland in June 1915. The infancy of Alexander Edward Charles Gibson – invariably known as Alick – can be followed in 'Baby's Biography', a kind of infant's logbook which Nora had brought from England. She enthusiastically filled in the sections devoted to such matters as Baby's First Toy (a little red man), Baby's Vaccination (23 October) and Baby's Food (firstly, Robinson's Patent Barley, barley water, and special milk). The headings are interspersed with florid illustrations, spaces for comments and photographs and vacuous verses. 'Creepity crawlity over the floor / Off on your first independent explore' begins one which accompanies the page entitled Baby's First Crawl. Nora duly entered the details: 'Baby made *his* first experimental crawl on the *21st* day of *February*. This statement is vouched for by *Nurse Jane Davis*. The distance covered was 2 *inches*.' Other verses plumb depths of mawkishness not even approached by Victorian ballads. Some of Nora's own entries rival their sentimentality and suggest an idealized view of motherhood which her numerous servants no doubt helped to sustain.

As the months passed Nora began to lose interest in the Biography. This is a pity, because a continuation would later have provided more information about Guy. But some entries are revealing. In the section headed 'Quaint Failings' Nora noted that at the age of eighteen months Alick spoke Hindustani and very little English. At two years Alick was speaking a hybrid of the two tongues. This was normal: like most other infants from families of quality, Alick saw more of his ayah than of his mother.

Nora's three pregnancies came in quick succession. Joan was born in August 1916, Guy just over two years later, on 12 August 1918. Guy was christened by Harold Wheeler, an Indian Army chaplain and friend of the family. As the elder son, Alick had been awarded a name that ran back in the family for over a century. Guy's first name was prompted by that of a family friend in Simla. Penrose, his middle name, derives from a place on the high road between Helston and Porthleven, once the seat of the Penrose family.

Nora was still only in her early twenties. Relieved of household chores and the mundane tasks of motherhood, she seems to have enjoyed her children, and by a later account Guy's infancy in India was happy. Children often flourished emotionally under the affection lavished upon them by doting servants. The chota sahibs Alick and Guy and missy baba Joan had bearers to attend to their wishes, and were cared for in turn by several ayahs, one of them a Eurasian nurse to whom they became devoted. (Even for infants, however, nanny's place in the social order was never forgotten. British children in India were bred from the cradle with a facility for issuing peremptory commands.) Whether playing outdoors, attending parties with other children, camping at Naldera, visiting distant cities, or being carried in baskets by bearers on tour, the early upbringing of the Gibson children was full of vivid experiences and warmth.

However, the childhood paradise was deceptive. India was a dangerous place for the sickly or unwell, and at the age of six Alick contracted infantile paralysis. Fortunately, he made a good recovery, although the attack left him slightly lopsided. Servants in the Gibson household applied their own remedy, encouraging Alick to go about with a dead chicken tied under his arm. This was a harbinger of drastic change. However happy young children might be, convention insisted that the influence of Indian servants would eventually become morally infective. Local schools, though often perfectly adequate, were regarded as suitable only for the sons of tradesmen. Hence, at six or seven, sometimes sooner, children of parents in the Gibsons' circles would be sent to boarding-school in a distant, chilly and unfamiliar land called Home.

In 1922 the children had a glimpse of Home when Nora took them to England for a holiday at Porthleven. Guy was now four, just old enough for small episodes of the long voyage from Bombay to lodge in his memory. In Porthleven the children encountered a new category of people called relatives. In place of orderlies and bearers there were smiling young aunts, very young cousins and Edward and Emily Strike, who hugged their grandchildren for the first time. Here too was the sea, hitherto only viewed from the deck of a steamer. With his brother, sister and other young relatives Guy was taken for picnics on nearby beaches where he dabbled in rockpools. When it was too stormy to go out, he could stare at the sea from the front windows of the clifftop house.

Back in the Punjab A.J. was now chief conservator of forests, and Guy's Indian childhood had barely a year to run. A boarding-school had been found for Alick, and it was decided that Nora should return to England as the younger children embarked upon their schooling. The pain of this decision was eased neither by the fact that sundered families were a norm for English children brought up in India, nor by the convention that any distress should be stoically concealed. But Alick, Joan and Guy were more fortunate than some. Air Chief Marshal Sir Arthur Harris, C-in-C Bomber Command, never forgot the banishment of his childhood. A couple of decades before, when George and Caroline Harris decided to send their five-year-old son away from India to school in England, he was 'left parentless and effectively homeless in order to receive an education in keeping with the official status of his family'.[2] But whereas Arthur was 'thrust into the care of so-called baby farms ... run by impecunious generals' daughters and vicars' wives', the Gibson children at least had contact with loving grandparents and a network of relatives.

So it was that in 1924 Guy had said goodbye to his ayah, given Mollie the fox terrier a final hug, and ridden for the last time in his father's majestic car. Six years old, he was back in England, awaiting school.

Separations

It appears that the Gibsons' marriage was under stress before the children were sent home and the decision that Nora should go with them may have been taken in acknowledgement of an ailing relationship. Intellectually austere and nearing fifty, A.J.'s mainspring was duty. Just thirty, good-looking and adventurous, Nora's liking for amusement perhaps outstripped A.J.'s ability to provide it. When the excitement of her fairy-tale marriage and the novelty of producing children had faded, India's opportunities for social drinking and flirtation began to replace them.

Whatever happened, Nora did not readjust well to life in England. For ten years she had been accustomed to material and social privilege. Abruptly deprived of both, her drinking approached the threshold of alcoholism. Nor did the prospect of lengthy terms of celibacy hold appeal. Sexually restless, Nora embarked upon an ill-concealed affair.

How soon Nora's behaviour began to impinge on her children we do not know. Alick was sent to preparatory school at Folkestone, while Joan was placed in a Cornish boarding-school. The school took male siblings up to the age of eight, and Guy went with her. From the age of six, therefore, Guy was removed from his mother for more than half the year. Perhaps it was just as well: Nora became increasingly volatile, sometimes alarmingly so, and the children's absences to some extent shielded them from their mother's increasingly erratic behaviour.

During holidays the lives of Guy and Joan were semi-nomadic, at some times staying with Nora in various hotels and rented accommodation, at others with relatives, most often with their grandparents in Porthleven. Grandmother Emily was a cheerful, homely lady who cared well for the children. Nearly twenty years later Guy looked back with nostalgia to these days, recalling Edward Carter Strike's love of his garden, and the fishermen who congregated beside the harbour basin on summer evenings.

Guy became fascinated by the harbour and by the life which revolved around it. At low tide on warm days he breathed its mingled smells of mud, seaweed and oil, and wandered between the pots, nets and tarpaulins which were laid out to dry. Sometimes he walked to the end of the pier to watch fishing boats departing to sea, pitching on the swell. When the tide was high he might join the company which gathered to see them return. At intervals a steamer – typically laden with coal, building materials and fertilizer – would negotiate the hundred-foot harbour entrance. Such arrivals were big events, accompanied by gatherings of bystanders and their sweethearts, the blast of sirens and shouts of enthusiastic children. Guy never forgot these scenes. Along with his grandfather's stories, they awakened a keen interest in boats and an abiding love for Porthleven's union of romance and practicality: characteristics rather similar to his own.[3]

For all these compensations, Guy's upbringing remained in partial shadow. In later life he was extremely guarded about the effects of his parents' behaviour, confessing little even to close friends. A.J. was more frank. Writing after Guy's death, he reflected sadly: 'His early years were not happy ones, and I could do so little to help.'[4]

When at the age of eight Guy followed Alick to St George's Preparatory School in Folkestone, A.J. was still on the other side of the world. After the children returned to England, he became conservator of forests in Bihar and Orissa, his last posting until retirement from the IFS in November 1929. However, in 1928 he was commissioned to report upon the establishment of a forest products laboratory in Australia, and in the following year his consultancy skills were put to further use in a report on power development for the Australian parliament.

Once back in England A.J. embarked upon a second career as a senior official in the Department for Scientific and Industrial Research. His unusual spectrum of skills – including Russian, mathematics and industrial planning – prompted gossip that he was working for British Intelligence. Perhaps he was; his government consultancy work continued well after final retirement and took him abroad during and after the war. However, the Department had a Forest Products Research Board and such evidence as there is suggests no more than that the expertise he had acquired in India was being put to logical use at home. A.J. took a flat in Flood Street, Chelsea. His contacts with the children were infrequent and emotionally distant.

Meanwhile, Guy's childhood continued along a well-worn itinerary for sons of the Imperial Service. Douglas Bader's childhood and education bear a close resemblance to those of Guy: his mother, Jessie McKenzie, was eighteen when she married Frederick Bader, twenty years her senior, in India. Douglas spent his infancy in India, there was a return to England and he was educated at a prep school in a south coast town – and St Edward's, Oxford.

School

Guy arrived at St Edward's School, Oxford, in September 1932, aged just fourteen, to begin a public-school career which would be largely undistinguished. The new school was harsh after St George's, and still took much character from its founder. Thomas Chamberlain had been an ascetic man, a stalwart of the Oxford Movement, who believed that life in Victorian Britain was too soft. Chamberlain set out to found a school where a rigid High-Anglican education could be had for reasonable fees. By 1932 the cost of educating a child at St Edward's was £120 a year – roughly half the outlay required by Eton or Winchester. Today St Edward's has a relaxed and liberal atmosphere. In the early 1930s it was quite different.

Alick had preceded his brother to the school, and Guy was allocated to his house, Cowell's, which then still retained signs of its origins as a detached stockbroker's villa, over the road from the main school. Inside, the building had been converted by the creation of small, cell-like day rooms for the boys and communal dormitories. Bounded by a cinder path and backed by sheds, the slightly shabby building looked out over a vast expanse of playing fields – the domain of the 'Gods', and training ground for Peter Cranmer, a school prefect in Guy's first year who in 1933 passed directly into the England XV. Beyond lay the spires of Oxford.

Alick no doubt warned his brother of the initiation which awaited him: the obligation to mount a table, recite poetry or sing and generally account for oneself at the whim of older boys. At the end, the victim was required to lower his shorts. New boys were imprisoned in Eton collars for the first few terms and had to wear all jacket buttons fastened. Senior boys and masters required subservience. Both specified a system of hierarchy, obligation and predetermined routine to which new arrivals were required to submit.

Guy did not immediately fit in. Initially he was lonely, taunted for being small and persecuted for his habit of attaching himself to others in a craving for friendship. Despite the protection of his elder brother, Guy was unpopular, as the insults carved on his desk lid told him.

But as the winter of 1932 grew colder, Guy gradually began to orient himself within the new order: the daily trudge from Cowell's to the main school buildings, the routine of rather formal lessons, the relentless pursuit of field sports – rugby this term, a sport at which Guy's stocky frame equipped him to settle down as a reasonably capable scrum-half. Next to theological correctness, St Edward's prided itself on sporting prowess. But even in games he never excelled.

As a new boy, Guy was required to fag for seniors – to clean their rugby boots, to fetch tea and toast and run freezing errands to the school shop. Meals were taken at long tables with benches in the school's neo-Gothic dining hall, which also doubled as a venue for special meetings and the rare spectacle of a public beating. The food was unimaginative: yellow cherry cake in huge, flat tins ('railway cake' – one cherry every station), great piles of pre-buttered bread which needed to be peeled apart before you could eat it and a more or less predictable main meal. According to one of Gibson's contemporaries, boys were 'almost permanently hungry'. Chapel was held twice daily, with a full cathedral service on Sundays.

Every new boy was required to conform to routine, and those who did so successfully were able to settle down happily – or as happily as anyone can without much privacy, comfortable accommodation or decent food. The penalty for transgressions was (from the boys) bullying or (from masters and prefects) beating. Grave crimes, such as 'unsuitable behaviour in chapel', gained the attention of the warden himself. Beatings by the Reverend Henry Ewing Kendall prompted a special fear in the boys. Being ambidextrous, he could counter fatigue simply by changing hands.

The austere regime did offer compensations. Guy's masters at St Edward's formed a distinguished group, none more so than his housemaster, A.F. (Freddie) Yorke. To the official historian of St Edward's, Cowell's under Yorke was 'one of the best houses in any school at any time',[5] a verdict amply supported by Gibson's contemporaries, all of whom remember him with affection and respect. Yorke held a special position in respect to Alick and Guy since he was *in loco parentis* – both housemaster and guardian. Though their father had returned to England, Guy and Alick saw little of him. Some of their vacations were spent at Osberton House, boarding with the family of one of the masters, the McMichaels. Occasionally Nora would arrive, often in an embarrassing condition, to take the boys for unexpected outings.

Both Gibson boys looked to Yorke for paternal support; as the elder boy, Alick was also a strength to Guy. Yorke had been wounded in the First World War. By the 1930s he had settled into the role of a bachelor schoolmaster, living a life of ordered efficiency, enjoying music and coaching the boys in rowing during the summer term. He liked to take long walks to Wytham with his colleague and close friend, the Reverend Ken Menzies – at least until Menzies' departure from the school in the summer of 1935, following a disagreement with the warden. As science teacher, some of Yorke's charges found his manner dry, but they recognized in him a quiet, natural authority. A room of noisy boys would soon calm when Yorke entered. Boys could approach him easily on any matter, and when they did so he was kindly, humorous and attentive. For Guy, Yorke's combination of wisdom and concern provided just the stabilizing influence that he now so badly needed. In time Yorke approached the role of surrogate father, and long after Guy left the school he continued to visit him.

The new year of 1933 brought a different routine, principally in the matter of sports. Despite his nautical interests, Guy preferred hockey to rowing, but was to achieve more in the summer game, cricket, where he became a moderately effective fast-medium bowler and a dogged batsman, on one occasion holding out long into the twilight in a last-wicket stand for Cowell's.

This academic year ended with a remarkable festival. The weekend gaudy of 1933 was announced as the school's diamond jubilee. After a traditional Friday evening choral concert, the main Saturday events were a mass PT display by the boys on the cricket field, under a blazing sun, followed by prize-giving and speeches. Guy stood within ranks of sweating boys to hear Kendall tell them it had never been the school's object to foster love of ease and comfort. Life's realities were hard, and the reward was to be sought by striving for the happiness of one's neighbours. Admiral of the Fleet Lord Jellicoe then defined the virtues necessary for a successful life in peace or war: loyalty, discipline, courage, unselfishness, keenness and sportsmanship. It would be difficult to find two more concise statements of the ethos of St Edward's School in the early thirties.

Years afterwards Sir Ralph Cochrane described Guy as the 'kind of boy who would have been head prefect in any school'. In fact, Guy was thought to be too easy-going for high prefectorial office, being promoted to house prefect, but no further. Qualities later recognized in Gibson either went unnoticed at St Edward's or, more probably, remained as yet undeveloped. His progress was unremarkable. The way in which Alick and Guy Gibson exercised authority made them popular with other boys: both were considerate to their fags, and Guy's manner with juniors was good-natured. He was rather self-consciously eccentric, cultivating a raffish air, and liked to represent himself as physically tough, refusing to wear a pullover even in the coldest weather.

Guy's enthusiasms lay in applied technology. Machines and devices had been about him since birth: cars, saw-mills, trains, pumps, winches, cameras. Photography was an abiding interest. Taking things to pieces to see how they worked, and reassembling them, was another. For a time he developed an enthusiasm for the mechanics of cinema organs. Although marked by the philistinism of the Imperial Service background from which he had emerged, Guy responded emotionally to films and music when performances gripped him.

Short and stocky with a slightly rolling gait, Guy had a natural manner and a winning smile. His strength of character won masters' respect and did something to redeem his mediocre academic performance and moderate sporting record. He was second XV material and a lance-corporal in the OTC, moderately able, tenacious, but never getting to the top of anything.

According to later accounts, Guy's ambition to fly had formed early. Certainly, as his time at St Edward's passed, he set his sights on flying as a career. But anxiety arose over whether he would gain the necessary qualifications. The summer examinations of 1935 brought credits in English, History, Latin and French (oral) – no science subjects or mathematics. A re-take later in the year added physics with chemistry, as a single, combined subject. Given that his father was a mathematician, that Freddie Yorke was a science teacher, and that Gibson was in the lower science VI form and enjoyed science-based pursuits, his School Certificate reveals an unexpected emphasis on humanities. It is as if he had inherited Nora's talents within his father's fields of interest.

Why did he want to fly? One reason may have been the glamour and excitement of the whole world of aviation in the 1930s. 'Mechanics and speed fascinated him,' according to one account. A master, Mr Emmet, had an old Bristol Fighter (bought for £15) which he kept in a nearby field, in which he would occasionally take boys for a trip. Perhaps that planted the seed. But it is important to grasp that Gibson's interest at this time was primarily in *flying*; the RAF came second, by his own word as a means to an end. The thought of fighting did not enter into it. His main ambition was to become a civil test pilot, and to this end he contacted Captain Jo 'Mutt' Summers at Vickers for advice. Summers told him to join the RAF in order to learn to fly. The public image of the air force may have added to its attraction. Some people in the 1930s considered that the RAF was not entirely respectable. Perhaps this held oblique appeal for a schoolboy whose dress and habits were not pointedly fastidious. So, in common with about one in ten boys at St Edward's, he opted to try for the armed services, applying for a short-service commission in the RAF.

They turned him down. It is generally believed that he was rejected because he was too short. It remains possible, however, that the persistent migraine attacks which had afflicted him in adolescence had something to do with it. Whatever the reason, Gibson persisted, and the RAF relented. Perhaps he grew a bit. So, though he was always to remain a visitor, Gibson left St Edward's School in July 1936. Ahead lay the prospect of a summer holiday in Pembrokeshire with Alick, and his eighteenth birthday.

Indulged in India, afterwards the victim of family stresses that for much of the time left him effectively parentless, at boarding-school since the age of six, how had Guy been prepared for the new life which would begin in the autumn? Outwardly he was a standard product of his Imperial Service and public-school background: instinctively conservative, suspicious of intellectualism, an amalgam of innocence and self-confidence, keen to ensure fair play, schooled from infancy in giving orders to members of other classes. Given the traditional separation between India and Home, Guy could have emerged from St Edward's a near stranger to his parents whatever their relationship. To an extent too he and Alick had weathered family difficulties by depending upon one another.

Yet Guy seems to have been damaged. Starved of sustained affection for more than a decade, he walled off inclinations to tenderness and guarded his feelings. A reflex of this, which the increasing complexities of adult relationships would expose, was a childlike inability to judge how others might be reacting to him. Perhaps that is why war's exigencies and supervening priorities would suit him so well, for they would provide short-term purpose and distraction from his own emotional limitations. More than this, war would offer a context in which some of his weaknesses could be converted to strengths. His self-confidence, fearlessness in dealings with those above him and ability to shrug off criticism would all be assets as a commander.

Nevertheless, his difficulty in receiving – or at least acting upon – the subtle signals of social behaviour left him vulnerable. Too readily, it seems, he would offend, misjudge, irritate, or even lay himself open to ridicule. Last, it may be that something of Nora's addictive personality had passed on to him. This was not so much a tendency towards alcohol (although he came to drink) or tobacco (he soon became a heavy smoker) as an emotional craving – a need to belong, to be accepted and an object of regard. In due course he found all these things in the society of operational flying.

Pilot

The Bristol Flying School, Yatesbury, had been opened as recently as 6 January 1936 for the training of *ab initio* student pilots at the hands of civilian instructors. Established under the 1930s RAF Expansion Scheme, the site reused the old Great War aerodrome on Yatesbury Field, between Chippenham and Marlborough, where Cherhill Down formed a dramatic backdrop to the circuit manoeuvres of students in their bright yellow Tiger Moth biplanes.

Gibson walked down Yatesbury's wide, tree-lined approach, to join the thirty-three other pupils of No. 6 Flying Training Course, on 16 November 1936. No. 6 Course had an anxious time ahead. November is not an ideal time to begin flying training and attempts to get off the ground were continually frustrated by unflyable conditions on the exposed, windswept airfield. For Gibson there were hours of idling in flying kit, rereading the training manual in preparation for ground school exams and nervously running through cockpit drills in a cold and gloomy hangar. The course was due to conclude by Christmas, when each student should have completed fifty instructional hours, but it was necessary to extend the training until New Year's Day, 1937.

Never strong at academic work, Gibson did not distinguish himself in the ground school examinations. But at least he had passed, with a flying rating of 'average'. The next stage for the remaining twenty-eight young men (six had failed) was some leave, then a journey to suburban north-west London. Here, at the Depot, 24 (Training) Group, RAF Uxbridge, they would meet the RAF proper – meaning drill, King's Regulations, service lectures and uniforms.

Transition from civilian to commissioned officer was rapid. Having mustered on 31 January, course members passed out with the rank of acting pilot officer after little more than a month. Next they returned to Wiltshire, to reassemble at 6 FTS, RAF Netheravon, for the next stage of their flying training.

Like Yatesbury, Netheravon was an airfield of Great War vintage. It lay on high ground overlooking the valley of the Avon, where the river bisects Salisbury Plain. Gibson's interest in these surroundings was slight. To him, farmers and agricultural workers were 'yokels' or 'peasants' – members of an inferior caste he imagined as dull. Never much interested in architecture, he thought most country towns boring and villages correspondingly more so.[6] He enjoyed rural pubs, and the long clear roads on Salisbury Plain were good for indulging in his off-duty sport of dangerous driving, but his ideal place for escape was a city.

Even so, Netheravon was a friendly area for a student pilot. Helpful aids to navigation were Stonehenge, some eight miles south–southwest and the nearby neolithic monument at Durrington Walls. Gibson had been to the area before. Annual camps of St Edward's OTC had been held at the nearby Tidworth barracks, where he had watched student pilots in fragile biplanes feeling their way around the summer sky. Perhaps those sights had helped to awaken his interest. Now, he was one of the thirty-one newly commissioned students who, joined by eleven leading aircraftmen, made up the three Flights of No. 5 Flying Training Course.

The input of new trainees to Netheravon was staggered, such that at any one time the base accommodated both a senior and a junior course. Formal qualification, marked by the flying brevet, was achieved within four months of a syllabus comprising handling of the Hind and Audax biplanes, airmanship, meteorology and navigation. Students then progressed to learn combat flying, automatically becoming the

'Advanced Training Squadron'. On completion of both courses – and very rapidly by today's standards – students would be passed fit for squadron service. Everyone agreed that the regime was 'like school'.

Training that spring progressed smoothly. In consequence, the award of the Flying Badge to forty-two students of 5 Course was notified on 24 May 1937. Among those listed was 39438, Acting Pilot Officer G.P. Gibson. Spring term was over and, as quickly as that, Guy had his wings.

Netheravon reopened on 7 June, when the veterans of 5 Course, now the Advanced Training Squadron, were joined by a new group of juniors. One afternoon Guy travelled over to Tidworth to visit the St Edward's OTC camp, where he talked excitedly about his chosen career to boys who gathered round to listen. Indeed, enthusiasm was his prevailing condition at this time. Although he seems to have been neither a natural nor an outstanding pilot, flying combined all those things which aroused him – speed, science, technology and a touch of social prestige – and his passion for it had become absolute.

Flying during this period was a run-up to the most demanding part of the course: the Armament Training Camp, at Sutton Bridge in Lincolnshire. Here the students would receive instruction in the deployment of armament, specialized by fighter or bomber groups. In theory they could opt for either fighter or bomber service. Though few multi-engined types were then in service with the RAF, bomber flying offered what opportunity there was to gain experience on these aircraft.

Many student pilots on short-service commissions preferred this option since they had joined the RAF, like Gibson, simply in order to learn to fly. Their real goal was civil aviation, and the steadier reputation of bomber pilots, plus multi-engined type experience, was a valuable asset. Gibson was among the bombers. He flew up to Sutton Bridge for a fortnight's stay on Sunday 1 August.

Sutton Bridge lay between Tydd St Mary and Wingland Marsh, a few miles from the coast. The weather over the fens that week was typically dank and misty, making morning flying hazardous. It was in these conditions that Philip Bailey, one of Gibson's colleagues in C Flight, took off in an Audax at 8 a.m. for an exercise. Another 5 Course pilot, Douglas Bagot-Gray, flew as Bailey's observer. The take-off was proficient enough. Exactly what happened next is unknown, but while still in the circuit the Audax crashed into a clover field 400 yards from the aerodrome. Both men were killed. Bailey had evidently decided to abort the exercise and bring the aircraft in to land, probably having lost confidence in just the kind of foggy conditions which may easily induce disorientation in the inexperienced. (The view from an Audax's cockpit was good, but the top wing blocked vision in a tight circuit. In poor visibility a practised pilot would intermittently straighten the aircraft up to keep the place of landing in sight.) At the inquest next evening, evidence was put to suggest that Bailey had mishandled the controls under adverse conditions. Douglas Bagot-Gray's body was taken down to Ewell, where he was buried on the Friday. He was twenty. Next day, Bailey was the twelfth unlucky student since 1923 to be buried in the school plot on the sunny south-eastern side of Netheravon churchyard.

Gibson celebrated his nineteenth birthday the following Thursday in the shadow of this incident. The deaths of the two students had blighted 5 Course's time at Sutton Bridge, reminding enthusiasts like Gibson that while flying was fun, it was also perilous. But training proceeded normally, and on 14 August the bomber group returned to Netheravon and continued practice at the Porton Range until the end of the month.

Gibson had passed each stage in training at the first attempt, but he won no special distinction. As a pilot he was classed 'average', and his final mark of 77.29 per cent in ground subjects was rather lower than the grades of some colleagues. Many of those who went on to achieve high rank and honours in the wartime RAF show, if we examine their careers, some early sign of promise in approach or attitude. Douglas Bader was a school prefect at St Edward's (where, before Gibson's time, he was also in Cowell's under Freddie Yorke) with an exceptional sporting record and a Cranwell flying rating of 'above average'. Leonard Cheshire's undergraduate career in the later 1930s had social lustre, in spite of which he achieved a good second-class degree. These are clues. With the young Gibson we find charm, frankness that would soon evolve into self-assertiveness, some dare-devilry and a sense of fun. But the strongest impressions he left on his instructors were fervour for the *idea* of flying and persistence. His tenacity was perhaps prompted by an inner realism about his own limitations and a defensiveness in areas where his weaknesses might be exposed. Certainly, there is no sign that he had that happy facility of doing things well and seeming to do them effortlessly.

No. 5 Course graduated on the last day of August at a parade reviewed by the AOC 23 Group, Air Commodore L.A. Pattison. Of the thirty-one graduating officers, twelve were posted directly on to bomber squadrons, four to general reconnaissance squadrons and four to fighters, reflecting the general distribution of forces in 1937. The remainder went either into further specialist training or to army co-operation. Though many of Gibson's contemporaries found themselves dispatched to squadrons in pairs or small groups, Gibson was to go alone. Leaving Netheravon on 4 September, a week's leave was in prospect before reporting to 83 (Bomber) Squadron, RAF Turnhouse.

Part Two

LONG WEEKEND

September 1937–November 1939

. . . our loyal, brave people . . . should know the truth.

They should know that there has [*sic*] been gross neglect and deficiency in our defences; they should know that we have sustained a defeat without a war, the consequences of which will travel far with us along our road; they should know that we have passed an awful milestone in our history, when the whole equilibrium of Europe has been deranged . . . And do not suppose that this is the end. This is only the beginning of the reckoning.

Winston Churchill, House of Commons, 5 October 1938

Apprentice

Almost two years to the day before the outbreak of war, Gibson jotted a postcard to his brother: 'A short line to say I . . . can't come up over the weekend as I have got to go up to Edinburgh to join my new squadron . . . Tell you what it's like later.'

What was it like? RAF Turnhouse lay in open country seven miles west of Edinburgh. In 1937 its facilities were modest: some temporary light hangars with corrugated iron cladding, huts, a few married quarters and a grass flying-field with an area of perhaps a thousand yards in all directions. Turnhouse was shared by 603 City of Edinburgh Squadron of the Auxiliary Air Force with its Hawker Furies, and 83 (Bomber) Squadron, which since August 1936 had been reforming with Hawker Hinds and could now muster nineteen pilots. 603 Squadron had more, but they were part-timers under the aristocratic command of Lord Hamilton of Clydesdale, reminiscent of a private regiment, and rumoured to turn up for training only when they were broke.

Acting Pilot Officer Gibson was assigned to A Flight, 83 Squadron, and placed under the eye of Plt Off. Anthony Bridgman. Bridgman had been shown Gibson's training reports, which he recalls were 'not especially good', and he reacted guardedly to the newcomer's manner, which seemed forcedly cheerful.

Bridgman took Gibson aloft to familiarize him with the area. They set out over the Firth of Forth and then turned west towards Stirling. Gibson was delighted, becoming particularly animated when they sped past a sanatorium at low-level. Upon return he enthused further, claiming that their pass beside the hospital had been so dramatic as to alarm the patients. Colleagues wearied of Gibson's retelling of this episode for months afterwards.

The Hawker Hind was a light bomber, a development of Sydney Camm's elegant masterpiece, the Hart, which in one form or another had been in service with the RAF since 1930. Popular at displays, aircraft of the Hart family epitomized the delight in line which is seen elsewhere in British inter-war engineering design. The Hind was a sound aeroplane which handled well, but its open cockpit, fixed undercarriage and limited endurance looked back to the Great War rather than towards battles to come. The Hind was scarcely able to hoist a 500-lb bomb-load half the length of England, let alone take one to Germany.

Yet it was flying, not international politics, which had attracted Gibson to the RAF, and for that life at Turnhouse was a paradise. On weekdays a parade was held at eight-thirty, when the colour was hoisted. By half past nine the Hinds had been wheeled out on the line for an inspection. Then the pilots emerged for the day's flying, which on the whole was haphazardly organized. 'It's up to you' was a familiar saying. Sometimes there was simulated bombing over the Firth of Forth. Formation flying was regularly rehearsed. So too were pilot navigation, map reading and cross-country exercises. Virtually all flying was done by day.

There was no watch office at Turnhouse, only a wooden hut inhabited by a duty pilot whose task was to book aircraft in and out, accept telephone notifications for aeroplanes setting forth for Turnhouse and adjust symbols in the signals square if the weather changed. When the weather was too poor for flying the pilots might do little more than sit around smoking and chatting, while the ground crew were given menial tasks such as sweeping out the hangars to keep them occupied. Work usually ended around five o'clock. The weekday routine was followed on Saturday mornings, but from midday on Saturday time was free.

Bridgman watched Gibson's progress. Although he did not particularly warm to him Guy seemed to have the makings of an adequate pilot. In the air he was apparently steady, obedient in forma-tions and not prone to taking risks. Some of his crew members knew better. They had noticed a happy-go-lucky streak. When out of sight he was prone to be 'very daring' and 'flaunted the rules by stunts and low flying'.

On the ground too Gibson could be tiresome, being 'by no means modest about his prowess on Hawker Hinds'. Many kept clear of him, repelled both by his compulsion to impress and by his inability to sense when his relentless chatter about flying or exaggerated gestures became socially counter-productive. One evening in the Mess Gibson ordered a packet of twenty Players. When this was delivered by the Mess waiter he airily handed all the cigarettes round to those present and then ostentatiously threw the empty packet on the fire. His obliviousness to the embarrassment caused helps to explain why not many looked for his company.

Alick, meanwhile, had embarked upon an engineering apprenticeship with British Thompson Houston in Rugby. During the next two years Guy was a regular visitor to Alick's house at Bilton Road, which – in the face of Nora's alcoholism and A.J.'s remoteness – to all intents and purposes he now regarded as home. From here the brothers would walk into the countryside, go fishing or spend an afternoon watching a game of football or rugby. There were military interests to compare: Alick had joined the Royal Warwickshire Regiment as a reservist. Their relationship was genial, mutually supporting, referring to each other in private as 'Old Alick' or 'Old Guy'. For a while they took to cycling the twenty-two miles to Leicester to visit a family known from Oxford days; there were three daughters, in one of whom Guy seems to have taken an interest. Later he reflected that he had then 'never really thought about women . . . they were just things that came and went in [sic] parties. Sometimes they were dumb, sometimes they were too intelligent . . .'[1] The indifference was feigned, although his view of female intelligence as being in some sense problematic was honest enough. In fact, he had a sharp eye for good-looking women. A girl who went out with him once or twice before the war recalls that 'he was only interested in one thing'. That could apply to many young men, but confirms that the nineteen-year-old Gibson was already sexually preoccupied, even if in that instance disappointed.

Alick's affections had settled on a girl called Ruth Harris. Since 1932 she had worked for a firm of solicitors in Rugby, where she was secretary to one of the partners. Ruth and Alick soon became close companions. Their shared interests included amateur dramatics and opera, the making of home movies and various outdoor pursuits. In August 1938 they became engaged. Guy got on well with her, and when 83 Squadron moved to Lincolnshire in the spring of 1938 his visits to Bilton Road became easier and more frequent. The East Midlands, indeed, now became a kind of Gibson heartland. He cared little for the countryside, but it was within a narrow triangular wedge of England bounded by Lincoln, Coventry and Boston that he was to live, pass many leaves, meet his wife and from which he would fly, for more than five of the six and a half years that were left to him.

Landscape and Tradition

Gibson thought Lincoln a dull city, but like many map-reading aviators he was thankful for the legacy of Roman roads which led to it. Roman artificers built a fine road north from the city which aims unswervingly for an ancient ferry crossing of the Humber. Ermine Street on maps, its local name is The Street or the High Dyke: 'High', because it sits atop an outcrop of limestone that runs northward through the county. A mile or two west an escarpment drops sharply to the floor of the Vale of Trent. This is the Edge and at its foot is a line of ancient settlements. One of them is Scampton.

Early in the twentieth century the Edge became a landscape of aerodromes. Westerly winds over the escarpment helped aeroplanes as they departed and slowed their speed over the ground as they returned to land. During the Great War airfields were established on the heaths at Bracebridge and Scopwick, at Waddington, Kirton in Lindsey, Harpswell and Scampton. Most were closed after the war, but from 1936 the RAF Expansion Scheme caused many to be reopened.

Consisting mainly of grass, these aerodromes lay within the English countryside with a comfortable ease. Scampton was remodelled in 1936 with new hangars on a pattern devised in consultation with the Royal Fine Arts Commission and the Council for the Protection of Rural England. For good measure there were also lawns, flower beds and lines of saplings. The station's modern facilities were popular, as were the choice wines being amassed for the cellar of the officers' Mess.

83 Squadron transferred to Scampton in March and was to share the airfield, and a spirited rivalry, with 49 Squadron for the next four years. Scampton's proximity to the bombing and gunnery ranges on Lincolnshire's east coast permitted a marginally greater degree of realism in training. And this proximity may have reminded the squadron why they were there, for the new bomber stations in Lincolnshire faced Germany.

The squadron was a settled and socially homogenous community. A number of pilots who had joined before Gibson's arrival – like Bridgman ('Oscar' in Gibson's book), James Pitcairn-Hill, Joe Collier and S.H. Kernaghan – were still there in 1940. They came from similar backgrounds (typically military, medical, clerical or colonial) and had passed through the same minor public schools. Bridgman, for instance, like Gibson, had been born in India. Pitcairn-Hill had inherited the religiosity of his father, a Presbyterian minister, and a fervent sense of duty. Neville Johnson, Ian Haydon and Jack Kynoch joined soon after Gibson. Kynoch was in his mid-twenties, older than most (he had preceded Gibson as a pupil at St George's, Folkestone), good-natured and admired as an athlete. Gibson later sketched him as someone with 'not too much sense of humour', perhaps because Kynoch was cool towards him. Allen Mulligan and Ellis Ross were 83 Squadron's two Australians, extrovert, friendly and widely liked. They arrived early in 1938, as did Bruce Harrison. Kenneth Sylvester (a 'tall, empty fellow' in Gibson's eyes) and Alan Vagg came in the summer and autumn of that year. A few were posted away. Fg Off. John Dallamore, for instance, was dispatched to Heliopolis in the spring of 1938. Remembered as fanatically conscientious, he would die in a hopelessly brave dive-bombing attack on an Abyssinian airfield. On the whole, however, the officers of 83 Squadron were a cohesive group and remained with the unit for several years. Promotion was accordingly slow: by December 1938 Gibson was half-way up the ladder of seniority among pilot officers on the squadron.

Once more the public-school house, its hierarchy, team spirit, shared mentalities, rituals and traditions, is the inescapable paradigm. Almost half of *Enemy Coast Ahead* is devoted to one year of Gibson's life in 83 Squadron. Apart from St Edward's, its community was the closest thing to a family that he had experienced since childhood.

The 'house captain', in this new hierarchy was Sqn Ldr Leonard Snaith. Dermot Boyle, his predecessor, had been held in unqualified respect, and 83 Squadron's members studied their new CO with keen curiosity. Snaith's pedigree seemed good, for it embraced the majority preoccupations with flying and sport. Apart from playing rugby for Bedford, he had been a member of the Schneider Trophy Team, and was a pilot of outstanding ability, witnessed in the gentle refinement of his landings. In other respects Snaith was less typical: unlike some of his officers, who were prone to rumbustious off-duty behaviour and raucous singing around pub pianos, he was a quietly sensitive man. Late in the afternoon he sometimes drove into Lincoln, where he would sit in the cool shadows of the cathedral and listen to choral evensong. Gibson's references to him in *Enemy Coast Ahead* are often patronizing. Snaith's view of Gibson was much more shrewd.

Boyle and Snaith were men of calibre who had helped to lay the foundations of Trenchard's small peacetime air force. Some of the older officers lacked their competence and commitment and attracted less respect. One of these was Scampton's station commander, a large man who drank a good deal and was sometimes to be found wandering aimlessly round the Mess inviting junior officers to try their luck in punching him. 'Go on,' he would say. 'Hit me! Hit me in the stomach!'

If officers were the prefects of this self-absorbed public school of the air, the sergeant pilots were fifth-formers and ground crew were juniors or fags. Although they shared the same flying duties, officers and sergeant pilots belonged to different castes. They seldom mingled, officers congregating in the flight office, sergeant pilots in the crewroom. Unnamed in the Air Force Lists of the period, the NCO pilots receive scant mention in Gibson's book, probably because he never really got to know them.

83 Squadron's other ranks formed a colourful culture. Many original members were Scots or Irishmen who found Turnhouse convenient because they could travel to and fro from nearby ferry ports on their monthly leaves. When the squadron moved to Lincolnshire this Gaelic contingent moved with it. A newcomer in 1938 was startled to find himself in the midst of 'Orangemen, IRA sympathizers, Protestants and Roman Catholics, Scots Presbyterians, English C. of Es. A rabid bunch when let loose in the pubs of Lincoln: the Saracen's Head, the Turk's Head, the Treaty of Commerce. Evenings in barracks were likewise enlivened by spirited rivalries between Scots, Geordies, Yorkshiremen or the local Lincolnshire "swedes".'[2] Fraternization between officers and airmen was rare. Accidental off-duty encounters might be rewarded with a half of bitter, but such gestures were unusual. Officers in any case would normally be in the cocktail bar or snug, while sergeants and other ranks drank in the taproom. A sports field was one of the few places where the two groups might mingle on equal terms, though even here the pre-war RAF regular was likely to be conscious of commissioned status when he met it – 'Tackle him – *sir*!'

Like any community, 83 Squadron had its bullies and nuisances. Many officers treated airmen with consideration, but there were exceptions. That Gibson was one of them is witnessed by his ground crew nickname the 'Bumptious Bastard'. Delays or reports of technical snags were too often greeted by petulant outbursts, and skilled technicians were irritated by his tendency to behave as if he knew more about their work than they did themselves. At first sight this reputation for self-indulgent tyranny contrasts oddly with reports of his tolerant affability at St Edward's. However, flight mechanics and electricians were more akin to the tradesmen's children of his Indian childhood than the social equals by whom he was surrounded at school, while his emergent self-conceit may be seen as an extension of the insecurity which had earned him disdain in his early schooldays. It is possible too that officer status had turned his head. Gibson would not have been the first easygoing teenager to display despotic tendencies after a pilot officer's ring had been sewn on his sleeve.

There were occasions when Gibson's impetuosity landed him in trouble. In August 1938 exercises were held to simulate war conditions. Hawker Hinds were dispersed around the aerodrome, the ground crews likewise, temporarily accommodated in bell-tents. At the end of the exercise the Hinds were returned to their hangars on the other side of the field. Each aircraft had been provided with a set of ballast weights in lieu of the gunner. Too impatient to linger while the weights were properly attached, Gibson ordered an airman to hold them in front of the rear cockpit. He then began to taxi at excessive speed. The Hind struck bumpy ground, the airman lost his grip, and the weights fell through the bottom mainplane, causing such damage that the entire mainplane had to be removed and replaced. This was not the only occasion when Gibson's impatience landed him in trouble. In October 1938 a Court of Inquiry fined him for negligence following a taxiing accident at Hemswell when he ran his Hind into a lawn-mower. But Gibson's reactions to Snaith's rebukes were characterized by an offhanded imperturbability that others found puzzling.

The incident of the dropped weights reminds us that most pre-war aircrew other than pilots were volunteers who flew in their spare time. Often they were junior aircrafthands, sent aloft by their elders to get them out of the way, and by an Air Ministry doctrine which held that only the duties of pilots could be considered as full-time occupations.[3] This quaint faith in amateurism was being challenged by Bomber Command's C-in-C, Sir Edgar Ludlow-Hewitt, but another year would pass before his arguments were heeded. Meanwhile, Gibson would often be roaming Scampton's workshops in search of 'spare bods' willing to fly with him, barking out their names with invitations they could not refuse. Clive Banham was one of them:

Discipline was strict and as we were only lowly 'erks' (Aircraftman 2nd Class) a pilot officer was held in respect and awe. As I recall Guy Gibson was autocratic in the extreme, ebullient, rumbustious and egotistical to a degree, but there is no doubt that he was a great pilot . . . he was mad keen on flying – on a ghastly winter's day he would say 'Banham! Let's get airborne and find sunshine' – sometimes we did . . .[4]

And here, behind Gibson's passion for flying even in the most marginal conditions, we glimpse another of Bomber Command's problems. In 1938 Britain's bomber force was almost entirely a fair-weather organization. Few of its pilots had experience of flying long distances under adverse conditions and fewer still were qualified for flying at night. In 1937 only 6.3 per cent of Bomber Command's flying hours were flown at night. The percentage for 1938 (8.9) was little better.[5] Such an air force, argued Ludlow-Hewitt, 'is relatively useless'.

Early in August the squadron was told that it would soon re-equip with a new bomber: the Handley Page Hampden. This was a twin-engined machine with a crew of four which on its first appearance in 1936 had been hailed as one of the most advanced military aircraft of the day. Excitement was aroused when the first of these odd-looking aeroplanes, faintly reminiscent of a glass-fronted tadpole, was delivered to 49 Squadron on 19 September. It was none too soon. While 83 Squadron had been engaged in a Home Defence exercise, probing the defences of Leeds in its elderly biplanes, efforts to mediate between Germany and Czechoslovakia over the Sudetenland had failed. During September some of the ground staff were sent on courses to the Handley Page factories at Cricklewood and Radlett in Hertfordshire. Many Londoners supposed that Britain was on the brink of war and a stream of cars, lorries, buses, vans and trucks carried fleeing citizens up the Great North Road. The fear which provoked their exodus was sudden attack from the air.

After Munich there were token preparations for war. Dummy hedgerows were daubed across the grass of the airfield. Hangars and other buildings were painted in camouflage of green, brown and charcoal. Contractors arrived to excavate for air-raid shelters. But there were few air-raid drills, and still no realistic training.

The Hampdens were arriving, however, and by the beginning of 1939 the squadron had received its full complement of sixteen machines plus five reserves. Few of the squadron's pilots had any experience of twin-engined aircraft, still less of such avant-garde devices as the retractable undercarriage, slatted wings or an enclosed cockpit. Arrangements for conversion were typically haphazard. Snaith arranged for some preliminary conversion flying on a Blenheim at nearby Hemswell and Waddington, each pilot doing two or three hours of dual flying before being initiated to the Hampden. The Hampden's narrow cockpit only allowed space for one person and when pilots first flew it a more experienced pilot stood behind the pupil shouting advice in his ear. The Hampden called for new skills and, not surprisingly, there were some errors. Few serious mishaps are recalled at Scampton, although up the road at Hemswell there was a period when it was rumoured that 'they were putting one in the ground every week'. An exaggeration, but one pilot did land wheels-up after forgetting that he no longer had a fixed undercarriage and at the end of February Bridgman overshot the airfield when landing at Northolt.

In the spring the Hampdens were flown up to Evanton, near Invergordon, for an Armament Training Camp. Here for a month the squadron engaged in concentrated high- and low-level bombing practice using small smoke bombs and firing live rounds at targets. Evanton offered a range of off-duty pursuits. Local girls were friendly, there were hikes up nearby mountains and bus trips to Ullapool. War was now widely predicted, but the expectation seems to have been oddly abstract. Knowledge and consciousness can be different things and the mood at Evanton was rather cheerful, more akin to a Boy Scout camp with aeroplanes than to rehearsals for war.

Gibson, meanwhile, had been sent for further navigational training at Hamble. This was an accelerated course, one of a number of recent measures to strengthen standards. He passed, although it was noted with disapproval that he did not attend to his studies with sufficient seriousness. 'Average ability,' commented his instructor, who nevertheless noted as an afterthought: 'Could do well.'

Late in the spring came the end of an era when the last Hawker Hind was flown out of Scampton. The Hind was taken aloft for an air-test around noon one quiet sunny day, banking hard over a column of newly arrived airmen who risked being put on a charge if they glanced up while marching to and fro past crisply edged lawns and white-painted kerbs. To those who saw the impending second war as a resumption of the first, the sight of this graceful departing biplane might well have symbolized the last hours of a long weekend of self-delusion. By now, indeed, Gibson was due to leave the RAF. He had served his contract. But the small print was to retain him.

Taking Leave

At the end of May 1939 the squadron moved to Northolt for a month of defence exercises with the Hurricanes of 111 Squadron. The Hampdens were rehearsed in formations which theorists argued would be proof against fighter attack. Box formation was practised on one day, rotation formation on another. Camera guns were used, but it is not clear how the results were analysed and several who took part have no recollection of any formal debriefings. Stronger interest centred on drinking with 111's pilots and trips to London's nightclubs. At the end of the month they returned to Scampton, little the wiser. While at Northolt Gibson had grazed the roof of a car with his undercarriage in the course of a misjudged landing. On this occasion he seems to have escaped punishment, perhaps because his pilot experience of the Hampden between January and June 1939 amounted to only eighteen hours.

Gibson was now twenty, and we have a clearer picture of his emerging adult personality: by turns amiable, boisterous, frequently thoughtless yet disarmingly open, occasionally displaying a mild hypochondria which can be a feature of late adolescence. At Scampton most of his abundant energy was channelled into flying, the rest into egotism. Whether talking about his flying or acting as master of ceremonies for 'We are Sailing to Khartoum' while standing on a pub piano, he liked to be at the centre of attention. Tolerant colleagues saw this as compensation for his short stature; others simply thought him insufferably bogus. His victimization of ground staff remained a failing. Occasionally he goaded flight mechanics by letting them crank the starter of the Hampden's Pegasus XVIII while sitting smugly in the cockpit with the switches off. The Hampden was prone to genuine electrical problems and an aircrafthand electrician recalls Gibson's petulance when he was unable to correct a fault. On the whole, however, these outbursts seem to have been induced more by misjudgement than malice. At other times there was a redeeming sense of humour and he seldom bore grudges.

Away from Scampton, perhaps because there was less of a part to play, Gibson's underlying amiability was more to the fore. His cheerful thoughtlessness is nicely illustrated by an intended Christmas present to Ruth's mother of a large carton of cigarettes. When Ruth pointed out that this would be an inappropriate gift for a non-smoking lady in her late seventies, his unabashed reply was, 'Never mind, she can pass them round.' Even when out of uniform, however, there was an urge to impress. Guy was envious of a cigarette case owned by Ruth. It was solidly made and closed with a satisfying clonk. He persuaded her to part with it. On another occasion, after the outbreak of war, Ruth's maiden name – Harris – gave rise to a rumour that she was related to Arthur Harris, the new AOC 5 Group, a story which Guy did nothing to contradict. Two leading characteristics made their mark on acquaintances. One was his irrepressible buoyancy and prodigal spirit. When in company Guy was often to be found buying drinks or presents. The other was his self-will. As a relative put it: 'He didn't listen. Guy did what he wanted.'

For two years Ludlow-Hewitt's analyses of Bomber Command's inadequacies had been expressed to the Air Ministry in a series of uncompromising memoranda. Yet as the months of summer and peace ran out there was little to disturb the stagnant complacency of those who had ignored him. The RAF Intelligence Summary issued in August noted such trivia as the languid progress of a Sunderland out to Singapore, its six stops (at Malta, Alexandria, Bahrain, Karachi, Calcutta, Rangoon) redolent of the Empire in which Gibson had been brought up to believe. An international air display at Brussels in July saw performances by British-built aircraft of the Belgian air force, such as an ancient Fairey Fox. 'It was gratifying,' wrote a correspondent, 'to hear Belgian officers talk of the good service which had been given by these aircraft, and of engines nine years old but still maintaining their reliability.' Following the death of a German who failed to recover from a series of violent flick rolls in a Jungmeister, the analyst smugly concluded that Luftwaffe pilots were 'not so well trained in the smooth handling of controls as the pilots of other nations taking part'.

Just over two weeks later something did occur which seemed out of the ordinary. On 25 July Gibson took part in a flight to the south of France. Few members of the squadron had ever flown so far and the purpose of their odyssey past Paris, Lyon and Avignon – ostensibly to show the flag – provoked curiosity. But interest soon subsided as training reverted to normal. In August there were Home Defence exercises, with simulated attacks on London, but these were fairly routine. And, as usual, there was no night-flying training at all. A week before the end of the month Gibson set forth on his annual summer leave.

He went to Pembrokeshire, for several years a favourite haunt and the scene of a number of ephemeral romances. He and Alick had spent holidays together in a house near Saundersfoot. Fishing and sailing occupied much of his time; in the evenings there were invitations to parties and dances. (Whether because of his height or lack of co-ordination, Gibson seldom actually danced.) A day or two before the end of August a telegram recalled him to Scampton. Freddy Bilbey, a biologist of his acquaintance who was staying near by, drove him to Oxford. On the way they watched lengthening queues of vehicles at filling stations and overtook cars piled high with luggage heading home, or away from home. In Oxford they paused for a meal and then went into a pub while Gibson waited for his train. The bar was crowded and he recoiled at the sight of young people he took to be students: 'drunken, long-haired, pansy-looking youths, mixed [sic] with foppish women'.[6] Gibson was probably no more intolerant of students than any other young officer of his background, although it is a delicious specula-tion that one of those degenerates might have been Leonard Cheshire. His reaction is nevertheless illuminating, for it reveals narrow conformities.

The journey to Lincoln took hours. It was to be the first of hundreds of trips he would make in crowded, stuffy, blacked-out coaches, tedi-ously prolonged by unexplained halts. Reaching Lincoln just before dawn, he found transport up to Scampton, declared his return and went to bed. While he slept, turmoil surrounded the railway stations at Lincoln and the nearby towns of East Retford and Gainsborough, as train after train disgorged thousands of young evacuees from the West Riding of Yorkshire. Long after nightfall groups of exhausted children dozed on pavements as harassed billeting officers argued with unwilling householders or struggled to read lists and numbers on gates in the black-out.

Up at Scampton vehicles, aircraft and equipment were dispersed, sandbags filled, anti-aircraft guns readied and precautions against sudden gas attack were nervously studied. Pilots stood by throughout Friday 1 September, anxiously aware that six of their aircraft had actually been loaded with bombs. Preparations for war were largely based on theories, one of which asserted the high risk of pre-emptive attack. Accordingly, around tea-time, the remaining serviceable aircraft were flown to Newton, near Nottingham, where it was hoped that they would be out of harm's way. Everyone else was confined to camp and at dusk Gibson joined others who withdrew to the bar in the officers' Mess. At one minute before midnight the teleprinter in Scampton's headquarters began to chatter, giving out orders for general mobilization.

Next day, Saturday 2 September, 83 Squadron kept six machines at stand-by until the evening. Gibson lounged with the other pilots in the hot sun who were smoking and disguising their tension by trivial chatter. Although Gibson later depicted himself as sharing the same sense of subdued agitation that gripped his colleagues, this was not an impression he gave to them. One remembers that he seemed thrilled at the prospect of war and interpreted his suspense as the exultant opportunism of someone who 'saw his chance'.[7]

The heatwave continued into the Sunday. Towards eleven o'clock pilots gathered around the radio in the flight office and fifteen minutes later listened to Neville Chamberlain's announcement that a state of war existed between Britain and Germany. As the news sank in, Snaith looked across at Gibson and broke the silence, saying drily, 'Now's your chance to be a hero, Gibbo.'

War

By early afternoon nine of Scampton's Hampdens, six from 83 Squadron, Gibson's among them, were being readied for an attack on German warships in the Schillig Roads and at Wilhelmshaven. Towards six o'clock, after postponements and vacillation about the bomb-load, Gibson and his crew were driven out to their aircraft and the Hampdens took off in two formations.

Gibson tells us that beforehand he was deeply apprehensive: 'my hands were shaking so much I could not hold them still. All the time we wanted to rush off to the lavatory; most of us went about four times an hour.'[8] Not only was he shocked at the prospect of going to war, but there was immediate uncertainty about what it was like to take off with a full bomb-load – something he had never done before. Moreover, although his experience of night flying was negligible, the delayed start meant that they would return after dark. If they returned, that is. He had no idea what to expect.

The story of this hopeless mission has often been told, most graphically by Gibson himself.[9] Bad weather hindered the finding of the German fleet, darkness fell and the operation was aborted. The only real achievement was that all who took part managed to return. When he touched down towards 23.00 Gibson could not have guessed that he was not to fly again operationally for another six months.

Despite the anticlimax many at Scampton were gripped by a sense of imminent apocalypse. It only seemed a matter of time, probably sooner rather than later, before real action would begin. Tension therefore remained high as next morning Hampdens were again readied for an attack on the German fleet. But no order to proceed was given. Gibson, meanwhile, fell victim to a much more direct attack. Entering the Mess at lunch-time, he noticed a large dog. As he stooped to pat it, the dog bit his hand and tore his tunic. Both injuries were sufficiently serious to require stitches. The bite nevertheless brought a compensation. On the following day, Tuesday 5 September, Alick and Ruth were to be married. The wedding had originally been planned for October, but uncertainty about the destiny of Alick's regiment had prompted them to bring the ceremony forward. Unable to fly, his arm in a sling, Gibson was given thirty-six hours' leave to attend.

Guy was in high spirits when the couple emerged from the Rugby registry office, and set out to subvert the proceedings by attempting to lure his brother into a nearby pub. Ruth restored order, retrieving her new husband and resuming their walk to the Grand Hotel for the reception. The catering was no more than an impromptu buffet, but a wedding cake had been made, and the gathering was enlarged by hotel residents and casual drinkers in the bar who mingled with the guests, their spontaneous good wishes contrasting with the lack of them from A.J., who did not attend. Nor did Nora, whose alcoholism was now so serious that she had been institutionalized in a nursing home. At length everyone paused for a brief and rather incoherent speech by Guy.

Next morning Ruth and Alick collected their badly hung-over best man and took him to a jewellers, with the aim of buying him a new watch. Guy resisted the gift, arguing that he would soon be killed and that the gift would be pointless. 'Don't do it,' he kept repeating, 'I'm a dead man.' His protests notwithstanding, Guy received his watch and was driven off in Alick's little Standard Nine for lunch. Afterwards the newly-weds delivered him to Leicester station and waved him off. Back at Scampton he found the airfield deserted. That morning, following yet more unfulfilled preparations for strikes against German shipping, fears of attack had caused Bomber Command to implement its Scatter Scheme, whereby aircraft at bases in eastern England were temporarily withdrawn to more distant airfields, or to places where German Intelligence would not expect them to be. 83 Squadron had been ordered to Ringway, near Manchester.

Their sojourn in Manchester was brief, riotous and socially intense. Unlike Lincoln, which Gibson thought boring, Manchester was a colourful city with bars, nightclubs and theatres. There was little flying and the aircrew lost no time in identifying favoured drinking places at the Slip Inn, Liston's Long Bar and the Piccadilly Hotel. 'The war occupied our minds and we all thought that we would be fighting for our skins within a month. So why not make merry while the sun shone?'[10] Mancunians threw open their homes to the visitors and while the published version of Gibson's book tells us that girls were 'plentiful', the original manuscript depicted them with unintentional accuracy as having been 'laid on'. On some evenings Gibson sought out colleagues for bar-room singing. On others he pursued a girl he calls Barbara, for whom he confessed a passionate affection which was not reciprocated. The life and colour of the Manchester episode are strongly caught in his book; in fact, it lasted no more than ten days and although elements of the squadron were intermittently scattered to Ringway for weeks afterwards, by mid-September Gibson was back at Scampton.

Training during the weeks that followed differed little from peacetime, save for lack of leave and the inconvenience of the Scatter Scheme. Periodically Gibson flew a Hampden for the twenty-minute hop to Newton, a popular assignment if it involved an overnight stay because of Newton's proximity to Nottingham. Like most of his colleagues, Gibson was mistrustful of the army's aircraft recognition skills and such flights were usually were made at low-level, undercarriage down, for purposes of identification.

Restless because of the inactivity, Gibson sought amusement in illicit low flying. One crew member recalls Gibson frightening bargees nearly out of their wits as he attempted to underfly a bridge over the River Trent – a manoeuvre which was said to depend for its feasibility on the state of the tide. On another occasion he flew to Scunthorpe to entertain the family of a passenger by an impromptu display. After circling the tall chimneys of the steelworks, he then roared up and down Scunthorpe's main street. Looking over Gibson's shoulder, the passenger pointed to his house and then to his mother and sister as they stepped out into the backyard, around which Gibson noisily pirouetted in a series of exceptionally tight turns. When the passenger went on leave, his mother told him of recent great events. The King and Queen had visited Scunthorpe to open a new blast furnace and it appeared that the RAF had given them an escort and provided an exhibition of flying.[11]

As October passed to November there was still little to relieve the tedium. However, a proposal to enlarge Scampton's flying field provided some interest. An adjacent farm, Aisthorpe House, had already been damaged by the impact of a Handley Page Heyford which had flown into its side several years before and the proposal to remove it completely to provide more space gave rise to the suggestion that it be the target for a bombing competition. The exercise took place on the morning of 17 November. Gibson was among those who watched and he found it surprisingly instructive. Most of the bombs either fell short, or bounced beyond the house to explode harmlessly elsewhere. Evidently they had much to learn.

Part Three

RITES OF PASSAGE

December 1939–November 1940

Love looks not with the eyes, but with the mind,
And therefore is winged Cupid painted blind.
Nor hath love's mind of any judgement taste;
Wings and no eyes figure unheedy haste.
And therefore is love said to be a child
Because in choice he is so oft beguiled.

A Midsummer Night's Dream, I.i

Eve

Evelyn Mary Moore was a dancer and the end of the second week of December 1939 found her in Coventry in the company of the revue *Come Out to Play* which had its provincial première at the New Hippodrome theatre. The cast included Jessie Matthews and her husband Sonnie Hale. The audience included Guy Gibson.[1]

Gibson was on leave, staying with Alick and Ruth.* According to his own account his first encounter with Eve was at a party. Eve's version differs. When the show opened she noticed a young RAF officer staring at her from the front row of the stalls. On the next evening he was there again and at the Wednesday performance Eve was faintly disconcerted to find herself under close observation once more. By Thursday the fellow had decided to introduce himself. During the interval Eve received a message: would she meet him after the show?

Eve later recalled her first impression of the man who stood at the foot of the backstage stairs: 'At close quarters he looked younger than ever; a mere boy who looked as if he should have been at school.' This was not so far from the truth: almost eight years stood between their ages. Whereas Gibson was only four months past his twenty-first birthday, Eve was nearly twenty-eight.

Fair-haired, not beautiful, Evelyn Moore was nevertheless decidedly attractive, with a dancer's long legs and compact frame. Gibson was magnetized by her and despite later infidelities his obsession endured for several years. In the words of a friend: 'Guy adored Eve. He could not get enough of her.' He also enjoyed the colour and energy of the theatre. Performers and musicians provided a welcome change from squadron society, yet there were characteristics of stress and extroversion common to both and the amalgam of contrasts and similarities enchanted him. 'The chorus ladies are in a special class both for looks and dancing ability,' wrote a reviewer, who continued, 'indeed dancing is the hot-spot of the whole show.' Among the cast were several household names, including the dancer and singer Peggy Rawlings, and

* Gibson dated his meeting with Eve to a three-day leave which began on 1 December 1939.[2] In fact, *Come Out to Play* opened at the New Hippodrome in Coventry on 11 December 1939 (a Monday), finishing on the 16th.

Hal Thompson, a former Broadway partner of Ginger Rogers. Gibson was enthralled.

They went to the King's Head for supper. After small talk about their respective backgrounds, Eve was surprised to find that Guy said little about himself, being more intent upon cross-examining her about life as a performer. Eve summarized the history of the show, which had been put together following the suspension of Sonnie Hale's previous project, a spectacular called *I Can Take It* which had been designed for the London Coliseum. The production had been shelved because, as Sonnie Hale explained earlier in the week: 'London is hopeless for big shows at the moment. There are not enough people there to fill a large theatre . . . Families have been evacuated and the floating population can't find its way around the streets in the dark.' *Come Out to Play* had emerged as an alternative.

Gibson drank a lot and then got down to brass tacks: did she have a regular boyfriend? Eve was startled by his bluntness, but said no, she did not. Guy seemed pleased, stating in a matter-of-fact way that he hoped henceforth her boyfriend would be him. Eve was surprised, perhaps amused, by the unabashed simplicity of this *démarche*, but accepted his invitation to lunch and supper on the following day.

Gibson was due to return to Scampton the next evening, but his captivation by Eve and the prospect of escorting her to a cast party caused him to tarry. He again drank a good deal, chatted with members of the cast and saw Richard Murdoch (Peggy Rawlings' husband, later to become the gentle satirist of the RAF in the BBC's wartime comedy series *Much Binding in the Marsh*). Eve introduced him to some of her glamorous companions from the chorus of 'Our Girls', including a close friend, Doreen Douglas, with whom she shared a dressing-room.

The party ended around three in the morning. Addresses were exchanged. Guy implored Eve to write to him. Bemused by the artless frankness of her new admirer, Eve was also flattered and intrigued. Her main impression of the figure who drove his second-hand Rover unsteadily into the night was that he seemed 'quiet and unassuming'.

Three days later Gibson's spirits rose when he received orders – or did he offer? – to join a contingent of pilots who were to fly some Hampdens down to a Maintenance Unit at St Athan for the fitting of IFF transmitters. St Athan was only twelve miles from Penarth, where Eve's parents lived. Bridgman (recently promoted squadron leader and appointed OC A Flight) and Gibson were among those who took off on this gloomy midwinter morning, reaching St Athan shortly after one o'clock. Released from duty, he set out in search of Eve.

Ernest Moore had lived in Penarth since his marriage to Edith Cole nearly forty years before. When Evelyn, their second daughter, was born on 27 December 1911, the family house was at 25 Cwrt-y-Vil Road, a hillside street of late Victorian villas in a middle-class area on the west side of the town. In the 1920s, as Ernest Moore's career as a loss adjuster prospered, the family moved a few hundred yards down the slope and round the corner to a larger house in Archer Road. Small in distance, the social jump was greater. Houses built on Archer Road after the Great War were on a more ample scale than those of Cwrt-y-Vil Road and although many of them, including No. 21, were semi-detached, their size and variety left the passer-by in no doubt that this was a neighbourhood of substance.

Eve had therefore grown up within the compass of a few hundred yards in a quiet seaside town. Originally hoping to be a dancing teacher, she found herself temperamentally unsuited to the work and struck out for a career in the theatre. For several years she worked as a dancer and a player of small parts. Her theatrical career was supported by her father who, according to Gibson, 'kept her financed fairly well'; at least, 'she was always staying at the best hotels and knowing the very poor pay that most girls get on the stage, I am sure she would not have been able to do this had not her father stepped in.'[3]

The cast of *Come Out to Play* disbanded for Christmas and it was to Archer Road that Eve had returned on the Sunday following her farewell to Guy. Now, while playing bezique with her mother in the drawing-room, Eve was informed by the maid that 'an RAF gentleman' was asking for her. Faintly irritated by the lack of warning, Eve went out into the hall. Sure enough, there was Guy, who explained that he had had to bring an aircraft down and thought that he would 'hop over to see you'. Guy was ushered into the drawing-room and introduced to Eve's parents. Over dinner Eve's father, who had already registered polite surprise at Guy's unannounced arrival, inquired where he was staying. Archer Road mores were tested further when Guy replied 'Nowhere', adding ingenuously that his bag was in the hall.

After dinner Guy took Eve into Cardiff to meet some of the other pilots who had arranged to meet for a drink. During the evening an

argument developed. Tempers rose and one of the officers turned on
Eve with insultingly bad language. Bracing himself to intervene, Gibson
was surprised to find that no support was necessary. In his words, Eve
'gave as good as she got'.[4]

Eve's display of spirit set the seal on his enslavement, but progress in
the romance was curtailed when next day he was obliged to return to
Scampton. In his absence the squadron had been readied for an attack
on the German pocket battleship *Deutschland*, recently renamed as the
Lutzow.* The operation was postponed but on the following day,
Thursday 21 December, it went ahead.

Although they had been put on alert for maritime duties on fourteen
occasions since the outbreak of war, this was only the second fully
offensive operation that members of the squadron had been detailed to
undertake. Gibson clamoured to take part, but only three aircraft were
required from 83 Squadron, this being a contribution to a larger force
of twenty-four Hampdens, including nine from 49 Squadron, and
eighteen Wellingtons. The three took off at 07.40 led by Flt Lt Joe
Collier. Gibson grumbled at his exclusion. Had he known what was to
follow he might have been less frustrated.

Over Lincoln the twelve Scampton aircraft merged with a dozen 44
Squadron Hampdens from Waddington. Due to lack of co-ordination
by operational planners the various groups of aeroplanes had been
airborne for some time, wasting fuel, before the consolidated formation
set forth at 08.25. Intelligence reports placed the *Lutzow* off the
Norwegian coast. The bombers made landfall at Listafjord in southern
Norway, whence they headed north, flying parallel to the coast. There
was no sign of the battleship. Near Bergen they reached the limit of
their range and turned west, heading now for bases at Lossiemouth and
Kinloss. But homeward progress was impeded by a strengthening
headwind, a low cloud base and squalls of rain and sleet. Navigational
uncertainty caused further problems, and the formation broke. Perilously low on fuel, it was not until late afternoon that the scattered
Hampdens started to make landfall. As the midwinter twilight deepened,

---

* Following the loss of her sister ship the *Graf Spee*, it was thought prudent to rename
her, lest the possible future sinking of a ship bearing the name of the fatherland be
interpreted as a bad omen by the German public.

Collier and Sgt Lyster landed at Acklington, Northumberland, in company with aircraft of 49 Squadron, one of which crashed on its approach. Another of Scampton's Hampdens force-landed and several more landed at Leuchars.

The search for the *Lutzow* was dogged not only by disorganization but also, in the end, by tragedy. When the approach of the Hampdens was registered by shore radar, fighters were sent up to investigate. As two Hampdens from 44 Squadron neared the coast north of Berwick they were intercepted by Spitfires of 602 Squadron. Several Spitfires shadowed the bombers for some minutes and then proceeded to shoot them down into the sea. A Court of Inquiry on the following day ruled that the onus had rested with the bombers to establish their identity. News of these events aroused considerable ill-feeling at Waddington and Scampton and hostility towards Fighter Command deepened when it was learned that one of the Hampdens had been limping in on one engine.

Gibson devoted a page and a half of *Enemy Coast Ahead* to the *Lutzow* operation and it has always been a puzzle why he said nothing about the chaotic circumstances in which it ended. In fact, he wrote about this at length, summing up the operation as 'one of the biggest shambles in history'. The censor cut the entire passage, perhaps because it revealed the depth of Gibson's prejudice against the Auxiliary Air Force. In another passage – also censored – he expanded his views:

... the auxiliary boys at that time had not quite been able to get the full hang of operational flying. It was true that years later they ... were to distinguish themselves ... but in the dark days of 1939 they were very light on the trigger. It was said that one particular auxiliary squadron had to its credit one Heinkel, two Hampdens, one Hudson and one Anson, all destroyed.[5]

At the time, however, Gibson's thoughts appear to have been fixed on Eve and next day, 22 December, he seized a further chance to visit her by ferrying another Hampden to St Athan. Progress on fitting the IFF equipment was agreeably slow and Guy was able to pass the following evening at Penarth.

As the black-out curtains were drawn in Archer Road that evening, Guy's mother was preparing to go to a party. Nora had discharged herself from the nursing home and returned to Kensington, taking a room in a guesthouse in Wrights Lane. Nora was on sufficiently good terms with the manager, Mark Terry, to ask if he would escort her across London. She planned to spend Christmas with friends in Denmark Hill and requested his company because the evening was foggy and 'it was very unsafe to travel'.

Around six o'clock Nora went to her room to change. Half an hour later Mr Terry heard screams. He dashed up the stairs and was horrified to meet Nora 'coming down all in flames'. Mr Terry lifted her up and then went to fetch a pile of bath-towels with which he tried to smother the fire. His efforts were only partially successful; Nora's crêpe de Chine evening frock continued to burn until the arrival of the housekeeper 'who stripped the burning clothing off her'.

Upstairs in Nora's flat, Mr Terry found an easy chair in flames, which he struggled to extinguish. An electric stove stood in the room and there were embers of a coal fire in the grate. The carpet had been scorched. Mr Terry thought it unlikely that the coal fire had had anything to do with the accident and wondered if the burning of the carpet had been caused by Nora having fallen on the floor.

About an hour later Nora was admitted to St Mary Abbot's Hospital, where she was found to be suffering from extensive burns about the body and legs, and severe shock. Still conscious, Nora explained that her dress had become entangled in the electric stove. Within months there would be large advances in the treatment of burns, but the Battle of Britain had yet to begin and the means of dealing with such depth of shock had yet to be evolved. Leonora Gibson lingered into the next morning, Christmas Eve, and then died.*

We do not know when, or by whom, Gibson was told of his mother's death. He returned to Scampton late in the afternoon of Christmas Eve and perhaps he was called to the telephone to be given the news. But there is no record of his reaction and his book conceals the entire tragedy, dwelling instead upon the furious gaiety which gripped Scampton on Christmas Day.

Christmas Day opened with a routine now tediously familiar: Hampdens being bombed up awaiting orders which did not come. Had the operation proceeded the aircrew might have been less at risk than from the hazards of an RAF Christmas. As in medieval tradition, when

* The inquest into Leonora Gibson's death was held at Paddington on 30 December 1939. A verdict of accidental death was returned.

roles were reversed and kings waited upon peasants, custom dictated that Christmas dinner should be served to airmen by their officers, who were obliged to withstand whatever abuse was hurled at them. The meal over, members of the two squadrons began to exercise their rivalry by roaring tribal chants. At this stage in the war the Germans ranked only second, after 49 Squadron, as 83's chief adversaries and when the proceedings became life-threatening the officers withdrew to visit the sergeants' Mess, where considerable drinking was accomplished, and afterwards continued to their own to embark upon a pitched battle. In the midst of it all Gibson was summoned to the telephone. It was Eve, calling to wish him a happy Christmas.

What did they talk about? Gibson's appetite for Eve was sharpened by the conviction that he would soon be dead. Thus far the torpid efforts of Bomber Command had allowed him a reprieve, but he guessed this to be no more than a postponement. Eve's opportunities for sexual adventure had been wider than those open to him, while her comparative maturity and theatrical background may have increased her attraction for a man scarcely out of his teens, impatient at the best of times and eager to make the most of whatever time was left.

Yet the appetite itself was an extravagant passion – an all-consuming infatuation which for the time being overrode everything and never entirely subsided. They had known each other for less than a fortnight. When they had met – or rather, as Eve tells us, Guy had *selected* her – Nora's death could not have been predicted. But was it by coincidence that Gibson had sought, in a calculating way, to plunge himself into a relationship with a woman who was not far from a decade his senior? Differences in age are acutely realized by people in their twenties. Too young to be his mother, Eve was nevertheless old enough to qualify as a youthful aunt, and it was in that sort of family circle that Gibson had passed much of his middle boyhood.

Reversing the issue, we must ask what it was that drew Eve towards – or, at the least, caused her not to retreat from – someone who in her own words resembled a schoolboy, and in modern slang could almost qualify as a toy boy. If a kind of surrogate motherhood – not to mention the Oedipal undertones that such a suggestion invites – seems absurdly far-fetched, Eve's own medical history at least gives pause for thought. Eve Moore was incapable of bearing children.

Pursuits

January 1940 began mild, but on the last Thursday of the month the thermometer plunged and England was paralysed by an immense fall of snow. At Scampton the aerodrome was cut off, the road to Lincoln was blocked and efforts to clear the flying field were frustrated by further snowfalls. Flying was impossible for three weeks, but ground crew were still required to keep the Hampdens flyable and the aircraft had to be bombed up when the squadron was on duty. The hardship of this futile ritual was increased by continuing paranoia about surprise attack, which dictated that the aircraft be dispersed in the open rather than towed into the hangars. Tents containing paraffin heaters were placed over the engines and ground crew were daily obliged to smear a de-icing paste resembling peanut butter on the leading edges of wings. Since the men had no protective clothing, the paste caked their uniforms and greatcoats. While flight mechanics, electricians and armourers worked in the frost and snow, their hands burned numb by the sticky contact of sub-zero metal, some of the officers relieved their boredom by roller-skating in the empty hangars.[6]

Unable to fly, the lovesick Gibson waited impatiently for the 4th of February, when the cast of *Come Out to Play* arrived in Sheffield for the start of their provincial tour. Armed with a forty-eight-hour pass, he travelled over to visit Eve the following weekend. By now he was getting to know the show rather well. There were song-and-dance routines, spectacular numbers like 'Chinese White', a rather good close harmony trio called The Radio Three and numerous sketches. Audiences liked an item called 'Landladies', a parody of the Mayfair set facing up to war work, but the highlight was a satire which paid 'mock-lugubrious tribute' to the heroes of the BBC. But their time together was depressingly short and Gibson was inwardly despondent when he waved Eve off from Sheffield station on the Sunday morning. The cast was leaving for Glasgow and it seemed unlikely that they would see each other for weeks.

Yet luck lay just ahead. By St Valentine's Day conditions had improved enough for flying to resume and part of the squadron was ordered to Lossiemouth for temporary secondment to Coastal Command. Ever alert to opportunities for the pursuit of Eve, Gibson pleaded with Snaith for permission to travel by train, leaving the Hampden to be flown up by a colleague. Eve was duly impressed by Guy's resourcefulness when he walked into the Glasgow Alhambra, exhausted but triumphant after an overnight journey. The management were now so accustomed to his visits that he was allowed to watch the show from the wings. At other times he sat in Eve's dressing-room, whence he was ejected every few minutes during each of the girls' fourteen changes of costume. Again, however, their time together was brief and after their second farewell in a fortnight Gibson set out for Lossiemouth.

He did not get far. Delays on the railway forced him to stop overnight in Perth. And here he had an odd encounter. Entering his hotel bar he saw two pilots he knew. Yet both were wearing civilian clothes and when he approached they turned away. Puzzled by their odd behaviour he went to bed. Later in the evening one of the men came privately to his room in order to explain. Their task was to ferry Blenheims to Finland and they had been ordered to impersonate civilian pilots to circumvent international law. Gibson was impressed: by comparison with the dull routine of his own war thus far, such cloak-and-dagger stuff seemed enviable.[7]

Always happy to be close to the sea and among fishermen, Gibson at first found Lossiemouth congenial. After the snow of Scampton it was also surprisingly sunny and warm. But there was too little to do, a routine of stand-by followed by stand-down, relieved only by excursions to bars and a practice flight to Wick in which he nearly came to grief during a formation take-off.

Then, on 27 February, Gibson scented action. Soon after breakfast the squadron was ordered to a briefing by Snaith and Sqn Ldr Sam Threapleton.* A German U-boat had been detected and they were to seek and sink it. Around mid-morning eight crews led by Threapleton took off, heading out over the North Sea towards the area which had been allotted for their sweep. Things now began to go wrong. After the aircraft had departed, Lossiemouth was notified of a change in the search area. This order should have been signalled to Threapleton, but

---

* Threapleton was in 83 Squadron. The squadron's command hierarchy was variable in 1939/40, as Snaith was absent for a while and then returned. Threapleton seems to have deputized.

due to what was afterwards described as the 'inefficiency' of the W/T station at Lossiemouth the message was not received.

Meanwhile, two submarines had been sighted. Threapleton was carrying a naval observer who identified the vessels as friendly, but because of difficulties with the intercom in Threapleton's aircraft it took time for this information to be passed back. During the hiatus a Very light was fired, and Threapleton opened his bomb doors. Seeing this, the captain of another aircraft, Sgt Ollason, assumed that an attack was imminent. Ollason attempted to obtain confirmation, but this was frustrated by poor radio reception and without waiting further he proceeded to bomb one of the submarines. Fortunately both for Ollason and the submarine, the bombs exploded harmlessly. Both submarines crash-dived and escaped.[8]

Gibson treated the incident as a joke.* But the attack prompted a searching inquiry and censure of those responsible. In the face of enraged demands from the Admiralty, it fell first to Gp Capt. Emmett, commander of the Bomber Wing at Lossiemouth, to explain what had happened. Emmett reported that Threapleton 'could not be excused' from responsibility for the bombing because he had not promulgated 'the detailed instructions to carry out the ordered exercise'. On the other hand, Ollason and his crew were 'very keen', 'above average' and had learned their lesson. He sought to excuse their impulsive behaviour by suggesting that:

. . . the surprise and excitement of spotting two real live submarines in the Mid North Sea caused the long pent-up war-like spirit and keenness to temporarily overcome the precautionary instructions drummed in by the continual theoretical teachings of the past.[9]

Emmett begged that 'not too severe a view be taken of the matter' and his plea was endorsed by Coastal Command.

---

* Gibson[10] tells us that all eight Hampdens attacked the submarine, and that when a second submarine was encountered shortly afterwards this was left alone in the belief that it was British, whereas (according to Gibson) it was a U-boat. This does not correspond with 83 Squadron's ORB, which records that '1 aircraft dropped bombs on an unidentified submarine, result unknown'. Nor is it consistent with Group Captain Emmett's report, which confirms that only one Hampden actually dropped bombs and that two Royal Navy submarines had been under threat.

The AOC-in-C Bomber Command was unmoved. Twelve days later Ludlow-Hewitt wrote to AVM Arthur Harris, who had taken over command of 5 Group shortly after the outbreak of war:

This reflects great discredit both on the Squadron concerned and on the Group to which it belongs. I have again and again drawn your attention to the necessity for the very thorough instruction and practice of an adequate and efficient briefing procedure and pre-flight preparation before departure. Your Group have also been urged to improve the low standard of wireless communication efficiency which has been known to prevail in the Group for some time. The incident clearly proves that insufficient attention is still being given to these important matters, and neither the Station Commander nor the Squadron Commander seem to have any conception of the importance which should be attached to the proper preparation of crews before any operational mission, or any idea of what ought to be done. An operation conducted in so slipshod a manner can only be accounted for by assuming that the officers of the unit have no idea of what constitutes efficiency . . .[11]

Ludlow-Hewitt concluded by instructing Harris 'to convey to Group Captain Emmett and Wing-Commander Snaith my displeasure at their failure to bring the units for which they are responsible to a satisfactory state of efficiency'.

Harris passed on the criticisms but also sought to deflect Ludlow-Hewitt's wrath away from his Group towards technical weaknesses of the Hampden. Harris had a low opinion of this aeroplane and missed no opportunity to expose its shortcomings. He also took issue with Ludlow-Hewitt's remarks about poor signals procedure, pointing to the Hampden's chronic problems of intercommunication. Chastened, Snaith used their remaining weeks at Lossiemouth to administer intensive practice in navigation, formation flying, intercommunication and bombing. The war was six months old. 83 Squadron had operated on only four occasions, yet on three of them their efforts had been marred by confusion, poor equipment or ineffectual planning. Less than a month remained before they would be called upon to fight in earnest.

Strike to Defend

Gibson liked nothing better than a good 'shoot up' and three days after the squadron had settled back at Scampton on 20 March he celebrated his return with an exuberant low-level trip in one of the squadron's Ansons. What the Anson lacked in speed he made up for by flying it close to the ground. Trees, steeples and chimney-pots flicked past as Gibson skimmed down the Foss Way to Newton in a style which caused his white-knuckled passenger to conclude that he was being flown by 'professional maniacs'. Such escapades were mirrored on the ground, where Guy had introduced his pregnant sister-in-law to the sensations of high-performance flying by whizzing his car in tight circles round a cinema car-park. Giddy behaviour enlivened what in Gibson's junior eyes had been six drab months of 'hanging around', now made worse by orders for intensive training in flying at night.

For Air Vice-Marshal Harris, on the other hand, those months of relative inactivity had been the greatest blessing he could have wished.

On the outbreak of war we had ... a force almost without reserves and without any adequate training organization behind it; any sustained campaign in the autumn of 1939 would very quickly have brought us to the end of our small supply of trained crews. And even what we had in the shop window, though there was nothing behind it, had to be bled white if we were going to provide the instructors, aircraft and unit organizations for the training that was essential to maintain the force for the bombing offensive of the future.[12]

Training was the key. Not only had the 'phoney war' allowed time for the readying of Bomber Command by experiment and the rehearsal of night flying, but at Ludlow-Hewitt's insistence seventeen squadrons had been withdrawn from the front line and converted to Operational Training Units. This decision was unpalatable to the Air Staff and even less welcome to the Cabinet. But it was the saving of Bomber Command and ironic that the end of Ludlow-Hewitt's term as C-in-C on 3 April 1940 should have coincided with the moment when his preparations were put to the test.

In that same week 83 Squadron's casualties began. On 6 April three Hampdens set out on a security patrol to discourage flying from the

German seaplane bases at Sylt and Borkum. One of the crews became lost. After nine hours in the air they ditched their Hampden near St Mary's lighthouse off the Northumberland coast. They drowned in seawater chilled at the end of an Arctic winter, at the coldest hour, shortly after four o'clock in the morning. If handled well, a Hampden which came down in the sea might stay afloat for some minutes; if badly, the men who struggled to escape from its rapidly flooding narrow spaces had a hard time of it. Thick flying clothing required by the poorly heated interior made matters worse. Once in the sea these garments soon became saturated and dragged their wearers down. It was a pathetic, useless way to die, especially when nothing had been accomplished.

Three days later Scampton was galvanized by news of the invasion of Norway. At breakfast time on 9 April a battalion of German parachute troops descended on to the Norwegian airfield at Stavanger. By mid-morning transport aircraft were arriving every few minutes, unloading troops, fuel and supplies. Defenders of ports were rapidly overpowered and after Oslo had been seized, reinforcements of men and materials poured into Norway virtually uninterrupted. Denmark was occupied simultaneously, to protect the Kattegat and Skagerrak and the channels between Jutland and the Danish islands which were essential for the passage of German shipping.

It was the narrowness of these waters, allied to the fact that they were only a few minutes' flying time from Danish airfields now teeming with German bombers, which prevented the Royal Navy from sending surface ships to intervene. Mines dropped from aircraft, on the other hand, could disrupt supplies to Norway and for the next month 5 Group were regularly engaged in delivering them. Here again they were fortunate – after a fashion. Mine-laying sorties provided a useful initiation to the disciplines of long-distance navigation and target finding at night. For the unseasoned, however, even these tutorials were fraught with peril.

Gibson flew his first on 11 April and in contrast to the nervousness which had seized him on his first sortie back in 1939 he tells us that he welcomed it. For several months he had been flying with a permanent crew, another development which reflected Ludlow-Hewitt's foresight. Plt Off. Jack Withers had trained as a pilot, but because the Hampden had no place for a co-pilot he was serving his apprenticeship as

Gibson's navigator/bomb-aimer until he gained a crew of his own. An artistic man, older than the squadron average, Gibson liked him not least because he was an accomplished pianist and therefore a useful companion on stand-down evenings. In the rear were LAC McCormack, the wireless operator/upper rear gunner, described by Gibson as 'scruffy',[13] and Plt Off. Watson, the lower rear gunner. Watson was about thirty, much older than the rest of them. A former armament NCO, he had volunteered for aircrew duties and had recently been commissioned. Privately, Gibson thought him a 'cool devil'.

They took off just after 11 p.m. as one of a force of eight 83 Squadron Hampdens sent to lay 1,500-lb magnetic 'M' mines in the channel of the Lille Baelt, between Jütland and Fyn. In an effort to disguise their real purpose, Gibson was instructed to reconnoitre several Danish towns and seaways, in addition to delivering the mine. As it turned out, the trip was more like a training sortie. Nothing untoward occurred and his abiding impression of the operation was its length: the Hampden did not return to Scampton until breakfast-time the following morning. Evidently, bombing was going to be exhausting.

Three days later things did not go so well. The area to be mined was the narrow strip of water between Middelfart and the Danish mainland. The weather was poor with high winds, low cloud and heavy rain. Forced almost to the level of the water by the low cloud, Gibson found his target (professing to have flown under Middelfart bridge in the process), climbed to the release height and had his first exchange of fire with a flak ship. The return was flown entirely on instruments through black rain cloud and electrical storms. Gibson touched down at Manston, Kent, after seven and a quarter hours in the air.

Four Hampdens had set off from Scampton the previous evening; three came back. Fg Off. Kenneth Sylvester had been with the squadron for two years and Gibson and 'Sylvo' had socialized in a casual way. Now Sylvester's Hampden disappeared. The aircraft made contact with Manston and obtained a homing bearing which brought its engines within earshot of listeners on the ground. But Sylvester could not find the aerodrome. Disorientated, he flew out down the Channel until his Hampden ran out of fuel. Distress signals were received at 04.00. Then silence. No trace of the aeroplane, or Sylvester, or his crew, was ever found.

Inexperience was their main enemy and on his next operation Gibson narrowly escaped a fate similar to Sylvester's. On 20 April Bridgman, Ross and Gibson were ordered to bomb German transport aircraft massed on the aerodrome at Ålborg in northern Denmark. It was raining hard as they went out to their aircraft towards 11 p.m. As they settled in their places Gibson discovered that one of the electrical systems was faulty. Cursing the hapless 'erk' who had been unable to restore it to working order, an ill-tempered Gibson transferred to a reserve aircraft. He and his crew took off half an hour after Ellis Ross, worried that the delay might cost them dear if Ålborg's defences had been aroused.

In the event they never found Ålborg, where Bridgman and Ross delivered their bombs in the teeth of ferocious light flak. Instead, they became lost, and when Withers eventually established their position near Copenhagen it was too late to continue. Gibson turned for home, crossing Denmark at low-level after daybreak, Watson and McCormack watching tensely for fighters. Gibson had little confidence in the Hampden's capacity to withstand a fighter attack in daylight. The mounts of their Vickers gas-operated 'K' guns in the rear were rickety and their field of fire was restricted, the upper pair being fitted with ramps as a precaution against the gunner shooting off his own tail. Gibson eventually landed at Lossiemouth, and accused Withers of incompetence until it emerged that they had been misled by a faulty compass.

Bomber Command awarded code-names to the seaways it was attempting to deny to German shipping. Different sectors were named after flowers or vegetables, and mine-laying was to be known as 'Gardening'. Thus the Lille Baelt between Jütland and Fyn was Carrot, and the compiler of the squadron's Operations Record Book solemnly recorded that the only successfully planted 'Carrot' on the night of 14/15 April had been Gibson's. Carrots had again been sown on the 17th, while on 21/22 April six Hampdens set forth to plant Daffodils. Daffodil was for Oresund (the Baltic Sound between north-east Zealand and Sweden) and two nights later seven more aircraft attempted to mine it. Only three, one of them Gibson, managed to locate the target. Lettuce (the Kiel canal) was the objective for two aircraft on the 25th – both unsuccessful – and on successive evenings at the beginning of May there was a horticultural festival when Hampdens visited Forget-me-not (Kiel harbour), Asparagus and Broccoli (areas within the Store Baelt) and

Nasturtium (part of Oresund). Within the first fortnight these efforts were rewarded by the sinking or damaging of at least five ships, although three of these were Danish train-ferries that routinely plied back and forth between Fyn and Zealand.

83 Squadron operated on eleven occasions during April and its members were becoming accustomed to the new routine. In the morning came the daily inspection of aircraft. Most servicing was done in the open and since the Lincoln Edge is a blustery place, even simple tasks could be complicated by wet weather or strong cold winds which caused greatcoated airmen to teeter atop tall ladders. If all was well, the aircraft would be signed for and there would be a short flight test towards lunch-time. By now the signs of an operation might be evident, with the towing of bomb-trolleys, the winching-on of bombs and delivery of pans of ammunition. Briefing came later in the afternoon; often this was perfunctory, discretion largely being left to individual crews over routes and times. On days when no operation was in prospect there were local training flights, followed by a trip to a pub or cinema in the evening. It was all fairly straightforward and although there had been losses, no one had yet been shot down. Ålborg's flak excepted, it was almost as if the adjustment to war was to be an evolution from older routines.

Or was it? At 6 a.m. on Friday 10 May Scampton's commander was informed that Holland and Belgium had been invaded. The squadrons were brought to readiness, personnel were confined to camp and crews waited for orders that would surely plunge them into their first real battle. Later in the day, crowded round wireless sets, they heard more momentous news. Chamberlain had resigned. Winston Churchill was prime minister.

For forty-eight hours they waited on tenterhooks; on Monday evening operations resumed, but only Gardening was carried out. Yet over that weekend the map had changed utterly. German units were in the outskirts of Rotterdam and by the time Gibson and Collier had returned from an abortive sortie to plant mines in the Kiel canal, Queen Wilhelmina and her ministers had left for England. When Gibson returned to the canal the following evening Holland had surrendered, and Belgium was being overrun.

The next night saw glimmers of a change of strategy. As usual several aircraft flew to lay mines, but three others were detailed to bomb road junctions in the Low Countries to impede German troop movements. One of them crashed on the way home, apparently as a result of navigational confusion. Then, on Thursday 16 May, less than a week after the assault on the Low Countries, Guderian's tanks now loose in France, the squadron was at last ordered to Germany. They sent five aircraft, to each of which a specific building or site was allocated.

This fastidiousness was based partly on Bomber Command's instinct for conservation, but more particularly upon vastly exaggerated expectations of a navigator's ability to pinpoint a target at night and of what an individual bomber could do to it if he did. On this evening, in fact, all five crews claimed success. More typical was what happened to them in the process. Bridgman's Hampden was damaged by flak while attacking a marshalling yard in Düsseldorf. Pitcairn-Hill's aircraft was holed by light flak when he bombed the aerodrome at Duisburg. The starboard wing of Sgt Stan Harpham's Hampden had a hole punched through it by a pom-pom shell. And to ram the message of peril home, the next night Fg Off. Ian Haydon was attacked by a nightfighter and Gibson's aircraft collided with a balloon cable while dive-bombing an oil refinery at Hamburg.

By 20 May Viscount Gort was already considering how the British Expeditionary Force might be evacuated from France. On this and following nights the squadron was sent to tactical targets in France, Belgium and Germany: French road bridges on the 20th; bridges, trains and aerodromes on the 22nd; railways, airfields and road junctions on the 26th. Gibson flew on 22 May and demolished a railway bridge over the Schelde–Maas canal. Four nights later he claimed success in blocking a railway tunnel near Aachen. But relative to the scale of events on the ground the effects of such actions were trifling and on both these evenings – as on many others – some aircraft returned early, either having failed to locate their targets or because of mechanical failure. Inexperience remained their weakness. When poor visibility caused Sgt Stanley Jenkins to be diverted from Scampton to Ringway in the early hours of 23 May, he flew into the side of a hill.

On 27 May Scampton was occupied by preparations for a 5 Group investiture by King George VI. Gibson was not much interested in the formality of such musters and in the keeping of his wardrobe he was ever the despair of his batman – another echo, perhaps, of his disjointed upbringing.

But, however he viewed the parade which was drawn smartly to attention by Snaith at half past three that Monday afternoon, there was an aspect of the occasion which caught his interest. The King was awarding decorations. Already several of Gibson's colleagues had become curious about his zest for operations, suspecting that behind it there might lie an urge to win medals. He always denied this and those close to him confirm that the pursuit of honours was not a leading factor in his motivation. Even so, his desire to be in the centre of things would outwardly be reinforced by badges of achievement. For Gibson, perhaps the award of a medal was less an end in itself than a means to an end. But on this occasion the matter was academic, because he was not among those who were decorated.

Around this time Gibson took a night off. Nottingham was a highly favoured place for socializing, with a traditional circuit of pubs that began at the Trip to Jerusalem, was followed by visits to the Flying Horse (the 'Airborne Nag'), Black Boy, Exchange, Dog & Partridge and Admiral Nelson and ended at the Palais de Danse where Billy Merrin and his Commanders would be playing and girls could be found. If for any reason a reveller missed his transport back to Scampton, a chilly night dozing on mail bags on Nottingham station awaited him until the first train left for Lincoln. Gibson takes up the account:

This particular night Oscar and I ran into trouble with a couple of MPs. We had been crossing the road to the Flying Horse without our hats on, when we had been spotted and these Army Red Caps had been extremely rude. We were both polite at first but after a while Oscar began explaining patiently but very cuttingly that we had both been over Germany for two nights running and that it wouldn't be a bad idea if great strapping men like them were in France doing a bit of fighting themselves . . . I will never understand why in time of war men who never risk their lives themselves must forever be watching those who do . . . Many people do not realize that the Royal Air Force is as much in the front line as anyone, the only difference being that we . . . possess a range which makes it possible for us to reach the scene of action in a few hours, while operating from peaceful surroundings.[14]

The incident introduces one of his frustrations: the impossibility of communicating to non-fliers anything of the schizoid life of the bomber pilot, whose hand could be tilting a glass in his local on one evening and bubbling up in blisters inside a burning aeroplane on the next. There were aspects of bombing he enjoyed, but the arbitrary juxtaposition of skylarks and flak, Lincolnshire lanes and German cities, and the tension between domestic routine and an undated warrant for execution, all drove him to distraction. Repeatedly Gibson evinced a sense of anger at his inability to explain this terrible paradox to anyone who was not already part of it. He struggled to make people *understand*, or at the least show deference to men who were, in the main, trapped in a bad dream.

Operations were cancelled on the evenings which followed the investiture. Gibson took advantage of the lull by telephoning Eve to invite her up to Scampton. *Come out to Play* had just finished its London run at the Phoenix theatre and Eve had a few spare days before the show opened in Brighton on 3 June.

Gibson met her at Lincoln station and shooed away several pilots returning from leave who had introduced themselves on the train. Guy drove her up to the aerodrome, apologizing for the fact that he would, after all, be flying that night. But his friend Ian Haydon would take her to dinner instead. Haydon and Eve watched Gibson 'in old Admiral Foo Bang take off with a lurch into the night sky'. Perhaps Gibson had volunteered, to impress.

Admiral Foo Bang? Some weeks before, several ground crew had been fooling in their barrack room. One of them was Douglas Garton, who had grabbed a broomstick, turned his hat back to front, and embarked on an impromptu performance as Long John Silver, lurching to and fro yelling, 'At the sign of the Admiral Ben Bow'. One of his mates was a former Halton apprentice nicknamed Foo (a catchword from a popular 1930s American comic strip) and during the ensuing horseplay Garton's chant was modified to 'Ben Foo'. From there it was only a step to christening an aircraft, which Garton duly did by painting *Admiral Ben Foo* on the nose of Bridgman's Hampden, adding the small heraldic device of a fouled anchor. Initially, Garton recalls, 'Oscar was not overly amused', but the idea caught on and in following weeks several other A Flight Hampdens were awarded 'Admiral' names: Admiral Imaz Dryazel (after the famous Guinness toucan), Admiral von Shicklgruber, Admiral Foo Bang. Much care was lavished on lettering and emblems, and Garton recalls how disheartening it was when such aircraft were promptly lost. At least one Hampden disappeared before its name was painted.[15] The Admirals appealed to Gibson's sense of fun and perhaps too for the way in which they fostered the exclusivity of a team. At any rate, he did not forget them and for the next three years aircraft he flew regularly were adorned with an Admiral name.

Next day came news of the squadron's first decorations. There were eight, five DFCs and three DFMs, awarded to the crews of Bridgman and Ross 'for reconnaissance and bombing of Ålborg aerodrome, and for work carried out since the outbreak of hostilities'. There was a stand-down that Saturday evening, and a large party in the Saracen's Head. The Ålborg raid was the first occasion when 83 Squadron had shown its real mettle. For Gibson, on the other hand, this had been the night of malfunctions and bungled navigation. Remembering this failure, he was not pleased to be excluded. On the Sunday he left for a week's leave, and travelled with Eve to Brighton. A day or two later, his jealousy subsiding, they sent a saucy postcard to congratulate Bridgman and Ross.

Boyhood's End

By the time Gibson returned to Scampton the following weekend some 330,000 British, French and Belgian troops had been evacuated from France. The French fought on a few days more, but it was all over. It was all over too for Ian Haydon, who had taken Eve to dinner the week before and was now in a grave near Aachen. There had been another loss in Gibson's absence and several important changes.

Snaith was about to depart for a new posting at Kinloss. He and Gibson had had their differences, Snaith having been a restraining influence on Gibson's irresponsible antics and wary of his cocksure manner. Yet Snaith had been in charge of the squadron more or less continuously since Gibson had joined it; he was part of the traditional community and Gibson seems to have viewed his going with genuine regret. Their new commander was Wg-Cdr J.C. Sisson, a man who flew on operations more frequently than Snaith and believed in leading from the front.

Continuity was disturbed more directly by news that Jack Withers had been given a crew of his own. This meant a reorganization within Gibson's crew. But everyone's crew had in some sense changed, for it was now general policy that all 'aircrew airmen' should be sergeants. This scandalized the older NCOs, mostly pre-war regulars who had worked for years for promotion and resented the idea that someone like LAC McCormack should have vaulted to the rank of sergeant overnight. Resistance was accordingly fierce and there were crude pressures to maintain the *status quo*. Gibson's opinion is unrecorded, although in common with a number of other officers, NCO airmen were beginning to find him more approachable and less likely to stand on his dignity when in their company off duty. The bonds of shared experience had begun to transcend the barriers of class.

Gibson administered a crash course in navigation to Watson, who moved forward to the navigator/bomb-aimer's position and was replaced at the rear by a Sgt Howard. Together they embarked upon one of the most gruelling spells of operational flying which Gibson ever undertook. During the next three weeks the squadron operated on seventeen occasions and Gibson flew on almost every alternate night from 9 June to the end of the month.

His bombing was improving. Most of these sorties ended in success and in all but two he reported that he had bombed the primary target – in one instance despite very bad weather. But more and more Hampdens were now returning scarred by flak; miraculously, no further crews were lost during the month, although one Hampden was engaged by a flak ship while mine-laying at the mouth of the Elbe and its navigator blinded. This incident made a lasting impression on Gibson, who seems to have feared permanent disability (or the relegation likely to go with it) as much, or more, than death.

But other pilots were beginning to wonder if he feared anything at all. By the beginning of July, according to the draft of his book, 'all our bomber crews were all in'. Bridgman confirms that as the weeks passed and evidence of the terminal risks they were facing became inescapably obvious, several pilots became badly stressed. Yet if Gibson shared in the mounting strain, this was not evident to those around him. He volunteered for extra sorties and his unconcern became a talking point.

Gibson's accounts of these raids and the social life between them make vivid reading. But they are not very good narrative history. Incidents, details, personalities and dates are transposed or remixed. This is a characteristic of many memoirs. Here and there, however, we may suspect Gibson's penchant for exaggeration. His account of Pitcairn-Hill bottling up a train by bombing both ends of a railway tunnel is questionable. Pitcairn-Hill attacked a different target on the

night in question and although he may have entombed a train on some
other occasion, records disclose that two months later another pilot
bombed a train entering a tunnel. Likewise, one wonders what really
lay behind Gibson's story of his near error in preparing to bomb an
airfield in Berkshire. He tells us that he had lost his way on return from
'the bombing of a German military headquarters at Ghent' on the night
of 13 June and assumed he was still over France. He cites his logbook as
evidence, but several other purported quotations from his log departed
from what he actually wrote in it, and squadron records tell a different
story. On that night Gibson was detailed to attack a target on the edge
of the Ardennes, and failed to find it.

Targets during June had typically been German industrial sites, oil
plants, roads, railways and shipping lanes. July saw a temporary change
of focus, with a series of attacks on the *Scharnhorst*, then in floating
dock at Kiel, and others on the *Tirpitz* and *Scheer* at Wilhelmshaven.
The *Scharnhorst* had dispatched the aircraft carrier *Glorious* in two
salvoes during the Norwegian campaign in June. Twelve aircraft led by
Sisson flew to seek her on the night of 1/2 July. Kiel was heavily
defended and only Kynoch reported hits on the battle-cruiser. Gibson
made what was afterwards described as an 'accurate dive attack', but
with uncertain results.

Three nights later 83 Squadron attempted to repeat the attack, but if
anything this was less conclusive than the first. Two crews failed to
locate the target and such was the ferocity of the light flak and the glare
of searchlights ('like putting your face into a bowl of milk') that in five
instances the whereabouts of the bomb bursts were unobserved. With
typical persistence Gibson made five trial dive attacks before releasing
his bomb on the sixth, but found that on each attempt 'we couldn't see
a thing'. One of those who took part recalls violent explosions caused
by guns which had been depressed to fire shells with close-proximity
fuses across the water. It was a fearful experience, from which several
crews returned badly shaken.

Gibson overshot on the final dive and his bomb exploded in the
town. The bombing of civilian dwellings was still prohibited, partly for
fear of reprisal but more particularly because of the gentlemanly attitude
to war which continued to prevail in the government and Air Ministry.
Theory still asserted that the selective bombing of industrial and communications targets would bring the German war economy to its knees.

Harris believed none of this, although then, as later, the chance of sinking a capital ship seems to have appealed to him, if only as a means of eclipsing the Admiralty. But where, now, lay the feelings of the crews?

One of the passages which was censored from Gibson's book concerns an NCO whose mother had been killed in an air raid. In the published version of *Enemy Coast Ahead* all we read is this:

He came to me that afternoon; his eyes were wet, but he was not crying. He wanted to come with us that night, to avenge his mother.

Such a spirit spelt doom for German cities in 1943 and 1944.[16]

In the original, it read like this:

He wanted to come with us that night to avenge his mother, and to do so in kind, and long after the briefing was over, a few pilots stayed behind. One of the deputy Flight Commanders carefully looked around to see that all senior officers had gone out of the room, then he made a short speech.

'Don't bother about the target tonight, chaps,' he said, 'a stick across the town will do for all, and may we kill as many people as possible to avenge Sergeant Knox's mother.'

Such spirit and such sign of revenge spelt doom for German cities in 1943–1944.[17]

Gibson placed this episode in September. In July 1940, when the Luftwaffe offensive against Britain had scarcely begun, it seems unlikely that such vengefulness should yet have been a factor which spurred crews to their targets, still less deliberately miss them in order to kill civilians. An active desire to kill mothers, children, the elderly, or patients in hospitals never ranked high in Bomber Command's motivation. (Harris later commented with chilling sarcasm that it was not his policy to bomb such people because they were already a burden upon the German economy.) Many bomber crews found civilian slaughter to be an aspect about which they cared not to think too deeply, or conditioned themselves to accept. In Gibson's case, however, the artless honesty of his story gives pause for thought. If this is not thinly disguised autobiography, or an episode he made up as a means of signalling his own feelings, then presumably there were such conversations at Scampton. Two years later we shall find Gibson urging his crews to the destruction of German cities, and promising retribution in his letters of condolence to bereaved mothers. Paradoxically, there is nothing in that which marks him out as bloodthirsty. Gibson's eagerness to kill Germans and his emergence as an outstanding commander stemmed rather from the directness in his cast of mind – a tendency towards the logic of the isolated case, shorn of all doubt and complexity.

By contrast with the frenetic activity during June, Gibson's operations in July were fewer and more widely spaced: 'Life became quite orderly and we felt rather like businessmen who spend their days in a year doing regular things.' Moreover, his self-esteem was lifted on 9 July when news arrived that he and Pitcairn-Hill had been awarded the DFC. The accolade cheered him on his way to an inconclusive raid on the *Tirpitz*, where the sky was scribbled with tracer, curling lines of Bofors shells and searchlights of impenetrable brilliance. Not everyone was able to relax after such experiences and while at this time Gibson seems to have had a capacity to shed stress in slack periods, others found it accumulative.*

There were distractions. On one day a consignment of mines in Scampton's bomb dump blew up. The explosion was of such force that it flung pieces of girders 'across Ermine Street and smaller pieces nearly to Welton and Hackthorn'. Gibson's memory of the incident places him in the grounds of Brattleby Hall, a tall Georgian mansion under the Edge just north of Scampton, in which a number of aircrew officers were billeted. The house was set in large grounds adjacent to Brattleby church and according to Gibson was owned by an elderly lady who struggled to keep it going. By his own admission,

We were not very good billettees; at least not very quiet ones. When we got back from a raid at night we were usually in high spirits. Often we would make such a noise that we waked [*sic*] up the whole household. Often we played silly games in her garden, such as trying to plunge through the rhododendron bushes on bikes without hurting ourselves or rolling on the

* Gibson's competitive impulse, enthusiasm for operations and – at this stage – apparent lack of operational stress are confirmed by Harris, who later wrote that, 'Not content with doing more operational flying than anybody else, he used to go out on additional nights just for fun and attempt to bomb the *Tirpitz* while she was building with 2,000-lb bombs with wing tip flares tied on them so he could re-direct his aim next time.'[18]

lawn in one great fighting mass cutting up all the grass, which must have broken her heart next day.[19]

Others remember Gibson's behaviour as rather worse than this. Returning from the pub one night, it is said that he entered the room of a young lady visitor and attempted to join her in bed. Next day there was a formal complaint and he was banished from Brattleby Hall.

This incident – and in today's scale of condemnation it is not clear where it might fall – again draws us to consider Gibson's relations with women. His casual conquests were legion and while the present case could represent anything from a bet or a dare to drunken opportunism after walking into the wrong bedroom (the Hall had no electricity), his outlook towards women in general was oddly disjointed. There is no doubt that he was a compulsive sexual adventurer, but he was also capable of intense relationships in which sex was relatively unimportant. It is almost as if he sought different women for different purposes, categorizing them either as whores or goddesses. His responses to the feelings he touched or scarred were likewise contradictory, veering between a generous sensitivity and indifference. Sleeping with women may have been another facet of his self-assertion.

From the end of July to 24 August Gibson did not fly on operations. Early in the month he took part in training for a low-level attack on the Dortmund–Ems canal which aimed to drain the inland waterway at the point where it is carried across the River Ems by a pair of aqueducts. In the event he was absent when the attack took place on 12 August and claimed two of his oldest colleagues.*

---

* Eleven Hampdens of 49 and 83 Squadrons set out shortly before 9 p.m. on 12 August. Two crews made diversionary attacks, Sqn Ldr J. Collier bombing lock gates at Munster, Sgt Sewell flying up and down the waterway to bomb river craft and shoot out searchlights. Defences around the aqueducts had recently been strengthened. When Pitcairn-Hill made the first attack from 150 feet he accordingly flew into a tangle of light flak, sustaining hits which shattered the perspex rear turrets, injured both his gunners and shot the wireless to pieces. But nothing struck the vitals of his aircraft, and he emerged from the barrage having delivered his bomb on to the aqueduct. Ellis Ross came next. By now the defences were fully alert to the method of attack and both Ross, and Alan Mulligan who followed him, were shot down. Mulligan managed to climb his burning Hampden to sufficient height for his crew to escape, although one man was killed and another died of his injuries. The next Hampden sustained bad damage, but

That day was his birthday. He passed it at Boscastle in north Cornwall, only afterwards coming to realize that had he been at Scampton he might well have been among those who perished. But just then, there were other things in his mind. Most immediate of them was Eve. *Come Out to Play* had finished. With no work in prospect Eve had gone home to Penarth, where she was cheered to receive a telephone call from Guy inviting her to join him for his long leave. After weeks apart, they met on Bristol Temple Meads station and set off for a holiday which was to be the longest they had so far spent together.

They stayed in the Wellington Hotel, went for walks, swam and sunbathed, lazed late in bed and read about the Battle of Britain in the newspapers. In the evenings there were strolls to the pub and opportunities for Guy to trade yarns with fishermen. On their walks Guy at last began to go into detail about his unhappy upbringing and brought Eve up to date with more recent events. He told her of his sister Joan, who by now had borne two children, one of whom had died. Against A.J.'s wishes she would soon marry an engineer. After a family conference A.J. had virtually washed his hands of her, leaving Alick, Ruth and Guy to rally round. For a while Joan and the surviving child had lived with Alick and Ruth, but Alick's unit had been transferred to Northern Ireland.

But how did Guy react to A.J.'s choice of wife? Two days before Guy's birthday, seven months after Nora's death, his father had remarried. Diana Katherine Hodges, a neighbour of A.J.'s in Chelsea, was now Guy's stepmother. However, far from being old enough to be his mother, at thirty Diana was only fractionally older than Eve and quite young enough to be his wife. (Age may have preoccupied A.J. too: at the wedding either he or the incumbent understated his own age by five years.) Guy's family had now effectively atomized. He was on his own.

They parted where they had met, on Bristol Temple Meads, but now with that sense of hollow depression that recalled the end of a summer holiday and return to boarding-school. This time it was worse.

---

bombed accurately and was nursed home. Last came Flt Lt R.A.B. Learoyd. Having seen two out of the previous four aircraft perish, he flew into the dense flak, dropped his bomb on the aqueduct and emerged, not intact, but still flying. Learoyd took his Hampden back to Scampton, where he circled for several hours with a maimed hydraulic system in order to land in daylight. The attack succeeded to the extent that normal use of the canal was denied for a month. Pitcairn-Hill was awarded the DSO. For his unflinching persistence, Learoyd was awarded the Victoria Cross.

Within days the seizure of parts of southern England by German forces might be a reality and they were surrounded by servicemen embracing wives, lovers, children, parents – perhaps for the last time. Wartime station platforms were ultimate boundaries, places of first and last touch, ecstatic greeting and glistening cheeks. There is an almost thoroughgoing lack of correspondence between Eve's account of her life with Guy, and of his with her. But at this point, the long kiss finally broken by the lurch of the train, their memories were as one.

Britain was now braced for invasion and in September 83 Squadron's attention was again redirected, this time to transport ships and barges lining harbour basins of the Channel ports. Gibson flew to bomb barges at Ostend on the 7th, Antwerp on the 15th and again on the 20th. Others remember the ferocity of the defences, especially the sinuous lines of glowing Bofors shells, lazy at first, then accelerating to unavoidable speeds. On the second of these trips Gibson's Hampden received a direct hit from a shell which passed through the cockpit, knocked the rudder bar from its pivot and severed the intercom. Deprived of communication with his bomb-aimer, Gibson nevertheless persisted and released the bombs himself.

Having survived so much, the valiant Pitcairn-Hill had been shot down two days previously during an attack on Le Havre. One by one the old stagers of the original group of 1937–38 were making their exits. For the survivors, operational flying now seemed crushingly onerous. Several were rotated out of the line, to be rested at OTUs. Of those who remained, some became withdrawn, others fretful, irritable or bellicose. Drinking increased and on one occasion Gibson took the place of a colleague who was too drunk to fly. His reprieve was brief: a few days later he was shot down. They were very tired.

German occupation of the Low Countries and Denmark had placed Lincolnshire's aerodromes within easier range of Luftwaffe bombers. Increased German night intruder activity added to existing difficulties of guiding Hampdens safely back to earth. Scampton's night-flying provision originally consisted of no more than a Chance light and gooseneck flares which fed from paraffin. Laying the flarepath was tedious and became even more so if the wind changed and the entire layout had to be picked up and set out anew. Loitering Ju 88s only made matters worse, for a gooseneck flarepath could not be extinguished in a hurry.

Scampton's electricians improvised an electrical flarepath, cutting holes in four-gallon petrol cans to accept 60-watt bulbs. Each line of lamps was connected to the Chance light generator, so the entire system could be extinguished at the touch of a switch. This was a great improvement, but brought its own risks. If an aircraft swung on landing it could become entangled in the cabling and cause the whole system to fail. Electricians would thus remain on duty until all aircraft had returned.[20]

It was during one of these vigils that a leading aircraftman was faintly surprised to see a de Havilland Dominie slip in and taxi up to his position. Out stepped an elderly man, who announced himself as Lord Trenchard. Trenchard was father and first Marshal of the Royal Air Force and theorist emeritus in matters of strategic bombing ('The moral effect of bombing stands to the material in a proportion of 20 to 1'). He was now on tour to gather his impressions. Within a few months he would produce a memorandum which argued that German society was uniquely vulnerable to collapse under the effects of sustained aerial attack.

After the bewildering changes of emphasis in their long summer campaign – Gardening, German industry, bottleneck targets, capital ships, barges – it may not have been obvious to Scampton's weary crews that a strategic air offensive was now under way. Yet a few weeks before, Churchill had written to Beaverbrook:

. . . when I look round to see how we can win the war I see that there is only one sure path. We have no Continental army which can defeat the German military power . . . But there is one thing that will bring him back and bring him down, and that is an absolutely devastating, exterminating attack by very heavy bombers from this country upon the Nazi homeland. We must be able to overwhelm them by this means, without which I do not see a way through.[21]

So Gibson's last operation with 83 Squadron was uncannily symbolic. Tactically it shows Bomber Command at a crossroads, being in some respects a synthesis of past habits and in others a signpost pointing along Churchill's 'one sure path'. At half past seven on the evening of 23 September Gibson's was the first of eleven 83 Squadron aircraft that took to the air, merging with a company of 129 Hampdens, Whitleys and Wellingtons heading for Berlin. No larger force had yet raided one German city, let alone been to the capital and a new theory – concentration – was being tested. In other respects tradition still ruled. Each aircraft was allocated to one of seventeen specific targets, thereby dissipating the effects of bombing by the 112 aircraft which actually reached the city. Gibson's target was the Potsdamer station which, according to squadron records, he found and attacked or, according to *Enemy Coast Ahead*, he bombed by estimation, on a timed run. Not all his colleagues managed nearly so much. One pilot complained of giddiness and returned early. Several, including Gibson's old companion Jack Withers, were defeated by the weather and bombed alternative targets. And Sqn Ldr Bridgman 'did not return to base'.

Bridgman's loss made a deep impression:

We waited all night; we waited until the grey darkness of the early hours became purple, then blue as the sun rose in the east over Lincoln Wolds and it became daylight. But Oscar never came back.[22]*

His Hampden had crashed near Bethen. Bridgman survived, and spent the next four and a half years in a prisoner-of-war camp. All his crew died, among them Gibson's former navigator, Watson.

That Berlin raid exemplified many of the difficulties that had dogged them – icing, groping for pinpoints, poor visibility over the target, unforeseen winds – and which since early April had claimed sixty-two of Gibson's colleagues. Fifty were dead, nineteen as a result of accidents. Only twelve were prisoners. Most of the rest had been seconded to OTUs, to invest their experience as the coming men of Bomber Command.

To Gibson, it seemed the end of an era. And for him, it was. Since the outbreak of war he had flown thirty-seven operations, thirty-four of them within little more than five months. On the day after Berlin he was told that, for the time being, he had done enough.

* To judge from the text alone, Gibson does not seem to have known of Bridgman's survival, as the publisher found it necessary to insert a note at this point to explain that 'S/Ldr Bridgman survived, to be taken prisoner.' However, in the introductory dedicatory list of lost colleagues this is already evident, as Bridgman is there described as 'Missing – Prisoner of war', suggesting that Gibson did know.

Pause

In Harris's eyes he had done more than enough. Historians have supposed that Gibson's emergence as a warrior-leader of outstanding calibre came later. In fact, even before he had packed his bags for transfer to No. 14 OTU at Cottesmore in Rutland, Harris had marked him out. Eighteen months afterwards Harris wrote that Gibson 'was without question the most full-out fighting pilot in the whole of 5 Group in the days when I had it'.[23]

The business of Cottesmore was the final training of pilots, W/T operators and air gunners. There were plenty of familiar faces among the instructing staff when Gibson reported for instructing duties on 26 September, for Cottesmore was a place where operationally tired aircrew from Scampton and Waddington were rested in exchange for newly trained crews. Several colleagues, including Jack Withers, went with him, and they had been preceded by Jack Kynoch and Sam Threapleton. But Gibson never settled there. He was only attached to 14 OTU for two weeks, and part of that time was passed on leave.

Eve invited him down to Wales. With no immediate prospects in the theatre, she had been thinking of joining one of the services. Guy had other ideas. Casual partners aside, Eve had absorbed him for the best part of a year. He had pursued her doggedly up and down Britain, and they had holidayed together several times. Now he decided that he would like to marry her.

Others – on small acquaintance – had found Eve rather worldly. Certainly, her years in the theatre had given her a taste for smart (some say gaudy) clothes, good make-up, social excitement and a life of her own. A mutual friend thought her 'a bit flighty'. Of lively temperament, sometimes volatile, she also possessed reserves of self-reliance, even steel, which would emerge in later years. None of that would have diminished her attraction for Gibson. The more interesting question is why he wanted to marry her and she him.

Part of it was loneliness. The family network – what was left of it – had largely fallen apart. Alick was now in Northern Ireland and everyone else in Guy's near family – brother, sister, father – had recently married. Why not him? Gibson wrote of his hankering after 'a little home life, which I had missed so far'. These words, a touch plaintive, were the nearest he came to openly referring to the disaster of his childhood. The kind of home life he envisaged is less obvious – Eve was someone to have at your elbow at a party rather than in the kitchen – although the desire to realize it before time ran out is easier to understand.

For her part Eve may have supposed that marriage would offer something new: fresh surroundings, variety, perhaps a little extra status. She had little interest in the RAF, but enjoyed Guy's spontaneity, admired his deeds and shared his urge to find or make fun. She was nearing thirty and the role of wife to a roistering 22-year-old emergent war hero may have held stronger appeal than broken fingernails and oily hands servicing trucks in the ATS, or hauling in barrage balloons. But no previous conjecture touches the probable root of the matter, which is that each held extreme feelings of sexual attraction for the other and that in 1940 expectations of permanence were measured in weeks or months.

Guy's proposal was typically blunt and prosaic, made one wet night under a dripping tree while walking back to Archer Road. 'Just like that; no fuss,' Eve wrote later, adding, 'but then, Guy wasn't a romanticist.' Perhaps not, in Eve's eyes, although behind the matter-of-fact manner of her boy there was a dreamer she seems never to have noticed. Anyway, she said yes and the engagement was announced on 8 October. The Moores did this sort of thing properly, placing notices in the newspapers and Guy, as a child of the IFS and an officer, was apparently *persona grata*. A day or two later he was posted to No. 16 OTU at Upper Heyford.

The Luftwaffe, meanwhile, was changing both its objective and its methods. Since late August it had been attacking cities, and during the autumn the weight of bombing shifted from daylight to night. Fighter Command, hitherto trained and equipped largely for defence by day, was left unprepared. AVM Trafford Leigh-Mallory, AOC 12 Group, and AM Sholto Douglas, deputy chief of air staff, made urgent appeal to Harris for 'some absolutely picked night pilots to leaven their inexperienced night-fighters'. Harris obliged, sending them what he described as 'a hand-picked bunch, of which Gibson was the best'. Gibson readily agreed to give up his OTU rest period in favour of something more interesting. For his part, Harris promised Gibson that 'when he had done his stuff on night-fighters' he would give him 'the best command within my power'.[24]

This remarkable bargain struck, Gibson was ordered to report to 29 Squadron at RAF Digby in Lincolnshire. He arrived at Digby on 13 November, his rest from operations having lasted just forty-eight days.

Part Four

STARLIGHT

November 1940–March 1942

We ran across the meadow scabbed with cow-dung, past
the crab-apple trees and camouflaged nissen hut.
It was curfew-time for our war-band.

At home the curtains were drawn. The wireless boomed
its commands. I loved the battle-anthems and the
gregarious news.

Then, in the earthy shelter, warmed by a blue-glassed
storm-lantern, I huddled with stories of dragon-
tailed airships and warriors who took wing
immortal as phantoms.

Geoffrey Hill, *Mercian Hymns*, XXII, 1971

Fighters

South of Lincoln the road to Grantham is threaded between villages that look west from the limestone Edge across the Vale of Trent. Coleby, Boothby Graffoe, Navenby, Wellingore, Welbourn: their names are intriguing, their sites ancient. East of the Edge lies an emptier region where churches stranded at the ends of lanes testify to extinct hamlets. Today this is gently undulating farmland, but the strict geometry of enclosure, opened out by modern agriculture, does not wholly disguise the waterless heath across which Georgian surveyors aligned their quickset hedges. There is a melancholy about this landscape which Gibson seems to have sensed when he was delivered to RAF Digby one afternoon in mid-November.* Hurricanes and Blenheims were parked on the grass, their engines covered against the drizzle. As the Anson which had brought him smalled into the dull sky, Gibson turned to make himself known to the adjutant of 29 Squadron, Sam France.

France seemed affable and his warm office offered a welcome retreat from the miserable afternoon. As they ran through administrative formalities, France explained that at night their machines operated from a small satellite airfield perched on the Edge at Wellingore Heath six miles to the west. Gibson's questions turned to 29 Squadron's personalities. France now became oddly guarded and Gibson began to wonder if all was well. His worries intensified when he was driven to the officers' Mess at Wellingore Grange, a building of Jacobean beginnings, admired for its oak-panelled hall and beamed ceilings. Despite cheerful log fires, the atmosphere here was hostile. Several officers acknowledged Gibson's entrance with sullen grunts. One walked out and slammed the door. Bewildered, Gibson was thankful when someone more genial introduced himself. This was Plt Off. Edward Graham-Little, one of five pilots who had been posted in three weeks before. With several of these newcomers

* Gibson arrived at Digby on 13 November 1940, whereas Gibson's service record gives the date of his transfer to 29 Squadron as 31 (*sic*) November 1940. Presumably the numbers were transposed by clerical error. However, records of 16 OTU claimed him as a member of their 'screened operational staff' as late as 26 November, by which date someone had determined that he should be posted to 58 OTU.

Gibson ate his supper and afterwards went across to the Red Lion to hear what had been going on.

Morale during the summer had been poor. Envious of those who flew Hurricanes and Spitfires, the prospect of flying Blenheims at night seemed pointless and depressing. Standards in training had fallen and the squadron had been withdrawn from Debden at the start of the Battle of Britain, when indiscipline became so serious that there was talk in Fighter Command of disbanding the unit. But 29 Squadron had been reprieved and a new commanding officer was appointed to restore its spirit.

Sqn Ldr Charles Widdows took command in July 1940. Twenty-nine years old, of medium height, slim and strikingly handsome, Widdows had the physique of an athlete and a hawkish alertness. Intolerant of fools, his rather imperious manner earned mixed reactions as he began to weed out pilots he thought had been 'training too little and drinking too much'. Whatever reservations some had about Widdows on the ground, however, no one doubted his abilities in the air. Since 1937 he had been a service test pilot with the Aeroplane and Armament Experimental Establishment at Martlesham Heath. Here he had test-flown the first production Spitfire and many prototype aircraft. So valued was his experience that after the outbreak of war he was at first barred from returning to operational flying. Rebuilding 29 Squadron was the eventual reward for his persistence.[1]

Widdows set about getting to know his pilots. Some of them promised much. Fg Off. J.R.D. Braham, known to all as Bob,* stood out for his determination and aggressive spirit. Fg Off. Charles Winn impressed Widdows by his skill in the air and good-natured charm on the ground. Plt Off. David Humphries and several more were recognized for their abilities. But there were others who one way or another in Widdows' eyes failed the test of the squadron's motto, *Impiger et acer*, 'energetic and keen'. Widdows accordingly engineered their departure and in their

---

* Wing-Commander J.R.D. Braham went on to become Britain's most highly decorated fighter pilot, being awarded the DSO, DFC, AFC, CD, Belgian Order of the Crown and Croix de Guerre. Braham was shot down and taken prisoner on 25 June 1944 while returning from a daylight intruder sortie over Denmark in a Mosquito, when screened from all but occasional operations. Braham attributed his defeat to a series of basic errors, committed under the influence of combat fatigue: circumstances not dissimilar to those that claimed Gibson twelve weeks later.[2]

place introduced younger pilots fresh from training school whose development he could mould. It was several of these men who had befriended Gibson. They also explained the reason for his frigid reception. Widdows was replacing his flight commanders and Gibson's appointment had displaced one of 29 Squadron's own men. In the following weeks there were further departures and one officer was stripped of his commission.[3] Not surprisingly the purges were unwelcome to the dwindling number of old hands. As an outsider, a former 'bomber boy' and as an instrument of Widdows' reforms, Gibson shared in this unpopularity.

Faltering morale was only one among many problems with which Widdows was having to grapple. His efforts to improve the squadron's cohesion were being undermined by 12 Group's direction that it be split and dispersed to distant airfields. Thus two or three aircraft were posted at Wittering, whence they were expected to guard the approaches to Coventry, Birmingham and the Black Country. Liverpool and Manchester were defended by a section run from a tent on the airfield at Ternhill in Shropshire. Humber ports and north-eastern cities were patrolled by a detachment stationed at Kirton in Lindsey. This scattering of men and machines meant that at any one time up to half of 29 Squadron's crews were absent. When back at Digby they were more like occasional guests than members of the community which Widdows was seeking to foster. Even Digby itself was a place of problems being overcrowded and also home to two Hurricane squadrons whose Canadian airmen, deprived of cereals and fresh orange juice, were in a state of moody unrest.

Night patrols had shot down only one German bomber in five months and they had recently lost one of their own crews to an attack by a Hurricane. Lack of combat success was mainly a result of the inadequacies of their Blenheim Ifs. The Blenheim handled well enough, but as a nightfighter it was ineffectual. Airborne radar was primitive and on the occasions when it worked its operators had difficulty in coaxing forth the data needed for successful interceptions. Ground control was thwarted by the poor range and unreliability of the Blenheim's radio. After dark the Blenheim was in effect both blind and hard of hearing.

Despite these woes, hope was at hand. Since September the squadron had been re-equipping with Beaufighter Is. True, the Beaufighters were only being delivered in ones and twos and as a new type being hurried into service their use was restricted by teething troubles. But these were robust and heavily armed nightfighters. Above all, they were fitted with more modern AI equipment.

Gibson went to bed in thoughtful mood. On the following evening Widdows took him to the operations room for an introduction to techniques of ground control. The date was 14 November and it was from the sector map upon a large table that Gibson witnessed the ruin of Coventry. The attack was opened by Pathfinder aircraft guided by X-Gerat. Their first incendiaries fell at a quarter past eight starting fires which beckoned more than 400 bombers which followed during the next ten hours. Gibson watched and listened intently as patrols were ordered up, but as the WAAF plotters quietly manipulated the flags representing incoming and outgoing enemy bombers it became obvious that the raid was proceeding with impunity. Only one of 29 Squadron's pilots even saw a German bomber that night. Fg Off. Peter Kells stalked a Heinkel out over East Anglia, fired and missed. Kells was the man who had slammed the door on Gibson the previous evening.

We may wonder how Gibson reacted to the implications of this grim board-game. Coventry had strong sentimental associations for him. Crews had seen the fires and there was mounting anger next day when men returning from daylight patrols described the shattered city. Privately for Gibson, as well as publicly for the nation, Coventry was now the place in whose name Nemesis would be invoked against German cities later in the war.

Having fought off the Luftwaffe during the great daylight aerial battles of August and September, the RAF was now incapable of preventing the same aircraft returning to wreck Britain's cities by night. Widdows knew the solution lay with the improvement of airborne radar. But that would take months; meanwhile, there were political demands for improvisation. A few weeks previously the squadron had received two Fairey Battles, hand-me-downs from units which had been fighting in France where they had perished by the score. The Battles were now used for futile and time-consuming experiments, towing flares at the end of a 1,000-foot cable in the hope of illuminating enemy aircraft. Trials showed the method to be counter-productive: not only did the flare endanger the tug by exposing it to attack, but it also destroyed the night vision of the fighter pilot. 29 Squadron's report concluded that the idea was open to 'serious criticism'. Gibson was more abrupt, dismissing the inventor of the method as 'a fool'.

In the eyes of some, even the Beaufighter was a mixed blessing. Rumours claimed it to be a 'suicide ship' and a few days after Gibson's arrival there was an incident which lent credence to such talk. Late in the evening of Sunday 17 November, Widdows was flying with Plt Off. Willy Wilson as his AI operator. Shortly before midnight the port engine failed. The Beaufighter toppled into a steep dive and Widdows, finding the aircraft uncontrollable, ordered Wilson to jump. As Widdows himself turned to escape, he looked down the dark tunnel of the fuselage and saw Wilson still wrestling to open the rear hatch. Widdows returned to the controls and managed to level the aircraft. He switched on the landing lights and with Wilson still aboard he proceeded to land wheels-up in a field near Sleaford, alighting with such delicacy that the tailwheel touched first before the Beaufighter ploughed through a fence and a flock of sheep. Typically, Widdows' confidence in the Beaufighter was unshaken. In time it would serve them well.

Winter Wedding

Four days after Widdows' forced landing Gibson was allowed the use of a Blenheim to ferry him down to Cardiff and, two days later, on Saturday 23 November, he was married.

Mr and Mrs Ernest Moore gave their daughter a good wedding. There was none of the hasty informality which had attended the marriage of Alick and Ruth the year before. Eve was admired in her sumptuous gown of ivory panne velvet, against which her spray of roses made a splash of red. Civilian men were in morning suits and after the service at Penarth's Anglican church there was a reception at the Esplanade Hotel with champagne and formal speeches. A.J. attended with Diana, father and son introducing their new wives to one another. The *South Wales Echo* added a little lustre with its headline: PENARTH ACTRESS MARRIES DFC AIRMAN. It was all very traditional, almost like peacetime.

But not quite. Eve and Guy were driven to a hotel near Chepstow and as Eve bemoaned the confetti which she discovered between the layers of clothing in her dressing-case, the sporadic thump of anti-aircraft fire reminded them that their honeymoon was to be brief. The hotel looked out across the River Severn. As Eve readied herself for dinner the next evening she could see flares in the direction of Bristol. By half past six a raid was in progress and later they turned off the lights and opened the black-out curtain to watch the whitish stalks of searchlights groping in the sky and the dull orange glare from multiplying fires. Next morning much of Bristol's centre was in ruins, its fate betrayed for miles around by a tower of smoke. Evidently there was work to do and after a day or two more Gibson returned to Lincolnshire. But this time there was no distressful parting: Eve came too.

In years to come Gibson would be vehemently opposed to aircrew living with their wives in the vicinity of operational airfields. His doctrine that war and wives are best kept apart was influenced by his own experience. From the first he found that a dual allegiance, to Eve and to the squadron, was difficult to sustain.

The first problem was to find somewhere to live. While Guy searched for a cottage they took a room in one of Wellingore's pubs. Eve was appalled by its meagre amenities. House-hunting proved fruitless and, mindful of Eve's loud complaints about the outside lavatory, a mattress which 'felt as if it had been filled with golf balls' and the difficulties of putting on make-up by candlelight, Guy agreed that they should move to a bed-sitting room in the Lion and Royal, a large pub on the main street of the adjoining village of Navenby. The Lion had electricity, and a bath.

Navenby was a small agricultural village of some few hundred souls. To an outsider little seems to happen in such communities. During the day there was nothing to do other than to go for walks or sit in her bedroom beside the gas fire, brooding upon memories of the bright society and easy friendships of the theatre. Eve disliked the landlady and found little to look forward to in her cooking. There were few opportunities to wear her expensive new clothes. Her solitude was broken only by occasional outings to the cinema in Lincoln or Grantham, or to tea at Wellingore Grange. Most of the other pilots were unmarried, so there was little companionship to be had from squadron circles. Lonely and unhappy, Eve reacted angrily to Guy's terse dismissal of her protests. Within days there were quarrels.

Up on Wellingore Heath, Gibson was becoming accustomed to the ways of the Beaufighter. The Bristol Beaufighter was a large, pugnacious-looking machine. The Mk I was armed with four cannon sheathed in the aircraft's belly. In common with most aircraft of the day its designers had made few concessions to the convenience of people who actually had to work in it. By comparison with the Hampden a Beaufighter was spacious and well appointed. But that was not saying much. Entrance for the pilot was by a ladder which pulled down from a hatch under the nose. The first rung of the ladder was quite high and although handholds were provided, short men burdened by heavy flying clothing needed practice before they overcame the awkwardness of hoisting themselves out of the hatchway into the fuselage above. Once inside, Gibson's small stature was more of an asset. The Beaufighter's interior was a hazardous place, full of jagged projections threatening scraped knuckles and barked shins. The distance from the forward hatch to the cockpit was only a few feet, but a raised transverse spar demanded more gymnastics before the pilot could settle himself at the controls. Once seated, however, the pilot found himself excellently placed. Vision ahead was magnificent and the Beaufighter's potential as a fighting machine was something that Gibson quickly came to relish.

Beaufighters were still in short supply and the beginning of December found the squadron in a state of transition. Widdows reorganized his crews into A Flight (Beaufighters) with four pilots and B Flight (still flying the superannuated Blenheims) with nine. He supervised his pilots' conversion to Beaufighters with scrupulous care, making sure that they became thoroughly familiar with the aircraft by day before taking it aloft at night. Gibson made his first flight on 1 December, practising circuits and landings at Wellingore. Next he rehearsed asymmetric flying, then a cross-country to Upper Heyford, followed by practice for instrument flying at night.

The weather on 5 December was very bad, with high winds and squalls. But Gibson was keen and went off anyway for eighty minutes of AI practice. He now discovered for himself what he had already been told: that successful nightfighting hinged upon teamwork. In the Hampden he had given the orders, but when hunting in the Beaufighter he had to accept that control lay not in the cockpit but at the AI operator's position some yards aft. Radar-guided interception was still in its infancy and some pilots found it difficult to subordinate their individualism to someone – often an NCO – who they could not see, using new-fangled equipment which they might not trust. It was only in the closing moments of an interception, when the pilot had been led to within visual range of his quarry, that he took charge of the attack. Pilots who were impatient, domineering, or otherwise failed to develop a close working relationship with their AI operators, shot down few aircraft. Successful crews flew together regularly, developed a high level of technical proficiency and a mutual faith in each other's abilities.

At first Gibson was paired with two AI operators, Sgt Taylor and Plt Off. Watson, one or other flying with him whenever the weather would permit. His first Beaufighter combat patrol came with Taylor on 10 December. It lasted just over an hour and, after stalking an aircraft which turned out to be friendly, they returned to Wellingore before midnight. Gibson and Taylor settled themselves in the dispersal hut and awaited further orders.

Intruders of 1/NJG2 were active over eastern England during the early hours and shortly before eight o'clock next morning Gibson and Taylor were scrambled to catch a Ju 88. Gibson chased it out over the North Sea for sixty miles. The pursuit was in vain: he could not overtake it and when eventually he fired ineffectually from a range of half a mile, the intruder fled into cloud. The job was going to be difficult.

Next evening, 12 December, a large force raided Sheffield. Gibson and Watson flew two patrols, each of nearly two and a half hours, but no enemy aircraft were seen. Gibson's determination now began to show itself. Bad weather grounded most of Digby's aircraft during the next few days, but Gibson's quest for mastery of technique drove him to squeeze in more training and AI practice.

Early in the evening of the 20th reports arrived of a large attack building up on Liverpool. Gibson was ordered aloft at a quarter to seven, now with a new AI operator. Once again the patrol was unsuccessful. Still on duty at breakfast-time the following morning, they were scrambled to tackle an intruder. They found it quickly – a Ju 88C-2 of 1/NJG2 – but even as they did so their quarry strayed within range of the anti-aircraft defences at RAF Manby, which promptly shot it down.

Intruders were becoming a nuisance. Wellingore and Digby were attacked on several occasions and three days before Christmas Plt Off. Ken Davison was in the circuit at Digby in a Blenheim, downwind with his undercarriage down, when he reported that 'tracer bullets came into the cockpit'.[4] Davison landed safely, his crew unhurt, but the prospect of a Ju 88 mingling with Beaufighters and Blenheims as they prepared to land remained an unnerving hazard for several months to come.

And so the cycle was repeated: duty towards dusk, one or two patrols during the night and back to the Lion and Royal some time after 9 a.m., where the normal routine of guesthouses was reversed to breakfast and bed. The shortage of Beaufighters and pilots qualified to fly them obliged Gibson to be on duty two nights out of three. Wellingore's facilities were then meagre, less unfinished than scarcely started. By the end of two nights on duty, waiting in the dispersal hut in full flying kit with nowhere to wash, Gibson recalled his bath water 'was quite black'. If he woke early there might be an hour or two to share with Eve before she drove him back up to the aerodrome. But daylight was weakening fast by half past three and on these midwinter evenings the Luftwaffe often came early. It was a difficult time for both of them. Gibson, ever eager for action, was frustrated by the lack of it, while Eve's despondency deepened as she huddled over her gas fire during his long absences. Neither of them had any eye for the recessive beauties of the Lincoln Edge in December. But amid Wellingore's mud and drizzle even a poet's first priority might have been a pair of dry boots and a place beside the Queen Mary stove.

On 23 December, the anniversary of Nora's fatal accident, Gibson nearly came to grief. There was a large attack against Manchester, but R/T failure forced him to abandon his patrol. Unable to communicate with his controller, Gibson was also denied a homing bearing. Layer cloud defeated his search for a flarepath and, low on fuel after hours of aimless flying, he began to contemplate baling out. Luckily, he glimpsed an Anson making its approach to an airfield, followed it down and landed at his former station of Upper Heyford. Walking into the Lion and Royal at lunch-time next day, he found Eve frantic and tearfully accusing. Where had he been? No one had remembered to call her to explain why he was overdue. Married for a month, she had assumed she was already a widow.

Over Christmas there was a lull when winter drabness was temporarily enlivened by parties. Wives and girl-friends were invited to a high-spirited Christmas dinner and were duly startled when Gibson marched into the Mess at the head of a procession of officers bearing burning yard brooms. But at the year's end there was little good to look back on. Britain's cities were being wrecked. German night bombers came and went as they pleased. On the last day of 1940 Sam France wrote:

It is disheartening for a night flying squadron . . . to go up night after night and never get a 'Jerry'. We can only hope that the coming year will produce some new method, or improved equipment to enable our pilots to contact more enemy planes and shoot them down.[5]

New Year

Towards midnight on New Year's Eve a Wellington low on fuel sought refuge at Wellingore and crashed in an adjoining field. Next morning Gibson and a friend walked out to look at it. 'We were the first there,' he recalled in *Enemy Coast Ahead*,

and the wind was whistling fiercely, sending up snow flurries around each foot as we tramped across the fields towards the gaunt skeleton of the Wellington, its tail fin sticking up in the air like an accusing finger. As we got closer we could smell that unpleasant smell of burnt aircraft, but when we got really close we could see quite clearly the pilot sitting still at his controls burnt to a frazzle, with his goggles gently swaying in the wind hanging from one hand.[6]

This seems vividly remembered, yet in one respect the impression is wrong. The Wellington had not burned. The dead pilot – a Pole, far from home – may have been sitting frozen rigid at the controls, but he had not been 'burnt to a frazzle'. Perhaps the fire was added for effect. But was it by coincidence that such an exaggeration was made around the anniversary of his mother's funeral? Around midwinter burns and burned people would again form a sub-text in Gibson's life.

During the following days Wellingore froze, testing the spirit of flight mechanics who serviced the Beaufighters in the open, wrapped heavy covers over engines and placed heaters inside fuselages to protect temperamental AI sets against condensation.[7] The cold deepened and on the 18th it began to snow heavily. Falls on the following day and through the next were swept by a rising wind into drifts that trapped Eve and Guy on their return from a party and halted the bus service to Lincoln. Eve rather welcomed the blizzards that kept German bombers away and Guy on the ground. But the interlude was brief. A thaw turned Wellingore to a soggy mess and for days afterwards such flying as there was took place from Digby.

In February conditions improved and Gibson teamed up with Sgt Richard James, who became his regular AI operator. As if making up for lost time, they flew together as often as possible, putting in hours of training in addition to their patrols. James found him a considerate and sensible pilot, attentive to his directions, and on 4 February their new-found empathy was rewarded by a brush with success. Luftflotte 2 was seeking the Rolls Royce factories at Derby, and other enemy aircraft were in the vicinity of Hull. They took off at half past six. It had snowed again during the day, but visibility was good and from their patrol height of 10,000 feet Gibson marvelled at the moonlit detail of Lincolnshire's whitened landscape. At seven o'clock the controller ordered them to Mablethorpe. Minutes later James reported a contact. This turned out to be another Beaufighter, but the tracking of it took them out over the Humber estuary, between Grimsby and Spurn Head, where Gibson's attention had already been caught by unexplained flares. The Intelligence Combat Report continues the story:

By coming up behind and below a line of about six flares the enemy aircraft was seen above and ahead illuminated dimly by the flares below it at 19.55 hours. Fire was opened at 500 yards range giving a 3-second burst. Enemy aircraft was lost to sight when flares went out, but had been picked up on AI meanwhile and was held and followed for a few seconds. No apparent avoiding action was taken by enemy aircraft which was lost in turns. The flares seemed to ignite about 100 feet below the aircraft and burned for about 15 seconds, being dropped in rows of six ... The aircraft's type could not be determined as it appeared as a dull silhouette and distinguishing features could not be seen. Using similar tactics the same or a second aircraft was picked up

by sight at 20.05 hours. A 3-second burst from 200 yards range was given and
the enemy aircraft was followed for a short period on AI. No return fire was
experienced and no damage to the enemy aircraft was observed during either
of these attacks which were carried out between 7,000 and 10,000 feet.[8]

In his book Gibson tells us that he was 'so excited' that he 'took bad
aim and missed' adding, perhaps fancifully, that the bomber crew had
taken fright and jettisoned the rest of their load into the Humber. 'It
was obvious that I was a very bad shot, but at least it was a beginning.'

It was indeed, and further encouragement followed next morning,
when Gibson and James were scrambled to deal with an intruder.
Gibson saw nothing, but James succeeded in obtaining contacts and
while they were airborne another crew attacked a homebound intruder
over the North Sea. No one had yet shot anything down, but their
growing experience with AI was beginning to suggest that before long
they would.

Towards the end of February, following incessant training and many
patrols, Widdows decided that a party would improve morale. The
Assembly Rooms in Lincoln were booked, cabaret performers and a
band engaged. The occasion was judged to be a sensation by those who
attended it and condemned as a disgrace by the local authority. Details
of such events are almost invariably beyond recall, with only
kaleidoscopic impressions remembered – noisy horseplay, drunken singing, debaggings and David Humphries being handed a Widdows'
Cocktail by its inventor and promptly passing out after drinking it. One
index of success for a 29 Squadron party was the amount of broken
glass underfoot at its end; by this measure the evening in the Assembly
Rooms is said to have been unsurpassed. Widdows was shrewd in his
timing. The party released pent-up energy and marked a paragraph in
their progress towards success.

Full moon in March was on the thirteenth night of the month. On
this and neighbouring evenings the Luftwaffe launched a series of heavy
attacks on northern cities. The 12th was clear and almost cloudless:
good for bombing, but ideal too for interceptions. Three hundred and
sixteen bombers converged on Liverpool and Birkenhead in an attack
which continued for over six hours. Gibson and James were airborne
for nearly two. According to Gibson they attacked a bomber, and he
afterwards wrote in his logbook 'One Hun destroyed'. This is a doubtful

and apparently private claim. 29 Squadron's records do not mention it and James reported only that they had 'contacted e/a with weapon [i.e. on AI] but lost owing false height indicated. Set found to be u/s.' If Gibson did open fire that evening, he was not responsible for any of the five bombers brought down over England that night, for each can be matched to another known combat. However, several hours later a Heinkel 111 of Stab KG27,* based at Tours, landed at St Malo in Brittany, with four crew who had been injured by a nightfighter. Perhaps they were Gibson's victims.

Next evening the bombers returned to Liverpool and there was a lesser attack on Hull. Now at last came the long-awaited victories. Braham shot down a Dornier Do 17z-2 which was attacking Hull and in the early hours of the 14th Widdows caught a Ju 88C-4 intruder. News of the victories prompted jubilation among the flight mechanics who clustered to greet and cheer the Beaufighters as they taxied to their dispersals. For months they had laboured in dark, wet and cold conditions, feeling the monotony and disappointments. Now the elation was theirs too. Widdows' victim had broken up in the air. He recalls his amazement that when the Beaufighter's four cannon were operated the aeroplane trembled with a firm vibration for two or three seconds – and the Ju 88 disintegrated before his eyes.

Later that day Gibson and James took off for a short flight to test their AI apparatus, which on recent trips had been giving trouble. In the evening came the build-up to a heavy attack on Clydeside, with a substantial secondary on Sheffield. Gibson and James were ordered to patrol off the Lincolnshire coast near Wells. Ground control directed them towards an incoming target and at 21.25 James picked up a contact and guided Gibson to its source. It was a Heinkel 111, piloted by Lt G. Stugg and heading for Glasgow.

Guided by James, the bomber came into Gibson's view at a range of about 400 yards. He stalked it from behind and slightly below, a tactic which minimized the risk of presenting the Beaufighter's silhouette to the rear gunner while outlining the Heinkel against the stars. Closing to 100 yards Gibson opened fire with a burst that was curtailed by a malfunction of his cannon. Gibson saw no strikes on the Heinkel but the absence of return fire made him wonder if he had killed the rear

* The headquarters flight of *Kampfgeschwader* (bomber *geschwader*) 27.

gunner. James worked to clear the jam while Gibson reduced speed to avoid overshooting and repositioned for a second attack. Alarmed, Stugg began to take evasive action, turning out to sea and putting his aircraft into a dive. The jam cleared, Gibson delivered a second burst which stopped the Heinkel's port motor. More cannon fire halted Stugg's starboard motor but also yielded a cloud of debris into which the Beaufighter flew, chunks of metal denting its wing. The Heinkel was now doomed and as it descended a crew member baled out. The bomber came down in the sea off Skegness. Stugg and his three comrades, including the man who jumped, all died.

Gibson and James were ecstatic. 'When I first saw him,' Gibson wrote, 'I had screamed over the RT full of excitement. When he was gliding down completely helpless I felt almost sorry for him ... we were so excited we could hardly speak.'⁹ Back at the Lion and Royal, Eve's usual question of 'Any luck?' was answered by his beaming face. Even the weather smiled. That morning in mid-March was sunny and warm, the first real hint of spring after·a hard winter. Later in the day Gibson drove over to Skegness and collected the Heinkel's dinghy as a souvenir.

Three days later winter returned. Appalling weather grounded everyone, but there were reports of intruders about. Gibson was determined to fly and was only dissuaded when the station commander ordered him out of his aircraft, warning him that the weather was too bad. This is an intriguing episode, illustrating Gibson's increasingly fanatical determination and willingness to 'freelance' in the absence of any immediate order not to do so.

Early in April the partnership with James was temporarily broken, and for a fortnight Gibson flew with at least three different AI operators. After several days with one man ('NBG' – no bloody good – wrote Gibson), he teamed up with Sgt Bell, who had been seconded from 219 Squadron. On 8 April they set forth on patrol. Shortly before midnight, a long-range nightfighter shadowed them as they prepared to land. With his navigation lights on and undercarriage and flaps down, concentrating on his approach, Gibson never saw the attacker. The German pilot opened fire just as the Beaufighter was crossing the hedge. Committed to the landing, Gibson put the aircraft down only to discover that the brakes had been damaged. The Beaufighter careered across the landing ground and through the hedge on the far boundary.

Gibson was unhurt, although Bell was wounded in the leg. Some pilots became nervous or excessively cautious after such narrow escapes, but Gibson had experienced worse in his Hampden days and apparently made light of it.

On 23 April, reunited with Richard James, after hours of more intensive AI training enlivened by an emergency landing on one engine, Gibson had an opportunity for revenge. Towards 11.00 p.m. they took off into a sky crowded with German aircraft. James obtained many contacts. One was a Ju 88 which they intercepted but then lost after the German took evasive action. Around 01.05 James guided Gibson within sight of a Dornier Do 215 near Boston. Gibson closed to 150 yards and fired. The Dornier's top rear gunner was alert and his return fire accurate. Gibson broke away, but contact was retained and they repositioned for a second attack. This time he saw the flashes of cannon shells as they struck the Dornier's fuselage. Again the rear gunner replied and the engagement was broken off, its outcome uncertain.

29 Squadron had served its apprenticeship and was beginning to get results. It was usual for squadrons to be rotated at intervals between different sectors. Widdows was accordingly keen for his unit to be transferred to a more rewarding area, and he invited AVM Trafford Leigh-Mallory, AOC 11 Group, to dinner in the hope of engineering a move.

Widdows' diplomacy was soon rewarded. On Friday 25 April 1941 the squadron was ordered to move to West Malling, in Kent. West Malling was a permanent station with good accommodation and its proximity to London raised hopes of more trade in the air, and more scintillating life on the ground. Widdows wasted no time. Later that day he and Gibson flew down to inspect the suitability of West Malling's runways. Some said the landing ground was too small to accommodate Beaufighters, but after the 450-yard run they had at Wellingore it seemed spacious.

Guy informed Eve that as he would be flying to Kent, she would have to take their car and belongings. Eve was alarmed: she was an inexperienced driver and had never driven such a distance in her life. Guy curtly insisted that she could manage perfectly well and took her out for a practice drive to prove it. Tempers rose and the lesson ended when Eve climbed out, slammed the door and announced that she would return by bus. In the event, her journey to Kent was uneventful, although with all signposts removed she had to pause every few miles to ask for directions.

Wellingore had been a strange place. Some had found it unfriendly and introverted. One pilot was startled to be evicted from his lodgings simply because he had had the temerity to ask for an extra blanket and there were reports of 'fifth columnists' – more probably inquisitive locals – who entered the airfield and clambered about upon their Beaufighters at night. When 29 Squadron arrived at West Malling they closed up behind Widdows for a low pass to leave no one in any doubt about their risen spirits. 'From Wellingore to West Malling in formation of 8' reads Gibson's logbook entry for 29 April, adding 'Everyone very pleased to leave.'

X-Raids and Orchards

They immediately found their stride. Four days after arriving at West Malling, on 3 May, Gibson dispatched an unidentified enemy aircraft near Shoreham with what he called 'a lucky burst'.* On 6 May a German bomber was damaged by Widdows and on the 8th Bob Braham destroyed another Heinkel. These victories were quickly followed by two more and Gibson might have caught another on the night of 10/11 May, when London was subjected to attack by over 500 German aircraft. They took off under a full moon shortly before midnight, but returned within half an hour, Gibson impatient because of faulty R/T. The problem cured, they took off again at 01.10. Afterwards Gibson wrote in his logbook: 'Saw two He 111; but cannons would not fire. Damaged one with Brownings – no claim.' Others did better. Fighter Command flew 325 sorties that night and eleven enemy aircraft were destroyed.

Gibson's account of events on that evening again illustrates his

---

* The victim may have been a Heinkel He 111P-4, based at Dreux, flown by Lt G. Becker, whose failure to return from an attack on Liverpool that night is otherwise unexplained.

compulsion to impress. It contains a purported extract from his logbook: 'Night defence of London. We saw four Heinkels. Cannons jammed each time.' Gibson also tells us of a 'very rude word written in the Remarks column' which was 'blacked out by the CO with an appropriate note'. But neither this entry, nor the word nor signs of its crossing out appear on the page and James's logbook confirms that there were only two contacts. Four or two? It hardly matters. What is revealing is that Gibson wished to magnify the scale of his disappointment. His purpose was to set the scene for an outburst of frustration in the next paragraph:

Four Huns! For months we had stooged around, thinking ourselves lucky if we saw one. Then we had seen four fat ones with bomb loads on, and they had all got away.[10]

He was becoming worried by his comparative lack of success, and as the summer advanced he grew bored.

The remaining days of May were occupied with training, unproductive patrols and the start of a series of visits to an RAF dentist for treatment which continued for weeks. In June Widdows was promoted station commander, his place at the head of 29 Squadron being taken by Wg-Cdr Edward Colbeck-Welch, a man for whom Gibson developed great warmth of regard. At the end of June Gibson himself was promoted to squadron leader. But the offensive against British cities had begun to subside and, having worked so hard at the craft of 'this nightfighting business', Gibson was impatient at the lack of opportunity to apply it. Logbook entries convey the growing monotony and frustration: 'X Raid. Returned.' 'X Raid. Nothing.' 'Stooge Patrol.' And so on.

There were targets about, but they were using new tactics. Recognizing that AI-equipped fighters were less effective below 5,000 feet, small numbers of bombers flew low across the North Sea to plant mines in the Thames estuary. 29 Squadron rehearsed new techniques to catch them, staying above their targets until contact had been obtained. Late in the evening of 6 July a Heinkel 111H-5 of 8/KG4, flown by Lt Franz Anderle, took off from its base in Holland for a mine-laying sortie. Gibson and James met it soon after midnight. A two-second burst finished the Heinkel instantly. It exploded and crashed into the sea off Sheerness, killing all on board. Gibson's self-esteem and sense of purpose were temporarily restored. He would need both, however, for while the victories of others continued to mount, Anderle's Heinkel was to be his last confirmed victim.

With Germany now fully engaged in Russia, enemy air activity over Britain lessened. In place of attacks during the winter involving hundreds of bombers, visitors now tended to come in groups of twenty or thirty. Their bombing too seemed relatively ineffectual, calculated more to annoy than cause real economic harm. On 12 July small numbers of raiders dropped bombs as far apart as Cornwall, Norfolk and Aberdeen. The next night raiders visited Great Yarmouth and five other places on the east coast; on the 14th, 17th and 22nd there were attacks on Hull; there was minor activity reported over East Anglia on the 29th. Raids on coastal towns like Bridlington and Yarmouth continued to claim civilian lives, but from Gibson's perspective it was relatively quiet, with much training and little action.

On the ground, by contrast, life was good. West Malling was a happy station, in enviable surroundings of woodland and orchards, sheltered under the North Downs. Eve adored the place and the social life which revolved around it. After a few weeks in a guesthouse they moved into a cottage in the grounds of the house occupied by Charles and Nickie Widdows. The cottage had no bathroom, but their neighbours were tolerant. The officers' Mess, in a large house called The Hermitage, was comfortable and popular. Eve was close enough to London to renew acquaintance with metropolitan friends. There were parties, trips to pubs and amateur dramatics in which Eve took part. In contrast to Wellingore, where the attitude of some local people towards squadron members had been surly, there was enormous local goodwill towards the RAF. Having watched the Battle of Britain overhead the year before, families opened their homes and larders to the young men from the aerodrome. There were soirées at which peacetime talents were resurrected. West Malling had its musicians, singers and mimics, and the wives clubbed together to put on a revue called *The Merry Wives of Malling* in which Nickie Widdows sang a rather wistful number about the life of a WAAF and Eve made a lasting impression by singing 'I'm a divorcee', dressed in scarlet. There were visits by royalty and the famous. Leave came frequently. As autumn advanced there was nothing to disturb Eve's contentment. They had even been given a puppy – a black mongrel, much Labrador in its parentage. One of Gibson's colleagues called him 'the black bastard'. Eve and Guy named him Nigger.

October brought a minor sensation when members of the squadron awoke one wet morning to find that a Stirling bomber had landed during the night. The Stirling was the first of the new generation of four-engine bombers and many at West Malling had never seen one at close quarters. After lunch the weather improved and some began to walk or cycle out to inspect the giant visitor. Late in the afternoon a knot of spectators gathered, curious to see how – or if – the bomber would manage to take off from the modest flying field. After each engine was tested in turn, the bomber taxied to the extreme edge of the aerodrome. The keeper of 29 Squadron's Operations Record Book was so surprised by what followed that he became quite lyrical: '. . . with roaring engines it moved off across the track and after an incredibly short run rose majestically into the air, climbed slowly and after circling the aerodrome set course for base.'

Gibson had now been with 29 Squadron for almost a year. Socially he was thoroughly at ease. Operationally he was less satisfied. A few evenings later there was a sharp attack on Dover, when Gibson and James intercepted three Ju 87s, opened fire and damaged two of them. Such engagements were rewarding, but the fleeting intensities of combat had become too infrequent to sustain him; there were long periods when nothing happened, and patrolling the French or Dutch coast more than once he and James discovered that they were themselves being hunted by German nightfighters. Yet several other crews, notably Braham and his celebrated AI operator, Flt Sgt Gregory, had begun to amass impressive scores. Gibson fretted about his lack of success, fearing that others might think him a failure. Worse, it seemed likely that he would soon be moved on. Anxious to evade posting to an OTU, and remembering the bargain struck with Harris a year before, he began to plot a return to Bomber Command.

After lunch on 9 November he flew up to Scampton in search of old comrades and to catch up on developments in the bomber war. The visit left him thoughtful, and depressed by news that Jack Withers had been shot down and killed by a Beaufighter. Five weeks later he was warned that a posting to an OTU was imminent. The news infuriated Gibson who, with a directness as characteristic as it was unorthodox, flew up to Grantham on the morning of 15 December to plead his case with HQ 5 Group. It was to no avail. Since November 1940 Harris had been Deputy Chief of Air Staff and was no longer in a position to exercise the patronage he had promised. Gibson described the interview as 'a waste of time' and that evening flew his last sorties with 29 Squadron. Glumly, he wrote 'Nothing about' against the entries in his logbook.

Christmas was near and there was a cheerful atmosphere next evening when West Malling's theatrical enthusiasts put on a performance of John Galsworthy's *Escape*. The production had been rehearsed under a professional director, whose patience had been sorely tested by absenteeism. Eve was playing the role of the prostitute and while Gibson was in Grantham trying to persuade 5 Group to re-recruit him, Mr Leon M. Lion was struggling to coax his company through a dress rehearsal – the first at which the whole cast was present. In the event the performance was held to be a great success. Gibson watched, but his thoughts were elsewhere. Persistent to the end, during the day he had telephoned several influential acquaintances.* But his efforts were fruitless. Fighter Command remained adamant. He was to be posted to 51 OTU at Cranfield, and he had to go.

Parting of the Ways

Eve and Guy had been married for just over a year. Since June they had been reasonably happy in their cottage, its spare bedroom often occupied by the visiting girl-friends of other pilots. They had made friends on and off the airfield and West Malling's surroundings did indeed seem like the Garden of England. With more to entertain her, Eve was less demanding and they quarrelled less.

As for himself, despite his self-doubts Gibson had done well. By comparison with bombing, nightfighting was relatively safe. This is not

---

* Did Gibson appeal direct to Air Marshal Sholto Douglas? According to Harris, when Gibson had embarked upon his tour on nightfighters Douglas had agreed that he should be returned to Bomber Command when he completed it. It is not known if Gibson was aware that Douglas had been party to the arrangement, but three months later Harris certainly remembered it.

saying much: the dangers of nightfighting were numerous enough, but they rested more in inexperience or misjudgement than in combat and these were threats he could reduce by his own efforts. Fate and Bad Luck, in Gibson's mind his most dangerous adversaries, were thus kept at bay. In September he had been awarded a bar to his DFC, the citation speaking accurately of his 'courage and utmost devotion to duty'. Although less successful than Braham in shooting down enemy aircraft – a comparison which paralleled the rivalry with B Flight, which Braham led, and may have rankled – Gibson and James made an effective partnership* and their score of three confirmed victims was a considerable achievement. Gibson left 29 Squadron with an 'above average' rating and – important for his subsequent career – had added vastly to his experience of instrument flying. He had also begun to take more responsibility, deputizing as squadron commander during several of Colbeck-Welch's absences.

So, when they looked back, both Eve and Guy remembered West Malling with nostalgia, their time of greatest contentment. But now things had to change. Guy refused to accept Cranfield as anything more than an irksome interlude, to be escaped at the earliest moment. This led him to argue that it would be pointless for Eve to go with him. Instead, she should return to Penarth. When Gibson knew his future they could reconsider. In the event, for the next two years the longest period that they would pass together would be a fortnight.

Two days before Christmas Gibson flew up to Cranfield to make arrangements for his new appointment as chief flying instructor. He returned to spend Christmas with Eve, but at the end of the month she was left alone in the cottage with only the dog for company. A few days later even Nigger was removed: Gibson flew down to West Malling to collect him, leaving Eve to pack their few belongings and return to Penarth.

51 OTU was equipped with an assortment of aircraft. Much training was undertaken using elderly Blenheim Is and IVs. There were the ubiquitous Airspeed Oxfords, but also some types which Gibson had not previously encountered, like Lysanders and Havocs. Gibson was soon reminded that casualties at an OTU could be higher than in an

---

* Richard James was a good AI operator. In 1942 he was posted to 96 Squadron, where he flew with the squadron commander, Wg-Cdr Burns. He survived the war.

operational squadron. Bad weather, inexperience and mechanically exhausted aircraft all took their toll. More machines and men could perish in a week at Cranfield than 29 Squadron had lost to the Germans in a year.

A blizzard at the beginning of February closed the airfield. Even under snow, however, Cranfield's atmosphere was lively. The narrow, class-based attitudes of the pre-war air force had begun to dissolve and many responded eagerly to the station's flourishing artistic and intellectual life. There were orchestral concerts and chamber music and, for those who found this too highbrow, Flt Lt Ralph Reader and his Gang Show came to perform. On 4 February an audience of over 250 crammed into an improvised auditorium to listen to a talk by Professor J.B.S. Haldane. Scores more were turned away.

None of this was for Gibson, who found little comfort either in the companionship of ex-29 Squadron stalwarts like Braham, who caroused with USAAF 8th Air Force men in the Key Club in Bedford. Braham's view of Gibson at this time in his own book seems significantly distant. Gibson was frustrated and lonely. He missed the society of West Malling and for weeks afterwards returned there whenever he could.

Flying at Cranfield was busy and Gibson's habit of writing up his logbook at irregular intervals meant that he often lost track of dates, aircraft, times and destinations. His logbook is a fascinating document. Many of its entries were made at a single sitting, discernible from changes of pen, ink or variable handwriting. There are larger contrasts between different phases of his career. During the early days at Wellingore he seems to have been on his best behaviour and made entries with uncharacteristic care. In the early summer of 1941 his remarks column begins to contain telegraphic asides and quips. At Cranfield one senses there was little to interest him: the entries are perfunctory, often wrong and heralded by the announcement in block capitals: 'WITH THE NEW YEAR I AM POSTED AS CFI TO 51 OTU CRANFIELD. THIS BEING HELD AS A REST FROM OPERATIONS!!!' Gibson treated his logbook as a kind of score sheet, as much a record of accumulated experience as of his flying.

Non-operational flying meant less leave and during February and early March he saw little of Eve. When he did manage to get across for a weekend he told her that he was 'browned off' and that 'this instructing lark' was driving him 'round the bend'. With time on her hands, Eve had joined the Red Cross in Cardiff and was working in its prisoner-of-war department.

On 22 February Sir Arthur Harris took over as C-in-C Bomber Command. Less than three weeks separated Harris's elevation and Gibson's redemption from his purgatory. The closeness of the two events was not coincidence. Harris had not forgotten the promise he had made to the young flying officer eighteen months before.

In any case, Harris was on the look-out for men like Gibson. His Command still offered the only means then open of taking offensive action against Germany. Yet the RAF's front-line bomber force remained puny and ill-equipped, and its growth was being retarded – in Harris's eyes – by admirals and generals who were diverting his bombers into other theatres faster than new squadrons could be built up. During Harris's first month as AOC-in-C the number of bombers he could raise for attacks against German targets averaged about 180. On a typical night fewer than a quarter of them would be likely to come within five miles of their target. The need for vigorous leadership at squadron level was high in Harris's mind.

Small wonder, then, that Harris ordered Gibson to his headquarters. What happened next is explained in a letter written by Harris on 22 March to AVM Slessor, AOC 5 Group:

Strictly Personal and Confidential

I am sending you almost immediately S/Ldr Guy Gibson. I understand that Fothergill who commands one of your Lancaster squadrons, though a good organizer, is not a fire eater and I am sure you will agree that these fine squadrons ought as far as possible to have the absolute pick. Gibson has only been a S/Ldr a year, but I desire to give him acting W/Cdr rank and command of a Lancaster squadron as soon as he can convert.

Harris then summarized Gibson's wartime career, concluding that:

Since leaving bombers he has done one 200 tour on nightfighters, has himself accounted for 7 Boche [sic] and raised his [sic] squadron to an extraordinary pitch of enthusiasm and efficiency. You will find him absolutely first class and as this is a two year old promise now in fulfilment I am sure you will agree to its consummation. If you prefer to put Gibson in place of any of your other squadron commanders that is for you to say, but in your absence today I gathered from Jackson Taylor, without divulging my reasons, that the replacement for Fothergill seems to be the most suitable move. Please let me know your views. Gibson is being made available at once and will take a week or so to convert before he gets going.'*

Harris's demands usually galvanized those to whom they were addressed and, on the following day, 23 March, Gibson was posted from Cranfield. However, this was only a holding measure, pending his posting back into 5 Group, and in another respect his new appointment did not follow in quite the way that Harris intended. Although Harris hoped that Gibson would go to 207 Squadron or one of the other two units in 5 Group already equipped with the new Lancaster, Slessor took Harris at his word about his discretion to decide otherwise. Gibson was given command of 106 Squadron, which flew Avro Manchesters. He would take over at the beginning of April. Meanwhile, he was sent on leave. Reunited with Eve for a week, he told her the news. Eve's heart sank, but Gibson was overjoyed.

* Harris's support for Gibson, based on a high opinion formed as far back as the summer of 1940, places Gibson's subsequent career in a new light. In Harris's eyes Gibson was already outstanding, a special figure, and his later selection to undertake special operations, culminating in the Dams Raid, can now be seen as following the fulfilment of early promise recognized by Harris, rather than simply as a result of his emergence to prominence during 1942.

Part Five

NEMESIS

April 1942–March 1943

I am the man who looked for peace and found
My own eyes barbed.
I am the man who groped for words and found
An arrow in my hand.
I am the builder whose firm walls surround
A slipping land.
When I grow sick or mad
Mock me not nor chain me:
When I reach for the wind
Cast me not down:
Though my face is a burnt book
And a wasted town.

Sidney Keyes, 'War Poet', [1922–43]

Shining Sword

Bomber warfare at night was exceptional to the history of battle in that until the Dams Raid in 1943 leadership was exercised away from the theatre of combat. Routes, tactics, altitudes and times were pre-arranged. Once airborne, although they might be in invisible company with hundreds of others, each crew was on its own. Their force was essentially atomistic. How well they performed and with what will they delivered their attacks were matters shaped by their training and motivation: characteristics bred in artificial rural villages, populated largely by young men, called RAF stations.

John Keegan has defined battle as

essentially a moral conflict. It requires, if it is to take place, a material and sustained act of will by two contending parties, and if it is to result in a decision, the moral collapse of one of them.[1]

On that definition, the Strategic Air Offensive as a whole was 'the battle' and individual raids within it were volleys and skirmishes. Later in 1942 the purpose of Bomber Command's four-year battle would be articulated in terms which have a clear affinity with Keegan's. Strategic bombing was intended to bring about

the progressive destruction and dislocation of the German military, industrial and economic system, and the undermining of the morale of the German people to a point where their capacity for armed resistance is fatally weakened.[2]

For a bomber crew, this 'sustained act of will' was spread across an entire tour of operations, which by August 1942 had been settled as thirty completed sorties. Only one man in two was likely to survive his first tour and for every one who emerged safely from a second, three could expect to be killed, maimed or taken prisoner. The figure of thirty sorties for a first tour was set partly for actuarial reasons, but it was also a threshold beyond which lay an unacceptable increase in the incidence of falling morale and psychiatric breakdown.

If we agree that

what battles have in common is human: the behaviour of men struggling to reconcile their instinct for self-preservation, their sense of honour and the achievement of some aim over which other men are ready to kill them,[3] then what was the honour, what was the aim, and how might a squadron commander reinforce them? Among bomber crews, most of the influences which would lead soldiers to fight were exercised at second hand. Leadership, compulsion and peer-pressure were mainly exercised between rather than during combat missions. In the air, the individual bomber captain became his commander's surrogate. He would answer to him on his return, but in the critical moments, when all instincts could screech survival before duty, he was on his own.

Such pressures were heightened by the bizarre divergence between life in rural England and the intermittent intensity of operations. And behind *that* polarity lay periods of transitional tension, extended scene-changes characterized by darkness, cold and deep anxiety, which could last anywhere between four and nine hours. Night bombing 'never was and never could be a mode of warfare to be conducted in hot blood'.[4] It was a theatre in which those who took part were at the mercy of their own imaginations. S.L.A. Marshall's observation that courage and cowardice are not 'alternative free choices . . . overriding all emotional stress' applies as much, or more, to the bomber crew as to any other kind of fighting man.

Which brings us back to Gibson, who grasped all this, even if he expressed it in more basic terms. He came to 106 Squadron with firm resolutions. Recognizing the dictum that the 'first and greatest impera-tive of command is to be present in person' and that 'those who impose risk must be seen to share it',[5] he determined to show others what was possible by doing it himself. If a successful bomber squadron was a complicated culture which sprang from technical efficiency, community and a clear sense of purpose, then all those aspects would have to be cultivated. To achieve that he would be rigorous but not always fanatical in matters of discipline; he would immerse himself in the life of the squadron on and off the airfield; he would reiterate the shared aim at all opportunities; and he would be ruthless in dismissing anyone who threatened his vision.

Gibson was playing a part he had seen acted elsewhere. Charles Widdows had been refashioning 29 Squadron when Gibson joined it, disposing of pilots he deemed unsuitable, replacing his flight command-ers, socializing during stand-downs but tolerating nothing casual or familiar when on duty. Colbeck-Welch was another admired model. Gibson knew from watching them that establishing the culture he wanted could take several months and that it might make him unpopular. He would live with that. It was all an extraordinary responsibility. How many twenty-three-year-olds would behave with greater maturity if placed in charge of 500 men and women, urging those to whom they are closest to actions that for many will end in their deaths?

Coningsby lies in the Lincolnshire fen country, overlooked by the lanky keep of Tattershall Castle. 106 Squadron had been there for over a year and when Gibson arrived in early April its crews had only just parted with the last of their worn-out Hampdens. The Avro Manchesters which replaced them were a disappointment and an immediate task for Gibson was to buttress morale against their low reputation. The first Manchester operations had been flown as long ago as February 1941, but operational use of the type had been curtailed by problems which centred on its Rolls-Royce Vulture engines. The Manchester's airframe was a huge advance on the Hampden, but its mechanical problems were irredeemable and by the time of Gibson's arrival a decision had been taken to re-equip all 5 Group's squadrons with the new Lancaster.

Gibson worked hard to gain a grasp of his new responsibilities. He talked informally to Charles Martin, 106's adjutant, and listened attentively to the off-duty chat and grumbles of his aircrew. He took time to familiarize himself with the Manchester and flew one down to West Malling to renew acquaintances and bask in the celebrity of his command. Sensibly, he seems to have curbed any impulse for an immediate return to operational flying, easing himself back with a mine-laying sortie to the Baltic towards the end of the month.

April 1942 was an outstandingly good month for 106 Squadron. The weather was fine; the squadron operated on eighteen out of thirty nights, six of them consecutively, and dropped the heaviest weight of bombs in the unit's history. Despite the Manchester's menacing record,[6] only two aircraft were lost. At HQ 5 Group and Bomber Command analysts of tonnages, losses, abort rates and aircraft serviceability noted an improvement on their graphs.

A leading feature of Gibson's new regime was his careful stewardship of crews. Harris was in a hurry. He needed to show what Bomber Command could do. Pressure was applied on squadrons to increase their sortie rates. In 1942 newcomers normally began their tours with several mine-laying trips. Such 'Nasturtium training' was intended to

acclimatize freshmen to operational conditions and Gibson refused to
be browbeaten into sending them to Germany until they had completed
it. Many of his exchanges with HQ 5 Group passed through Coningsby's
operations room, the degree of Gibson's vehemence being measurable
from the number of exclamation marks awarded to his comments in the
daybook.* Reports of Gibson's refusal to tolerate outside interference
soon circulated, although in the sergeants' Mess his reputation had yet
to recover from a foolish display of high-handedness. Gibson had
summoned the NCO aircrew to an introductory meeting. When he
entered the crewroom none of the sergeants stood up. Gibson misjudged
their mood and the savagery of his reaction to their informality was not
quickly forgiven. Nor did many NCO aircrew forget his caprice in
attempting to dismiss a sergeant he scarcely knew, apparently for no
better reason than that he had made up his mind – wrongly, as it turned
out – that the man was unworthy of his squadron. Gibson was intermittently prone to making such misappraisals and while his iron defence of
squadron interests earned admiration, this was tempered by misgivings
over what seemed to be unreasonable outbursts or persecution. His
nickname in the hangars and workshops was soon decided: the Boy
Emperor.

Fully reinstated to operations, Gibson's zeal was soon evident. On
25/26 April he flew on a raid to Rostock. This was the third night
running on which the Baltic port had been attacked and several crews
from 106 had been given the special target of the Heinkel aircraft works
at Marienehe outside the town. Gibson's second pilot was Plt Off.
Ronald Churcher, who recalls that Gibson elected to return at low-
level. Passing the Danish island of Langeland, they noticed a number of
U-boats moored in an orderly line. Gibson promptly began to circle at
about 1,000 feet in order to inspect their discovery. Churcher watched
apprehensively as German sailors ran back and forth on the submarines
and the crew braced themselves for the storm of light flak which
seemed likely to be unleashed at any moment. Gibson, however, was
unperturbed and loitered until sufficient information had been noted to
make a useful report to Naval Intelligence.[7]

By early May the Lancasters were starting to arrive. An *ad hoc*

---

* Gibson's willingness to argue with his seniors may have been strengthened by his
special relationship with Harris.

system of conversion training was introduced, whereby one or two crews were seconded for Lancaster experience while Manchester operations continued. Everyone rejoiced in the Lancaster. It was reliable, it was roomy, it was good to fly and, as bombers went, it was unusually fast. Its four Merlin engines were everything that the Vultures were not – dependable, efficient and delivering power that soon established the Lancaster's reputation as a lifter of great loads. For Gibson, a special attraction of the aeroplane was its carrying capacity. The Lancaster's bomb-bay was huge, its uninterrupted length capable of holding any bomb produced until the end of the war. For Harris the Avro Lancaster was the 'shining sword' in the hands of his Command.

Gibson first ran his fingers along the blade of this new weapon in mid-May. According to the account in *Enemy Coast Ahead* his initiation was at the hands of Flt Lt John Hopgood. But that flight took place seven weeks later. The pilot on this first occasion was one of 106's outgoing flight commanders, a man whom Gibson assessed as being operationally exhausted.

While Gibson was being initiated to the Lancaster, his commander-in-chief was pondering the need for some singular, dramatic operation to demonstrate the potential of Bomber Command as a strategic force in its own right. After successful raids on combustible medieval towns like Lübeck and Rostock, Harris decided that the time had come to demonstrate that 'bombing could be a decisive weapon' and to provide both aircrew and ground staff with the 'stimulus of some definite achievement'. To do this he proposed to commit his entire front-line strength and the whole of his reserves in a single operation.[8] This would mean the temporary impressment of instructors and crews nearing the end of their training. It was a gamble. Failure would strengthen critics who argued that Bomber Command had no independent strategic role and might paralyse training for months. Success, on the other hand, would silence the sceptics and reinforce Harris's demands for the concentration of resources in Bomber Command. Maybe for more reasons than one, therefore, the operation was code-named Millennium. And so, on 30 May, under a full moon, more than a thousand aircraft took off to attack Cologne.

106 Squadron contributed eleven aircraft to the thousand. Gibson was not among them. He was ill and for the next fortnight he languished

in hospital.* His exclusion from Millennium caused him annoyance not simply because he had missed Bomber Command's greatest *coup de théâtre* so far, but also because it had introduced new tactics. Gibson loved innovation and was frustrated to miss the first employment of the bomber stream. It was a tactic Bomber Command would use for the rest of the war, devised to saturate German defences, whereby all aircraft 'would fly by a common route and at the same speed to and from the target, each aircraft being allotted a height band and a time slot in the stream to minimize the risk of collision'.⁹ Millennium was a triumph and, having assembled his mighty force, Harris promptly used it again, launching over 950 aircraft against Essen two nights later. Bombing on this occasion was chaotic and results negligible. Gibson's impatience deepened, but after his discharge from Rauceby in mid-June he was still unfit and was ordered to take two weeks' convalescent leave. He flew down to St Athan in the station Oxford to join Eve. She was waiting at the edge of the airfield and waved ecstatically as the aircraft taxied in.

They went to Portmeirion, in north Wales. Guy was relaxed and in good spirits, and day after day the weather was hot and still. So smooth was the sea that Guy's normal leavetime hobby of sailing was ruled out. Instead, the couple swam, drove into the mountains of Snowdonia, walked and sat talking in the long light of the midsummer evenings. They browned on beaches and in the heat against the whir-ring sound of grasshoppers Guy reminisced about his childhood in India. Guy seldom discussed flying with Eve and would change the subject if she mentioned it. But there were times when he became introspective, talking quietly of the death he anticipated, sooner or later. Eve was perplexed by this calm fatalism. She was now thirty, her husband twenty-three and – in her own words – 'not a boy any longer'. For Eve, at least, the leave ended with a sense of despond-ency. On the last day they drove down the coast to the aerodrome at Llanbedr, amid the sand dunes near Harlech, whence the Oxford that

---

* The cause of Gibson's hospitalization has not been established. A colleague recalls that at one point he suffered from *otitis media*, a complaint of the middle ear not uncommon among aviators and potentially ruinous to a flier's career if not properly treated. He also suffered from headaches. It is possible that these troubles were linked, for example, in a sinus complaint. But these are speculations.

had delivered Guy to her seventeen days before now reappeared to take him back to war.

Pilot Officer David Shannon had joined 106 Squadron during Gibson's absence, three weeks after his twentieth birthday. Even more youthful in looks than in age, he came with an 'above average' assessment from the OTU at Kinloss where he had been flying Whitleys. In the year ahead the lives of Shannon and Gibson were to become closely intertwined. The son of an Australian politician, Shannon had entered the RAAF at the age of eighteen. Called up in January 1941, his first instinct had been to join the navy, but his impatience at finding a long queue at the Adelaide recruiting office caused him to go round the corner and sign up for the RAAF instead. During initial flying training he earned a reputation for excessively wild behaviour on the ground. In the air, by contrast, he impressed his instructor, who considered Shannon the best pupil he had ever taught.

In the autumn of 1941 Shannon and several hundred others were sent to England. The SS *Marapoia* took them from Sydney across the Pacific via Fiji to Los Angeles. From there they were moved to San Francisco, thence by a succession of trains to Halifax, Nova Scotia, and a convoy to Liverpool. It was an extraordinary journey, coloured by the spontaneous hospitality of well-wishing strangers, but typical of many whereby tens of thousands of young men emerging from their teens were shipped around the world, away from their ranches, villages, farms and towns, and systematically fed into the fire of the European war. There were many Dominion aircrew in Bomber Command. Gibson's relations with them were often strong. He enjoyed their openness and he was moved by the fact that they had volunteered to come. It was so with David Shannon.

Shannon's first week at Coningsby was uneventful. He was sent aloft in an Oxford to familiarize himself with local surroundings, then on a cross-country to Abingdon. Three days passed. Shannon now had his first ride as second pilot in a Lancaster. This trip was more noteworthy: the captain was Sqn Ldr John Wooldridge, OC B Flight, and their destination was the Focke-Wulf works at Bremen. It was Shannon's first operation and the third and last assembly of the 'Thousand Force' which had raided Cologne nearly a month before.

Hitherto Shannon had seen nothing of Gibson, who was still away.

Lancasters had been arriving in his absence and on his return Gibson
immediately began to make up for lost time in gaining experience with
the new type. On 4 July Gibson flew with Hopgood and on the
following day he assembled a crew and took them for a cross-country.
Two sergeant pilots flew with him, apparently for purposes of audition,
and on his return Gibson marched into Wooldridge's office and began
to vent his exasperation over their shortcomings. Whether they really
were inexpert, or (as Shannon thought) simply frightened of him, is not
clear. Nevertheless, he demanded someone better. Wooldridge suggested
Shannon.

Shannon was not scared by Gibson and the fact that he had more
Lancaster experience than his commander helped him to go about his
tasks efficiently, impressing Gibson by the way in which he could
anticipate commands.[10] Gibson was pleased. On 8 July came an operation, Gibson's first in a Lancaster, and Shannon flew with him as
second pilot/flight engineer. They went to attack the submarine yards at
Wilhelmshaven. 'Flak light' noted Shannon in his logbook. 'Good
prang' wrote Gibson in his. 'Opposition fairly accurate' was the verdict
in the squadron's ORB. Photographs showed that most bombs had
fallen on farmland well away from the port.

Three days later came Shannon's second operation with Gibson, to
the submarine works in the Baltic port of Danzig. It was an epic trip,
the outbound leg flown in daylight. The weather was appalling, with
low cloud and heavy rain. They arrived over the target late, in gathering
darkness, and did not attack the primary, turning instead to a ship in
the harbour – which was missed – and to engage a flak ship. Shannon
recalls little opposition on the outward flight, but the sheer length of
the sortie was gruelling. They were airborne for almost half a day. The
two frequently changed places, to stretch their legs and ward off cramp.

A week after this odyssey, Gibson took Shannon on a Moling sortie.
Moling operations were carried out by day in conditions of 8–10/10ths
cloud, with the aid of Gee – a navigational system, recently introduced,
which combined home-based radio transmitters and an airborne
receiver. Within its limited range of 400 miles, Gee enabled a navigator
to fix his position to between four and six miles. That range included
Essen and it was to this notoriously well-defended target that Gibson
was ordered late in the morning of 18 July. Home of the Krupps
armament factories and steelworks, Essen was bad enough at night

without the risks of fighter attack in broad daylight. Gibson was
appalled and even he was relieved to receive a recall signal as they
approached Vlissingen. They jettisoned their bombs and were safely
back at Coningsby by tea-time.

Or at least most of them were. Wooldridge landed away at Mildenhall,
possibly in order to allow Gibson's wrath to subside following a
subterfuge whereby Wooldridge had appropriated his favourite
aeroplane. Gibson was not amused. He burst in to Coningsby's ops
room after he landed and demanded a formal interview with his flight
commander. What passed between them next morning is unrecorded,
but Gibson was intolerant of any who took liberties with his command.

Wooldridge was a colourful figure, sporting a luxuriant moustache
which made him look every inch the gung-ho pilot. Some thought him a
little foolish. Yet appearances are deceptive. Just as Shannon looked
like an escapee from the sixth form, but in fact was one of the most
disciplined pilots with whom Gibson ever flew, so Wooldridge's
caricature exterior concealed a remarkable combination of creative
talent and courageous spirit. A good organizer, popular with crews for
the wry humour of his calm and clearly spoken briefings, Wooldridge
was also an author and a composer who had studied for several years
with Jean Sibelius. While Gibson passed a stand-down roaring songs
with aircrew in a bar, Wooldridge might be writing or tuning into the
broadcast of a Vaughan Williams symphony. Gibson, with his mistrust
of aesthetes and intellectuals, never quite found his measure.

Friendships between bomber crew were often in the nature of intense
personal associations rather than developed relationships. Past and
future were largely suspended. Living only in an uncertain present,
commitments ordinarily calling for thoughtful judgement, like marriage
or godparenthood, were sometimes entered in a spirit of nonchalance.
What bound men together was not an interest in each other's
backgrounds or prospects so much as fear and shared experience or,
more occasionally, elation or catharsis. Few of Gibson's friends knew
much about his background, or anyone else's. Nor, in many cases, was
there time to find out.

Who were his friends? Gibson's drive towards solidarity of purpose
put him at the centre of an inner circle of like-minded 'press on'
companions. These included Hopgood, Whamond (a Rhodesian doctor
with a robust sense of humour), Robertson (a New Zealander, OC

A Flight until his death on 27 July) and several more, including crew members like Frank Ruskell, John Wickens and Bob Hutchison who flew with him on a more or less regular basis. On a personal level Gibson warmed to Shannon for his attractive blend of quick-witted, sometimes dry humour and directness. Shannon's only blind spot was drink. Alcohol did not agree with him and Gibson played an almost fatherly role, taking care of his protégé and shepherding him out of trouble.

Hopgood is another special figure. Tall, deceptively languid, a veteran of one tour and now embarked on a second, Gibson thought 'Hoppy' a 'good squadron type', which was understated language for his highest praise: someone who immersed himself socially and professionally in the work of the squadron and was always eager to fly. Ten months later Gibson recruited Hopgood for the Dams Raid and was self-accusing when he did not come back.

Off-duty pastimes included swimming, games of water polo against US or Canadian rivals, or shooting over the nearby fields of friendly farmers. Apart from carousing in local pubs and chasing girls in Boston dance halls, a favourite haunt for the inner circle was the home of a doctor in Horncastle. This gentleman offered apparently limitless supplies of food and drink and kept open house for Gibson's friends. Not everyone who qualified for this special intimacy wished to share it. Wooldridge kept his distance. So did some others, wary of what they perceived as an almost manic intensity in Gibson's enthusiasm for war and blood-brotherhood.

Under Gibson's leadership, 106 Squadron began to wield the shining sword to increasing effect. When, after collecting the secretary of state for air and several senior officers from Norwich on 25 July, Gibson noted, 'I brought these gentlemen up to see a crack station,' one senses he was only half joking. Or perhaps not at all. A special culture was evolving in 106, manifested both in the air and on the ground. Its leading feature was an unusual enthusiasm for operational flying. In this, as usual, Gibson led by example. It was not rare for wing-commanders, their nerve shaken and the end of a second or third tour in sight, to become increasingly selective in the operations upon which they chose to fly. If Gibson practised selectivity, it was towards the tougher missions. This communicated itself to the sense of community and purpose in 106 Squadron as a whole. If he could do it, they could, and if he had survived, so might they. When orders came that aircraft should be fitted with night cameras to record where bombs had fallen, Gibson was at first suspicious, next tried the technique himself and then encouraged the whole squadron to become 'photo-minded'. Aiming-point photography became a tournament within and between squadrons. Certificates were awarded to successful crews and by late summer 106 Squadron was well on the way to pre-eminence.

Gibson's tersely effective briefings were animated by a crusading zeal. 'We've got to do this,' he would often say, standing in a characteristically defiant posture, legs apart, hands on hips, or punching the palm of one hand with the fist of the other. Several colleagues were puzzled by the depth of his loathing towards Germans and wondered if he was fighting the war on a personal basis. Charles Martin echoed Gibson's feeling in his record-keeping, sometimes turning aside from routine entries to annotate names of targets with stentorian lines such as 'Munich, shrine of the Nazis, and their birthplace'. When crews were lost, Gibson's letters to next of kin, even when drafted by Martin, were frequently augmented by paragraphs he wrote personally. Typically, such lines contained not only messages of solace but also promises of vengeance.

Gibson's enthusiasm for getting on with the war permeated squadron life. Punishments meted out for minor misdemeanours were not the mindless tasks beloved of military disciplinarians, but late work directed to the care and maintenance of aircraft, engines or weapons. Hitch-hiking flight mechanics might find themselves picked up by their wing-commander, who would rather return them to their duties promptly than adhere to protocols which asserted that officers and other ranks should not associate. A former aircrafthand, earlier ignored, was greeted as a long-lost brother when Gibson ran into him in a pub and discovered that he had completed a pilot training course. On the other hand, in purely social surroundings Gibson tended to keep his distance from lower ranks. Many aircrew were accustomed to a large degree of informality: 'You were on first-name terms with the officers, and NCOs went out boozing and having meals with them,' recalls Alex Kinnear, a rear gunner at Coningsby. However, one night Kinnear and his friends

drifted into a lovely little pub in Boston . . . and there was Gibson. He looked round, then turned his back on us. He didn't say 'Hello, boys'. He made it

clear that he didn't want anything to do with us. We just drank up and found
another pub. There were plenty of them.[11]

Gibson's standards were inflexibly high. As Kinnear's crew were
preparing to take off on a raid one evening, the self-destruct device on
their Gee set exploded. Conscious that they were 'sitting on a heavy
load of bombs and incendiaries', the cabin full of smoke, they 'scrambled
out pretty quickly'. Minutes later Gibson drew up in a jeep. He was 'in
a hell of a temper'. Implying that the crew were cowards, he said,
'You've got four good engines, you'll bloody well go and bomb
Germany.'[12] On another occasion the pilot of a crippled Lancaster
managed to return to Coningsby, landing with only one wheel down
without causing further harm to his crew, three of whom were already
injured. Elsewhere such an achievement might have earned an instant
medal. Gibson was not so easily impressed. The crew had not delivered
their bombs.

Although driven by an unremitting aggression which he expected
everyone to share, Gibson did not squander lives. Against the times
when his standards look excessively harsh, we may set those when he
was generous. Men troubled by family problems were sometimes sent
off on extra leave and Gibson's spontaneity could extend to the loan of
an aeroplane as a taxi. When told that the mother of one of his pilots
was dying, he immediately arranged for a Lancaster to take the man to
her. Of course, the bereaved pilot would be back on duty all the sooner,
but that does not alter the effect of the gesture.

The start of a tour was a time of high risk and Gibson saw to it that where
possible inexperienced crews were nursed into operations with one or two
easier sorties in new aircraft. Freshman pilots were sometimes initiated by
Gibson himself. Right from the start, however, crews were expected to
display the same determination as their commander. He was intolerant
towards any who did not and ruthless in screening crews of doubtful
reliability. Coningsby's senior medical officer was practised in discriminat-
ing between luckless new crews who experienced genuine problems and
real malingerers. Even so, some were not given the benefit of the doubt.
Gibson's judgement of character and ability could be perversely inaccurate
and a number of pilots were victimized or unnecessarily alienated because
he had made up his mind that they were irresolute. Gibson ruled by a
combination of exhortatory energy, example and asperity.

He was given to solitary vigils, sometimes driving to a remote corner of the airfield, there to sit brooding. Perhaps he was thinking of Eve. His insistence that the squadron should come first, that its business was bombing and that war should be practised without distraction had led him to declare his flat opposition to aircrew 'living out' with their wives. On the other hand, it was still the case, as one WAAF noted, that Gibson 'could not get enough of Eve'. He talked about her to anyone who would listen, telephoned often and kept a glamorous portrait photograph beside his bed. Behind this obsession, however, there was growing strain. At the end of the summer Eve found work in London, and now shared a flat with a girl-friend in St John's Wood. Eve tells us that she decided to move because 'Wales was so far from Lincolnshire'. Convenient as it may have been for her husband's forty-eight-hour leaves, London also offered independence for herself during the weeks between. News of Eve's vigorous social life filtered back to Gibson and on at least one occasion there were rumours that he made an abrupt journey to confront a crisis.

Conversely, there were opportunities for casual liaisons on and around the airfield which he often took. With his winning smile, boyish charm and growing glamour, willing partners were not hard to come by. Nor was he always subtle in his approaches: one WAAF remembers his habit of pressing himself unambiguously against her in the ops room. Few connected his remoteness from Eve with celibacy. But in a life reckoned by the day, when a long life equated with a tour, what does that tell us? As we shall see, there are aspects of Gibson which take us into regions beyond gossip and reveal a gentler and more vulnerable humanity.

Byword

After a particularly successful raid on Düsseldorf at the end of July, Air Vice-Marshal Coryton, AOC 5 Group, wrote formally to Coningsby's station commander, extending his congratulations on the 'effort put up by your squadrons' which was 'worthy of the highest praise'. The squadrons were 'now almost a byword in the whole Command'. It was this reputation, prefigured by Harris's faith in Gibson's commitment and abilities, which led to 106 being singled out for training in preparation for a special operation.

Since the beginning of the year work had proceeded on a bomb designed to rupture the innards of large warships. Its working principle involved a hollow charge which when detonated against armour plate would blow a plug of metal into the ship, followed by the entrance and explosion of the bomb itself. The bomb was developed in several versions, a large weapon weighing 5,600 lb, and a smaller edition. Experiments argued either for its dropping from very low level, or from a greater height using a drogue parachute. 106 Squadron was selected for training in the use of two kinds of bomb-sight which could be used to deliver this 'Bomb CS Type DR' (Bomb, Capital Ship (Disc Ring)).[13] For low-level attack a select group of crews practised with a rather complicated tachometric bomb-sight; in high-level training they used the Stabilized Automatic Bomb-sight (SABS).

Gibson made it clear to Coryton that attacking battleships from low-level was not a practical proposition. Losses would be catastrophic. During the second half of August training therefore switched to precision bombing from altitudes around 8,500 feet. Gibson flew with Sqn Ldr D.S. Richardson, a bombing instructor from RAF Manby who came to tutor them in use of the SABS. Eventually, on 27 August, nine crews set off to the Baltic port of Gdynia, seeking the *Scharnhorst* and *Gneisenau* and the new aircraft carrier *Graf Zeppelin*.

The raid was a failure. Unpredicted haze masked the harbour and although Gibson made at least twelve runs through the flak, Richardson could not gain a clear view of the *Gneisenau*. Others fared no better. None of the warships was hit. The circumstances of the failure were outside their control, however, and both Coryton and Harris noted the thorough preparation and resolution in pressing the attack. So did members of Gibson's crew, at least one of whom was unnerved by the perfectionism which had caused him to make repeated passes. The Gdynia raid set a precedent, connecting Gibson and his squadron with the idea of special training for delivery of a special weapon.*

Bombs and tactics developed apace. During August the Pathfinder Force had been formed and on 1 September 106 followed it to Saarbrücken – Gibson's Lancaster laden with an early 8,000-lb high-capacity bomb, enclosed by specially fitted, bulged bomb doors. Some of the Pathfinders inadvertently marked the smaller town of Saarlouis and it was here that the main weight of the attack – and Gibson's monster weapon – fell. Eighteen months later Gibson's honest account of the error in his draft of *Enemy Coast Ahead* drew critical pedantry from the Air Ministry censor, who asked how Gibson's confession that 'judging from the photographs there wasn't even a sign-post left standing' at Saarlouis could be reconciled with the official communiqué which had described the attack on Saarbrücken as an 'outstanding success'.[15]

From time to time the squadron had its tragedies. On 13/14 September three crews were shot down in a single night. All were captained by 106 stalwarts, including Sqn Ldr Howell, one of the flight commanders. Gibson reacted to such losses with undisplayed grief,[16] and smouldering resentment that he metabolized into yet grimmer determination to destroy future targets.

Meanwhile, Gibson had been told that 106 would have to move. Coningsby's grass flying field was unsuitable for the heavy Lancasters and was due to be upgraded with hard runways. On 28 September an advance party left for their new home at Syerston, in Nottinghamshire. The main body departed two days later and at their going were cheered by personnel of the station headquarters. The aircraft were flown out

---

* There are discrepancies between records of this raid which remain unexplained. In his book Gibson tells us that, 'we saw our huge bomb fall into the water about four hundred yards away from the *Gneisenau*', and that afterwards he reflected, 'That's the worst of one big bomb: you go a long way to do your best, then you miss.'[14] The logbook entry confirms the use of SABS, but continues, 'After the 12th run, we bombed *Gneizenau* [sic] but missed it with our 6 × 1,000 lb bombs by 100 yards. Bad luck.' 106 Squadron's ORB gives Gibson's bomb-load for the Gdynia attack as '6 × 1,000 lb RDX'.

next morning. 'Proceeded,' wrote Martin, 'does not accurately describe their departure . . .' Coningsby and its area had often been

treated to 'shoot ups' but all previous ones were eclipsed this morning. One regrets to record that such a farewell incurred grave displeasure in authoritative [*sic*] circles but few could have failed to have been impressed by such a superbly thrilling display of flying. Without doubt, Coningsby will not forget the departure of 106 Squadron![17]

An unwritten convention on such occasions was that one low pass might be tolerated. But some pilots went beyond tradition, one pair streaking back and forth over Coningsby's buildings, wingtip tucked into tail, so low that there were allegations of broken windows. Infuriated, Gibson ordered the offenders to be placed under station arrest when they arrived at Syerston, an order he rapidly countermanded when it was pointed out that the miscreants would otherwise be unavailable for a raid on the Dornier works at Wismar.

Heartland

Syerston belongs to that central region of the English countryside which is curiously unspectacular yet touches the core of English identity. Nottinghamshire beside the Foss Way was moulded by medieval farmers, whose fields and furlongs are still outlined by dog-rose hedges, and Danish ancestry in the names of places. Villages hereabouts are sociable clusters of houses and farms, mostly clad in warm, glowing brick. For fliers there were nearby landmarks, like the soaring steeple of Newark's parish church. Beyond the Trent, cradled in a hollow, lies Southwell, a Georgian town with a cathedral that Gibson regularly overflew. Near by stood Kelham Hall, helpfully conspicuous to incoming aviators, if less well understood as a hotbed of High Anglicanism that had forged the ethos of so many of their public schools.

Little of this impinged directly upon Gibson, for whom cultural history weighed less than science and practicality. In any case, he was too preoccupied to give much thought to his surroundings. Yet both from the air and on the ground Syerston was a place which gathered to a focus the materials of Gibson's adult life and the purpose of his war. If Cornwall was his childhood Lyonesse, the East Midlands was the landscape in which he came of age. Seen from a cockpit, the Foss Way threaded Lincoln, Leicester and the neighbourhoods of distant Rugby and Coventry together at a glance, linking the world of bombers to memories of family and late adolescence. Off duty, there was a good walk to be had down the tree-clad bluff to the Trent, with the promise of a pint or two at the pub on the opposite bank for anyone who took the ferry across. Newark was companionable, full of good brewing and the Bell at Bingham was a favoured haunt for the inner circle. Even more alluring was Nottingham, half an hour distant by car, relished by J.B. Priestley for the atmosphere of its Goose Fair, by aircrew for its pubs, dance-halls and cheerful promiscuity; and by Gibson for Margot's Bar – and pretty barmaid – in the Black Boy Hotel.

Gibson established a close rapport with the station commander, Gp Capt. Augustus Walker. An extrovert rugby international, Walker had a reputation for 'Hun hate' as large as Gibson's own and a wealth of recent operational experience. Like Gibson, he immersed himself in the life of the station and the first week found both of them intrigued by orders for exercises which involved upwards of eighty 5 Group Lancasters flying in sub-groups of threes and sixes in daylight at low-level. This promised something interesting, but the exercises were interrupted for other operations, including a raid on Cologne from which three out of eleven 106 crews did not return. Gibson took this badly. Like the tragedy at Bremen the month before, the losses included a flight commander, Sqn Ldr Charles Hill. A newcomer called John Searby had talked to Hill before the raid and asked how he got on with Gibson. Hill had replied, a little guardedly, 'All right – as long as you're willing to fly over Germany he's happy.' Searby met Gibson for the first time next morning:

He had been flying the previous night and was under some strain. He asked me what I had been doing before joining him – and heard me out with obvious distaste – impatient and barely polite. He was a small man – with a fresh complexion and, I thought, cocky as they come. I was brief but he cut in:

'You can forget all that – it means nothing. Anything you may have done before you came here is nothing. *This is the real thing.*' He got up from his

desk and walked to the window, hands thrust deeply into the pockets of his
uniform jacket. Then, 'Ops are what count here – and anyone who doesn't like
it can get out.'

I began to dislike him, but sensed that this was a bad moment; the letters to
the next of kin of the men who were missing lay on his desk awaiting signature
– three Lancasters and their precious crews was a nasty knock.

Once again: 'Forget it – it means nothing.'

I saluted and left the office; there was no more to be said – no time for trivia
– no welcome but the blunt truth – and his unspoken words amounted to this –
'You are a general duties officer – Flying Branch – so, bloody well fly and
prove it.'[18]

Next day, 17 October, the purpose of the low-level rehearsals became
clear: an attack on the Schneider armament and locomotive works at Le
Creusot, close to the Franco-Swiss border, in Vichy France. Gibson was
now all smiles. 'He liked anything out of the common run,' recalled
Searby, '. . . the Ruhr and similar well-pounded targets were all very
well . . . but the barest hint of something unusual brought a gleam to
his eye.'[19] A mass daylight attack by Lancasters *was* unusual and
Gibson's navigator, Frank Ruskell, took a cine camera.

They departed around noon and flew down to Oxfordshire where
they circled Upper Heyford until ninety-four Lancasters had assembled.
Led by Wg-Cdr L.C. Slee of 49 Squadron, keeping below 1,000 feet
to avoid detection by *Freya*, the formation proceeded out beyond
Land's End, southward into the Bay of Biscay and then east, dropping
below 500 feet as they entered France. They kept low for the remaining
300 miles inland to the target, rising to their bombing heights in the last
minutes. No fighters intervened, although several aircraft collided with
birds.

Le Creusot was reached just after 6 p.m. It was growing dark, but in
the light of the sunset crews were impressed by the 'vast area' of
factories, workshops and warehouses. During the next ten minutes
some 140 tons of high explosive and incendiaries were aimed at this
complex, while a subsidiary group of six Lancasters, including Gibson
and Hopgood, flew to the nearby Montchanin transformer station,
delivering ten 500-lb bombs apiece to the main buildings and discharging
thousands of rounds of ammunition into the transformers. Opposition
was negligible, although Hopgood attacked from below safety height

and his aircraft sustained serious damage from the blast of his own bombs. A Lancaster from 61 Squadron, 106's sister unit at Syerston, went in so low that it flew into the side of a building.

The rest returned safely, many aircraft landing away from Syerston because of poor weather, after a round trip of 1,700 miles. Most crews were jubilant: 'Not the slightest doubt . . . primary target effectively attacked . . . raid was so successful as it was brilliantly executed . . . 100% successful . . .' Gibson was unconvinced and his misgivings were proved right. The greater weight of bombs had fallen not on the industrial area but on a nearby housing estate. Analysts at Bomber Command concluded that:

. . . the accuracy of the bombing had been far less than was expected. They thought this was partly attributable to the failing light and the smoke which soon began to drift across the target, but they also thought that the tactics adopted had been inappropriate and that the bomb-sights had not been properly used. They suggested that the outcome was the penalty of employing night crews in complex daylight operations without giving them more than a few days' training.[20]

Like the Augsburg raid six months previously, Le Creusot revealed as much about Bomber Command's limitations as it did of its strength. The ability of a flock of Lancasters to penetrate so far into Europe in daylight rested largely upon the fact that the Luftwaffe's fighter defences were concentrated elsewhere. However, Le Creusot did show that it was feasible to circumvent this screen, and that lesson was now put to new use.

Four days later, crews were surprised to be briefed for a raid on Genoa. This was a dauntingly long flight – nine and a half hours – and Gibson called at Manston on his way back to refuel, and again at Chelveston in Northamptonshire. To judge from the jokey corruptions of these place names in his logbook he was in high spirits. Genoa was considered 'pretty cushy'. Next day they went again to Italy, this time Milan, in daylight. Gibson rejoiced in the panic they caused. The Lancasters scattered leaflets as well as bombs, warning of the end of Mussolini's regime. A Fiat fighter approached them, but did not engage. 'A marvellous trip with most magnificent scenery over the Alps,' recorded Gibson, who later recalled how during the flight out they were urged on with ecstatic waves from French farmers and families. Contact with outside emotion is virtually unknown in aerial warfare. There were no garlands or uninhibited kisses for bomber crews in the late summer 1944. Now even fleeting glimpses of real people reminded them why they were there.

The Italian raids caused a sensation at Syerston, contributing to a feeling that they were engaged in deeds that advanced the progress of the war. 'Le Creusot, Genoa, and now *Milan*,' enthused 106's diarist, '– three great raids within a week.' Morale rose further when it was realized that their attacks on the Italian fleet had been designed to help pave the way for the North African offensive. Then came autumn fog and drizzle and for eleven days Italian targets were spared.

Poor weather often caused the diversion of returning bombers and Gibson advised Searby of the excellent amenities to be found at night-fighter stations. Thus, when fog prevented several of 106's Lancasters from returning to Syerston after visiting Turin on 18 November, Searby and Gibson both found themselves at Middle Wallop. Initially Gibson was in good spirits; it would emerge that seven of the eight 106 crews had returned with excellent aiming-point photographs. Searby was impressed by Middle Wallop's runway lighting and by the WAAF who brought him tea the next morning. Next day Syerston remained fogbound and in the evening a party developed in the Mess. Searby records that Gibson was tense, aloof from the fun and behaving edgily. The station commander asked if all was well. Gibson's self-control then slipped and in a sudden outburst he accused Middle Wallop's resident nightfighter crews of being 'too bloody safe'.[21] The incident was smoothed over, although its significance was not lost on Searby, who noted his commander's growing irritability under the accumulating burdens of operational stress and responsibility.

Equally revealing is Gibson's increasing faith in Searby. After the strain of their first meeting, Searby's thorough airmanship and persistence in completing difficult sorties had convinced Gibson that his new flight commander was a good type after all. On the ground too Searby had emerged as an able administrator and before long Gibson was content to leave the squadron in his hands when he was away.

Gibson made one more trip to Turin and in addition to an 8,000-lb bomb he took 5 Group's flak liaison officer as a passenger, and a cine cameraman. Extended 'actuality' footage of Bomber Command operations before 1944 is surprisingly rare and much of what there is was made on personal rather than official initiative. In Gibson's case a progression can be followed from still photography through amateur filming to a professional cameraman as an extra crew member. Whether the films were intended for analysis or as souvenirs it seems likely that once again we are in the presence of Gibson's desire to communicate to a wider audience what the bomber war was really about.

What was it about? Essentially, we are told, it was about delivering bombs and little else. Gibson had become a monomaniac, his entire being devoted to the organization and execution of air raids, to the motivation of aircrew and the driving of ground staff who worked incessantly to keep the squadron's aeroplanes serviceable. The Admiral names had been continued from 83 Squadron days: *Admiral von Censored, Admiral von Gremlin, Admiral Prune, Admiral Chatanooga*, all adding in minor but telling ways to squadron identity. Most of his social life was similarly channelled. Even when in London he spent much time at Shepherd's Tavern in Hertford Street, a favourite haunt of bomber crews and a place to trade news about the careers of kindred spirits. But often now he returned early from his leaves. He was addicted to stress and found it increasingly difficult to relax or disengage, appearing restless or truculent at one moment, cheerful or charming the next.

There were now three concentric cadres of 106: the ground staff, aircrew who had yet to prove themselves or chose to keep their distance and the inner circle. It was Gibson's achievement that the squadron worked so well, but newcomers could find its society enclosed and their commander unforgiving. Sgt 'Buzz' Freeman and his crew arrived at Syerston in October, fresh from a Conversion Unit. Although Freeman's navigator, Plt Off. Ron Williams, had achieved a high rating and Williams in his turn had a high opinion of Freeman's abilities as a pilot, the crew was not considered to be of operational standard. Four weeks of training followed. They had gone some months without leave, but a request for leave was denied pending the completion of an operation.

On 23 November, almost six weeks after joining 106, Williams wrote to his parents in a state of depression. Three days previously they had been detailed to take part in an attack on Turin, but had been forced to abort their sortie because of a defective turret. The trip did not count towards their tour and because of their early return they were under suspicion of being faint-hearted. Other aircrew within 106 Squadron were victimizing them, putting it about that they were a 'jinx crew' and suggesting that they would never operate successfully. Shrugging off this macabre gossip, eight nights later Freeman again took off for Turin. This time they reached the target and completed the sortie.

Yet no leave was forthcoming. Instead, Freeman's crew waited with mounting frustration as for the next seven days 106 Squadron did not operate. Then on 9 December they were briefed for another operation against Turin. Williams takes up the story in a letter to his parents:

Approaching enemy territory recently Buzz began complaining that he felt sick and didn't think he was up to taking us all the way. He got worse and couldn't see the instruments properly. We turned back and the kite was all over the place. But with the help of 'George' [the automatic pilot] . . . and the Flight Engineer we got back O.K. and landed.

There was a lot of cross-examination. I had to sign a statement of what happened – while Buzz was at SSQ, and the next day the M.O. examined him and grounded him. Buzz has to go before a medical board and it is certain he will never do ops here. The remainder of us decided to do our best to keep together, but it looks like a vain attempt. Another pilot tried to get three or four of us all together and we were very agreeable, but the Wingco said he had already fixed him up except for a Flight Engineer so we lost him, and there are five left.[22]

By 11 December the remaining members of Freeman's luckless crew were listed as 'awaiting posting'. On the following day they were summoned to an interview with Gibson. Whatever Gibson said did not endear him to Williams, who felt that they had been unjustly treated. Three months after joining 106 Squadron, Williams was posted to 1660 Conversion Unit at Swinderby for recrewing. A month later he was back at Syerston, this time as a member of 61 Squadron. We shall meet Williams again.

Maggie

On 8 December 106 Squadron went to Turin. As usual the Lancasters queued up along the perimeter track awaiting their turn to take off. Syerston provided twenty-three machines on this evening, twelve from

61 Squadron and eleven from 106. Gibson was not flying. At half past five he and Walker were watching from the control tower.

On the far side of the airfield stood Lancaster K of 61 Squadron, a reserve aircraft which had been readied for use in case one of the others became unserviceable. Lancaster K's bomb bay held eight containers of 4-lb incendiaries and a 4,000-lb 'cookie'. Her bomb doors were open. Possibly as a result of vibration caused by the other Lancasters taxiing near by, the carriers of incendiaries fell out of the bomb bay on to the hard-standing.[23] Some of the bombs ignited.

Walker and Gibson saw the developing glow and the fire-tender setting forth to deal with it. Lancaster K's dispersal point was not far from Syerston's main bomb store. Fearing catastrophe, Walker ran from the watch office to his car and proceeded to drive at high speed, threading his way between moving Lancasters across the airfield. Gibson watched through binoculars as Walker got out of his car and approached the Lancaster, gesticulating frantically at the fire-tender crew who were 'moving up to investigate the possibility of extinguishing the fire'. According to Searby, Walker himself seized their long hooked rake and started to drag burning incendiaries aside. This desperate work was still in progress when the 4,000-lb bomb exploded.

So great was the detonation that its mighty thump was felt twenty miles to the east at RAF Hospital, Rauceby, where just at that moment two theatre nurses in the Burns and Orthopaedic Unit were seeking to persuade their sister to allow them to volunteer for an evening's work with one of the hospital's mobile surgical teams. Minutes later the telephone rang with an urgent request for surgical assistance at Syerston. Flt Lt Russell, the duty surgeon, the two nurses and an anaesthetist set forth.*

The team's vehicle was driven through the black-out at high speed with masked headlamps and no little risk. As they rounded a corner in Newark a policeman narrowly escaped being run down as he began to cross the road. At Syerston's main gate the guards waved the ambulance through and an airman jumped on to the running-board to guide them to the medical centre.

---

* Although Syerston's ORB states that the Mobile Surgical Team was led by Flt Lt Braithwaite, Margaret North, one of the members of the team, is sure that they were led by Flt Lt Russell. Fenton Braithwaite may have been the surgeon who operated on Walker later in the night, when Walker had been transferred to Rauceby.

Russell and his team were led down into a bunker beneath the Sick Quarters Annexe. Walker lay on a stretcher on the concrete floor. An orderly knelt beside him, clutching the dripping stump of Walker's right arm which had been severed just above the elbow. Near by were seven other casualties from the fire-tender crew. One of them, Sgt Cocker, had lost a foot. Another, an aircraftman called Thwaite, had a compound fracture of his skull and cerebral laceration. Thwaite died three days later.

The medical team was watched by a semicircle of hushed onlookers. Walker was conscious and for someone who had just been blown many yards across an airfield was in reasonable spirits. But Walker was also in shock and most seriously injured. Fearing that he would be unable to withstand transfer to Rauceby, Russell prepared to operate on the spot. The orderly crouching on the floor was by now in considerable discomfort. Cpl Margaret North, one of the two nurses, offered to change places.

While Russell worked on to establish Walker's condition, other members of his team set up plasma drips, prepared bandages and administered a blood transfusion. North, meanwhile, was in an awkward position on the floor, clasping the oozing stump of Walker's arm. Looking sideways, she saw pairs of legs and asked the owner of one of them to move forward to provide support for her back. After a short pause the legs shuffled forward.

'Is that better?' asked Gibson.

Russell now decided that Walker might after all be strong enough to survive the journey to hospital. Walker was carried to the ambulance together with LAC Hughes, who had been in charge of the crash party. Walker's transfusion continued in the ambulance and two hours later a surgical amputation took place in the Annexe theatre for crash and burns cases at Rauceby. The operation finished at 4 a.m.

Next afternoon Cpl North walked into the officers' ward of the Annexe. Walker lay in bed in a corner of the room. His wife sat beside the bed, as did a boyish-looking officer who sat on the other side, his chair tilted back against the wall. North, her rank concealed by a white theatre gown, told the officer to sit properly lest he end up in her theatre. She then turned cheerfully to Walker to ask how he was. North explained that she had a personal interest in his welfare by saying, 'You and I held hands last night.' Walker smiled and Gibson roared with laughter. Gibson then asked, 'What do you do around here? What is this place?'

North explained about the Crash and Burns Unit and offered to show him round. She told him of the victims of failed take-offs who arrived in the hour or so after bombers set forth on raids and the greater numbers who were brought in disfigured by frostbite, electrical burns, chunks of flying metal and fire after the aeroplanes returned. She told of the phosphorus which fizzed in wounds. She showed him the grievous injuries of the 'guinea pigs' (so called because of the pioneering work done on their burns), their faces and hands seared, and the work of Fenton Braithwaite, their resident plastic surgeon, and the visiting consultant from East Grinstead, Archibald McIndoe. Gibson was taken to a room close to the officers' ward in which stood three deep baths. Here some of the worst burns victims were submerged in saline solution, an excruciating treatment which could cause the bravest to howl and curse with pain. Along the corridor was the room where Bill Howell, the unit's clinical photographer, processed the sequences of pictures which followed the progress of patients from admission to reconstruction.

Gibson was quietly attentive. At length he asked: 'What do they call you?'

'They call me Butch,' said North. 'Who are you?' North had no idea who Gibson was, although she was already much taken with him.

'Just call me Guy,' said Gibson. 'What are you doing tonight?'

Margaret North admitted that she had no plans.

'Would you like to come out for a drink?'

Anxious to accept, Margaret was nevertheless wary, being conscious of her non-commissioned rank and the presumption against fraternization with officers.

'Yes, but . . .'

'Yes, but what?' persisted Gibson. North explained that beneath her gown she was only a corporal.

'Bugger that,' said Gibson cheerfully. 'We'll go anyway.'

And so they went out. Gibson drove Margaret to a quiet pub where they sat in the back room. Margaret sipped shandy and Gibson talked. He talked of Syerston, of colleagues, of administrative problems and frustrations. Margaret listened quietly, saying little, sensing a man who was very tired, unsettled, morose. Gibson spoke of Eve and his devotion to her seemed strong. But Eve was not a part of the bomber world. The strain of trying to explain 'what it was like' to wives and girl-friends was commonly too great for aircrew to begin to attempt it. On leave at home Gibson would make light of his work, talk about other things, or retreat into silence. But Margaret lived among aircrew. She knew about ops and flak and the symptoms of the condition that Rauceby nurses called 'bomb happy', when young men trembled in a species of shock. She was a member of the extended family of Bomber Command. So she listened and it was into her understanding ear that in coming weeks Gibson became accustomed to pour out his worries, annoyances and dreams.

After this first evening Gibson became a frequent visitor to Rauceby. His arrivals seeking Margaret were as often as not unannounced, heralded by a boisterous greeting of 'How's my Maggie? Cut up any good men today?' Nigger was usually on the back seat of his small black car which rattled as they drove around country lanes to rural pubs where the risks of anyone recognizing them were small. Margaret seldom knew where they were going or had been: all the signposts had been removed. Occasionally they were more adventurous and went to the cinema, a couple of times to the Picture House at Grantham to see Bing Crosby musicals. Maggie soon found that Guy had 'rather a soft spot for musicals', perhaps because of his first-hand acquaintance with their production.

Margaret and Gibson found each other good companions. Gibson's conversation was wide-ranging. Although much of it centred on his responsibilities at Syerston, he sometimes ventured into unexpected areas. 'Do you like opera?' he asked one day. Margaret confessed that she did not like it at all and was startled at the thought that opera might be one of his hidden enthusiasms. 'It isn't,' agreed Gibson, 'but I'm interested; I'd give it a try.' Books, burns and flying converged in the writing of Richard Hillary, whose book *The Last Enemy* Gibson had just read and about which he talked one evening. 'Have you read *all* those?' inquired Margaret when Gibson delivered a tall pile of volumes to Walker. Then she added: 'Why don't you write a book?' Gibson grinned. 'Maybe I will.'

They talked a lot about the work at Rauceby. Gibson was fascinated by its technical aspects and deeply interested in the work on the 'guinea pigs'. This curiosity may have been inspired simply by his admiration for the devotion shown by Rauceby's staff towards injured aircrew. But as December passed there were signs that his interest in Rauceby and growing affection for Margaret North were linked to deeper emotions.

One day around midwinter Margaret was told by a colleague that Gibson was in the building. She eventually found him sitting beside a patient in the Burns ward. The victim was an air gunner, scarcely more than a boy, remote behind bandages that concealed fatal burns inflicted by a flare that had ignited within his aeroplane. Gibson had been there for some time. On arrival he had seen the boy and said gently, 'My name's Guy Gibson. Can I sit with you?' The boy had made no reply: he could not talk. Gibson attempted no conversation either, but simply sat close to the bed so that the occupant should not feel alone as his life ebbed away.

Margaret, *The Last Enemy* and Rauceby are linked by burns. Guy never told Margaret how his mother died, saying only that she had 'been in a home'. There were times when she sensed that he was on the brink of talking about some painful personal matter, but the subject seemed too deep for words.

On other occasions Guy was wholly relaxed and liked to reminisce about moments of contentment in his boyhood. A favourite memory was when he had drifted off to sleep with the perfume of the honeysuckle arbour on the evening air at the home of a relative at Combe Martin. One evening sitting in front of a bright fire in a pub Gibson's eye alighted upon a picture of a house. 'That's like Honeysuckle Cottage,' he said and thereafter the furnishing of the cottage became a game of private fantasy between them. At various times it was provided in their imaginations with solid oak antique furniture, beamed ceilings, an ingle-nook fireplace and always lots of dogs. When Margaret asked what Guy planned to do after the war, he simply smiled and said, 'We'll be at Honeysuckle Cottage.' '*We?*' inquired Margaret, a little warily. But the dream deepened. By early January they found themselves talking as if they were actually living at the cottage and would discuss what to do on particular days. There was the sea near by; today Guy would go fishing. Ah, but the flower garden called for care; or perhaps they should go to Exeter for lunch? With Margaret, Guy travelled back into a land of lost content and forwards into an imaginary future.

Late one afternoon shortly after Christmas Guy telephoned Margaret at Rauceby. He was in bouncy mood.

'Have you got any civvies?'

'No,' said Margaret, who had long ago discovered that there was a limit to what could be crammed into the one kitbag and single suitcase which it was possible for her to carry.

'Well, could you dig some out?' pressed Guy. 'There's a dance I want to take you to this evening, and there'll be quite a few officers there.'

Thrilled by the invitation, Margaret was none the less apprehensive when she accepted it. 'What's the problem?' inquired the VAD clinical secretary as Margaret put down the receiver. Margaret explained, friends gathered and the junior theatre sister looked her up and down. 'You're about my size,' she said. 'Come upstairs and try something on.'

The 'something' was a red two-piece outfit with white cuffs and collar, a swirling skirt and a small jacket with a nipped-in waist. It fitted perfectly and the girls agreed she looked good. But Margaret glanced down and was alarmed by the incongruity of her service-issue shoes. A nurse produced another pair – rather elegant – and these too fitted. Others contributed a handbag, a pearl necklace, pearl clip-on earrings and a silk stole. Margaret's friends stepped back to admire their Cinderella.

'What about stockings?' asked Margaret. No one had any. Margaret was gloomily contemplating the whiteness of her legs when one of the cooks disappeared, to return a minute or two later bearing a cup of brown powder. It was Bisto. The friends set to, completing their camouflage with a pair of seams drawn in with eyebrow pencil.

Despite the assurances of her friends, Margaret remained nervous and self-conscious. The occasion was out of the ordinary for her and she had heard enough about Eve's keen interest in clothes and fashion to worry if she would be up to the standard to which Gibson was accustomed.

'My God!' said Gibson when he saw her. 'Where did you dig all that up? You look fabulous!' Margaret relaxed.

Dinner was unusually lavish – for Margaret an event in itself in the midst of wartime austerity – and the evening went well. Much later the two were sitting side by side, Gibson with a drink in one hand and his pipe in the other. He absent-mindedly leaned forward and brushed Margaret's shin with the back of his hand.

'Don't do that!' hissed Margaret with intense urgency.

Gibson recoiled, apologizing anxiously lest his gesture should have been misinterpreted.

'No, it's not that,' whispered Margaret. 'If you rub it, it'll come off.' She explained about the makeshift leg make-up. Gibson began to laugh and continued to giggle for the rest of the evening. The episode amused him for days and in private he renamed Margaret 'Bisto Legs'.

Gibson's moods swung sharply from euphoria to depression. After a highly successful attack in late December he sang and whistled cheerfully as he drove Margaret down the hospital drive, rhythmically banging the steering-wheel. Gibson rejoiced at the safe return of all his crews. By contrast, on a Thursday in mid-January Gibson began the evening in such quarrelsome ill-temper that Margaret ordered him to stop the car, demanding that he either calm down or take her home. Gibson fell quiet and apologized.

His outburst was caused by the failure of Flt Lt Gray Healey and Flt Sgt M.A. Phair to return from an attack on Essen. Phair had been an outstanding pilot. He had contributed many aiming-point photographs to the squadron's record and was near the end of his tour. Healey's loss was a special source of grief to Gibson, who earlier in the day had written a long and generous letter to Healey's mother, expressing the hope that he might be a prisoner of war. Midway through his second tour, all Healey's operations had been flown with 106 Squadron. He and his crew personified its spirit. The crew included several of the squadron's most experienced men. Michael Lumley, Healey's wireless operator, was a particularly popular and convivial figure. He had forty-one operations behind him. Pennington, the navigator, had accomplished thirty-two. Although Healey had been due back at Syerston before midnight, Gibson had waited up until dawn, hoping for news that they had come down in the sea.

Three weeks later they heard that all the crew had been killed. Gibson wrote again to Healey's mother, implying that their deaths had been caused by flak: '. . . it must have been a direct hit, and I am quite certain that he and the rest of the crew suffered no pain.' Perhaps Gibson's speculation was intended to console. He was not to know that their deaths at around half past seven on that freezing evening had been far from instantaneous. Healey's Lancaster had been attacked over Holland on its way to Essen by a nightfighter. The Lancaster caught fire. As it descended a running battle developed between the fighter and Healey's gunners, who continued to retaliate almost until their burning aircraft hit the ground.[24]

Gibson was now nearing the end of his third tour of operations. The loss of good and highly experienced friends like Healey not only touched him deeply but reinforced his view that his own survival was due to chance. His own death would be equally arbitrary. On several occasions he confided to Margaret that he knew that he was 'not going to come through this'. The crushing responsibilities of command on someone scarcely older than an undergraduate were beginning to tell. Off duty with Margaret, it was not necessary for him to maintain any façade of confidence, or to conceal depression.

A few days after the loss of Healey and Phair, Gibson turned up at Rauceby late in the afternoon. He found the theatre sister and asked for Maggie. Gibson looked grey and drawn and retreated to his car until Margaret should appear. Sister Stevens found Margaret and passed on his message, adding that her visitor looked in bad shape. 'I've seen that kind of thing before. You'd better go out to him.'

Margaret found Gibson sitting in his car, staring forward through the windscreen and gnawing obsessively on the stem of his unlit pipe. He was shaking uncontrollably. At length he pleaded, 'Please hold me.' Margaret reached out and hugged him. Gradually the tremors subsided and after half an hour Gibson had recovered his composure. 'Ops last night?' asked Margaret, who had seen similar cases before and had dealt with several in the same way. Gibson nodded. He never referred to the incident again and at their next meeting his customary ebullience seemed restored.

Margaret's role as a confidante may have been misinterpreted by her WAAF colleagues, some of whom looked upon Gibson's attentions with unconcealed envy. Privately Margaret adored him, but felt unable to make this known and made no attempt to steer their affectionate companionship towards anything more serious. For his part Gibson behaved with uncharacteristic circumspection. He made no advances. Rauceby nurses were well used to the clumsy gambits of married aircrew hopeful of a casual leavetime fling and equally practised in evading them. But with Gibson nothing like this ever occurred. Margaret gathered that his marriage was under strain, but he was not disloyal to Eve in anything that he said. On the other hand, within the space of scarcely a month the gentle intimacy of their relationship was becoming clear and on several occasions Margaret sensed that Guy was on the verge of addressing this in new terms. But the conversation that might have opened matters out did not take place until much later. While Guy openly drew Margaret into his dreams, he seemed incapable of talking about the reality of what their deepening friendship might mean.

The result was a rapidly growing sense of frustration on both sides. Margaret was aware that Gibson was a rising star within the RAF and that before long he would be given some new job, presumably on the ground, and elsewhere, which would set them apart. What was the point of getting involved? When faced with hypothetical inquiries about his future with Eve, Gibson took refuge in generalized replies to the effect that 'It would all come right.' Difficulties were compounded by the irregularity of his visits. Dates on consecutive evenings might be followed by a week of absence. Gibson often punctuated these gaps with cheery telephone calls, but he was by no means the only airman expressing interest in Margaret North, who was faced with the increasingly difficult choice of maintaining an intermittent friendship with an attached man, or acquiescing to the attentions of suitors who lacked the disadvantages of being married, of senior commissioned rank, and absent.

Matters came to a head in February when after a gap of some days he telephoned and found Margaret strangely distant.

'I haven't seen you for a while,' she said.

'It's been a busy time,' Guy replied. 'What have you been doing?'

Then Margaret admitted that her off-duty hours had been occupied by the determined attentions of a sergeant. Guy fell silent. Sensing the effect that this news had had and hoping to force unstated feelings into the open, Margaret continued: 'In fact, he's asked me to marry him.' Guy said nothing for a long time. Eventually he broke the silence.

'Don't do it.'

'Why not?' replied Margaret in a matter-of-fact way, adding impulsively: 'No one else seems to want to.'

Another long silence.

Then Gibson argued, 'You don't love him.'

'How do you know?'

The conversation continued in similar fashion, long silences being punctuated by Gibson repeating, 'Don't do this.'

Margaret North's marriage, like countless others in wartime, followed swiftly. The week before the wedding, depressed and emotionally confused, Margaret wept. A friend found her crying and coaxed forth

much of the story. Why did Margaret not cancel the wedding? There
was still time. But the marriage which Margaret North did not want, to
a man for whom she did not particularly care, had acquired an inevitabil-
ity of its own.

Gibson made one final attempt to prevent it. On the morning of the
wedding itself, Saturday 20 February, he telephoned Margaret and
pleaded with her to think again.

'Are you really going to go through with this?'

'Why – what's the worry?'

Even now Guy could not bring himself to explain. Unwilling or
unable to muster the words needed for analysis, he could only make
statements.

'I don't want you to do this,' he kept repeating.

It was left to Margaret to force the essence of the issue into the open.
'Guy, you are spoken for.'

There was a long silence. Margaret waited, alert for any hint of his
real feelings. At length Guy said, 'But I need you.'

'Eve wouldn't let you go, would she?'

Gibson sighed in a tone suggesting that this was an issue. Then he
asked, 'Would you come if I called?'

'Yes.'

'Do you really mean that?'

'Yes. You know I would.'

Margaret North was married a few hours later. The wedding took
place in the parish church at Quarrington, about a mile from Rauceby.
Alert guests might have caught the sound of Gibson's Lancaster high
overhead as it proceeded to a bombing range on the coast. For some
weeks Gibson had been working on a bomb-sight of his own invention
and after his telephone call, perhaps spurred by the need for distraction,
he took to the air to test it. Gibson was enthusiastic about the results
which according to his logbook gave an average error of 150 yards from
10,000 feet. By the time he returned to Syerston Margaret North was
Mrs Margaret Figgins and, for the time being, Gibson had lost his
confidante.

For Freedom?

Gibson's breakdown in the arms of Margaret North came the day after one of his most celebrated flights: a sortie to Berlin with an impressive young radio journalist called Richard Dimbleby as his passenger. Gibson disliked 'visiting firemen' and news of distinguished visitors often caused him to become uncooperative. Yet, like so much else about him, his reputation for brusqueness towards outsiders is an over-simplification. He had a keen interest in innovations that would help to prosecute the war and saw public awareness of what Bomber Command was doing as an essential part of that process.

Dimbleby and his colleague Stanley Richardson arrived at Syerston on 8 January and were temporarily attached to the station pending an operational flight. Dimbleby took a keen interest in Syerston's work and Gibson 'couldn't do enough to smooth his path'.[25] The two men may have felt some special affinity over the project, for the idea of an actuality broadcast had met with much resistance at the BBC and was viewed with deep suspicion by the Air Ministry. So they were being watched and both had a vested interest in the successful outcome of their experiment.

Berlin had not been raided for more than a year and there was a stir at briefing on 16 January when the target was unveiled. 'An attack on the Reich capital inevitably creates an atmosphere of particular excitement,' noted Charles Martin. They took off just after half past four, rolling past Gp Capt. Bussell, Walker's successor as station commander, at the end of the runway. Bussell was in the habit of saluting each bomber as it took off – a gesture which Gibson rather liked, despite the fact that Bussell's wife had referred slightingly to Gibson in his hearing as 'that boy'. As they climbed, Dimbleby looked about and counted between thirty and forty bombers, 'seemingly suspended in the evening air'. With the Lancaster still gaining altitude, a kink in the tube of his oxygen supply caused him to pass out. The flight engineer untwisted the tube and restored him to consciousness.

Crossing the enemy coast Dimbleby saw his first flak:

It was bursting away from us and much lower. I didn't see any long streams of it soaring into the air as the pictures suggest: it burst in little yellow winking flashes and you couldn't hear it above the roar of the engines. Sometimes it closes in on you, and the mid or tail-gunner will call up calmly and report its position to the Captain so that he can dodge it . . .[26]

As they approached Berlin Dimbleby was awestruck by the lattice of searchlights – 'a tracery of sparkling silver' – and shocked by the intensity of the flak, which 'closed right round us'. The blast of one close burst tossed the Lancaster upwards. Dimbleby was not to know that half of Berlin's flak personnel were absent that evening and that the barrage was lighter than usual. Nevertheless, it was fierce enough and Shannon's Lancaster was hit, returning on three engines. Looking down, Dimbleby watched in fascination as thousands of incendiary bombs burned: 'All over the dark face of the German capital these great incandescent flower-beds spread themselves.' Their own load was a single 8,000-lb high-capacity bomb. Sub-Lt Muttrie, a Fleet Air Arm bomb-aimer on secondment to 106, could not see the aiming-point on their first run. Gibson elected to go round again. Dimbleby was struck by the effect of flying out into the surrounding darkness before they re-entered the dazzle over the city. The second run was likewise unsatisfactory and the bomb was only released on their third. As they left the target, corkscrewing into the night, Dimbleby was overcome by the tension and physical buffeting. He leaned forward and vomited down the ladderway into the bomb-aimer's compartment in the nose.

'A good trip and fairly successful,' wrote Gibson in his logbook some days later, adding: 'The residential quarters got it! Dimbleby broadcasted next day.' In fact he didn't; the Air Ministry delayed transmission until the following Monday and 106 Squadron's record, based on debriefing in the early hours of the 17th, was more cautious about the outcome:

Thick haze made pin-pointing difficult. Three runs made over target before dropping 8,000-lb bomb from 18,000 feet near the red marker flare. Results not seen. Believed that bomb fell in Berlin but trip disappointing due to weather.

By later standards the force was not large – about 200 aircraft, all four-engined – and the results of the raid were not counted as particularly successful. The aiming-point at Alexanderplatz railway station was masked by haze and bombing was scattered.

But all this was of secondary interest in comparison with the broadcast, which was a triumph. Listeners were enthralled by the immediacy and incidental detail of Dimbleby's account. For the first time radio journalism allowed the public some inkling of what really lay behind an unemotional Air Ministry communiqué which announced that, 'Last night a strong force of our bombers attacked Berlin ...' After all its earlier hesitation, the Air Ministry too was pleased. Members of 106 clustered round their wireless sets and liked what they heard. Dimbleby 'did not let us down' noted the adjutant. 'It was not a "line-shoot" but a very fine tribute to Bomber Command crews in general and to Wing-Commander Gibson's crew in particular.' Dimbleby was particularly moved by a brief but unequivocal telegram from Bomber Command High Wycombe. It read 'Good work'.[27]

Gibson knew the wider significance of the broadcast and wrote to Dimbleby to thank him. Dimbleby replied, confessing his fear during the raid, but stressing the importance of his 'unique chance to see for myself what is being done week after week in the name of Freedom ...' This pleased Gibson deeply. Not only had Dimbleby caught an echo of his squadron's motto – Pro libertate, 'For freedom' – but he had also recognized that his glimpse into the inferno was what a bomber crew would experience every week. Gibson's difficulty in articulating the sheer routine nature of the terrors faced by his crews had long been a source of frustration. Now Dimbleby had supplied the words he lacked – an Aaron to Gibson's Moses – and millions had heard them.

Dimbleby himself had already had a taste of what it was like to be an object of public incomprehension. On his way back to London from Syerston on a crowded train he

... managed to find an empty seat and sat down. As they pulled out of the station some uniformed soldiers looked into the compartment. Seeing it was full they stood outside. Dimbleby was the only civilian in the carriage apart from an elderly woman sitting opposite him. She looked up sharply: 'I should have thought that a lucky young man like you would have the good manners to give up his seat to one of our fighting men.' He was too tired to reply.[28]

And while Dimbleby was preparing his broadcast at the BBC, Gibson was at Rauceby, shaking with silent sobs.

No one else seems to have questioned his invulnerability. Colleagues recognized signs of strain, but most assumed 'Gibbo's' operational ardour to be limitless. Gibbo himself, on the other hand, was well aware of his limits and knew that he was approaching them. During his last weeks at Syerston he began to count the number of sorties he had flown: 'This is my 67th bombing trip' (after Berlin), 'My 169th war flight' (after Cologne, on 26 February) and so on. In fact, his next sortie, to Milan on St Valentine's Day, was a memorable success. The city was easily seen by moonlight and after he had bombed it Gibson flew around for twenty minutes to enable the cameraman he had brought with him to take movie pictures. 106 brought back six aiming-point photographs from that operation and crowned the squadron's celebrity:

It was a remarkable success and has earned all concerned praise from the highest quarters. This magnificent record combined with recent successes has put the squadron on top of Group Photographic Ladder.[29]

Gibson had been with 106 Squadron for eleven months. During that time he had moulded one of the most efficient and dedicated units in Bomber Command and added a further twenty-nine sorties to his operational record. He had also lived through a year of experiment: the thousand raids; the introduction of Gee, the Lancaster and the bomber stream; raids preceded by specialized training; the inauguration of the Pathfinder Force, flares, skymarkers and target indicators. The growing complexity of bombing demanded planning and co-ordination undreamed of in 1940. Routes, raids, loads and tactics were now planned in minute detail, even to the point of adjusting the mix of bombs to correspond with the condition (intact, semi-ruined, destroyed) of the hapless city to be visited. A good deal of Gibson's work was accordingly now centred on meetings and committees, convened for purposes of organizational and tactical planning. During the winter Gibson had become an increasingly familiar figure at HQ 5 Group in Grantham, where he and Air Vice-Marshal Coryton had discussed the possibility of developing 106 as a squadron for special operations, an idea reported to Harris, who was likewise following the career of the restless young man he had appointed a year before.

Coryton left Grantham at the end of February. Gibson was sorry to see him go, but intrigued by his successor, Air Vice-Marshal the Honourable Ralph Cochrane. After Coryton, Cochrane seemed cold, almost clinical, but made up in intellectual ability what he seemed to lack in human warmth or personal experience of operations. Appropriately enough, Gibson's first meetings with Cochrane, and last as commander of 106, were connected with planning for the first use of a technical innovation which would revolutionize bombing. Its code-name was Oboe: it was a distance-measuring system between an airborne radar and transmission stations on the ground. Although limited in range by the curvature of the earth, Oboe provided a means to mark targets in the Ruhr through cloud or haze.

Was it the success of Dimbleby's broadcast which led Bomber Command's PR department to arrange for Edward Hunt to be at Syerston early in March on the day when Oboe was first used? At any rate Hunt, a journalist on the *Sunday Express*, wrote of his 'rare good luck' in being the 'only civilian to have visited any RAF operational station' during Bomber Command's raid on Essen on the Friday night of 5/6 March. Under the headline THIS WAS IT! amplified by THREE TONS OF BOMBS ON ESSEN EVERY FOUR SECONDS FOR 35 MINUTES, readers were told that this attack had been 'by far the most outstanding show of the last six months and perhaps the heaviest and most concentrated air attack of the war'. For once, journalistic hyperbole was not far from the truth. PFF Mosquitoes equipped with Oboe had marked Essen regardless of its usual shroud of industrial haze and with further PFF assistance over 360 bombers had proceeded to lay waste a large area between the Krupps armament works and Essen's centre. Over 5,000 houses were destroyed or badly damaged. Bussell commented to Hunt: 'I have never seen crews come back looking so cheerful . . . Krupps is a whale of a target with its ten groups of huge factories, steel works, blast furnaces and coke ovens.' Gibson – 'who has taken part in seventy-two bombings and ninety-nine fighter operations' – talked to Hunt in similar terms:

It's the most excellent prang I have ever heard of. I wish I could have gone myself. Everything seems to have worked right. It was absolutely perfect. Taken all round I should say that Essen has had it at last. Our losses have been incredibly small for the results achieved.[30]

Elsewhere in that issue of the *Sunday Express* was an article asking, 'Why all this bosh about being gentle with the Germans after we have beaten them when ALL GERMANS ARE GUILTY!' The theory of collective German guilt, to which Gibson later subscribed, fitted well with area bombing: up to 482 Germans had just been killed at Essen – a new record.

Gibson flew one more operation with 106. It came on the following Thursday and was to Stuttgart. In the squadron diary it was noted that:

There were no incidents of particular interest but W/Cdr G.P. Gibson DSO DFC made almost the entire journey at 4,000 ft owing to failure of one of the engines. Incidentally this was the Wing Commander's 72nd bombing raid and his 'swan song' with 106 Squadron.

Gibson took with him a freshman pilot, Fg Off. Walter Thompson. After the war Thompson wrote a book of his own, and for connoisseurs of the fallibility of memory it is interesting to compare his account with Gibson's in *Enemy Coast Ahead*. According to Thompson they lost two engines, both because of flak; according to Gibson's book they lost one, through mechanical failure. Thompson reports their touchdown back at Syerston as 'more in the nature of a controlled crash' and was inwardly cheered to find that even someone of Gibson's reputation was not infallible. But his memory of their first meeting a few hours earlier captures the force of the personality who had led 106 Squadron for a year: 'Not a tall man, but firmly and squarely made, his smile lit up the day.'[31]

Upon his return from Stuttgart Gibson received a summons from HQ 5 Group. His term as commander of 106 was over and he was to present himself for interview with Cochrane. Gibson travelled over to Grantham next afternoon, returning in the evening for a farewell party. John Searby was to take over as commander of 106, a compliment to both of them.

Curious friends asked what Cochrane planned for him. Charles Martin recorded Gibson's answer in the squadron diary for 14 March: 'Wing Cmdr G.P. Gibson DSO DFC was posted from the squadron today to form a new squadron.' Then Martin looked back over an eventful year:

He commanded 106 Squadron for 11 months and during that period some notable successes were achieved. The squadron completed conversion from Manchesters to Lancasters and under Wing Commander Gibson's command it was and retained the reputation of one of Bomber Command's leading squadrons, figuring conspicuously in most of the more important and spectacular raids – the '1000' raids, Danzig, Le Creusot and Milan to mention but a few. His own personal record is remarkable. With the squadron he flew on 29 raids, winning the DSO in October [*sic*],* and his operational sorties, in figures, are 72 bombing raids and 199 fighter hours.

Exactly how many sorties Gibson had flown remains uncertain (see Appendix III), but whatever the total it was a phenomenal achievement. Upon his return from Stuttgart on 12 March, Bussell had recommended the award of a bar to his DSO. The dispassionate Cochrane thought that 'in view of the recent award of the Distinguished Service Order' a second bar to his DFC should be considered. Harris brushed this aside, adding in his own hand: 'Any Captain who completes 172 sorties in outstanding manner is worth two DSOs if not a VC. Bar to DSO approved.' And now a new squadron?

Most authorities have accepted Gibson's account in *Enemy Coast Ahead* which described his posting to Group HQ under the pretence of helping to write a book 'for the benefit of the would-be bomber pilot'. Gibson recollected that he had been at Grantham working on this unlikely project for 'one or two days' before Cochrane sent for him. Yet it seems that Gibson had already been invited to form the squadron on the afternoon of 15 March. All sources agree on the question which had preceded this invitation. Cochrane had leaned forward and asked: 'How would you like the idea of doing one more trip?'

* Gibson was actually awarded the DSO in November.

Part Six

JAVELIN

617 Squadron, March–July 1943

As many arrows loosèd several ways
Come to one mark,
As many several ways meet in one town,
As many fresh streams meet in one salt sea,
As many lines close in the dial's centre;
So may a thousand actions, once afoot,
End in one purpose, and be all well borne
Without defeat.

Henry V, I.2

Testing Times

At about tea-time on Sunday 21 March Guy Gibson drove through the main gates at Scampton in his Humber shooting-brake. A witness recalls the impression of the Napoleonic figure who emerged outside the Mess: small, conspicuous, active, demanding and impatient, with a dog that followed him everywhere. Contrary to regulations, the dog slept in his room.

Scampton's four hangars stand in an arc on the south side of the airfield. Gibson's new squadron – as yet without a number – was given accommodation in No. 2 Hangar, with rooms along the hangar's side, adjacent to the flying field. Gibson's office was on the first floor. On this day it was empty but for a table, a chair and a telephone.

One of the most remarkable aspects of the Dams Raid was the organizational achievement behind the formation of the squadron which was to undertake it. In modern management terms a wartime bomber squadron might be compared to an engineering company with a turnover of several millions, or a medium-sized international airline. The running of such an enterprise itself called for ability and stamina; to set one up virtually overnight required talents in even greater measure. Yet the establishment of 617 Squadron, like the making of the world, took just seven days and much of the essential work was accomplished within the first three.

The secret of Gibson's success in administration was that he had little interest in it at all. Delegation therefore came easily and colleagues who knew what they were doing were left to get on with it. Gibson nevertheless had a keen eye for outcome, if not always for detail, and inefficiencies were quickly purged. An adjutant had been drafted in, but he was unequal to the whirlwind pace. Gibson dismissed him as 'useless' and summoned Flt Lt Harry Humphries from Syerston.

Meanwhile, Gibson's chief immediate associates on the ground were two senior NCOs. Flt Sgt G.E. Powell and Sgt J. Heveron, formerly of 57 Squadron, were old friends. Fortunately for Gibson they were also exemplary administrators. George Powell came from Wrexham. 'Sandy' to his friends, he was a thoughtful, rather softly spoken man with a north Welsh accent. Those who listened closely found him a source of delightful Malapropisms, as he 'scruntinised' documents and called for a 'nomial roll'.

Powell rustled furniture, sought essential supplies and billeted some 500 bewildered incoming personnel, while Jim Heveron dealt with other aspects of management. 'The first week is a blur,' recalls Heveron. 'We worked till we dropped.' During the first few days Gibson was seldom to be seen. A virtual stranger to his helpers, he left most administration to Heveron, who scrounged typewriters and other basic office equipment in order to do it. Heveron dealt with all paperwork and periodically left piles of documents on Gibson's desk for signature in the rare moments when he was in his office. 'At the moment,' sighed Gibson on one of these occasions, 'you could put a piece of toilet paper in front of me and I'd sign it.' Heveron was tempted to try, but he noted that Gibson was 'a bit of a martinet, with a shortish fuse' and thought better of it.[1]

When his helpers met obstruction, this volcanic temperament could be an asset. Disobliging administrators surrendered to his demands and supply officers watched as their jealously guarded stores were thrown open to provide trestles, aircraft jacks, propeller stands, trolley accumulators, winches and half-a-hundred other items which the new squadron needed.

Some members of the core team on the ground were recruited by Gibson himself. One of them was Fay Gillon, a 21-year-old WAAF officer in Intelligence Ops, serving Scampton's existing resident unit, 57 Squadron. Gibson sent for Sec. Off. Gillon after he had been at Scampton for some days.

'Sit down,' said Gibson, as she entered his spartan office. 'The first thing is: can you keep a secret?' Gibson's misgivings about the general inferiority of the opposite sex were made even plainer when he added: 'I don't often ask women this.'

The Intelligence Officer assured Gibson that she was well able to keep secrets. Gibson probed further, checking his understanding that Gillon was married and that her husband was overseas. Gillon surmised that the reason for these questions was that as a married woman she would be unlikely to have boy-friends with whom she might talk about squadron matters.

'Right,' continued Gibson, 'this is what I need.' And he proceeded to explain that Gillon's duties would be to liaise between the organizers of the flying training programme and HQ 5 Group. Low-flying routes were to be cleared with Group, not least in order to forestall civilian protests. To ease communication Gillon was given an office next to that of the navigation officer. Les Munro (a newly arrived New Zealand pilot) and his crew were summoned. 'Fix the office for Fay,' said Gibson. Paint was found left over from the decoration of Gibson's office and they scavenged furniture for Gillon's new room.[2]

Pilots and crews were beginning to assemble. Gibson tells us that he chose all the pilots from personal knowledge and that he had selected them while he was at HQ 5 Group the previous week. 'It took me an hour to pick my pilots. I wrote all the names down on a piece of paper . . .' Gibson also reports that the pilots were all tour-expired and that he picked them because he 'believed them to be the best bomber pilots available'. As a final touch Gibson describes them all waiting in the Mess at Scampton on the evening of the day of his arrival.[3]

In fact, the first pilots did not arrive until the following Thursday and a number did not appear until the end of the month. Nor did Gibson choose them all. As John Sweetman's careful dissection of 617's membership has shown:

Not all the pilots were personally known to Gibson . . . the majority were not decorated (including six of the pilots); and far from having finished two operational tours some had not done one. Many who would fly to the German dams in May 1943 had completed fewer than ten operations against enemy targets, and some of the flight engineers were actually on their first.[4]

A third of the pilots came from just two backgrounds. One of them was 57 Squadron, from which six were originally transferred. The other was 106 Squadron, to which Flt Lt John Hopgood, Flt Sgt Lewis Burpee and Flt Lt David Shannon had formerly belonged. Hopgood and Shannon had previously left 106, Hopgood to an OTU and Shannon to 83 Squadron which he had joined only a day or two previously. Gibson telephoned his friend, explaining that he was 'putting things together' for a new squadron and inviting him to join it. Shannon was keen and conferred with his crew. Apart from Walker, the navigator, they declined to accompany him.[5]

Gibson did ask for some other pilots by name. One of them was Flt Lt Harold Martin, whom he had met during an investiture at Buckingham Palace. Martin had talked about the virtues and techniques of very low flying. Martin's crew, which included Flt Lt Jack Leggo, the squadron's navigation officer, began to arrive on the last day of March.

Why did Gibson over-simplify and exaggerate the circumstances in which 617's crews were recruited? The root of the mythology is found in an article which appeared in the *Sunday Express* later in 1943. This purported to be by Gibson and fragments of it appear, reworked, in *Enemy Coast Ahead*. However, as we shall see, the article originated as propaganda and Gibson did not write it. Gibson did nevertheless advise the author, who credited him not merely with the selection of all his pilots, but of the entire squadron.

Perhaps the statement in Gibson's book reflects his subconscious perception of what a squadron was. As we have seen, beyond his usual attitude which divided the membership of a unit into those who risked their lives and those who did not, there was a further distinction between his inner warrior band of officer pilots and those others who flew but with whom he had little contact. One hundred and thirty-three men flew to the dams on 16 May. Many of them saw little of Gibson beforehand and some only spoke to him once or twice during his entire command.

Gibson was still ignorant of his task. On the morning of Tuesday 23 March Gp Capt. H.V. Satterly, Cochrane's senior air staff officer, telephoned Barnes Wallis, an engineer at Vickers, to arrange for Gibson to visit him. Wallis was extremely busy, but agreed to meet Gibson the following day.

For nearly four years Wallis had been exploring ways of delivering sharp and overwhelming blows to the industrial capacity of the Axis powers. In particular, he had been investigating methods of attacking dams. Wallis had found that some types of dam were vulnerable to explosive charges within the water, provided that these were placed immediately adjacent to the dam wall and detonated at a particular depth. Such accuracy was wholly outside the scope of normal bombing. In order to overcome the problem of delivery Wallis had developed an ingenious technique which involved the release of a weapon, called Upkeep – a form of depth-charge – from a low height in a way which enabled it to skip across the water, lose momentum, be halted by the dam and then sink to explode at the depth and position required. A smaller version of this weapon, known as Highball, was being developed for attacks against capital ships.

Official vacillation over whether to proceed with the tactical develop-ment of Upkeep had continued until late February. Then Wallis had been told that the attack was to be made. This left absurdly little time and placed Wallis and others under crushing pressures. For technical reasons the dams could only be attacked in May, when their levels were full. If for any reason the Möhne could not be attacked before 26 May, it was considered that the whole enterprise would have to be postponed until early 1944. Yet development of Upkeep was incomplete. It had not been tested at full size, its eventual form and important aspects of construction remained unsettled and details of the mechanism required to impart backspin to the weapon at the moment of release had still to be decided. Moreover, the aeroplanes which were to deliver Upkeep had yet to be modified to accommodate it. All these matters had to be resolved within a period which allowed the crews who were to make the attack sufficient time to rehearse. It was a daunting task. For practical purposes Wallis had two months. When Satterly telephoned him on Tuesday 23 March the first of them was nearly over.

Next day Satterly called Gibson to Grantham and there directed him to his meeting with Wallis. According to Gibson he was driven south down the Great North Road, beyond London, to 'an old country railway station'. (Interest in England's geography was never one of Gibson's strengths; the layout of the rail system suggests that this was actually somewhere west of London.) From here he took a train to Weybridge, assuming the change to be for reasons of security. At Weybridge he was surprised to be met by Mutt Summers, the Vickers test pilot who had advised him to join the RAF all those years ago. The two said little during the short drive to a country house at Burhill and at about twenty past four in the afternoon Gibson was ushered in to Wallis's room.

In the months ahead the relationship between Gibson and Wallis became unusually close. But at this first meeting neither man was sure what to expect of the other. Wallis may have been too busy to give Gibson much forethought, but the arrival of this exceedingly boyish, rather vital, smiling and heavily smoking man forced him to confront the fact that fulfilment of his project was to be more than a matter of science. A large human dimension would also be involved. At this moment it was Gibson who represented it.

For his part, then or later, Gibson may have reflected on their unalikeness. Gibson had met few real intellectuals and mistrusted most of those he had. Wallis must have counted for something because he had designed the Wellington, but Gibson was ever prone to jumping to conclusions on the basis of sketchy impressions and it may have been some time before he began to connect the quietly precise utterances and lateral thoughts of this restrained, preoccupied, almost unworldly man with the huge violence that was latent in his ideas. In the event, it was their differences that made for success. Gibson and Wallis personified action and theory. Together they would achieve a fusion of both.

At the outset, however, there was awkwardness when it emerged that Gibson had no idea of the target and that Wallis had no authority to divulge it. Embarrassed by the hiatus which had brought Gibson to his office for a briefing he could not properly provide, Wallis confined himself to the working principle of his weapon and described the limits of flying which would be needed to deliver it. Gibson was then shown two films of trials demonstrating a half-size version of Upkeep.

Gibson was intrigued, but daunted by the requirements in flying and privately guarded over the tactical feasibility of a task he did not yet know. Wallis was asking if it would be possible for his crews to dive from 2,000 feet to attack from a height of 150 feet over smooth water at 240 m.p.h. at night. Gibson was unsure, but promised to experiment and report back.

Gibson's return to Scampton gave him ample time for reflection on forthcoming difficulties and to brood about the target. This was not a matter of simple curiosity. If it was heavily defended then the restrictions of height, direction and distance imposed by Wallis's weapon offered little hope to the crews being asked to deliver it. And since virtually the only thing he did know about the target was that it would be approached over water, Gibson's thoughts naturally turned to capital ships and U-boat pens. It all seemed very ominous.

Next morning Gibson conferred with Humphries, who had arrived the previous afternoon to take over as adjutant, and summoned his flight commanders, Sqn Ldrs Melvin Young and Henry Maudslay, to outline the basic needs in training. The squadron had now received a number – 617 – and in the following days it would be provided with some ordinary Lancasters with which to train.

Meanwhile, a meeting was in progress at the Air Ministry at which further details of the operation were taking shape. The need for stringent security was emphasized. Scampton's mail would be censored, its telephones tapped and, in order to remain inconspicuous, senior officers visiting the station should wear 'fore-and-aft' caps and not be adorned with gold braid. Dropping trials for Highball would begin on 11 April, those for Upkeep six or seven days later.

Highball would be a problem. The Admiralty expressed enthusiasm for it and a Mosquito squadron for its use was being formed in parallel to 617. However, both at this and previous meetings Admiral Renouf had insisted that Upkeep should not be deployed before Highball. The Admiralty feared that if the principle of the weapon was disclosed, Highball would be compromised. For the same reason, the Admiralty wanted Highball itself to be employed simultaneously against a number of targets, which might include the *Graf Zeppelin*, Italian warships and capital ships in Bergenfjord, possibly in Altenfjord, and elsewhere. No solution had yet been found to the problem of recovering the Mosquitoes which delivered Highball to distant targets like Narvik. There was talk of sending them on to land in Russia, or even ordering the crews to fly their aircraft into Sweden and abandon them.

None of this was appreciated by Gibson, who still did not know his own objectives, let alone that his mission to destroy them was being jeopardized by inter-service argument. However, six days after his arrival at Scampton, Gibson and Scampton's CO, Charles Whitworth, received a memorandum from Satterly which provided a more detailed schema for 617's training, in preparation for an attack on 'a number of lightly defended special targets'. By now preliminary training had begun and Gibson ordered reconnaissance sorties to photograph three groups of lakes and reservoirs in Wales, the Yorkshire Dales and Leicestershire.

On 29 March Cochrane summoned Gibson to Grantham and there explained that 617 Squadron had been formed to attack dams. With a sense of relief Gibson examined models of two dams, the Möhne and the Sorpe. At its meeting on 21 March, the day of Gibson's arrival at Scampton, the committee had been told that the breaching of the Möhne would be a 'major disaster' and that the destruction of the Eder would have 'far-reaching' effects on Germany's inland transportation. It was then questioned whether several dams could be attacked in the same night and there was talk of raids on consecutive evenings. Four days after the targets were revealed to Gibson, Mr O.L. Lawrence, an analyst at the Ministry of Economic Warfare, gave his opinion that 'The destruction of both dams [the Möhne and the Sorpe] would be worth more than twice the destruction of one.'[6]

Meanwhile Gibson's own crew had started to assemble. Contrary to the impression given by R.C. Sherriff in his screenplay for the film *The Dam Busters*, only one of its members was previously known to him and there were several of whom he had a rather low opinion. Flt Lt Robert Hutchison was an old comrade who had regularly flown with him as his wireless operator in 106 Squadron. At the end of Gibson's tour Hutchison had departed to a Conversion Unit at Wigsley, but scarcely a week after their separation he agreed to rejoin him. (It is interesting to speculate whether Gibson issued similar invitations to any other aircrew who had flown with him regularly at 106 Squadron and, if so, why they refused.) Following him came Plt Off. Harlo Taerum, a Canadian navigator who had also been at Wigsley after a tour with 50 Squadron. Taerum arrived on 3 April and may have been recruited at Hutchison's suggestion, just as it may be that Plt Off. Frederick Spafford, the bomb-aimer, was nominated by Taerum. Spafford and Taerum had been friends for the best part of a year. The rear gunner was Flt Lt Richard Trevor-Roper who had amassed fifty-one operations in the course of two and a half tours. He too came from 50 Squadron.

In the draft of his book Gibson described Flt Sgt George Deering, his Canadian front gunner, as 'pretty dumb' (tactfully changed to 'pretty green' in the published version) 'and not too good at his guns and it was a bit of a risk taking him'. This was rubbish, as Deering had flown thirty-five operations. Gibson's misapprehension may have arisen because for much of the time he saw little of his crew socially and even less of its NCO members.

The network of 50 Squadron alumni and friends which produced the core of Gibson's crew failed to furnish a flight engineer. Flt Sgt John Pulford, formerly of 97 Squadron, joined them on 4 April. Gibson had a low opinion of Pulford, thinking him dull and incapable of independent thought.[7] This may say more about Gibson than Pulford, for Gibson never listened to him long enough even to notice that he came from Yorkshire rather than London. In the cockpit of Gibson's Lancaster there was a distinct air of master and servant. In the fuselage as a whole his crew represented Britain's class structure in microcosm and the pattern of the Empire beyond.

By the beginning of April Gibson had decided on a rough plan of training. During the first week of the month all crews would practise low-level navigation. In the second, emphasis would shift to flying at

150 feet over still water at night. Thereafter, from 16 April, crews
would rehearse the full operation. In the event, the low-level navigation
exercises continued into the third week of the month. These were long
cross-country flights with interchangeable legs and precisely specified
turning-points. On 3 April Martin's route took in Stafford, Caldy
Island, Penzance and Harwell. Shannon did not fly his first until 6
April. The route criss-crossed England from Scampton to Sudbury,
thence to Langham, up to Ripon in the West Riding, south-east to a
given co-ordinate (a point on the River Trent), to Didcot, Wainfleet and
back to base. Two days later Shannon flew another route which took in
Stafford, Llanwddyn (Lake Vyrnwy), Caldy Island, Porthleven, Wells,
Halstead, Potter Heigham and Wainfleet. Censorship of letters was not
yet so strict as to prevent Sgt Gordon Yeo, Young's front gunner, from
writing to his parents in Barry, South Wales, to describe a low-level
cross-country which had taken him past their home earlier in the day:

We have just got back from a trip of 5 hours, we were flying quite close to
Barry this morning, we flew right down the coast and came back round
Cornwall and Bridgwater a lovely trip we were flying in our shirt-sleeves half
the time as it was so hot.[8]

Other crew members recall impressionistic scenes. Take-offs
westwards from Scampton disturbed horses and landgirls below the
Lincoln Edge. Stampedes of farm animals were common. April is a busy
time for ground-nesting birds. Flocks of plovers inhabited the grass field
at Scampton and there were generally futile attempts to drive them
away by motoring back and forth in a van. Once a pheasant crashed
into Shannon's cockpit. Insects posed problems as the sudden appearance of a smudge on a windscreen could cause a pilot to refocus and
confuse his vision. Several aircraft scraped trees. Maudslay's Lancaster
returned one day with foliage entwined in its tailwheel. Gibson
cautioned Martin after a similar episode. Church steeples stood taller
than trees, and in some of the areas where 617 practised there were
plenty of churches.

By the middle of the second week the appearance of noisy Lancasters
skimming low over lakes and reservoirs had become a talking point in
local pubs. Incessant low flying also provoked complaints. Squadron
staff found themselves dealing with an increasing number of testy calls
from Grantham. At first Gibson was too preoccupied to be bothered by

them, but the nuisance grew to such proportions that he drove down to HQ 5 Group to confront the critics and bluntly stated his indifference to anything which interfered with essential training.

In parallel with the first week of navigation exercises, Gibson was in discussion with specialists whose advice was sought in solving particular problems. On 2 April he was visited by Wg-Cdr Dann, who assisted in development of a trigonometrical bomb-sight that was used to release Upkeep at the correct distance from the Möhne and Eder. Fixing height over flat water was another difficulty, as Gibson found when he made experimental runs in the Derwent Valley near Sheffield at twilight. At first he thought of using a trailing wire, but this was unsatisfactory and for a time Gibson was troubled. A solution was found involving a pair of spotlights in the belly of the Lancaster, the lamps angled so that their beams converged when the aircraft was at the correct height. Experiments followed and after some days the method was adopted.

Gibson's practice flights had to be fitted between meetings with visiting technical specialists, trips to Grantham and conferences and committees further afield. This was a punishing schedule, made no easier by his need to maintain the momentum of a training programme which by the end of April had accumulated over 1,000 hours of flying. From the start he worked hard to produce a culture which demanded the utmost commitment from everyone. The standards he demanded had to be maintained whether he was in view or – as much more often – not. His priorities were soon evident to a pair of zealous service policemen who arrested a member of 617's ground crew for a dress offence and then found themselves berated for interfering with his squadron's efficiency. Ground crew who elsewhere had been accustomed to taking things easy when their aircraft were not operating now found themselves driven as never before. Gibson was also active in weeding out aircrew who for one reason or another did not meet his standards. A number were scarcely at Scampton long enough for their names to enter 617's records. During April two complete crews were dismissed and a third departed following an argument over the competence of one of its members.

Squadron opinion about Gibson was divided. In matters of summary discipline Heveron observed him to be generally lenient; others recall him as 'straightforward but strict'. Eileen Strawson, his WAAF driver, found him considerate, with a relaxed attitude towards such things as the petty regulation which asserted that she should wear her cap while driving even in the hottest weather.[9] In the eyes of others, however, Gibson was a tyrant. At times his stress broke surface and men who committed trivial errors were subjected to enraged outbursts. Gibson's impatience is illustrated by the case of an NCO pilot who held the door open for colleagues as they assembled in his office for a training briefing. Entering last because of his gentlemanly gesture, the flight sergeant was astonished to find himself on a charge for being late. Some 617 aircrew avoided Gibson when off duty, leaving him to socialize elsewhere. In fact, Gibson had little time to himself, although occasionally he would pack a few colleagues into his car and take them swimming at the baths in Lincoln.

On 13 April Gibson took his bombing leader, Flt Lt Robert Hay, to Reculver in order to view trial drops of scaled-down versions of the mine. They travelled down the day before and finding themselves without duties passed the afternoon in unaccustomed contentment, ambling along the seafront at Margate. Two weeks previously the police had sealed off the area around Reculver's ruined Anglo-Saxon minster, and it was near the church that Gibson and Hay joined Wallis and a small audience of civilian and service officials at nine o'clock the following morning. Twenty minutes later they caught the snarl of a Wellington diving in order to gain the high speed – nearly 290 m.p.h. – at which Upkeep was released. The mine behaved impressively, bouncing much as Gibson remembered from the films. A second performance, using a Lancaster, followed just after eleven o'clock. This was not successful. The release height was higher and the mine broke up.

During the afternoon work proceeded at Manston to strengthen a third Upkeep for a further trial that evening. Gibson and Hay did not stay to watch, but borrowed a Miles Magister from 137 Squadron for a local flight to reconnoitre the dropping area. About ten minutes after take-off the engine failed and Gibson was obliged to force-land near Birchington. He seems to have handled the emergency very well; the Magister was prone to a vicious stall if the nose was held too high in a long glide, but he managed to put the aircraft down in the only field available. Anti-glider obstacles caused much damage, but Gibson and Hay were unhurt.

Gibson inaugurated a policy of including some ground staff on training flights, ostensibly to provide them with first-hand experience to enhance their appreciation of the work that the squadron was doing. Fay Gillon was his first passenger. The flight was at night and involved dummy attacks on a number of reservoirs. Five days later Gibson invited another WAAF for a low-level cross-country. This was Ann Fowler, with whom David Shannon had been becoming increasingly friendly. The trip was made in daylight, using synthetic night-flying equipment which had recently been introduced. The fitting of amber celluloid on the Lancaster's cockpit canopy, coupled with blue-lens goggles worn by the pilot, reproduced the effect of flying at night. This caused a minor sensation when Ann's Elizabeth Arden make-up appeared livid under the filtered light, like the mask of a clown. Gibson thought this so hilarious that he summoned members of the crew to the cockpit to share the spectacle.[10]

Once airborne, Ann Fowler watched horses, cows and sheep scatter as the aircraft skimmed northwards over Yorkshire and on up to the Caledonian canal in Scotland. She noted strict discipline in the aircraft, although Gibson took odd liberties – for example, by neglecting to ensure that Taerum's directions were repeated.

By now the squadron had moved fully into the second phase of training. A new routine emerged of low-level practice bombing and spotlight altimeter runs. Following further trials with Upkeep Wallis had concluded that the release height would have to be reduced. On 24 April Gibson attended a meeting at Weybridge at which he was asked if it would be possible for them to attack at sixty feet. Three days later he telephoned Wallis to confirm that it could be done.

Throughout the training Gibson remained nervous about security, solemnly warning his WAAF driver not to repeat any conversations she overheard. Towards the end of March he had mustered the ground crews in a hangar, standing on the bonnet of his Dodge to deliver a talk on the standards he expected, emphasizing the need for absolute confidentiality about their work. Anyone breaching this rule, Gibson warned, 'will be shot'. His warning notwithstanding, several cases of loose talk were detected and Gibson was unsparing in his anger towards the culprits. A day or two before the operation, mail ceased altogether.

Security elsewhere, however, was a different matter and Gibson was at least twice confronted by lapses which caused him deep alarm. On one occasion a member of the Intelligence Operations staff returned from a meeting in London and confided to Fay Gillon that details of the operation were common knowledge at the Air Ministry. Gillon immediately sought out Gibson and a private conversation followed in his car.

'Sir,' said Gillon, 'do you know what I have just heard? All about the special op. Where and when.' Gibson was horrified and immediately set out to demand that the rumours be silenced.[11]

On 2 May Gibson was astonished to discover that Plt Off. Watson, 617's armaments officer, had been shown a file containing sectional diagrams of 'certain objectives', a map of the Ruhr which showed the targets and 'very secret details in connection with Upkeep'. Gibson's annoyance was intensified by the fact that Watson had been on attachment to Manston for three weeks and had been shown the file within three days of his arrival. This moved him to point out in an angry memorandum to 5 Group that 'P/O Watson . . . thus knows more about the operation than either of my flight commanders and at the time, more than I did myself.' Gibson added that following a long talk with Watson he was 'satisfied that he understands the vital need for security and that the disregard of security will lead to the most distressing results'. Next day Cochrane dispatched a blistering note to Bomber Command HQ which concluded that 'This information is of a Most Secret nature, and it is criminal that he should have discussed it with junior officers.'[12]

Countdown

On the afternoon of 29 April Gibson attended a meeting at ICI House in London. Gibson and Wallis had come straight from Reculver, where earlier in the day they had witnessed a more or less successful trial drop of an inert Upkeep. Gibson's workload was already daunting, but in the next fortnight his commitments multiplied and burdens increased. Around him work proceeded on the balancing of mines, the fitting of VHF radio sets, the development and testing of drills and procedures. On the 2nd, 3rd, 5th, 11th and 14th of May Gibson was flying. Meetings and Upkeep trials took him to Reculver (1st), Manston

(4th, 7th, 13th), Grantham (5th) and London (often). At Scampton there were reports to be read or drafted, discussions to be held, decisions taken, questions of discipline to resolve – and visits by Cochrane, Trenchard and Harris. Privately, Harris remained pessimistic, dismissing Chastise as 'barmy'.

It was not until 13 May that a successful drop of a live Upkeep was made, five miles out to sea off Broadstairs. Gibson watched the test from a second Lancaster. After skipping seven times there was a pause of several seconds as the Upkeep sank to the depth set for its detonation. Then the sea whitened in a shuddering disc, followed in an instant by a massive column of water that reared upwards for a thousand feet. Gibson stared, awestruck, as the tower and its ragged pinnacles of spray remained momentarily poised and then dissolved in the spring sunshine.*

Gibson's hard-driven programme of training, meetings and travel left little time for meals or sleep. Fg Off. Alan Upton, a medical officer at Scampton who sometimes flew and socialized with Gibson, detected no special signs of stress. Even so, Gibson was not well. In *Enemy Coast Ahead* he describes himself as beginning 'to get ill . . . irritable and bad-tempered, and of all things there began to grow on my face a large carbuncle. I went to the doctor.' Upton confirms that Gibson reported to him, but recalls Gibson complaining of pains in his feet. Upton diagnosed gout – a hereditary metabolic disorder which can be acutely painful and may be triggered by fatigue or worry. Upton advised Gibson to discontinue flying and rest for two weeks. Gibson ignored him.[13] A colleague recalls: 'It didn't seem to dampen any of his enthusiasm or activities, and we all took it as a joke.' There were moments when he sought time alone. Occasionally when being driven between meetings, Gibson would order his driver to pull over, then he would leave the car to walk away and stand, motionless, staring at the sky.[14]

By early May, unlike his commander-in-chief, Gibson believed that Operation Chastise could succeed. In earlier weeks there had been times when he had been daunted by the challenges. But any doubts he had kept to himself and one by one the problems had been conquered. Incessant, intensive training had produced a hard-working organization

---

* The film of this explosion survives in the film archive of the Imperial War Museum.

which knew what it was about and was ready for its task – whatever it was.

Some time in these last hectic days Gibson snatched a few hours to visit Margaret. With Chastise imminent, he seems to have needed to make his peace with her. After nearly three months they found themselves back in the quiet rear room of the pub in which their understated and unfulfilled relationship had begun. At first there was some inconsequential and strained conversation. Then Gibson asked: 'Are you happy?'

Margaret thought for a moment. 'I suppose so. How's Eve?'

Gibson replied with a lack of conviction: 'All right,' and then inquired: 'How's Douglas?'

Margaret answered with an identical inflection. 'All right.'

The glum symmetry of the situation caused both of them to burst out laughing. The friendship, at least, was saved. In better spirits, they went into Grantham to see *Casablanca* which had just opened at the Picture House. Guy was much taken with the film and whistled its café tune as they left. As usual, Margaret was left unsure of his real feelings when they parted. Guy gave no hint of what was to come.[15]

It was not far ahead. At noon on Tuesday 11th Gibson took off to make his first drop of an Upkeep. His aeroplane was ED932/AJ-G, a machine he had been flying regularly for some days and which would take him to the dams. This was a Type 464 Provisioning Lancaster, an aircraft specially adapted for Upkeep with a cutaway bomb-bay. The converted Lancasters contained gear which rotated the mine for several minutes before release, imparting backspin to assist its bounce across the water. All went well. Gibson noted in his logbook: 'Upkeep. Dropped from 60 ft. Good run of 600 yards.' Two other crews dropped mines that day and more practised at Reculver in days following, flying at right-angles to the shore and bouncing their mines off the sea and on to the beach.* Gibson watched them, noting how fractional differences in altitude, height of release, speed and water conditions could vary the

---

* Films of these trials, recently rediscovered in the archives of the Imperial War Museum, give graphic witness to the behaviour of Upkeep. Unlike Highball, which covered long distances with great elegance, Upkeep, dropped over the sea, gives an impression of skipping across syrup, each rise back into the air accomplished with a greater struggle than the last.

behaviour of the mines. There were also mishaps. Several Lancasters were damaged by the columns of seawater thrown up by their practice mines. Maudslay and his crew nearly came to grief; releasing Upkeep too low, water snatched away bits of their tail unit and spectators watched with alarm as the Lancaster crossed the beach trailing a mist of spray from water which had entered the fuselage. Yet, despite these dramas, Gibson was becoming increasingly confident.

Not all crews had the opportunity to practise with Upkeep and Gibson tells us he made a division between the 'best bomb crews on the squadron', which would go to the Möhne and Eder, and others who were 'really to act as a diversionary force and to attack the Sorpe' or be a mobile reserve.[16] This does less than justice to the significance of the Sorpe, which Bomber Command had been told was pivotal to the purpose of Chastise and was indicated as next in importance to the Möhne in the draft Operation Order which Gibson received from Satterly, via Whitworth, on 11 May.

Meanwhile, argument continued between the vice-chiefs of staff over the question of simultaneous use of Upkeep and Highball. The Highball trials had encountered difficulties* and whereas 617 Squadron was ready, 618 Squadron, the sister unit in Coastal Command, was not. Admiralty demands that Chastise be postponed were referred to the chiefs of staff, who were now in Washington with Churchill. On Friday 14 May Sir Charles Portal, the chief of air staff, signalled that Chastise should proceed.

That night there was a tactical exercise which as far as possible was designed to simulate the routes, tactics and target geographies of the eventual operation. Air Commodore Charles Whitworth, Scampton's station commander, flew with Gibson, who took off at 22.00 to deliver practice attacks on Uppingham Lake and Colchester Reservoir. Fay Gillon flew as a passenger with Martin's crew on that evening and immediately afterwards wrote down her impressions. She called her memoir 'Dress Rehearsal'. Nothing in it has been changed.

A sunny day. The navigation officer of 617 Squadron, an Australian Flight Lieutenant, sitting at his desk at the end of the crew room. Log sheets and

---

* Experimentation with Highball continued until after the war. Further research is needed to explain why this interesting weapon was never used.

maps lying all over the place. The room full of young men chattering intently, talking 'shop', in great high spirits. The Wing Commander coming in and walking up to Jack saying: 'All OK for tonight Jack old boy? Here's the programme, OK? Bang on. Oh, Fay, by the way, would you like to come? If so, you can go with Mick. Sorry I can't take you myself this time, because the Station Commander is coming with me.'

The last bit of work, checking with Ops and Flying Control etc. Then rushing up to the mess for tea and getting a chit from Admin. for permission to fly. Back to the Squadron H.Q. and getting into slacks. Locking up, and helping Jack dole out Bomber Command codes and flimsies. Mick shouting: 'Come on Jack you are always last.' Jack, pushing the last things into his sack and fastening up his harness. Running out of the hangar with him, and joining Mick and collecting my helmet, Mae West, and parachute, and clambering into the bus with the rest of the crews of P Popsie, W Willie and F Freddie. Out of the bus, and up into the huge black Lancaster P for Popsie. Bob the bomb aimer first, then Mick the pilot, Ivan the flight engineer, Jack the navigator, me, then Len Toby and lastly Tammy, the rear gunner. Jack laying out all his maps and checking the compass. Mick and Ivan starting up the engines. First the starboard outer and starboard inner, then port out and port inner. The gathering roar of the engines. Ivan, synchronizing the revs. Plugging into the intercom: and answering Mick's 'hellos'. Then Mick letting off the brakes, and taxiing into position on the port side of the Wing Commander in G George, with Hoppy on his starboard side. A signal from the Wing Commander and all three of us simultaneously creeping down the runway and gathering speed. The terrific roar and power of the engines, then the last bump and we are airborne. A course given by Jack, and Mick settling down to formate on the Wing Commander. Me, clambering into the flight engineer's seat and watching eagerly and intently as we go rushing out to sea over Mablethorpe, and into the gathering dusk. Gliding right down, practically into the 'drink' and getting a QFE. Dropping a smoke float to check the wind, and then a burst of firing from the Wing Commander's plane, followed by a burst from all three of us, missing each other by inches. Tammy and Toby, the gunners, enjoying it tremendously. On and on, with the moon slowly rising and the mist clearing. Looking back, and seeing the other two formations following closely behind. Then, land looming up ahead, crossing it a quarter of a mile starboard of track, according to Bob the bomb aimer: 'OK thanks Bob,' from Jack. Then suddenly, the target, glistening in the moonlight. The voice of the Wing Commander coming over the VHF: 'Stand by number 2 and 3, number 1 going in to attack.' The formation breaking up, and we are circling above, while a Lancaster is dimly seen diving down and down and out of sight, merging with the ground detail. Then a huge explosion and a flash of light. Right on target, then: 'Attack completed, go in number 2.' The same procedure for Hoppy, but no results observed. Then our turn. Mick doing a big circle to get into position, grim determination on his face, and Jack and I with our noses glued to the perspex. Down, down, twenty feet more, ten feet more, five feet more, steady, steady on an altitude of sixty feet and the run along the water. 'Bomb's gone!' from Bob and then the pull up, up into the sky at full revs. Mick's voice vibrating 'Number 3 calling, attack completed Sir, over.' 'OK Number 3, set course for base,' from the Wing Commander.

Alone, one Lancaster alone in a huge dark sky, dashing along over the tree tops, over the roofs of houses and around the chimneys and steeples. Crossing the coast again and an alteration of course from Jack. In again over land right on track and picking up the maze of aerodrome lights with our own beacon flashing the call sign. Home! Circling and calling up on the R/T and the reply from Flying Control: 'OK P Popsie, come in to land,' from the WAAF R/T operator. Rushing down the flare path, throttling back, flaps down and gradually losing speed to the end of the runway. Taxiing in to dispersal and turning her into wind. One engine switched off, two, then three and four. Silence, so complete after so much noise. Then the crew bursting out with cracks and jokes and clambering out into the waiting bus. Looking around at their faces and noticing happiness and satisfaction on all of them. 'Enjoy it, Famous?' to me, from Mick. Me: 'Wonderful, absolutely wizard.' 'Come in and have the odd pint of beer with us, Famous.' Back to the mess and a pint of beer and eggs and bacon for supper with the boys. Then the Wing Commander arriving with a beam of appreciation on his face. 'Bloody good show boys.'[17]

Next day, Saturday, was hot. Immediately after lunch Cochrane flew up to Scampton to warn Whitworth and Gibson that Chastise would take place on the following day. Gibson returned to Grantham with him for a brief meeting with Satterly and Dunn (5 Group's signals officer) to discuss the Operation Order. Meanwhile Wallis arrived in a Wellington flown up from Weybridge by Summers, who brought the aircraft to a stand in front of No. 2 hangar and there awaited Gibson's return. Wallis and Gibson walked out to inspect some of the modified Lancasters. Standing in the late afternoon heat, they talked in what was to be their last moment of quietude for several days.

1. Indian scrapbook: (*clockwise, from top left*) Nora Gibson; Alick at three weeks with his nanny and bearers; Nora, Harold Wheeler, Alick, orderly and Alick's bearer; Guy, Joan and Alick, Simla, *c.* 1922; AJ with Alick and Nanny

2. Guy's first visit to Porthleven, summer 1922, in a page from Nora's album: Alick, Hope (a cousin), Joan and Guy

3. Out for a drive. Alick sits in the car, Joan and Guy on the running board. Lahore, 1923

4. Guy, a month after his eleventh birthday with Nora and companion, shortly before returning to boarding-school

5. Guy at St Edward's School, Oxford

6. 83 Squadron at Scampton, spring 1938. War was only fifteen months away. James Pitcairn-Hill (*left*) and Leonard Snaith are seated centre. Gibson sits to their right, next to Allen Mulligan

7. (*top*) Hawker Hind of 83 Squadron. This aircraft was relinquished in 1939 as the squadron re-equipped with Hampdens

8. (*centre*) Factory-fresh Hampden I, probably Gibson's L4070 – Admiral Foo Bang – at the Handley Page airfield, Radlett

9. (*left*) Alick and Ruth after their wedding, 5 September 1939. Gibson, recuperating from a dog bite, is flanked by Winifred Butler (*right*) and Marjory Gabor

10. Eve Moore in *1066 and All That*, 1935

11. Richard Hearn instructing bathing girls, including Eve Moore (*far right*) in a scene from *Nice Goings On* at the Strand Theatre, 1933

12. Four of 'Our Girls' in 'Ta Ra Ra Boom De Ay', a scene from *Come Out to Play*: the show which captivated Gibson in 1939 and introduced him to Eve

13. January 1940: 'There was snow everywhere; it blocked the runways, blocked the hangar door, it got into the aeroplanes, it made life unbearable' (*Enemy Coast Ahead*, p. 56)

14. Gibson and Eve at Brighton, June 1940

15. 83 Squadron's Bruce Harrison (*left*) and James Pitcairn-Hill, August or early September 1940. Pitcairn-Hill was killed in action a few days after this photograph was taken

16. Flak and searchlights in action at Wilhelmshaven, 20/21 July 1940, during an attack on the *Tirpitz* and *Admiral Scheer*. Gibson did not take part in this raid, but the ferocity of the defences gives an impression of what he faced when he attacked the *Tirpitz* a few days previously

17. 'Bob' Braham, Gibson's comrade and fellow flight commander on 29 Squadron in 1941

18. Gibson – top tunic button undone, 'fighter boy' style – and 106 aircrew at Coningsby, summer 1942. Behind are two Avro Manchesters

19. Sqn Ldr John Searby, probably at Syerston, January 1943

20. John Wooldridge, formerly a flight commander of 106 Squadron, seen here as CO of 105 Squadron

21. Margaret North, October 1941

22. Flt Lt David Shannon at Syerston, January 1943

23. Gibson with colleagues at Syerston, January 1943. The group includes 106 Squadron stalwarts David Shannon (*far left*) and Don Curtin (*second from right*). Curtin, from Long Island, USA, was killed on the last operation of his tour, 21 February 1943

Stills from cine film of an Upkeep trial at Reculver in the week before Operation Chastise

24. A Lancaster (possibly flown by Sqn Ldr Henry Maudslay) releases Upkeep

25. Tail is enveloped by a plume of water thrown up by the mine

26. Damaged Lancaster continues, shedding bits and trailing a stream of water

27–8. Barnes Wallis (*in front of officer, arms outstretched*) and Gibson (*at right of main group*) are among those who watch an inert Upkeep being bounced off the sea at Reculver, probably 11 × 14 May 1943. In the next photograph (taken from the cine film, a few frames later) the mine has bounced off the beach between a pair of masts positioned for sighting purposes, and careers on over the seabank in a cloud of shingle

29. Lancaster AJ-G with Gibson at the controls making a low pass at Reculver, probably 11 May 1943

30. A 617 Lancaster taking off for the dams at sunset on 16 May 1943

31. Survivors and colleagues relax at Scampton. (*Left to right*, *seated*) Mick Martin, Joe McCarthy, Geoffrey Rice, David Maltby, Fay Gillon (Intelligence Ops), Les Munro, Richard Trevor-Roper; (*standing*) 'Doc' Watson (Armament Officer), Bob Hay, Jack Fort, David Shannon

32. Reconnaissance photograph of the breached Eder dam

33. King George VI at Scampton, 27 May 1943, flanked by Gibson and Air Commodore Whitworth, the station commander. Behind are Air Vice-Marshal Cochrane (*right*) and the Lancaster in which Gibson flew to the dams

34. Members of 617 Squadron in boisterous mood on their journey to the investiture, 21 June 1943

35. Gibson and Eve on the day he received his VC at Buckingham Palace, 22 June 1943

36. General H. H. Arnold, Chief of the USAAF, hangs the Legion of Merit about Gibson's neck during a ceremony at Bolling Field, October 1943. Air Marshal Sir William Welsh looks on

37. Sir Archibald Sinclair, Secretary of State for Air, talks to Gibson during an inspection of 54 Base controllers at Coningsby, 3 September 1944

38. Portrait of Gibson by Gordon Anthony, one of several taken during a studio sitting. This one has seldom been seen, and captures a hint of boyishness and uncertainty

39. Scene from the last sortie: flares going down over Rheydt on the evening of 19 September 1944, recorded from a Lancaster of 463 Squadron about fifty minutes before Gibson's death

At six o'clock Gibson escorted Wallis to Whitworth's house for a private meeting to which Young, Maudslay, Hopgood and Hay had been summoned. The two flight commanders, deputy leader and bombing leader were now initiated into the aims and tactics of the operation. With his customary clarity Wallis explained the principles of Upkeep and the economic significance of the dams. Gibson worked through the operational details, pausing to consider his colleagues' comments. The informal conference lasted nearly four hours. As the six men stood to leave Whitworth appeared, looking anxious. He brought news that Gibson's dog had been killed by a car.

Gibson put on a brave face and returned to his office. Wallis retired to his bedroom in Whitworth's house. Pausing before sleep to write up the day's events in his diary, he concluded with the words 'Nigger Killed'. Rational, austere and generally unaffected by other people's pets, Wallis later denied any thought that Nigger's death might be some sort of omen. Yet Wallis's biographer notes that this was the first reference to an animal in any of his personal writings for forty years.

For his part, Gibson was deeply shaken and possibly also apprehensive lest news of his dog's death should become a source of demoralizing gossip. Gibson had little time for jinxes or omens, believing only in an arbitrary fate, but the superstitious anxieties of other aircrew were well known. Here was one more worry. Deeper than this was the grief of a real bereavement. Nigger had been Gibson's constant companion for two years, a link with Eve and a focus of strong – at times almost childish – attachment. Back in his room towards midnight he found himself 'looking at the scratch marks on the door Nigger used to make when he wanted to go out, and feeling very depressed'.

Gibson did not sleep for long. Rising around 5.30, he again found his feet acutely painful and paid a call to Upton's surgery before breakfast. Gibson insisted that he would have to fly that day. Upton asked if this meant that he would be operating. 'Yes,' replied Gibson, adding his now-familiar threat, 'but if you tell anyone that, you'll be shot.' Upton considered prescribing aspirin or codeine, but decided that pain-killers might dull Gibson's alertness.

Sunday 16 May had dawned clear and as the morning passed the day warmed. Soon after midday Wallis and Gibson briefed the pilots and navigators. At two thirty they were joined by the bomb-aimers and gunners, all of whom now settled to study and memorize details of photographs, maps, routes and models. The Möhne, Eder and Sorpe were their principal targets. Three further dams, the Lister, Diemel and Ennepe, were targets of 'last resort'. Gibson was emphatic about the need for first-time success, warning that if the dams were not breached they would have to return the next evening, adding darkly that if they did so they would all 'probably get the Victoria Cross' – a grimly sarcastic warning of the mightily strengthened defences that would greet a second strike.

Final briefing came at six o'clock. Gibson introduced Wallis, who calmly explained the economic case for attacking dams, how the dams were built and why Upkeep could destroy them. (In conversation with Martin afterwards Wallis stressed: 'You are going to shake the dam, not hit it.')[18] Next came Cochrane, who emphasized the military importance of the attack and the paramount need for secrecy afterwards. In view of the media coverage which promptly followed, words attributed to Cochrane by Gibson have a special irony:

You boys are off on a raid which will do a tremendous lot of good and damage, but you may never read about it in the news. It may be a secret until after the war. So don't think you are going to get your pictures in the papers.

Cochrane ended: 'I know this attack will succeed.'[19]

Gibson worked through details of the various waves, routes and procedures. The company then broke into smaller groups, testing each other on codes, call-signs, routes. Around half past seven the crews took a quick meal. Afterwards, in ones and twos, some dispersed to their quarters, reappearing soon afterwards at the crewrooms to collect parachutes and gear.

After the urgency and intensity of preparations there was now nothing to do but wait. In the long remaining minutes men loitered in the evening sunshine and lengthening shadows cast by 617's hangar. Here they stood or sat, smoking and chatting quietly. Others reclined on the grass. The mood was subdued. For nearly half of these young men this was to be their last evening on earth. Gibson arrived in his car. Outwardly calm, he walked among colleagues and spoke briefly to several. A year before Hopgood and Gibson had fallen into the habit of holding a ritual conversation before each operation. After such exchanges they always came back. But on this evening Hopgood knew better. Talking to Shannon, he confided that he knew this was 'going to be a tough one' and that he did not expect to return.[20]

Around half past eight vehicles arrived to take the crews to their dispersals. Cochrane came out to Gibson's aeroplane, AJ-G, to wish Gibson well and a photographer asked him to pose with his crew. Then came the start-up sequence and taxiing out, all choreographed and carefully timed.

As the Lancasters of the first wave paused, waiting for the signal which would send them forth, we may wonder if Gibson believed in his heart that Operation Chastise would succeed. Looking back, the task ahead and the odds against achieving it seem immense. For many members of other crews this question may scarcely have arisen, for it was only afterwards that the full nature of the raid became properly apparent to them. But those who were close to Gibson, his inner circle of officer pilots, were in a better position to judge his expectations. When David Shannon prepared to take off on that Sunday evening he had not the slightest doubt that the outcome would be anything other than successful. He attributes his certainty to Gibson's unfaltering confidence, which had been spread to everyone close to him.

Waiting in his Lancaster, nursing his feet, Gibson might have pondered some odd coincidences. The squadron letters – AJ – were his father's initials and the final preparations had coincided with his father's birthday. It is curious too that Gibson's own aeroplane bore the letters AJ-G. G also stood for George, England's patron saint, invoked in that passionate call to arms at the start of Agincourt. It was later claimed that *Henry V* was Gibson's favourite play and that he was wont both to quote from it and liken colleagues to its characters. With hindsight, perhaps even at the time, the parallel was there: a feat of arms by a handful of men, against the odds, which would go down in legend.

Chastise

At twenty-eight minutes past nine an airman at the control caravan signalled with a green light from his Aldis lamp, and the first machine (Flt Lt Robert Barlow, AJ-E) started its take-off run. Shortly after half past nine, Gibson, Hopgood and Martin taxied forward and lined up for take-off. Two minutes later the green Aldis flashed. Gibson gathered the cluster of throttle levers against the palm of his hand and eased them forward. Cochrane and Wallis were among the knot of spectators who bade them farewell as the three Lancasters began to roll. Heavy with fuel and mines, the trio gathered speed more ponderously than usual. Eventually airborne, they crossed the northern boundary of the airfield and briefly flew parallel to Ermine Street while they gained a little height. Then they turned south-eastwards. Gibson looked at the three towers of Lincoln cathedral, shadowed against the setting sun.

At intervals, the others followed. By the time all aircraft of the main force had left it was dark. The sky was cloudless. It grew chilly. A light mist settled upon the aerodrome.

Lancaster AJ-O was the last to return. Flt Sgt Bill Townsend landed in broad daylight, having raced against the dawn across Germany and fought their way out of Holland. AJ-O crossed the airfield boundary at a quarter past six with one of her engines shut down and forward vision blurred by an oil-smeared windscreen. After an ungainly landing Townsend drew the Lancaster to a stand and with Sgt Powell, his flight engineer, went through the after-landing routine, switching off the booster pumps, the master-engine cocks and ignition. One by one the engines fell silent. In the sudden quiet the faint metallic tinkling noises of the cooling Merlins mingled with the sounds of skylarks and then of approaching vehicles and enthusiastic voices. Operation Chastise was over.

Sgt Chalmers, AJ-O's wireless operator, was the first to emerge. Standing in the door towards the rear of the fuselage he looked down and saw senior officers clustered at the foot of the ladder. One of them called out peremptorily, 'Is the skipper there?' Chalmers replied that he thought Townsend was still at the controls. Slightly dazed, he descended to a succession of vigorous handshakes from Cochrane, Whitworth and others, including the unrecognized questioner, who was Harris.[21]

Townsend had taken off at 00.14, only twenty minutes before the landing of the first Chastise aircraft to return. This was AJ-W, flown by Flt Lt Munro. Bound for the Sorpe, AJ-W had been hit by light flak in the vicinity of Vlieland and was forced home. Within six minutes another damaged aircraft had landed. Approaching Afsluitdijk among the Dutch islands Plt Off. Geoffrey Rice in AJ-H had misjudged his height. AJ-H hit the water twice with a smack that wrenched the Upkeep from her belly and caused substantial structural damage. Alarmed and depressed, water spouting from his Lancaster, Rice had turned for home.

Survivors of the first and second waves began to arrive shortly after three o'clock. Flt Lt David Maltby landed at 03.11, Martin eight minutes later, closely followed by Flt Lt Joe McCarthy. Then there was a pause. Crews who had proceeded from the Möhne to the Eder were now awaited. For forty minutes there was silence, until bystanders heard the motors of Shannon's approaching Lancaster. AJ-L touched down at 04.06, Gibson at 04.15 and Plt Off. Les Knight five minutes later. Gibson had been flying in his shirt-sleeves. His hair was glistening with sweat and he was exhausted by the pain of controlling his aeroplane's rudders with gouty feet. A second pause, this time for well over an hour. Then Flt Sgt Cyril Anderson arrived at five thirty, and Flt Sgt Ken Brown several minutes later. After Townsend at six fifteen some aircrew loitered, staring into the eastern sky, willing more to return. But no more came. Eight of the nineteen crews had been lost.

Wallis, Harris and Cochrane had known the outcome of Chastise within minutes of the breaching of the Möhne and Eder dams. After the main force had departed they were driven down to Grantham where, together with Satterly and other senior officers, they followed the progress of the attacks through coded signals received in HQ 5 Group's ops room. As the assault on the Möhne proceeded there was rising tension as the W/T signals announced a nil outcome for each of the first four attacks. Then at 00.56 Hutchison signalled Nigger – code for the breaching of the Möhne. The dignity of Air Marshaldom was overwhelmed, even Wallis raising his arms in a series of involuntary spasms. Now there was free conversation, mutual congratulation, handshakes of triumph and relief. The vigil resumed, until at 01.54 the signal Dinghy announced that the Eder too had been broken. Wallis's vindication was now complete. Well aware of the political significance of what had been achieved, Harris telephoned Portal in Washington. The party then drove back to Scampton in jubilant mood to await the crews' return.

In Scampton's ops room debriefing was in progress by half past four and as each crew told its story a picture of events was pieced together. As expected, the line of approach to the Möhne had been relatively straightforward, but the time available for settling each Lancaster at its correct height and line over the lake before releasing Upkeep had been perilously short, a matter of nine or ten seconds, whereas both during and after their approaches the Lancasters had been exposed to an intense barrage of light flak from positions on and near the dam. The visitors heard of Hopgood's doom: how his Lancaster had been hit and was burning as it began its final approach; the late release of his mine, which bounced over the dam, exploding beside the power station beyond; and of the last seconds of AJ-M, Hopgood's struggle to gain sufficient height for his crew to escape, which had ended in a sudden, sickening, flash. They were told of Gibson's efforts to divide the attention of the defences by flying parallel to and slightly ahead of Lancaster AJ-P during Martin's attack. Although Martin's aircraft was badly holed, he and Gibson performed a similar service for Young, and again for Maltby. Young's mine had levered open the beginnings of a breach; when Maltby's Upkeep exploded a large length of the dam gave way.

Even finding the Eder had been a feat: leaving the Möhne, Gibson and the remaining aircraft of the first wave had found the terrain increasingly hilly, with many lakes to confuse them. At the Eder there had been no flak, but the position of the dam within a steep-sided valley and a tree-covered peninsula which projected into the lake and interrupted the line of approach had both been a cause of difficulty and peril. Shannon made at least four dummy runs and when his mine was finally released it caused material damage to the dam wall. Maudslay's Upkeep was delivered on the third attempt. Released late, it had detonated against the parapet. When Knight's mine went off it blew a ragged round plug of masonry out of the dam, almost as a large bung might be forced from the side of a barrel. A vast spout of water issued from the hole and the masonry subsided into a wide breach. The airmanship needed for these three attacks had been no less than astounding.

At the Sorpe things had not gone so well. Only two aircraft reached it. Moreover, this dam was of different construction from the Eder and Möhne and called for a different method of attack. The Sorpe was essentially a massive wedge of earth of triangular section enclosing a central concrete blade. Here Upkeep was neither spun nor bounced, but dropped as a conventional depth-charge from an approach aligned along the length of the dam. The aim was to damage the crest of the Sorpe 'to cause leakage on a sufficient scale to force the Germans to empty the reservoir in order to effect repairs'. The surrounding terrain and rising mist posed great difficulties, as the Sorpe had to be approached by diving into and across the valley. This left little time or space in which to clear high ground beyond. Emerging from his third attempted run, Upkeep still on board, Brown succeeded in recovering flying speed only by putting his Lancaster into a stall turn. Only after numerous dummy runs did McCarthy and Brown release their mines. The two Upkeeps caused damage to the crown of the Sorpe, but no breach.

Other dams planned to be attacked that night were the Lister, Ennepe and Diemel. Of these, only the Ennepe was reported to have been attacked, by one aircraft.*

There was more – much more – to relate but by 07.25, when a PRU Spitfire left Benson to take the first post-raid photographs, a reasonably clear outline of the night's events had formed. After breakfast various scenes developed. Photographers appeared, catching the jubilant smiles of the survivors in posed groups outside the Mess. Most retired to bed, although the bar had been opened and some embarked upon a party which continued for much of the day. Around mid-morning a select group which included Ann Fowler and Flt Off. Eileen Ainslie (another of the WAAF officers with whom Gibson and other aircrew were friendly) converged upon Charles Whitworth's house. The mood was festive and before long a number of them began to dance a ragged conga which moved through the house, culminating in the seizure and triumphant

---

* John Sweetman's suggestion[22] that Townsend mistakenly attacked the Bever dam instead of his intended target, the Ennepe, has not found universal acceptance.

display of Whitworth's pyjamas when the procession reached the station commander's bedroom.

In the midst of it all Ann Fowler found Barnes Wallis, attired in a dressing gown, standing aside in quiet misery.

There were tears in his eyes. Before the raid he had said to Gibson, 'You know, I hardly look upon this as an operational mission. My job has just been to develop something which will break down a dam wall. I look upon this raid as my last great experiment . . .'[23] His absorption in the theory, mechanics and technical details of Chastise had left him unprepared for the human cost. Fifty-six of the young men to whom he had spoken seventeen hours before were gone.* The losses left him deeply shocked, and Ann found him inconsolable. Later in the morning Gibson tried to coax Wallis out of his despondency, but lack of sleep coupled with the racking tensions to which he had been exposed left him defenceless against self-reproach. After lunch and a final word with Gibson, Wallis departed.

Meanwhile, Gibson had been investigating the early returns and Anderson's unfulfilled sortie. Munro and Rice were soon exonerated. Anderson received less sympathy. Instructed to attack the Diemel dam and the last to take off, at 02.28 Anderson had been redirected to the Sorpe. By this time flak and searchlights had driven him away from his track, the navigator was uncertain of their position and a fault had developed in the rear turret. For forty minutes Anderson scoured the area, but at 03.10, with light seeping into the eastern sky, he abandoned the sortie and returned to Scampton with Upkeep still on board. Never pleased by bombs brought back, Gibson dismissed what he saw as Anderson's excuses. This had been an operation in which every weapon counted. A single Upkeep, exactly placed, might dispose of a dam. Gibson was in private mourning for lost friends who had struggled to deliver their mines. He could not stomach this failure and at the end of the interview he told Anderson that he and his crew would be posted from the squadron.[24]

Congratulations poured into Gibson's office through the day from Sinclair, Trenchard, Portal (via Harris), Slessor and Cochrane. Before nine o'clock a personal written message from Cochrane awaited him:

---

* Fifty-three out of the fifty-six died. Three survived to be taken prisoner.

All ranks in 5 Group join me in congratulating you and 617 Squadron on a brilliantly conducted operation. The disaster which you have inflicted on the German war machine was a result of hard work, discipline and courage. The determination not to be beaten in the task and getting the bombs exactly on the aiming-point in spite of opposition has set an example others will be proud to follow.

Gibson turned to join Heveron in the main duty of the morning: sending fifty-six telegrams to the next of kin of those who had been lost. Gibson wanted follow-up letters to be written within the day, although dates on those which survive show that the task was not finished until the following Thursday. Most were written to a standard format, but Gibson maintained his practice of adding a personal paragraph or supplementary note for men he knew. Eileen Ainslie helped them, also writing personal letters of condolence to bereaved parents in parallel with those sent officially.*

While Gibson and Heveron worked, the destruction unleashed by 617 continued to spread. A flood wave some thirty-six feet high had been advancing down the lower Möhne valley and, one after the other, villages in the Eder valley had been swamped. By breakfast-time inundation of the Ruhr and Eder valleys had drowned roads, bridges, railways, thousands of farm animals, and people. A lot of people. Chastise set a new record for the number killed by an RAF operation against a German target. Nearly 1,300 people had died, including 493 forced labourers and prisoners of war – mostly Ukrainian women – drowned at Neheim-Hüsten. At Fröndenberg and Bösperde, thirteen miles from the Möhne dam, the aerial camera of the RAF caught poignant details, like the wreckage of a passenger train which had been stopped in its tracks and derailed by the tidal wave. Only much later did anyone hear of pathetic individual episodes, as at Wickede where the driver of a railway locomotive had frantically sounded his whistle, urging passengers and bystanders to flee. Destruction along the Eder valley was catastrophic. As 617 went to lunch the floods arrived in the city of Kassel.

---

* On 20 May, for instance, she wrote to Mrs Astell, reassuring her that 'we will never forget your precious Bill', and saying how he was 'loved and appreciated' by those around him.

In the afternoon Fay Gillon encountered listless groups of aircrew.[25] Some were wandering about outside the hangars. Others sat in crewrooms. In one room several exhausted airmen sat dozing, their heads resting on tables. This rather sombre, dazed mood is recalled by others. Chalmers had an impromptu meeting with other members of his crew and through their conversation came a dawning realization of the momentous nature of what they had done. But for many the prevailing mood was characterized less by elation than by anticlimax. The full significance of the attack was not yet grasped and much of the talk turned on the enormity of their losses.

Late in the afternoon the BBC broadcast the first communiqué from the Air Ministry which told them, and the rest of the nation, what they had done. Soon afterwards Gibson withdrew for a few minutes to telephone Eve. Eve had heard the news and was nonplussed when Guy scarcely mentioned it. Unbeknown to her, Scampton's telephones were still tapped. Gibson was presumably wary of talking about what had happened. Instead he baffled her with mundane questions about what she had been doing in London.

Early in the evening there were more posed photographs outside the Mess. Then those hardier souls who were still awake were taken by bus to a party at Woodhall Spa. Gibson went with them. He was in high spirits and Ann Fowler described his behaviour on this evening as 'extremely amorous'. His social artlessness is nicely caught: interspersed between cheerfully blatant attempts at seduction, he held a professional discussion with another squadron commander on operational tactics. Back at Scampton Jim Heveron was still typing letters. Gibson had not forgotten him. Around 10.30 p.m. a Mess waiter appeared bearing a bottle of beer, 'with the Wing-Commander's compliments'.[26]

Did Harris and Cochrane weigh prospects for a follow-up raid to deliver the *coup de grâce* to one or more of the remaining dams? The Sorpe, in particular, because of its economic linkage with the Möhne, was a prime target. Much in the spirit of Balaclava Gibson expressed himself 'ready to go again'. But a second raid would have to be undertaken at once, before the Sorpe could be fortified, and there is no sign that this was seriously entertained. In any case, resources for a second strike were insufficient. Both 617's flight commanders were missing, only twelve crews were available to fly and a mere four aeroplanes were fully serviceable. Losses to be expected on a second raid would be even larger than on the first and few of the survivors had practised the specialized method of attack which the Sorpe required. There was also the added risk of losing Gibson. After so many rehearsals there was to be only one performance.

In any case, aerial photographs revealed that some damage had been inflicted on the Sorpe. In following days Gibson was optimistic that the original aim of attacking it – to decommission the reservoir – might have been achieved. On the Thursday he wrote to congratulate Wallis on his invention, which had 'worked like a dream'. He began: 'Now that the floods are subsiding and the tumult dying down (wait for the Sorpe) . . .' Those who had actually seen the Sorpe, however, had their doubts. Its great embanked mass – in Robert Owen's words, 'More like a landscape feature than a dam' – seemed unlikely to yield to any number of mines.

In relishing 617's achievements, Gibson may have underestimated its weaknesses. If more crews of the second and third waves had reached their targets, the economic impact of Chastise would have been sensational. It was a sensation in any case, but without the Sorpe, incomplete. Harris understood this perfectly four years later when he wrote:

There would, of course, have been a better chance of breaching the Sorpe dam or other Ruhr dams . . . if so many aircraft had not been lost on the way to the target, and if the whole squadron had been able to attack.[27]

He might have added that the cruel truth behind this incompleteness was that not all of the crews had been able to meet the stringent requirements of the raid and that the frantic haste with which Upkeep had been developed had not allowed all crews to practise its use. Planning, practice and precision had destroyed the Möhne and Eder. Anything less, even fractionally less, was insufficient. Minor navigational errors and momentary lapses which in normal circumstances would have been trifling had all cost Chastise dear. By luck, one of Taerum's errors had not affected the outcome. Misjudged winds over the North Sea had caused Gibson to make landfall in the wrong place. Altering course to correct the error, he had passed within a mile or two of the Dutch town of Steenbergen and virtually flown over the site of his future grave.

On the Tuesday Cochrane returned to congratulate the squadron upon its achievement. Gibson made a speech and 617's aircrew were then released from duty and sent on seven days' leave. They left Scampton as heroes, for it was on Tuesday that the first full reports and photographs were published in newspapers. Around midday passengers on the bus into Lincoln found RUHR RAILWAYS STANDSTILL AFTER DAMS RAID emblazoned across the front page of the *Lincolnshire Echo* and looked up to find themselves sitting beside some of those who had been responsible. At Lincoln's stations 617 aircrew departing to the four corners of Britain mingled with travellers who had been reading in their newspapers of 120,000 homeless, rumours of civil disorder in Duisburg and Mülheim, 'many cities flooded', an 'inland sea' around Kassel and 4,000 drowned. All the national dailies carried large front-page stories, many illustrated with reconnaissance photographs of the Möhne. Under the headline FLOODS SWEEPING RUHR FROM SMASHED DAMS the *Daily Sketch* described the effects of the raid as a 'major victory' for the RAF which had caused the 'most shattering blow of the war' to the manufacture of German armaments. Someone at the *Sketch* remembered the Book of Job: 'Hast thou marked the old way which wicked men have trodden? Which were cut down out of time, whose foundation was overflown with a flood' [22. 15–16].

A speech by Sir Archibald Sinclair in the Albert Hall on the previous evening was widely reported. 'Bomber Command – the javelin in our armoury – struck last night a heavy blow of a new kind at the sources of German war power.' If Bomber Command was a javelin, 617 was its tip.

National Hero

It was not only in Britain that news of the attack, and of Sinclair's speech, caught public imagination. *The New York Times* devoted its front page to the story, under the strident headlines RAF BLASTS 2 BIG DAMS IN REICH; RUHR POWER CUT, TRAFFIC HALTED AS FLOODS CAUSE DEATH AND RUIN. Elsewhere were photographs of the targets and of Gibson. (American self-esteem prompted a paragraph which compared the Eder and Möhne to dams in the United States. It was noted with apparent relief that whereas the Eder was, or had been, only 134.48 feet high, the Boulder dam in Colorado stood to 726 feet.) Even Goebbels was impressed, confiding to his diary that the raid had been an 'act of war against the state, but one to be admired, for the English had navigated and planned so thoroughly': an accurate summary.

Chastise provided Churchill with a propaganda victory that was uncannily timely. Press freedom in the United States and Canada was greater than in the UK and there were many in North America who had been voicing doubts about the efficacy of Bomber Command's campaign and its counterpart by their own 8th Air Force. Within hours of the raid, Sinclair had furnished Churchill with a summary of its outcome, adding that 'W/Cdr Gibson directed the operation via R/T and after dropping his weapon flew around shooting at the flak. He returned unscathed.'

Results of the raid, magnified by media excitement, provided Churchill with just the example he needed to silence American critics. Chastise also helped to boost confidence among the Canadians, who were contributing so many of their sons to the war effort. On the afternoon of 18 May Churchill was joined at the White House by W.L. Mackenzie King, the prime minister of Canada. Their conversation centred on the bomber war, which Churchill described as very effective. Churchill pointedly referred to the destruction of the two dams and the great damage and loss of life which had resulted. As if anticipating later criticisms, Churchill spoke of Germany herself as having started the war of bombing and argued that she had only herself to thank for it.

Public euphoria mounted rather than lessened in succeeding days, with newspapers carrying ever more dramatic photographs and estimates of damage. Even the Ministry of Information, which ordinarily found that public interest in air raids was short-lived, knew it had a sensation on its hands. Yet in the midst of it all Gibson suddenly found himself alone. With all the aircrew and half the ground staff away, an unfamiliar quiet descended on 617's headquarters. For two months he had laboured incessantly in the cause of Chastise. Always at the centre of events, driving everyone near him, overriding obstacles, bustling from task to task, quelling doubts, surrounded by some of his best friends, he had been driven by the imperatives of a great enterprise. Now he was simply very tired, bereft of some of his closest colleagues and overtaken by self-recrimination and uncertainty about his own future. Even the praise being heaped upon him was ominous. An Air Ministry spokesman said, 'Wing-Commander Gibson has done as much for his country and the Royal Air Force as it is possible for any man to do. We could ask no more.' That was precisely the problem. Having given so much, what else was left to him?

There was not even a dog to walk on the airfield, where several of 617's flak-riddled Lancasters remained dotted about, parked where they had stopped, like monuments to a departed age. He was, in the words of a close friend, in a 'desperate state'. Apart from the sense of anticlimax, each one of the fifty-six letters of condolence forced him to confront the thought that since he had recruited several good friends to the squadron it was he who had been the instrument of their deaths. Much of his grief centred on Hopgood. But for Gibson's summons there was no reason why Hopgood should have flown operationally again.

Gibson's feelings about the cost of life in Germany are harder to ascertain. Some days before Chastise he had watched his WAAF driver – a farmer's daughter – wring the neck of a cockerel which had become entangled with their car. Gibson had winced at her businesslike action, asking, 'How could you?'[28] Yet he had long been inured to his own business of bombing people and in public he admitted regret, but not remorse, for their deaths. Gibson the animal lover, on the other hand, seems to have felt bitter repentance for the farm beasts and pets which had drowned in their thousands.

Later in the week Gibson revisited Rauceby. Upon arrival he was surrounded by a knot of nurses and other admirers who were anxious to receive an account of the great exploit about which they had been reading. But Gibson was circumspect, saying no more than that the raid had been a 'bit of a do'. Gibson talked to Margaret about David Shannon and Ann Fowler, who had just become engaged. He spoke of Shannon as 'my pal'. He also talked a good deal about Ann.

'You're very fond of Ann, aren't you?' asked Margaret, once more resigned to her role as a listener.

Gibson agreed and then groped for words. 'Ann,' he said at length, 'is a really good mate.' It may have been otherwise, but presumably out of his deep regard for David Shannon, Gibson seems to have come to terms with Ann Fowler as a kind of honorary man.

On Friday Gibson was given weekend leave and travelled to Penarth to join Eve. Next day he went into Cardiff with Mr Moore to his club. Here they encountered an OSE who afterwards confided that he had never met a more 'modest, charming, unspoilt and gallant lad' – adjectives uncannily close to those used by the North American Press a few weeks later. On the Sunday morning, Harris telephoned Gibson at Penarth with the news that he had been awarded the Victoria Cross. Afterwards Gibson was subdued. According to Eve, he said little other than to lament Hopgood, Maudslay and other lost companions. 'It all seems so unfair, somehow,' was all he could find to say. Nevertheless, friends were contacted, Gibson's stepmother was telephoned (his father was away in the United States on 'government business') and an impromptu family party ensued.

The gathering at Archer Road included Mr Moore's friend, the OSE, who was so inspired by Gibson's achievement that he wrote to share it with the secretary of the St Edward's School Society, noting with nostalgic pride that it 'was only what I expected to find from an Old Boy of St Edward's'. Gibson and the Dams Raid had already conferred new prominence upon his old school and Warden Kendall had sent his congratulations to Gibson shortly after the attack. Kendall also hoped that Gibson might be able to visit the school during June. Gibson replied on 25 May: 'I should love to come back to see Teddy's some time but you know how it is. However if it is humanly possible I will make the 18th June as I'm looking forward to seeing you again.' At the bottom of the page Gibson added: 'P.S. Was Awarded V.C. yesterday.'[29]

The Dams Raid had caught everyone's imagination. Two days after the attack a message was passed from Buckingham Palace to the Air Ministry indicating that the King wished to make a two-day visit to the RAF and USAAF. Back at Scampton Gibson was informed of the royal visit which was expected on the coming Thursday. Whitworth had been working on the programme over the weekend and although it was stressed that the visit was to be informal and that all airmen were 'to be at usual work', the schedule was timed to the minute and required considerable preparation.

David Shannon was still away and Gibson asked Ann Fowler to his room to sew the crimson ribbon of his VC on to his tunic. She set to with needle and thread, listening as she worked. The mood of depression had not lifted. Gibson sat hunched on the bed, chin cupped in his hands. His celebrity seemed not to touch him. He was morose and his thoughts returned to his dog. 'My Niggy's dead,' he said over and over again.

Details of the decorations awarded to 617 aircrew were entered in the squadron's Operations Record Book for Monday 24 May, but the sewing on of the VC ribbon preceded the official announcement in a supplement to the *London Gazette* on the Tuesday and was embargoed in general release to the Press until Friday. This became a matter of fleeting controversy when the *Daily Express* pre-empted the official announcement by printing a large photograph of Gibson next to the headline DAM LEADER TO BE MADE VC. Other newspapers carried similar stories. The episode moved a Conservative MP to ask a parliamentary question. Captain Balfour, the under secretary for air, explained that, 'The official announcement was deferred in order that other awards in connection with the dam operation could be published at the same time.'[30]

It is unclear what consequences, if any, this trivial breach of protocol may have had for Gibson. But by now a new fact was dawning on him. Snaith's words nearly four years before had been prophetic. As a national hero, someone known to millions and the epitome of Bomber Command's achievement, he was now virtually proof against public reprimand and disciplinary action. Always inclined to 'do what he wanted', Gibson had gained a large measure of liberty. In time this would leave him vulnerable.

Meanwhile, publicity continued unabated. Away on leave, 617's aircrew found themselves fêted. Taxi drivers waved away their fares, publicans poured free pints, strangers invited them into their homes for meals and drinks. Shannon passed his week's leave with Walker in Bradford and recalls how he was at real risk from alcoholic poisoning, so numerous were the drinks thrust towards them everywhere they went.

On Thursday the 27th came the royal visit. The King and Queen arrived at one o'clock and were immediately taken to the officers' Mess for lunch. The royal party was small, the Queen being accompanied by a lady-in-waiting and the King by an equerry. Wallis had been summoned from Weybridge and was seated next to Gibson, who was placed opposite the King.[31]

This was virtually the first chance Gibson and Wallis had had to talk about anything other than planning for Chastise and, while the breaching of the dams dominated conversation, it is interesting to watch a growing personal intimacy between the middle-aged scientist and the young pilot. When talking about Gibson, Wallis sometimes referred to him, entirely unslightingly, as 'the boy'. For his part, the formality which caused Gibson to address the scientist in letters as 'My dear Mr Wallis' was soon relaxed to 'My dear Wally'. Wallis now had an unquestioning faith in Gibson and their relationship developed genuine warmth.

After lunch and official photographs the royal party was taken out on to the tarmac where two Lancasters had been positioned opposite No. 2 hangar. In front of the aeroplanes aircrew of 57 and 617 Squadrons and a contingent of WAAFs were drawn up around three sides of a square. Gibson, Whitworth and Cochrane walked with the King. Gibson introduced 617's pilots who in turn presented their crews. By some oversight the Queen was escorted by an officer who knew no one on the squadron and accordingly managed to muddle many of the introductions.

After the inspection the King was escorted to inspect one aircraft, aircrew and ground crew of 57 and 617 Squadrons, and thence to 2 Hangar crewroom to see models and photographs of the dams. Here Gibson and several of the aircraft captains talked at length about their training for the attack and answered the King's questions about its undertaking. Then Wallis took over, accompanying the King into the hangar to view a 617 Lancaster loaded with an Upkeep.

Later, with Cochrane and the royal contingent gone, the atmosphere relaxed and a party to celebrate Shannon's twenty-first birthday began in the officers' Mess. Shannon was one of its earlier casualties. Ever vulnerable to drink, at about nine o'clock he fell over and caught the side of his face against the corner of a magazine table. Unimpressed by the consequential black eye, Ann Fowler stalked off and left him to be put to bed by others. Hangovers notwithstanding, there was more parade-ground formality for 617 on the following day when Sir Archibald Sinclair, secretary of state for air, inspected the squadron.

That afternoon Gibson travelled to Sheffield for his first exposure as a public figure. The occasion was the opening of Sheffield's Wings for Victory Week. He passed the night as a guest of Lord and Lady Riverdale at Riverdale Grange, Fulwood, where arrangements had been made for him to be interviewed by the Press. Gibson reminisced about

his nightfighting experiences hunting German bombers during the Sheffield blitz in 1940. The legend of Nigger was also now placed in the
public domain. 'This is the first time I've been interviewed,' Gibson is
reported as saying. 'Hope it will be the last too.' But it was not the first,
and certainly not the last, the next being the following morning when
he was paraded for a photo opportunity on the lawn. Here Gibson
stressed the importance of Wings for Victory weeks and urged that
Sheffield's citizens should 'back up our work by giving until it hurts'.

After lunch Gibson was escorted to the town hall where he was given
pride of place beside Mrs Churchill who was to take the salute from a
large parade. With them were a number of officers, civic dignitaries and
such illustrious figures as the National Savings regional commissioner
and the Sheffield Wings for Victory queen.

Thousands gathered along the pavements. Owners of shops opposite
the town hall opened their upper floors so that smaller children should
be able to see. After the parade a throng of enthusiastic onlookers
surged forward to surround Gibson. Among them was a schoolgirl who
recalls forcing her way to the front of the crowd and finding Gibson
mobbed by ecstatic well-wishers seeking to shake his hand, pleading for
his autograph, or simply trying to touch him. If he had been in any
doubt before, Gibson now knew for certain that he was a star.

After some minutes Gibson was rescued from the mass of frantic
admirers and together with Mrs Churchill was led into City Hall. *The
Times* reported part of his address:

I had the displeasure of watching from the air your city burn during the air
raids of 1940. I knew there would come a time when we should do the same to
the enemy. It is said that the British can take it. We can also give it and are
engaged in blasting the middle out of Germany.

These lines catch several traits of the emerging public Gibson. 'Displeasure' has that accent of arch formality which is familiar from
public-school magazines or after-dinner speeches by chairmen of minor
companies and there is a touch of rhetoric in the message of retribution.
Yet uncomplicated directness is the strongest characteristic. Moreover, a
speech should never be judged from the page. When saying, 'It is said
that the British can take it,' Gibson was quoting Churchill, looking
sideways at Clementine Churchill in order to emphasize the point. The
Sheffielders loved it.

Meanwhile the Press had discovered Eve, who tells us that her telephone 'never stopped ringing'. There is every sign that her appearance in national newspapers on the day after Sheffield was the result of a calculated decision by the Air Ministry to widen and prolong the Press coverage. On the previous day reporters had been invited to her flat. She posed for photographs, talked of the new swimming-costume upon which she had expended her last coupons, answered questions about her dog (Wiener, a dachshund), her reading habits (she preferred historical fiction to 'sentimental stuff') and concurred with her husband's public – though, as we shall see, not necessarily his private – view that 'it is better for all RAF wives to do a war job' and not live too close to where their men were stationed. This message, sugared by trivia, carries the stamp of Bomber Command orthodoxy.

His Sheffield weekend over, Gibson proceeded on leave. The couple journeyed to a hotel near St Ives in Cornwall where, at last freed of any obligation to look cheerful or heroic, Gibson slumped into exhausted introspection. He passed much of the time fishing. When ashore, Eve found him withdrawn, his thoughts unshared. He refused to discuss the raid. At times he was irritable and the sense of fun which had once made him such good company was less evident. Eve too may have had her problems. As an actress, fame had eluded her; now she was a focus of huge publicity as a result of her husband's actions.

There were deeper strains. With Chastise over, Guy had begun to look for a house near Lincoln and to press Eve to come and live in it. Eve came up to Scampton, where her presence caused some awkwardness. 617 was a family to which she did not belong and she did not endear herself to some of its members, one of whom recalls her manner as 'very offhand'. Nor did Eve's loud clothes and extravagant hat go down well. In the event, Eve refused to leave London. Gibson was disappointed. Ever the centre of attention, leader of hundreds of men and women, his inability to command the support of his own wife was a cause of inner frustration.

Gibson kept his promise to revisit St Edward's, joining Warden Kendall and the prefects to dine at High Table in Hall. What followed is curious, and revealing. When dinner ended, Warden Kendall invited Gibson to address the boys. 'What, am I to speak?' replied Gibson, apparently taken aback. Some of the staff withdrew, leaving Gibson with the boys. One of them was George Beldam, then fourteen, who recalls the mood of rapt anticipation which descended. 'Most chaps,' began Gibson with disarming informality, 'when they come back, say they didn't work at all.' His tone then acquired fierce intensity. 'Well, all I can say is: don't believe them. *I worked like hell!*'

And that was all. A shocked silence followed, as the realization dawned that nothing more was going to be said. Then Gibson came down briskly from the top table to offer an affectionate smile of recognition and a handshake to an old school servant who was standing in the centre of the room beside a food trolley. The impact of his peremptory speech was increased by this display of warmth, which had not been directed towards the boys and from which some of them felt excluded. For them, George Beldam remembers, the message was that war 'was an earnest business, which simply had to be got on with'.[32]

For the moment, however, Gibson's war was on the home front. While the future both of Gibson and of 617 remained undecided, the morale-boosting value of both remained large. During the remaining part of June and July Gibson made several further public appearances, including a Bombers for Britain parade at Gloucester and another Wings for Victory event at Maidstone on Saturday 19 June where he visited a scout troop and obliged photographers by solemnly clasping the troop's banner and reaffirming his boyhood promise.* At 5.00 p.m. the audience was rewarded by the spectacle of four 617 Lancasters, flown by Maltby, Munro, Shannon and Martin, roaring low over the town.

On the following Monday a party of 617's members came to London to receive their decorations and to celebrate. Their excursion made a welcome break from intensive training which had resumed in Gibson's absence. The first three weeks in June had seen a resumption of low flying. More spotlight altimeter runs, Upkeep trials, cross-countries to reservoirs and several tactical exercises all seemed to point to another special operation, perhaps with casualties as heavy as the last.† Many were ready for a fling.

The railway company wisely reserved two coaches for the group which left Lincoln early in the afternoon. One was colonized by 617's more rumbustious personalities, who began flinging empty beer bottles

---

* It appears that Gibson had been a Boy Scout and, according to John Maynard,[33] his father was involved in the scouting movement.

at bridges and invaded the locomotive during stops at Grantham and Peterborough.

Drinking late left some of 617's members the worse for wear before the palace investiture on the following morning. This was a proud occasion, as much for the squadron as for individuals, and was attended by wives, sweethearts and parents. Not only did Gibson emerge from it the most highly decorated airman in the British Empire, but thirty-three other members of the squadron received decorations: honours on an unparalleled scale which added lustre to 617's achievement. The King was in North Africa and in his absence the investiture was taken by the Queen. Care was taken to avoid any repetition of the confusion which had marred her introduction to 617's crews at Scampton the previous month. This time Queen Elizabeth was well briefed and surprised several 617 members by her knowledge of their backgrounds. A remark so commonplace as 'Ah – you're the boy from Peterhead' could leave a young man flabbergasted.

Outside the palace photographers, newsreel cameras and the Press were waiting. There were posed photographs of the thirty-four, interviews, then informal snapshots for family albums. Newspaper coverage was wide and enthusiastic as ever and in following days the MoI made much of the international composition of 617 in its releases to newspapers overseas.

That evening A.V. Roe & Co. Ltd gave a celebratory dinner at the Hungaria Restaurant in Lower Regent Street. Roy Chadwick, designer of the Lancaster, honoured earlier in the day with a CBE, was there; so too were Wallis, colleagues from Vickers and other visitors. The menu caused a sensation, less because of the misspelling 'Damn Busters' on the printed card than for the food, which was completely outside the rationing of the period. Free spirits were available; memories of the speeches are accordingly vague. Avro presented Gibson with a silver

---

† During the first three weeks of June 1943 David Shannon was rehearsing intensively to a pattern which resembled practice before Chastise. Between 2 and 20 June his logbook includes five low-level cross-country exercises, two sessions of spotlight altimeter runs, two tactical low-level exercises, two tactical trials with Upkeep and a further visit to the Sheffield reservoirs. Correspondence between Harris and Cochrane during the month confirms that a further single operation for 617's remaining crews involving Upkeep was indeed in prospect. Possible targets mentioned included transalpine tunnels, inland waterways, and – most promisingly – dams in Italy.[34]

model of his Lancaster. Then there was a group photograph, organized by calling people to take their places in turn, Gibson in the centre at the front, ground staff to the rear.

Later they were joined by a group of show-business personalities who had been eating in the main restaurant. Among them were Jack Hylton, Elsie Carlisle (the singer with Ambrose's band) and Arthur Askey, who were persuaded to come down to entertain the company. Elsie Carlisle sang a *risqué* song. Arthur Askey surprised everyone by playing the piano instead of telling jokes.[35]

Late in the evening the party broke up in noisy disarray. Some of those who were awaited in hotels by their wives and girl-friends slipped away; others fanned out through surrounding blacked-out streets, shouting and fooling. One group made its way into Trafalgar Square, where Sandy Powell, 617's flight sergeant in charge of discipline, scaled a lion. Gibson was last seen roaring down Regent Street on the back of someone's motor bike.

Accounts of the investiture and the Hungaria dinner have been published before and it may be asked why their trivial particulars should have been mentioned so often, or why a souvenir menu should now be worth several hundred pounds. The answer is simple enough: it is the function of a legend to be retold. It is also a characteristic of legends that they contain small details which must be repeated with each retelling. Real events can make perfectly good legends which are defined not by whether they are fact or fiction, but by the audience which requires them.

Almost from its beginning the story of 617's breaching of the dams joined that group of historically based tales – like King Arthur, or Robin Hood – which defy all efforts at scholarly revision. Since the war's end one historian after another has queried the significance of Operation Chastise. Some have dismissed it as a costly failure. One journalist described the Dams Raid as 'a conjuring trick, virtually devoid of military significance'. In his book *The Right of the Line* John Terraine records that

It is with a sense of sickness, as one considers the high endeavour in every aspect, and the inexpressible degrees of skill and courage called for to bring it to fruition, that one learns that the effects produced 'were not, in themselves, of fundamental importance nor even seriously damaging'.

– a view derived from the *Official History of the Strategic Air Offensive*, though not fully representative of the official historians' verdict.[36] Yet little of this has touched the public, for most of whom Chastise remains an unquestioned triumph. Attempts to demythologize the Dams Raid have been less rebuked than ignored.

If legends are proof against historians, it may also be that the pendulum swings of historians' opinions between success and failure have done more to confuse than to clarify the issue of what Chastise actually did achieve. Yet, while the outcome of the Strategic Air Offensive itself remains controversial, it is difficult to see how the 'success' or 'failure' of a single raid might be measured.

Attempts to rate the significance of Chastise in purely economic terms are ultimately futile and arguably have diverted attention from several of its most far-reaching consequences. One of these concerns the sheer rhetoric of the operation. Another lies in the fact that Chastise marked an epoch in the development of aerial battle at night. Gibson, as a personality and as a commander, was central to both.

The theatrical impact of the Dams Raid was unparalleled. In the eyes of some, however, showmanship equates with emptiness or superficiality – a 'conjuring trick'. Such scepticism existed at the time. Air Vice-Marshal Donald Bennett, AOC 8 (PFF) Group, later pointed to the achievement of the Mosquitoes of the Light Night Striking Force in mining the Kiel canal after only a few hours' practice, comparing this 'with some others of Bomber Command, who always had to go in for intense training for a considerable period before they undertook any special duty and, without being unduly rude, had to ensure that the Public Relations Department was well informed'.[37] Yet there was nothing remotely superficial or intangible about the effects of Chastise. The worth of the raid to Churchill in Washington, to Harris in his argument for the supremacy of the bomber and to the public in its need for buoyancy of spirit, have all been mentioned. To these must be added the influence of Chastise upon the RAF in general, and Bomber Command in particular.

The congratulatory messages piled up on Gibson's desk were inspired by more than warm approval. Chastise was in every sense an operation of extremes. In its depth of training, requirements of support on the ground, in navigation, flying limits, concentration and the application of technology, the Dams Raid set new standards. This was in contrast to Bomber Command's normal wartime activities, which were more in the nature of a grindingly sustained act of will on the part of members whose imperfections were taken for granted. By confronting and – in part at least – overcoming the chronic difficulties of night bombing, 617's *coup de théâtre* reinforced the self-esteem of everyone associated with Bomber Command. Against this background the abnormality of the operation hardly mattered. Its individual failures and proportionately catastrophic casualties were well understood at Grantham and High Wycombe, but it was the spectacular damage, inflicted by a handful of crews, which seized attention at the time and has held it since.

As an ambassador for this achievement no one better than Gibson could have been found. Resolute, youthful, smiling, active, directly spoken, outwardly modest, he appeared to personify all that was best in British manhood and the values for which the war was being fought. The raid he led was conceived neither as a legend nor as a propagandist's dream; that it quickly became both had much to do with Gibson's image. In July Harris might have ordered the bombing of repairs to the Möhne. Instead, he arranged for Gibson to go to America, to publicize the work of Bomber Command. Later, when Harris wrote about the bomber offensive the passage which deals with the support of the Press immediately preceded his account of the breaching of the dams.

Chastise was yet more important for the extent to which it redefined the possibilities of aerial battle. For three years Bomber Command had worked as a kind of remote machine. On the evenings when it fought it had been wound up – like an alarm-clock, as Cheshire put it – aimed and sent forth by commanders who in most respects had less influence over its subsequent progress than did the château generals over their infantry in the First World War. Operation Chastise had departed from this pattern by interposing the judgement of a commander on the spot. One of the real innovations was the use of VHF radio. This enabled Gibson to pace the attacks, to consult, to improvise and – in theory – to redeploy reserves. For the first time an aerial attack at night took on the character of a battle in which there was control as well as commitment. The results of this lesson were soon applied more widely. The first night attack co-ordinated by a controller – 'master bomber' – was launched by 5 Group just over a month later. By 1944 the influence of an individual master bomber could extend well beyond the specifics of target marking. Gibson did not invent the role of controller – that emerged from teamwork – but he was the first to play it and to prove that the part was viable.

Dog Days

During July there came a change of mood. Gibson already knew that he would not be allowed to fly again operationally for the foreseeable future, if ever. In the immediate aftermath of Chastise he had been busy enough to put aside the question of what he would do for the rest of the war. After the investiture, however, there was little to distract him. The future promised nothing interesting. Chastise had been the culmination of three and a half years of incessant action which had raised him to the status of a national hero; yet precisely because of that status, inaction was all that he could now expect. The bomber war had been his life, yet he would be excluded from its climax. Suggestions of an administrative job filled him with gloom.

The cheerlessness of his predicament was driven home by the arrival of replacement crews. Gibson led by example and most of his closest male friendships were forged through shared action. Excluded from such intimacy, it seemed that although Gibson remained in command of 617 he could no longer properly lead it. That task for the time being devolved to the flight commanders: David Maltby (A Flt), who had been promoted to squadron leader and Sqn Ldr George Holden (B Flt), one of the newcomers.

Holden was unpopular. Fair-haired, a man of slight build with a thin smile, remembered as 'hopeless' and 'weak', he was also given to displays of foolish arrogance. The squadron operated thrice during July. Italian power stations were raided on the 15th. The aircraft flew on to Blida in North Africa and attacked the docks at Leghorn on their homeward flight nine days later. Leaflets were dropped on Genoa, Milan, Turin and Bologna on the 29th. On this occasion too the aircraft continued to Blida. It was on one of these stopovers that Holden appalled his companions by gleefully driving a jeep at high speed into a flock of goats and goatherds.

Forbidden to fly in the shuttle operations, Gibson used some of his time to extend consideration towards those who did. Chalmers, for instance, had been abruptly recalled from leave in Harrogate by a telegram and within hours had found himself in the air on the way to Africa. Knowing that the return of the squadron would be delayed, on the next day Gibson sent a telegram to Chalmers' wife to let her know that her husband was safe. Mrs Chalmers was unwell at the time and grateful for Gibson's thoughtfulness. Both she and her doctor were delightedly astonished when some days later her husband returned bearing a box of grapes and bananas.

Gibson's first recorded flight since the Dams Raid was described in his logbook as a 'low-level to Cornwall' on 2 July. Gibson departed Scampton at 17.15 and returned three hours later, noting his flight as being in Lancaster KC-A. In fact, the aeroplane Gibson flew was A J-J. The error may seem trivial, or at least no more than characteristic of Gibson's disregard for detail in his personal record-keeping. However, Gibson's logbook displays a high level of inaccuracy throughout July, when nearly half of his thirteen entries contain errors of date or destination and at least one flight was omitted altogether. Taken together, they suggest his mind was elsewhere.

The success of Chastise aroused fears that a reprisal might be launched against British dams and on 3 June Wallis had attended a meeting to consider counter-measures. Searchlights which could dazzle attacking pilots were expected to be most effective. Subsequently Wallis recommended that Gibson or another 617 crew member be invited to test such defences. Wallis stressed his preference for Gibson, arguing that his determination was unsurpassed and that accordingly his report 'would be conclusive'.

Anti-aircraft defences were provided for reservoirs near Sheffield where 617 had undertaken much of their training. These included apparatus for the generation of a smokescreen in the Derwent Valley and an entry in Gibson's logbook for 4 July concerning a 'Smoke exercise' probably refers to this.* On Monday 19 July Gibson flew to Grantham, apparently to be briefed on the testing of dam defences in Wales, and then on to Fairwood Common, an aerodrome on the Gower

---

* John Matossian's suggestion that Gibson was rehearsing for an attack on the *Tirpitz* at this time[38] accords unjustified mystery to events which are otherwise well explained. Apart from the substantial evidence for other Upkeep targets which *were* under consideration between June and September 1943, and the testing of dam defences, Matossian's interpretation of the 'Smoke exercise' as preparation for dealing with ship defences is difficult to accept. The close range at which Upkeep was released would have rendered it unsuitable for assault on the *Tirpitz*. Highball, released at greater range by faster aircraft, was the weapon intended for capital ships.

peninsula, whence he took off after dark to assess the effectiveness of dazzle in defence of a dam. This may have been at Caban Coch, part of the Elan Valley reservoir system near Rhayader, which had been identified as a vulnerable target. Gibson flew to London next day for a meeting at the Ministry of Aircraft Production in Thames House. The meeting had been convened to discuss the future of Upkeep, but Gibson took the opportunity to brief Wallis on the results of the tests on the previous evening.

Upkeep was still under active consideration for further use. A list of potential targets included several embanked points along the Dortmund–Ems, Wesel–Datteln and Mittelland canals, hydroelectric dams in Italy and the Rothensee ship lift. Another application concerned Upkeep's potential for piercing anti-tank walls and coastal defences, the weapon being released with forward spin and bounced in off the sea. It may have been one of these techniques – the latter evidently a harbinger of invasion – which six days previously had drawn Gibson, Maltby and Hay, 617's bombing leader, to inspect targets at Shoebury Sands. The targets were intended for further Upkeep trials and Gibson arrived early in the afternoon to view them at low tide. Three days later he returned in a Lancaster, landing first at Southend and then proceeding to Shoeburyness for the dropping of what was probably a live Upkeep.

Other projected Upkeep targets would require the release of the mine over land. Experiments to test the feasibility of such tactics had been started early in June, and it was the land-based use of Upkeep which formed the main topic of discussion during the meeting at Thames House on 20 July. The anticipated target was a large viaduct and it was agreed that a mock-up representing the piers of such a structure should be erected at Ashley Walk to assist further trials.

Back at Scampton, Gibson was flattered to receive a summons to lunch at Chequers on the following Saturday, 24 July. Eve was invited too, although by her recollection it was not until late on the Friday evening that Gibson remembered to tell her. Eve was first astonished, then alarmed at the thought that she had no suitable hat. 'Borrow one' was Guy's curt instruction.

Eve, resplendent in a borrowed hat, met her husband at noon outside the Dorchester, where a car sent by the prime minister collected them. Forceful young men were on Churchill's mind that day. Earlier he had dispatched a minute to the chiefs of staff about Brigadier Orde Wingate, leader of the Long Range Penetration Group which had been fighting behind Japanese lines in Burma. Describing Wingate as 'a man of genius and audacity', Churchill had him in mind as commander for the 'army against Burma . . . This man, his force and his achievements stand out,' wrote Churchill, 'and no mere question of seniority must obstruct the advance of real personalities to their proper stations of war.'[39] Churchill might equally have been thinking of Gibson and it is perhaps significant that he had just summoned Wingate home 'for discussion' at the moment he had arranged to meet Gibson.

After lunch Eve and Guy sat with Churchill to watch a film. Films were one of Churchill's few sources of relaxation. On this occasion, however, the viewing was not for entertainment. The film had been edited together from snippets smuggled out of occupied Europe. Its subject was the Holocaust. Churchill was deeply moved. Gibson was appalled and in the longer term the deep impression it made reinforced his determination not to be sidelined from the war.

The afternoon was hot and before the couple departed Churchill took Eve aside for a walk in the grounds. As they strolled through the rose garden, Churchill made kindly conversation and then started to talk about Guy's future. Preparations were in hand for a conference in Quebec and Churchill had decided that Gibson should accompany him. The conference, code-named Quadrant, was the supreme secret of the hour and it is unlikely that Churchill would have mentioned anything about it to a relatively junior officer's wife. Nevertheless, Eve tells us that the prime minister warned her that Guy would shortly be sent away.

Gibson had an appointment with Sir Charles Portal at five thirty that evening. Portal was no doubt curious about what had earlier passed between Gibson and the prime minister, but the purpose of the meeting probably centred on his forthcoming trip abroad. Gibson's presence in the Quadrant party has normally been explained by the need to find some honourable non-operational role for him. That was a consideration, but a prime motive in sending him to America was political. How far Portal went in explaining this is unclear, but Gibson's mission in America was to be more important than he ever knew.

A few days before the Dams Raid Harris had written a personal letter to Churchill in which he warned that American public opinion was worryingly unsupportive of the European bomber offensive. Harris's recent conversations with Averell Harriman (Roosevelt's special envoy to Britain since 1941, then US Ambassador to Moscow) and US air force generals had convinced him that American preoccupations lay chiefly with the war against Japan. This was being reinforced by an unhelpful alliance of 'Anglophobes (especially ex-Isolationists)' and admirals and generals who did not want the bomber 'to emerge as a Prima Donna in this war's offensive'. If American bomber forces were to play their part in Europe, Harris argued, it was essential to convince the American public of the priority of the bomber offensive. A 'resounding declaration' was needed to counter criticisms of American daylight bombing which had been overheard in Britain and distorted in United States media 'to such an extent that there is now widespread publicity to the effect that the British have no faith in an American Bomber Offensive against German targets and that it is no good *per se*'.*[40]

Operation Chastise coincided with Churchill's visit to Washington three weeks later and such was its impact on American perceptions that political commentators might have wondered if the raid had been deliberately staged to provide Britain's prime minister with just the opportunity he exploited so successfully when he addressed a joint session of Congress. Churchill turned the tables on the sceptics: when Germany had been defeated, Britain would assist the United States in concluding the war against Japan. Of course, from other evidence we know the political timeliness of Chastise to have been a product of luck rather than calculation. Nevertheless, the value of Chastise in underscoring Churchill's 'resounding declaration' would accord with his intense personal interest in the operation, and the urgency with which news of its outcome was brought to him.

Meanwhile, things were going well for Harris. As Gibson emerged from his meeting with Portal into the sultry heat of that July evening, bomber crews across eastern England were assembling for briefing. Protected by the first use of Window – that devastatingly simple

---

* Harris tells us that he made 'a personal appeal' to Churchill to enforce a period of rest upon Gibson, and that it was Churchill who 'arranged for Gibson to be detained for a short period travelling round air bases to talk to American airmen'.[41] Newly found evidence shows that Harris wished Gibson to be protected from adulation, and to return to Britain as soon as Quadrant was concluded. The lecture tour was to be an afterthought, arranged opportunistically after Gibson arrived in Canada.

countermeasure against radar-predicted searchlights, flak and nightfighters – Bomber Command was about to put Germany's second city to the torch.[42]

617 Squadron did not take part in the attack on Hamburg, but next day Gibson quizzed colleagues from 57 Squadron about the effects of Window. That Monday was hot. Tuesday was hotter still. In the morning, while armourers and mechanics sweltered to ready 57 Squadron's Lancasters for the next blow against Hamburg, Gibson received a telephone message which again demanded him in London. After lunch he flew down to London to be given a briefing from the Ministry of Information, under whose auspices his overseas trip would be made.

At some point amid these hectic days of journeys and meetings Gibson found time to see Margaret. Just as he had sought her out on the eve of the Dams Raid, so his imminent departure overseas seems to have stirred him to make what might be his last visit for many months. A rumour had reached him that she was leaving the WAAF and when Gibson drove down to Rauceby she confirmed what he had heard.

'God, you're not pregnant, are you?' asked Gibson.

'That's for me to tell you,' said Margaret defensively, but then added, 'Why – do you want to be the godfather?'

'Yes, of course. I'd be glad to,' said Gibson, cheerfully adding to the list of children for whom he already stood sponsor. But Gibson missed the christening, just as his sudden departure prevented him from fulfilling his promise to David Shannon and Ann Fowler to be best man at their wedding.

Late in the morning of Monday 2 August Gibson took off on his last flight as a member of 617 Squadron. The Lancaster was one of the Upkeep aircraft and, appropriately enough, Gibson's regular crew was with him. So was Holden. Gibson's logbook records portentously that they made an 'Attack on special objectives', but Holden logged the trip as a cross-country.* Taerum accounted for it as a tactical exercise, its route taking in Uppingham lake. The flight appears to have been an

---

* Alan Cooper's claim[43] that this flight was a Crossbow operation does not withstand scrutiny. Apart from the contrary logbook evidence of those who took part (Gibson, Taerum and Holden), attacks on Crossbow targets (V1 launching sites) did not begin until November 1943.

abridged version of earlier Chastise exercises, with the purpose of instructing Holden in the technique for releasing Upkeep. The next day Gibson departed. Holden inherited his crew, and the command of 617.

Gibson arrived in London on Tuesday afternoon, announcing to Eve that next day he would be 'leaving for overseas'. In the evening they dined out. Towards midnight Guy said farewell and left to join a party of some 200 people who mustered to board a special train to Scotland. The mood of their parting is difficult to gauge. Reassured by her talk with Churchill, Eve later professed relief that Guy was going somewhere safe, tinged with a mixture of envy that she could not go with him and pleasure at the prospect of presents, like nylons, which Guy promised. However, it is not clear that she knew where he was going, and Gibson's feelings at the prospect of leaving Eve to her own devices for several months cannot be guessed. But for him, perhaps, it was a new kind of adventure, which overrode other anxieties.

Churchill's party arrived at Faslane early next afternoon and was taken out to the *Queen Mary*, anchored in the Clyde, aboard an old Channel steamer. The *Queen Mary* set sail at about half past five. Leaving the battered Old World for the New, Gibson's spirits rose. He liked ships and he liked the idea of Canada. He was in the company of Britain's leader and her most senior military planners. This was better than the administrative posting he feared so much. That had been postponed – at least for a time.

Part Seven

AMERICA

August–December 1943

I have taken steps to inform the Air Ministry that I do not
want Cheshire to go to America after our experience with the
way that they spoiled young Gibson.

Air Chief Marshal Sir Arthur Harris to Air Vice-Marshal
the Hon. R.A. Cochrane, 24 July 1944

Quadrant

Gibson was in distinguished company. Fellow passengers included Lord Louis Mountbatten (chief of combined operations), Sir Hastings Ismay (minister of defence), General Morgan and his planning staff, Averell Harriman, Portal and the other chiefs of staff. Churchill was accompanied by his wife and his daughter Mary travelled as his ADC.

For Churchill and the chiefs of staff the main business of the voyage was to examine war plans for the coming year. These included Overlord, the scheme for the cross-Channel invasion of France. But Churchill also set aside time for private meetings in which he probed ideas and gathered opinions. One such encounter was with Orde Wingate, who had reached England on 4 August, dined with the prime minister that evening, and less than twenty-four hours later found himself on his way to Canada 'with little but a bush shirt and a toothbrush'. Gibson too was bidden to the prime minister's stateroom for confidential discussion. Both men were to give first-hand accounts to the combined chiefs of staff of dramatic and unorthodox operations which had yielded results that were disproportionately large in relation to the forces committed.

In other respects Wingate and Gibson were outsiders. Most of those aboard the *Queen Mary* had been on similar missions before and formed socially exclusive parties. Several who attempted to befriend Wingate found themselves rebuffed by his 'stern concentrated spirit'.[1] Gibson, by contrast, seems to have entered more readily into shipboard conviviality. He chatted to Mary Churchill, for whom he 'had all the aura of a hero'. She was struck by the '"school-boy" cherry-cheeked fair good looks' of the young wing-commander and found him 'very agreeable and debonair to talk to'.[2] After dinner on the last evening of the voyage, Gibson was invited to address the entire party on the Dams Raid. His talk seems to have fixed the attention of the audience, for several members noted it in their diaries. Churchill may already have been pondering the young man's aptitude for a political career.

The *Queen Mary* docked at Halifax, Nova Scotia, the following afternoon. Churchill's party transferred to special trains which would take them to Quebec. Here was luxury. The trains were equipped with huge baths and the richness and variety of the food were welcome after the Woolton Pie and powdered egg diet of wartime Britain. As the train made its way across eastern Canada – a Hebridean landscape, in the opinion of John Martin (principal private secretary to Churchill) – onlookers speculated upon the identity of its passengers. Some assumed that the Pope was among them. Others thought it was Stalin. Whenever the train stopped, crowds collected and Churchill was recognized with waves and cheers.[3]

They arrived at Quebec in the afternoon of Tuesday 10 August, little more than a fortnight after Gibson's Chequers luncheon. The British prime minister was greeted by his Canadian counterpart, Mackenzie King, and travelled to the ancient Citadel, overlooking the city. Most other members of the mission were lodged in the Frontenac Hotel.

Gibson enjoyed Churchill's continuing favour during social rounds preceding the conference. On Wednesday Gibson accompanied the prime minister to a select luncheon with Mackenzie King, who described him in his diary as 'a fine young boy'. Another present was a senior scientist who was working on a project known as Tube Alloys. It is doubtful if anything behind this mysterious code-name was revealed to Gibson, although the informal, intimate conjunction between the scientist and the bomber pilot *par excellence* gives pause for thought. Tube Alloys was the research programme to develop an atomic bomb.

In mundane contrast, Gibson spent the balance of that wet afternoon visiting a RCAF recruiting centre. This initiated him into a role in which, over the next fourteen weeks, he was to prove himself a master: Gibson became, quite simply, a professional hero. His duties were to make speeches, raise morale, praise the British Commonwealth Air Training Plan, assert Britain's long-term commitment to the Pacific war and boost confidence in the Strategic Air Offensive. The extent of this exposure was to be huge: something very different from a parade in Sheffield or a raffle in Maidstone.

The next day was his twenty-fifth birthday. After buying some perfume to send to Eve, Gibson was taken to meet several hundred journalists from around the world who had gathered for a Press conference arranged in his honour.[4] Their host was the Canadian air minister, the Hon. C. G. Power, who introduced Gibson and chaired the questioning that followed. The occasion was a cause of anxiety to its organizers. Tensions then existed between Britain and Canada arising from Canadian dissatisfaction with the relative credit given to British and Dominion servicemen. Power was at the centre of this issue. He was also a heavy drinker. Fearing that his air minister might do or say something indiscreet – as indeed a few days later he did – Mackenzie King had demanded that Power promise to abstain from alcohol throughout. Thus far he had kept out of trouble. But only just. Next day he embarked upon a bout of drinking and fled Quebec.

Clearly Power was erratic, and against this background it is difficult to give much credence to his explanation of Gibson's visit. 'We asked for him,' Power told the assembled Pressmen, 'so that our young men might be inspired from him to try to emulate his example, and they could hear at first hand what operational problems are in actual combat.' Yet, as we have seen, the Canadians did not ask for Gibson, who had been dispatched as an envoy, in part to help improve Anglo-Canadian relations. But neither does Gibson's own account entirely ring true.

'Last Tuesday,' he explained,

I was up in Lincoln carrying on my duties when I got a message to report to London. I thought that it was simply the usual conferences with the Chiefs of Staff. I was told to get on a train and – the rest of it secret – I found myself in Canada in a very short time. And I can't tell you how mightily pleased to be here I am too.

In casually compressing the time-scale, Gibson appears to have been enacting a policy of disinformation, ultimately for German consumption, to suggest that Churchill had flown the Atlantic. Later in the tour this was elaborated when Gibson was named as the pilot of the bomber in which Churchill had travelled.

With introductions over, Gibson fielded questions.

'Did the Möhne and Eder raids fulfil your expectations for the damage done?' asked one reporter.

'It almost surpassed our expectations, as far as the floods were concerned,' replied Gibson. 'And the full effect will not be felt until late this September when the Ruhr goes pretty dry.' Dispelling a rumour that the Dams Raid had been the brainchild of a German Jewish refugee, Gibson stated (accurately) that, 'The possibilities of attack had been under study for a long time. It was the genius of British engineering combined with the work of the operation boys that made a success of the project.'

What about the opposition? Flak still 'came up like a curtain of steel', but 'In my opinion, German fighter pilots are definitely deteriorating. They're getting bad, especially in closing to attack.' Knowing his audience and mindful of the opinion-forming role in which he had been cast, Gibson turned to the American reporters. 'Your Fortress boys know all about that. I base my opinion on their losses.' American daylight bombing was 'absolutely terrific. What we miss at night they get in the days.' What did he think of Flying Fortresses and Mitchells? 'Great planes.'

The Pressmen knew of Gibson's intimacy with Churchill. Did the prime minister address him by his first name? Gibson laughed.

'No. He calls me "Dam-buster".' To the question of whether Germany could be defeated by bombing alone, Gibson chose (on this occasion) a diplomatic answer. Smiling, he said: 'In Bomber Command we are taught to think that.' Would he like to bomb Japan? 'I should give my right hand to bomb Japan.' After a pause he looked round and added, 'I don't think I expressed it forcibly enough.' Laughter greeted Power's comment: 'I may say that my friend was warned not to be too bloodthirsty in his remarks.'

What did Gibson think of Canadian aircrew?

'RCAF fliers are just as good as RAF fliers. The RCAF, in my opinion, is just like the RAF. We fly under the same flag. We wear the same uniform, and we fight the same enemy. We are very good pals too. Those who come over to us are jolly well trained. I don't know anything about their training. That's what I'm going to try to find out.'

Gibson had told the Press just what they wanted to hear. Their reports were ecstatic and must have given Gibson some satisfaction, if he took the time to read them next day:

From the first second, the unassuming young wing-commander captured his audience. The difficulty is to find words to describe him . . . short . . . fair . . . blue eyes . . . unspoilt . . . alert . . . intelligent . . . with a saving sense of humour.

As he stood there he might have been in a sweater and shorts, his feet firmly planted, his hands behind him. He might have been feeling the turf with his cleats . . . He is not tall. He has a boyish face, sturdy body. He has the kind of a smile and manner that weaken even the boldest of the correspondents who firmly believe they are hard-boiled.

Perhaps Guy Gibson never dreaded any of his operational flights as much as he did the ordeal of going under the gun at a press conference . . . when hundreds of correspondents faced him, but he left the conference with the pressmen applauding and joining in a chorus of judgement – what a boy.

Gibson remained in Quebec until late August. On the 14th he visited No. 1 Air Gunnery Ground Training School at Quebec airport to give the first of many speeches praising the British Commonwealth Air Training Plan. President Roosevelt arrived in Quebec on the 17th and that evening a sherry party and dinner were held at the Citadel to welcome him. Anthony Eden (Britain's foreign secretary) arrived next day, along with Brendan Bracken, minister of information and head of the department responsible for Gibson's tour. Churchill wished the president to meet Gibson and a private session was arranged.

During this period Gibson met, and was seen with, most of the senior political and military leaders of the western Allied nations. It is unlikely, however, that he saw more of C.G. Power. Returning to Quebec a week after Gibson's Press conference, Power checked into a hotel and downed three bottles of whisky in quick succession before crawling round the public rooms of the building on all fours. Farcically, he had also lost his trousers.

On Tour

The formal business of Quadrant had already opened when Gibson left Quebec on 20 August. The previous day had been occupied with a graduation ceremony at No. 8 Air Observer School, where he presented flying badges to newly qualified airmen from Canada, Britain, Norway, Australia and France. Since 1940 the British Commonwealth Air Training Plan contingents in Canada had grown to enormous proportions. Prolonged spells of clear weather, uncluttered skies and an absence of enemy air activity all made Canada ideal for the preparation of RCAF and RAF aircrew, who were trained in huge numbers before posting to OTUs. Gibson's first job was to visit students nearing the end of their training, to stimulate their appetite for the task awaiting them over Germany.

Accompanied by AVM Billy Bishop, the first war ace and fellow VC, Gibson began his tour by flying to Ottawa via Montreal, and then on

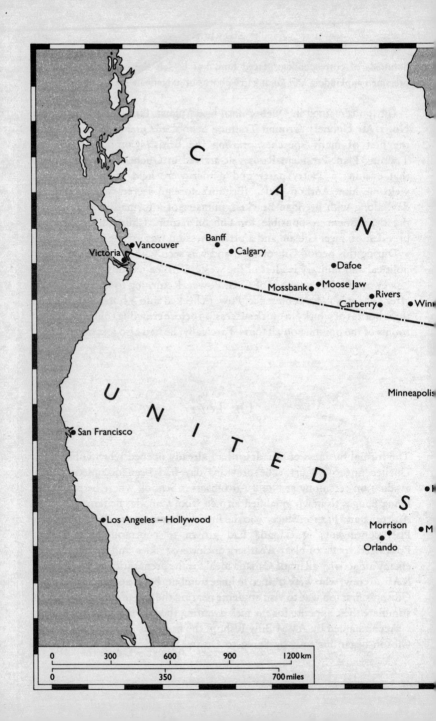

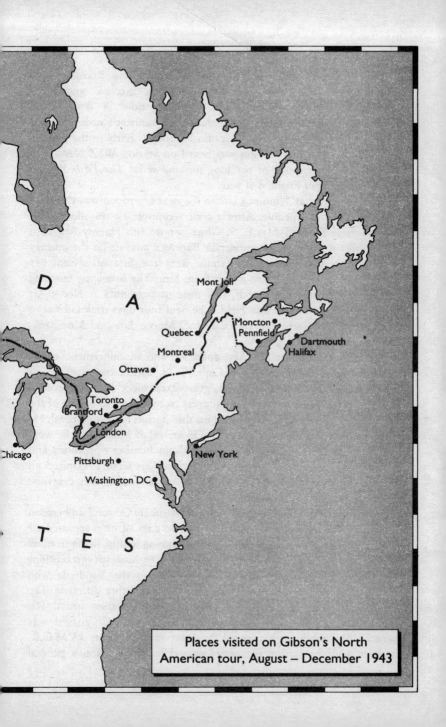

Places visited on Gibson's North
American tour, August – December 1943

an itinerary which included Toronto, London, Jarvis, Brantford and Centralia, receiving civic honours, attending aircrew graduation ceremonies and making speeches. Churchill, now in Washington, retained an interest in him and on the prime minister's orders he was diverted to New York to make a radio broadcast. Early in the evening of Sunday 5 September Gibson was heard on Station WJZ New York as a guest in an episode of the long-running serial *The Fifth Year*, a dramatized story of England at war.

Gibson's arrival at Winnipeg late in the next afternoon was therefore three days behind schedule. After a civic reception, he travelled across town to meet Mr and Mrs E. S. Glinz, whose son Harvey had been killed whilst flying as front gunner in Barlow's aircraft on the journey to the Sorpe dam. The Glinz family were the first of several 617 Squadron relations to receive a visit from him. The following morning was devoted to another speech, this time to personnel at No. 5 Air Observer School at Stevenson Field. The next four days took Gibson to training bases at Carberry, Rivers, Dafoe, Moose Jaw and Mossbank, before his arrival at Calgary.

Gibson excelled himself in these speeches, and announcements of his coming aroused enthusiasm. Gp Capt. T. B. Bruce, commanding 33 SFTS at Carberry noted how the 'great excitement' which preceded Gibson's visit was rewarded by an address 'voted by all to be one of the best and most interesting talks heard on this station for a long time'. He scored another victory two days later. On arrival at Moose Jaw he went straight to the station cinema to speak about bomber operations and the Dams Raid. Just as Power had promised, his lecture 'inspired all present' and next morning all flying was suspended so that everyone else on the station could hear him.

By the time he reached Calgary on 11 September, Gibson had been on tour for a little over three weeks: twenty-two days of uninterrupted air travel, receptions, public exposure, speechmaking and of living in hotel rooms and unfamiliar Messes. Despite enthusiastic receptions everywhere this was a punishing schedule, and the hundreds who pressed to meet him were strangers. Calgary was rather different. The mood of expectancy before his visit was greater than usual. His programme had been published in advance and Currie airfield was opened to the public for his arrival. At 6.00 p.m. the mayor, AVM G.R. Howsam and the station personnel waited to give Gibson a general salute. In the front of the crowd was a middle-aged lady from 15th Avenue West. Gibson recognized her at once.

'I'm awfully glad to meet you,' he said. 'You are the living image of him, you know – or rather, he is the living image of you.' Gibson then gave Mrs Taerum his impressions of her son. 'Terry is a great boy and a great navigator. He got the whole squadron to the dams.'

The official welcome from AVM Howsam was robust. 'You have come here,' said the AOC 4 Training Command, 'to tell our instructors and aircrews things which they are very anxious to know. These are things they are going to do in the future, like dam-busting, Cologne-busting, Hamburg-busting and finally busting Hitler's phoney fortress of Europe.'

Gibson's reply was rather less emphatic. 'Thank you,' he said, 'for coming out to look at me. This is the first welcome of this type I have had since coming to Canada, and I deeply appreciate it.'

If the Calgarians were generous to Gibson, they expected a lot in return. His schedule for that Saturday evening alone included a radio interview broadcast from the control tower at Currie, a motorcade through the streets, a reception and another radio interview. A more private duty was meeting LAC Robert Young, the Californian younger brother of Sqn Ldr Melvin Young, 617's deputy leader who had been killed on his return from the dams. Now, aged twenty, his brother was about to qualify as a wireless operator.

On Sunday evening Gibson returned to Calgary from a day at Banff and visited Mrs Taerum at the family home. The two spent several hours together and Gibson was able to give her news of Terry, who remained on operations with 617, now flying as Holden's navigator. Mrs Taerum took to Gibson. His cheerfulness, natural manner, physical build and even his voice reminded her so much of her son, she said. Her weekend had been a special occasion: 'Meeting Wing-Commander Gibson was one of the proudest and happiest moments of my life. He is one of the nicest persons I have ever met.' So Taerum's death the following Wednesday was an especially cruel coincidence. Together with Holden, Spafford, Hutchison and Deering, he was killed during a low-level raid on the Dortmund–Ems canal. Their Lancaster came to earth, hit by light flak, on the outskirts of Nordhorn, its 12,000-lb blast bomb still aboard.

By the time Gibson received this news he had travelled five hundred miles from Calgary through the Rocky Mountains and had reached Montreal via Vancouver and Victoria. His public reaction was muted and the real impact of the deaths is difficult to gauge. Losses of old friends could affect him deeply, but Gibson's biographical sketches of his Chastise crew in *Enemy Coast Ahead* are so full of avoidable errors as to suggest that his fund of shared experience with them was less than legend claims. Nevertheless, he might have been with them. In Quebec he had explained his survival as due 'to the luck of the roulette wheel'. Through the cocktail-party chatter, Fate was eyeing him from across the room.

Whatever his feelings, the pace did not slacken. Between leaving Montreal on 21 September and arriving at Ottawa on the 27th, his itinerary took in training bases at Bapotville, Mont Joli, Pennfield Ridge, Debert, Dartmouth, Halifax, Greenwood and Moncton. Finally, reaching Ottawa, having made friends with 'one very nice air hostess' who was nostalgically remembered in his logbook the following year, Gibson had the welcome prospect of a week's rest at the Seignory Club before setting off once again, this time for the United States.

Most of Gibson's appearances in Canada had been before groups of airmen. In America his audiences were far more diverse, with an emphasis on civic bodies. He began in Washington, and then travelled to New York for another major Press conference, at the offices of the British Information Services in Rockefeller Plaza. After a circuitous trip across the central states and down to Florida, he returned to Washington where, on 19 October at Bolling Field, General Arnold invested him with the American Legion of Merit.

The decision to bestow this most prestigious of awards was taken quickly, in circumstances which reflect both upon the organization of the tour and the Americans' attitude to Gibson and Chastise. US awards to British servicemen normally generated paperwork extending over several months. In Gibson's case the first reference in British records occurs only twelve days before the ceremony, revealing once again the abruptness of the decision that Gibson should tour America. Much more revealing, however, is the exclusivity of the distinction itself. British policy dictated that American awards would not in general be accepted for actions which had already earned a British medal. The policy was intended to avoid duplication of awards, and instead allowed for the Americans to confer medals upon Britons to whom they wished to express particular gratitude. Hence, Air/Sea Rescue crews who had saved American lives were common recipients. Cases in which an outstanding action was deemed to have taken place represented one of the very few exceptions to this ruling. Just how rare such exceptions were can be judged from the fact that aside from Generals Montgomery and Alexander, Gibson was then the only British officer to hold the American Commander's Insignia to the Legion of Merit.

Gibson's next stop was Chicago, where he was received at a cocktail party by the British consul general and addressed the city Association of Commerce and personnel at the Glenview Naval Air Base. Then came Minneapolis, a speech at the Navy Day rally and another to his most improbable audience: the Minneapolis Traffic Association.

The social highlight of the entire tour soon followed: a fortnight's stay in Hollywood as a guest of the cinema tycoon Howard Hawks. Though he gave one Press conference in Los Angeles, the remainder of Gibson's time on the west coast was passed in private, without much publicity. The obvious interpretation is that he was resting, the opportunity to laze by swimming pools and mix with film stars being a reward for the gruelling tour. By Gibson's own account, he spent his time there 'accumulating circles under my eyes'.

Yet his visit to Howard Hawks had a further purpose. On 31 July Sqn Ldr G. Allen Morris, the air attaché at the British Embassy in Washington, had written to Harris:

Did you know that Howard Hawks, one of the biggest film directors in the States, has commissioned Dahl to write a script for him on the bombing of the dams? He wants to start right away and is actually building a scale model of the Möhne Dam 300 feet long together with models of Lancasters 9 feet long powered by engines which would actually fly. This all will cost $150,000. I am sure you will be interested to hear this, apart from the fact that Dahl's fee, which will be considerable, will go to the Benevolent Fund. I know this is none of my business, but since films are in my opinion the best means of reaching the public I do feel that the Air Attaché's office should be given every possible releasable detail at the earliest moment.[5]

'Dahl' was one Flt Lt Roald Dahl, the assistant air attaché in Washington, with whom Gibson had already had a meeting earlier in his tour. The projected film was given encouragement by Bomber Command's PR Department, and Gibson's visit to Hawks suggests that Harris's response to Allen Morris's request for technical advice had been positive. But the film was never made. When Wallis saw the provisional script he condemned it as absurd. Following his vehement protests the project was scrapped, although there may have been other reasons why it did not proceed.

Another project which did go ahead was a long article entitled 'Cracking the German Dams' which appeared in the December issue of the magazine *Atlantic Monthly*.[6] Gibson was credited as the author and American newspapers were quick to print new stories about the Dams Raid which drew from it. The article is important in relation to Gibson's career because parts of it were reused almost verbatim in *Enemy Coast Ahead* – and because Gibson did not write it. Gibson certainly assisted the author, but several months later he apologized to Wallis for its embarrassingly inaccurate aspects, excusing it as propaganda written by someone else.

Who did write 'Cracking the German Dams'? An obvious candidate is Roald Dahl. Dahl and Gibson had met and Dahl's attested link with the film suggests that the British Embassy in Washington was the centre from which these propaganda enterprises were being co-ordinated. Some of Dahl's earliest writing under his own name was published in *Atlantic Monthly*. More suggestive still is Dahl's reappearance a few weeks later, advising Gibson on his choice of publisher for *Enemy Coast Ahead*.

Conjecture aside, 'Cracking the German Dams' is integral to that part of Gibson's book which describes the origins, training and execution of Operation Chastise. The amount of material which Gibson transferred into *Enemy Coast Ahead* was not large, and the fact that he did so does not weaken his claim to be author of the book as a whole. More relevant is the discovery that Gibson had been working with a writer (who had also been an operational pilot and whose advice on artistic matters might therefore be accepted) and the opportunity that this provided for some of the writer's basic craft – keep it simple, short sentences – to rub off.

Gibson's last duty in Los Angeles, on 10 November, was to address 120 people at the inaugural meeting of the City War Chest, before a trip to San Francisco and yet another Press conference. Then, after making his way back to Montreal, he travelled home in a Liberator being ferried to Britain, arriving at Prestwick on 1 December 1943. A senior member of staff from the Bristol office of the MoI 'visited' Prestwick on the same day, apparently to greet Gibson and make a preliminary report on his tour.

Four months had been spent away from Britain, the war and Eve. Around 150 speeches had been delivered in at least forty different venues. More than ever, Gibson was now an international celebrity.

Alcohol and Adulation

Gibson later described the American tour as one of the most exciting things ever to have happened to him. Equally, the celebrity who had thanked the people of Calgary for 'coming out to look at me' intensely disliked being exhibited as a war hero. He came through this gruelling schedule because he had just got on with it, in his usual workmanlike way.

Gibson had also justified a trust placed in him by his seniors at Bomber Command, and by Churchill. Before the first major American tour by a group of British servicemen, led by Sqn Ldr Nettleton VC in 1942, Anthony Eden had written to the secretary of state for air, Archibald Sinclair, to say that whilst the idea of sending such men seemed good, in general:

. . . such a tour would have many pitfalls. The personnel would need to be not only gallant but simple, sincere and level-headed – or strong-headed, for it will not be easy to preserve these qualities under the torrents of alcohol and adulation with which they will be deluged, and such tours of fine fellows can degenerate disastrously.

Eden's reservations were prescient. At a time when famous airmen were sometimes plied with free drinks by landlords in order to attract these popular heroes to their establishments, the effects of sudden fame upon brave but otherwise quite ordinary and very young men was a justifiable source of official concern. Gibson proved resistant during the tour, but only just so. He later confided to David Shannon that his social drinking during the tour had been prodigious. George Leonard, a navigator from Syerston days, encountered Gibson at a hotel in Montreal where he was giving an after-dinner speech to the RCAF Veterans' Association. Thankful for a familiar face, as soon as his talk was over, Gibson hailed Leonard and strode over to join him. 'Come up to my room,' he urged, 'I've got a bottle.' Leonard obliged, and between them they drank half of it. His companion came away with the clear impression that the lecture tour was 'not Gibson's cup of tea'.[7]

It may have been the after-effects of the tour that caused Harris to write so ruefully to Cochrane in July 1944, complaining of the way the

Americans had 'spoiled young Gibson'. Harris was disappointed to find that his protégé's head had been turned. At the start of the tour journalists had described him as 'unspoilt'. Back in Britain five months later Gibson's sense of his own importance seems to have expanded. During 1944 a number of those around him would retreat from his egotism. This set him apart from the very people – operational fliers – with whom he most wished to associate, and his frustration and loneliness may have deepened because of it. The influence of America, indeed, may offer a key to the lack of advancement in Gibson's career after his return.

Despite such reservations, Gibson obviously enjoyed himself and was influenced by the experience in several ways. One curious aspect was his adoption of Americanized speech. This might be guessed as a product of journalistic translation. But that Gibson really did say such things as, 'the job was no cinch', called aeroplanes 'ships', the Möhne dam 'the big baby' and cars 'automobiles' is corroborated by a reporter who noted that the wing-commander was peppering his speech with American terms. This was seen as a charming courtesy, but it also represents the development of a genuinely Americanized idiolect in Gibson himself. Parts of *Enemy Coast Ahead* are written in a kind of American slang, indicating that Gibson's way of writing (or speaking) had been invaded by transatlantic expressions. Reported speech also implies that Gibson's American vocabulary expanded during his time abroad. In Quebec he spoke English. When he met Mrs Taerum in mid-September she observed that he sounded like her son. By Los Angeles in mid-November, he was on the way to sounding like a native. Gibson's ear for ambience may reflect another of his strengths: adaptability. Equally, his continued use of Americanisms back in Britain might be compared with his habit after 29 Squadron days of leaving the top button of his uniform jacket undone, fighter-boy style, as a badge of experience.

We do not know how Gibson's speeches in America were composed, or by whom. But their content, together with his answers to Press questions, emphasized two main themes which cannot have been personally inspired and probably came either at the suggestion of the prime minister or via the MoI. First, Gibson took pains to stress the important contribution of Canadian aircrew to the bomber war. Secondly, he reiterated his keenness to take the war to Japan when hostilities in

Europe had been successfully concluded. Both aspects merit further
consideration.

As we have seen, Gibson's tour coincided with a period when
relations between Britain and Canada were strained. By 1943, Canadian
aircrew were going to Britain in huge numbers (Canada eventually
supplied 73,000), yet at this date all victories were being trumpeted in
the name of the RAF alone. A British War Cabinet Memorandum
dated 14 August 1943 reported the Canadian premier's anger: Britain's
treatment of Canada, he thought, was more appropriate to a colony
than a Dominion. Canadian contributions to recent campaigns in North
Africa, Sicily and Italy had barely been reported because, as C.G. Power
protested in September, Canadian war correspondents had been denied
inclusion in a recent Press tour of the Mediterranean theatre. This story
was given lengthy coverage in the uncensored Canadian Press. In the
Montreal Daily Star the headline POWER TELLS RCAF NEWSMEN TO
IGNORE RAF MUZZLING stated the problem as seen through Canadian
eyes, or at least those of Canada's intemperate air minister who was,
amazingly, still in office. From the British viewpoint, the meagre publicity afforded to the Canadians was also becoming counter-productive.
Reports from the air attaché in Ottawa to Portal during 1943 express
serious concern over dwindling recruiting figures for the RCAF. To
reverse this, an intensive recruiting campaign was run in the autumn of
1943, coinciding with Gibson's tour.[8]

All this explains much of what Gibson had to say about the RCAF.
As he said in Quebec: 'The RCAF, in my opinion, is just like the RAF.
We wear the same uniforms, fight the same enemy, and we're very great
pals too.' Or again, in Calgary: 'There is no difference between a
Canadian, an Englishman, a New Zealander, or anyone else. We are all
white people, fighting under the same flag, against the same enemy,
with the same planes.' (This was an unfortunate remark, given the
Asian and Afro-Caribbean contribution to the war effort; Gibson was
referring here to the Japanese.) His speeches were intended to emphasize
familial unity between the Commonwealth forces. Though Gibson's
ostensible purpose in Canada was to visit aircrew under training, an
anticipated side-effect of his civic appearances was to improve recruiting
rates through the glamour and publicity surrounding the 'Airman VC'
of so many Press reports. And whilst it would be unjust to see any
cynical motive in Gibson himself when he visited Chastise families,

whoever arranged the meetings and briefed the Press had publicity and recruiting in mind. He was there to tell the Canadians that their countrymen had taken part in the single most dramatic air victory of the war, and that the British cared. Gibson's tour was probably one factor responsible for a three-fold increase in RCAF recruiting rates between August and November 1943.

Secondly, the war against Japan.[9] Early in June 1943 the secretary of state for war had noted with concern a tendency among servicemen and the public alike to assume that with the defeat of Germany the war would be over. His memorandum stressed the need to ensure that people should realize that the war with Japan would still need to be prosecuted:

This could only be done if prominence to this aspect of the war was given in speeches by Ministers and other prominent persons, and in newspaper articles and broadcast talks ... we must therefore inculcate the idea that while, of course, our first object is to defeat Germany, much will remain to be done, especially in the Far East, in order that the job may be finished once and for all ...

The memorandum stressed that the Dominions should be similarly reminded. At the same time, there was political tension between Britain and the United States over whether Britain would meet its commitment to carry the war into the Far Eastern theatre once the defeat of Germany had been accomplished. Several of Churchill's speeches in America attempted to dispel this fear and Wingate's proposals for future Chindit operations and the invasion of Burma helped to reinforce his case. The Japanese issue, in which the MoI under Brendan Bracken was closely involved, also informed Gibson's speeches. His pronouncements on Japan were double-edged. He stressed first the deplorable conduct of the Japanese towards Allied prisoners of war and, in turn, his own enthusiasm for retribution. 'I don't like Japs,' said Gibson, before 300 air cadets in Vancouver. 'I'm longing for the day when I can fly over Japan, because I know a little story about how the Japs have treated some of our prisoners.' For the Americans, in New York, he had the following reassurance: 'There is one thing I wish to clear up. I've heard it said that the war would be over for Britain when the war in Europe was over. Let me put you right. As a bomber I can say that it's the wish of all of us to get over Tokyo first. We will be in there until the finish, sure as eggs.' Or in San Francisco: 'I think I will fly with a bombing fleet over Japan. Mark my words, you'll see 4,000 bombers over Japan one day.'

Gibson's audiences naturally expressed curiosity about the Dams Raid. Gibson answered their questions with what initially may appear to be a surprising frankness, apparently giving much technical information on the release of Upkeep. For example, in Los Angeles: 'We found, finally, that mines would do the trick *if* they were dropped *exactly* in a five-yard square at *exactly* 240 m.p.h. from *exactly* 50 feet altitude.' He also explained how 617's crews had used spotlamps to solve the problem of fixing height over water. But, interspersed with these largely factual details, came items which look like disinformation. Saying that he was getting 'weary with censorship', Gibson told an audience that crews had trained for night flying by simulating darkness using goggles and 'taking pills', floating for German consumption the idea that the Allies had developed a biochemical aid to night vision.

If we assemble all Gibson's discussions of the Dams Raid (as only a contemporary German Intelligence officer or a historian would), it looks as if a subtle Intelligence strategy lay behind them. Yet this was not so. Probably because of the haste in which his tour was arranged, Gibson had received no specific briefing on what could or could not be said publicly about Chastise and Upkeep. It was only after his return that the security problem was raised. Early in December 1943 Barnes Wallis wrote to Sir Stafford Cripps (minister of aircraft production):

On reading the English versions of the accounts which W/Cdr Gibson has given the American press representatives of the method which was used to breach the . . . Dams I am impressed by the difficulty by which the boy [*sic*] is faced in attempting to give a convincing account whilst at the same time revealing nothing of the truth.

While I have never been faced with an American reporter I can realize from the acute cross-examination [to] which their English brethren can subject one how great the strain must have been in a land where refusal to grant interviews with the press is unheard-of.

Wallis, who had enclosed his own publicity material on Chastise, concluded by assuring Cripps:

I have made the present account fit almost entirely with the statement W/Cdr

Gibson has made to the American press so that it will not be necessary for him to retract or modify anything that he has already said.[10]

Gibson was debriefed on his return and security matters were raised. So on 17 December, Sir Richard Peck of the Air Ministry, having seen Wallis's earlier correspondence, replied to Wallis:

A few days ago, and before receipt of your letter, I had a talk with W/Cdr Gibson on this very question of security measures to safeguard the secrecy of the weapon and I asked him how he had handled the matter during his tours in Canada and the United States.

He took exactly the same line that we took originally in the announcement about the attack, namely that it was a large mine which had to be dropped close to the face of the dam between it and the torpedo net protection which appears on the photographs. For this reason it was necessary to fly very low, in fact at an exact height, in order that the mines could be dropped within the very narrow limits involved.

This account of the matter has been accepted, he assures me, everywhere he has gone.[11]

Wallis was not quite correct in thinking that Gibson had revealed 'nothing of the truth' about how Upkeep was released. More or less accurate airspeeds, heights and times had been specified, as well as the method of height-fixing. In fact, Gibson really only omitted the specific ballistic properties of the weapon, and the fact that it spun. Since the Germans had captured an intact Upkeep on 17 May, retrieved from the crash of Barlow's Lancaster, so Gibson's comments might have been of some use in a technical appraisal of the weapon.

Apart from his propaganda speeches Gibson seldom rose to speak on the broader questions of politics and international relations, and had nothing much to say when he did. 'I hate war. I've seen too much of it. There is only one way to stop it, and that is to have united nations and free trade . . .' is a sufficient example. But he spoke at length, on several occasions, about strategic bombing. In comments on the moral aspects of the Dams Raid, Gibson said that he regretted the civilian casualties, but argued that responsibility lay in Germany: 'if the Germans had any sense', he said, they would have cleared the valleys below the dams.

On the strategic role of bombing, Gibson's speeches reveal more surprising opinions. Contemporaries argued whether bombing alone could achieve Allied victory by destroying the material infrastructure of Germany and eroding the morale of her people. Harris firmly believed that, given proper resources, such an outcome was within the capabilities of Bomber Command. Though he supported Harris, Churchill was not so consistent an adherent to this doctrine, especially as far as the likely civilian response was concerned. In 1940 he had argued for a 'devastating, exterminating' campaign of bombing as the only means then available for continuing the war. In 1917, on the other hand, he had observed:

It is improbable that any terrorization of the civil population which could be achieved by air attack would compel the Government of a great nation to surrender . . . In our own case we have seen the combative spirit of the people roused, and not quelled, by the German air raids. Nothing we have learned of the capacity of the German population to endure suffering justifies us in assuming that they could be cowed into submission by such methods, or indeed, that they would not be rendered more desperately resolved by them.[12]

Like Harris, the American military theorist Major Alexander Seversky believed in the ability of the bomber to bring about absolute victory. Unlike Harris, he advocated precision tactics over the area bombing practised by Bomber Command. In 1942 Seversky argued that area bombing was failing to affect German civilian morale and that the role of a strategic bomber force devolved upon the refinement of bombing accuracy, such that:

Attacks will increasingly be concentrated on military rather than on random human targets. Unplanned vandalism from the air must give way, more and more, to planned, predetermined destruction. More than ever the principal objectives will be the critical aggregates of electric power, aviation industries, dock facilities, essential public utilities and the like.[13]

At the time of Gibson's tour, Seversky was in the ascendant. As recently as 10 June, Bomber Command had been presented with Pointblank, a new directive which 'reasserted the firm American Air Force belief that German military operations could be fatally weakened by attacks on six selected target systems, comprising some seventy-six targets in all.'[14]

Who was right? As we have seen, the question was asked as early as Gibson's first Press conference in Quebec. Did he believe, inquired a correspondent, that the war could be won by bombing alone? Gibson laughed. 'In Bomber Command we are taught to think that.' He meant that, in Bomber Command, Harris taught them that they could win the war by themselves. A month later, in Calgary, Gibson echoed Churchill's earlier opinion, given above, and stated that 'in view of the German character' it was 'debatable' whether they could be defeated by bombing. Every bombing raid helped to shorten the war, but there would be no single raid after which the Germans would be forced to admit defeat. In a set-piece speech in Montreal, he took the matter further:

We have a creed in Bomber Command. We are taught that we can knock Germany out of the war by bombing her. I am not a Seversky man myself but, of course, when I am at home I have to subscribe to that creed. But even if we cannot bomb Germany out of the war, we can soften up the country. And it is fairly obvious that if a country is softened up first, it is easier for the land forces to attack and win. In effect, it is shortening the war. Take Hamburg, for example. It is not only the nine square miles of the city and district which are destroyed. It is the whole area, and that means that Hamburg cannot now produce the former 60 submarines, nor all the ships, guns, tanks, the city produced before. The same applies to Essen, Düsseldorf, Cologne, and a score of other large cities. These places are producing only 15% of their former totals.

This speech was given before the Air Force Veterans' Association at the Mount Royal Hotel, Montreal, on the evening of Monday 20 September 1943. In the audience were senior serving officers – two air vice-marshals and several high ranking naval and army personnel. They heard a veteran bomber pilot reveal personal views on the policy behind the operations which it had been his duty to execute. These views contrasted with those of his AOC-in-C, Sir Arthur Harris, who within two months would write to Churchill stating that saturation bombing of Berlin would 'cost Germany the war'. True, Gibson's perspective was shaped by the directive which had been issued at Casablanca in 1942, that bombing would bring about

... the progressive destruction and dislocation of the German military, industrial and economic system, and the undermining of morale of the German people to a point where their capacity for armed resistance is fatally weakened.[15]

Explicit in Gibson's speech, however, was an acceptance of the need for an invasion and a land offensive on the Continent. Indeed, his words read more easily as a paraphrase of the thinking behind Pointblank and of the strategy of interdiction which preceded Overlord than as an endorsement of Harris's view. Here, perhaps, lie clues to the private conversations between Churchill and Gibson on the *Queen Mary*, where Overlord and operations to prepare for it had been under active discussion. We do not know whether Harris ever discovered what Gibson had been saying to the Americans on the subject of strategic bombing. A more pertinent question is what Gibson imagined the consequences might be if Harris found out. Perhaps he no longer cared. What disciplinary action could possibly be taken against him now? In America he had said that flying over enemy territory was now ruled out because, after Chastise, Hitler had listed him as a war criminal: 'My life won't be worth tuppence if I come down in Germany.' Gibson evidently believed this, for he told his father that he was on the Germans' 'black list'. He may simply have considered that if he could no longer fly operationally then for practical purposes his career with the RAF was over. And by now, the object of Gibson's loyalty had shifted from Harris to the prime minister by whose attention he had recently been flattered. Before long, this would bring unexpected rewards.

Homecoming

Soon after breakfast, almost four months to the day since his departure, Gibson returned to Aberdeen Place. Eve was shocked by his appearance. He was pale, he had lost weight and, although exhausted, he seemed neurotically restive. Scarcely had he unpacked than he left for Lincolnshire.

Gibson's agitation was driven by an outside hope of a return to operations and his need to renew contact with 617 Squadron. For all he knew he might still be part of it. But he was completely out of touch. Hence, when Gibson marched into the Mess at Scampton demanding, 'Where's the squadron?' he was crestfallen to be informed that 617 had moved to Coningsby in August. Gibson reacted by ordering that the squadron be telephoned, and asking for a car.

At Coningsby Gibson was greeted by the few founder members who survived to recognize him. Shannon was still there, so too Martin, McCarthy and one or two more. It was explained that following Holden's loss Martin had been appointed as Acting CO. However, Martin's term as leader had recently ended. 617 Squadron was now commanded by Wing-Commander Leonard Cheshire.

Gibson's reaction to this news is not recorded. The two had probably never met, although their paths had crossed briefly when Cheshire visited Scampton back in July. Cheshire recalled that when Gibson returned, his remaining friends greeted him with joyous acclaim. Sensitive to their loyalties, Cheshire withdrew. It was Gibson whom Cheshire felt he was replacing, and the sensation of being in Guy Gibson's shadow was now made stronger by the return of the man who cast it.

Gibson regaled Martin and Shannon with stories of his American tour, describing its punishing schedule of lectures, travel and drinking. Martin teased him about an absurd article entitled 'How we Smashed the German Dams' which had just appeared in the *Sunday Express* under Gibson's name. Gibson was embarrassed to find that this was none other than the ghost-written piece from *Atlantic Monthly*. The *Express* had republished it without his knowledge, presumably with the encouragement of the MoI.*

Gibson then visited HQ 5 Group, apparently to lobby for an operational job. Instead he was declared 'Non-effective sick' and told to go away for a month's rest. After that, at the beginning of January, a posting awaited him at the Air Ministry.

But this is not quite all. Gibson attended at least one debriefing meeting at the Air Ministry quite early in December and at some point around this time a new idea was put to him, or an old one resurrected: would he like to write a book?

---

* The appearance of this article in the *Sunday Express*, and the publication of excerpts from *Enemy Coast Ahead* in the same newspaper over the winter of 1944–45, raises the possibility that Gibson may have been one of those hero-celebrities who were paid large retainers by Beaverbrook in return for articles that were ghost-written.

Part Eight

'CHURCHILL'S YOUNG MEN'

January–May 1944

Appointments in London

Guy Gibson is remembered in the public imagination chiefly for two things: as the leader of the Dams Raid and as the owner of a dog which perished under a car on the eve of the attack. The ultimate reason for this celebrity is the vivid account in his own book *Enemy Coast Ahead*. Begun after the month's convalescence on his return from America, serialized in the *Sunday Express* during the winter of 1944–45, then fully published in 1946, *Enemy Coast Ahead* has been in print with only brief interruptions ever since. In various editions it has sold hundreds of thousands of copies.

Given the prominence and permanence that the book has achieved, it is odd how few have sought to inquire into how and when it came to be written. It is by any standard a remarkable piece of writing. That it should have been written at all stands as a large achievement. Few authors write best sellers. Fewer still write them before they are twenty-six.

The success of *Enemy Coast Ahead* prompted a number of Gibson's acquaintances to ask whether he wrote it unaided. One contemporary at St Edward's commented:

Frankly, I was astonished by his war career. And on reading his book . . . was even more puzzled. I found it difficult to relate this first-class racy exciting account . . . with the schoolboy I had known.

Others, including friends and colleagues like Shannon and Widdows, have made similar comments.

Their doubts are reasonable. On the evidence of his letters and administration Gibson's command of written English was mediocre. Moreover, it is questionable whether someone so impatient would have summoned the strength and control to produce the sustained piece of writing which *Enemy Coast Ahead* is. Many have assumed that Gibson had help.

Yet Eve, the manuscript and other evidence all argue otherwise. In the summer of 1944 Gibson submitted a draft of the book to the Air Ministry for comment and approval. This typescript survives.[1] In its original form it is full of intolerant asides, insubordinate comments, gnomic criticisms, social prejudices, wicked jokes, and – in places –

sheer bad writing, that together leave little doubt that for most of the time we are in the presence of the authentic Gibson. Much of this was purged, first by the censors, in places possibly by Eve (some references to her were modified or excised: 'blonde' in the original, for instance; she is 'fair haired' in the published version) and latterly by subtle editing. The ghost-written article from *Atlantic Monthly* was reworked and expanded in the final chapters, and some other sections suggest external influence. The book is curiously variable, like contrasting movements from a symphony, and there may be more than one hand behind bits of it. The comments on the censor's work, however, seem to be entirely Gibson's, and the longhand corrections and interpolations are made in green ink, which corresponds with entries in Gibson's logbook in 1944. Moreover, a manuscript note from someone in 106 Squadron is addressed to him, so he was co-ordinating the work. Clearly, the book was substantially Gibson's own. So the question becomes not whether he wrote *Enemy Coast Ahead*, but how.

Gibson could have been led to the idea of writing by several influences – not all of them obvious. One was Roald Dahl, with whom Gibson had worked in Washington and who negotiated with a New York publisher on Gibson's behalf. Another might have been H.E. Bates, who was at the Ministry of Information and in contact with the literary agents Pearn, Pollinger & Higham who acted for Gibson from early 1944. Several publishers expressed interest in the project; it is possible that one of them suggested it. Early in January Hamish Hamilton wrote to Gibson. Geoffrey Harmsworth, editor of *The Field* and an RAF Intelligence officer, recommended Hutchinson. Hutchinson had published Cheshire's *Bomber Pilot*, but withdrew when they were told that the question of the number of copies to be printed in the first edition was of prime importance.[2] In March 1944 Michael Joseph said they would guarantee a print run of 50,000, and it was they who published the book in 1946.

Superficially, therefore, it looks as if Gibson embarked upon his book at the suggestion of a colleague or at the prompting of a publisher. It was to be a commercial venture, written with an independent voice. By early February work was under way. Gibson wrote to Wallis:

My dear Wally . . . at the moment in my spare time I am writing a book about the first four years of this war from a bomber pilot's point of view. I hope that

the facts that I have to tell about our training etc. will do full justice to all
those behind the scenes . . .[3]

Phonetic errors and guessed spellings abound in the typed draft,
suggesting that Gibson's initial ideas were committed not to paper but
to a dictaphone. Thus 'lecture room' appears as 'log room', (Douglas)
Bader is 'Barder', 'ring sight' emerges as 'ring side', 'deflection' as
'deflation' and – most enjoyably – 'World War Two' as 'world war
too'. 'Trouncing' was misheard as 'trancing' – a mistake which may
echo Gibson's slightly drawling manner of speaking.

Gibson corrected the draft, adding substantive as well as literal
alterations in his own handwriting and making interpolations. During
this phase of work there are signs of an outside influence – or influences,
for it is notable that several passages referring to Eve were now altered.
Many of Gibson's ruder first thoughts are moderated, unkind descriptions of colleagues are softened or deleted and there are small changes
which improve the text out of all proportion to their number. This
looks like the work of a professional. But the changes are in Gibson's
hand. Did he have a critic at his elbow?

Thus far there has been nothing to contradict Eve's statements that
Gibson wrote the book unaided. In her own memoir Eve recalled how
Gibson had written *Enemy Coast Ahead* while he was living in London
early in 1944. Shortly before her death in 1988 Eve Gibson sent word
which 'was very clear on this point. Gibson wrote it all himself. There
was no ghost. They had a flat in London at the time and he used to
come home and write all week-end . . .'[4]

After Gibson's death, the publishers asked whether Eve thought the
text needed a ghost. She replied, 'No, it is right, it is young, it is Guy,
leave it alone.'[5] In fact, Michael Joseph did make changes, but these
were small. However, the cumulative influences of the censors, the
publishers and the putative mentor, all acted to moderate Gibson's
voice. Each added a new layer of polish, softened his prejudices and
eliminated more criticisms of those around him.

Gibson went to some lengths to obtain material from his old squadrons. In the main this was a matter of names and dates. At Gibson's request Jim Heveron travelled to London armed with details about 617
Squadron and the Dams Raid. In the foreword Gibson denied that he
had ever kept a diary, but hearsay has it that he was keeping notes during

1939–40. John Searby recalled how when working at Bomber Command HQ in the latter part of 1944 he was shown a draft of *Enemy Coast Ahead* and remembered a passage which Gibson had shown him, written in longhand in an exercise book while he was still at Syerston.[6] This might suggest that Gibson had been working on the book since 1942. More probably it refers to an extract from 106 Squadron's ORB which Searby had seen in draft and which Gibson incorporated verbatim.

Controversy over whether Gibson wrote the book unaided has distracted attention from why he decided to write it at all. Heveron remembers that when Gibson called him from the Air Ministry he complained that he had been *ordered* to write the book. This is what Gibson rather implied when he wrote that, 'I never even dreamt that the lot would fall to me, in 1944, to try to describe the work of air crews in Bomber and Fighter Squadrons.'[7]

The statement that the lot had *fallen* to Gibson strongly implies that he did not embark upon his book because he wanted to, or in response to a publisher's invitation. Rather, it signals the likelihood that his posting to the Air Ministry at the beginning of January 1944 – ostensibly to the Directorate for the Prevention of Accidents – was a cloak for the writing of a book and that the project had been conceived by others as an exercise in propaganda. From the point of view of the MoI or the RAF's publicity machine – now being tested by Bishop Bell's criticism of strategic bombing in the House of Lords – the representation of the bomber offensive through the medium of an apparently independent book written by a national hero had clear appeal.

This hypothesis explains Gibson's access to a dictaphone and a typist, and also why he was using Air Ministry time to write a book rather than to prevent accidents. We are given a context for the expertise of his unknown adviser and an explanation for how he managed to complete the draft so rapidly – within no more than four months, perhaps in two. Gibson's absence from his office during much of February – to be discussed in the next chapter – becomes easier to understand if he had few routine duties to discharge. And of what other aspect of war, apart from fighting, did Gibson now have experience? He had just returned from four months of intensive opinion-forming in North America – on behalf of the Ministry of Information.

*

If that was the plan, it nearly backfired. At the outset Gibson detested his assignment. When Heveron visited Gibson he 'found him in a small back room in the Airworks, he had let his hair grow long, and was very depressed, almost in tears when he saw me'.[8] Gibson took revenge for his incarceration by writing in terms that were indiscreet, sometimes merciless, in their criticism of Bomber Command's leadership in the early stages of the war. But perhaps even this was part of a larger plan of which Gibson was kept unaware. The RAF's propagandists knew enough about him to guess that he would be likely to produce a book which would be irreverent, yet generally favourable to Bomber Command. By allowing Gibson the appearance – even in his own eyes – of writing as his own man, they would capitalize on his public reputation.

None of this can be proved – but the art of successful propaganda lies in disguising that that is what it is. The explanation fits all we know. Yet again it places Gibson as an instrument of others rather than as an initiator. Exploited by image-makers in 1943, Gibson's role as an author was an altogether more subtle vehicle for the ends of those who sought to project a favourable picture of the Strategic Air Offensive, then and in the future, after the war was over. For example:

We never thought we could win the war by bombing alone. We were out to destroy German industry, to cut their transport system, to stop them building U-boats and ships and to make their channels unnavigable by mines. We were out to bomb them until they found themselves weak and punch-drunk from our blows, so that they would fall back before our invading armies. This in turn would save the lives of our own men – the young men of the Allies on whom the future of this world depends.[9]

There are several themes here. The importance of the young was an issue iterated by Gibson himself. The view of bombing policy echoes his speeches in the USA and tilts more towards the perspective of the air staff than to High Wycombe. Compare Gibson's words with a recent comment from the late Air Vice-Marshal S.O. Bufton, then director of Bomber Operations on the staff of Sir Norman Bottomley (deputy chief of air staff):

... it was never the policy of the Air Staff or of the Combined Chiefs of Staff to attempt to win the war by bombing cities. There was never a Directive to this effect. The policy was to attack cities containing specific targets until the

Pathfinder force could be developed to a point where Bomber Command could attack the specific target itself. But Bert Harris did not give the Pathfinder force the support it needed, and went on to win the war 'his way', by attacking cities.[10]

In its later chapters, at least, *Enemy Coast Ahead* projects Air Ministry orthodoxy.

In one respect, however, Gibson's manipulators did miscalculate. They may not have reckoned with the possibility that he would actually become absorbed in the project, perhaps even enjoy it, and take it in directions for which they had not bargained. Yet this is what happened. As the story unfolds the early raucousness and clumsiness give way to something no less vivid, but more measured and controlled. Eve's memory of him working on the book with enthusiasm during March and April is significant. Gibson's normal domestic pleasures lay in tinkering with engines or going out to drink with friends: to find him concentrating on writing suggests that the project had turned into something which was fully engaging. In the event this did not interfere with the plan, although there would have been a much sharper edge to the book if officialdom had permitted his criticisms of those around and above him to stand.

A striking aspect of *Enemy Coast Ahead* is its eclecticism. Influences are found in popular journalism, the movies and – at least before the polishers took a hand – in Gibson's own manner of speaking and the patois of bomber crews. Today that idiom sounds false, and its vocabulary of words like 'wizzo' and 'bang on' seems embarrassingly forced. But that is as it was before the ridicule of *The Goon Show* and 1960s satirists consigned the accents of Bomber Command to the archive and concealed the crucial point that for much of the time their stock-in-trade had lain less in noisy exuberance than in understatement and irony.

Gibson was also working within a popular literary culture which today is almost invisible and forgotten. Its materials were writings which appeared in cyclostyled home-made newsletters and magazines that circulated on RAF stations during the war. Such media were ephemeral, and examples are accordingly rare. Those that survive are of the greatest interest.

Take, for instance, the August 1944 issue of 54 Base's house-magazine

The Gen, wherein is found a short story entitled 'Aiming Point'. Outbound on a raid, after a long silence, the captain says aloud to himself, 'Tomorrow, leave . . .' and then switches on the intercom:

'Everybody OK?' I asked.
One by one they answered.
'You all right, Dave?'
'Sure, Skip.'
'Leave tomorrow, eh?'
'Yes, wizzo.'[11]

Compare the dialogue Gibson (or his anonymous ghost-writer in the USA in 1943) attributes to his crew on their return from the raid on Stuttgart in March 1943:

During these moments there had been little talk, but once we were clear of the target area all the boys on board started talking.
'Leave to-morrow.'
'To-morrow we go on leave.'
'I'm going fishing.'
'I'm going to sleep.'
'To-morrow we go on leave.'[12]

Gibson did not draw on 'Aiming Point' for his own book; the issue is rather that there were amateur writers on squadrons who provided accessible models, and drew their dialogue directly from what was being said around them. Some of them were rather good. Here the author of 'Aiming Point' describes the awakening of German defences:

The searchlights came on suddenly, sharply, in bunches of ten or fifteen at a time, growing out of the ground in a vast circle round the target. And now the real flak started, spattering the sky with tiny particles of light, and then the long streams of tracer like coloured spray from a fountain, curving away into the darkness.

Some of the most interesting passages in *Enemy Coast Ahead* concern Gibson's social outlook and political views. The book contains laboured digressions on such themes, and his first thoughts were often a good deal more strident than those printed. Today we might characterize these as being well to the right, rather incoherent, in some respects extreme or intolerant. But that would be to over-simplify. Many of

Gibson's ideas were the luggage of his social background, less actively espoused than carried around. His dislikes included conceit, pomposity, intellectuals, social degeneracy and politicians who by their ineptitude or socialist leanings threatened the moral fibre of Britain's citizens and the fabric of her Empire. He hated not only Germany but also Germans, and fainthearts who refused to stand up against them he despised.

But what did he believe *in*? Running through the book is a single idea of great force: the need to wrest political power from old men who periodically sacrificed the younger generation in order to retain it. The book itself is virtually a metaphor for that, for most of it is about the lives, deeds, endurance and sacrifices of men in their late teens and early twenties. Even while *Enemy Coast Ahead* was being written another platform for this idea was offered to him, with consequences that clearly influenced the book.

Member for Macclesfield?

Gibson had first been introduced to Mr Willard Garfield Weston, Conservative Member for Macclesfield, shortly after the Dams Raid. A Toronto-born businessman, Garfield Weston's trade was manufacturing foodstuffs in a business empire which spanned the Atlantic and eventually developed to become Associated British Foods Ltd. In order to concentrate on his post-war business interests, early in 1944 he decided to relinquish his parliamentary seat and took a familiar route out of office by announcing that he would not contest the next general election. Since an election seemed unlikely until hostilities were over, Weston's decision allowed time for the selection of a new prospective candidate.

During his close relationship with Churchill and acquaintance with Weston, Gibson had been judged fit by both men to represent the Conservative Party in Parliament.* By the first week of February 1944,

---

* According to Eve Gibson (via Lady Wendy Martin), 'Garfield Weston told Churchill he wanted to retire at the end of the war and suggested Guy Gibson to follow him. Churchill was keen and it was put to Guy.'

with work on *Enemy Coast Ahead* well under way, Gibson had already been approached with the suggestion that he might stand. He found the idea appealing and told Eve that they had been invited to stay for a weekend with the Weston family at Marlow. Apparently this was the first Eve knew of her husband's new ambition.

After a six-hour journey in thick fog they arrived to a reception of genuine warmth. Eve later recalled, 'Of the nine Weston children, eight were at home that weekend and except for the two youngest, each played a musical instrument – they had their own orchestra. They were the happiest, nicest family I have ever met.'

The candidacy was not, of course, in Weston's gift. His opinion was influential, but the decision rested with the Macclesfield Conservative Association, to whom Gibson would need to present himself, in competition with others. It was probably at this weekend party that Weston briefed Gibson on the procedure for standing as a candidate, and arrangements were made for Gibson's first foray into political life. Lord Vansittart was due to visit Macclesfield the following week as part of a lecture tour in support of his Win the Peace campaign. It was agreed that Gibson should use this occasion as a chance to 'see and be seen' in the constituency.

Macclesfield is in Cheshire. In the 1940s it was a medium-sized town, with a population mostly engaged in textile manufacturing. For several centuries the town's economy had largely been based on silk, now made in the mills which spread over the western foothills of the Peak District. The core of Macclesfield was marked by a few fine eighteenth-century buildings, paid for with the proceeds of silk, supplemented by the red-brick workers' houses which clustered around the chimneys of the mills. Some of Macclesfield's wartime production was given over to parachute silk, and airmen visited from time to time to inspect the work and be photographed by the Press. In contrast to Weston's experience in business and manufacturing, an asset to the member for such a constituency, nothing of Macclesfield's way of life was remotely familiar to Gibson.

On the Wednesday following their visit to Marlow (9 February) Eve and Guy met Mr and Mrs Weston in Macclesfield. Lord and Lady Vansittart joined the party at the Macclesfield Arms Hotel for a dinner hosted by Garfield Weston. Weston took pains to ensure that Gibson would meet everyone who mattered: the mayors and town clerks of

Macclesfield and Congleton were invited, along with various JPs, local councillors and other dignitaries.

Next day Gibson was taken on a well-publicized programme of visits around his prospective constituency. Appropriately enough, the first was to the Avro works at Woodford. Here, with Eve and Garfield Weston, he renewed acquaintance with Roy Chadwick, and Garfield Weston was taken aloft for a brief flight in a Lancaster. Next he drove back to Macclesfield to visit the Waters Green silk mill owned by Councillor Edmund Lomas (a guest of the previous evening) and spent a couple of hours chatting to staff and looking round. Time was also found for a visit to Adlington Hall at Prestbury, a country house then in use as a branch of St Mary's Maternity Hospital, Manchester. By teatime Gibson had been seen in the company of war production workers, silk workers, doctors, nurses and (essential for an aspiring politician) babies. Last of all, Gibson had the opportunity to be seen with a prominent political figure. After another reception back at the Macclesfield Arms on that Thursday evening, he appeared on the platform beside Lord Vansittart.

Vansittart was a vociferous and controversial figure. A former permanent secretary at the Foreign Office, on retirement he had spurned the dignified anonymity favoured by many former civil servants and had thrown himself into a political campaign directed against Germany, German cultural conditioning and German values. In 1932 he had predicted that within the decade Europe would again be drawn into war by Germany. By 1944 his Win the Peace campaign led him to speak at venues throughout Britain, where he put forward an uncompromising manifesto for the treatment of post-war Germany. He proposed a charge of collective culpability against the whole of the German people, not just the seniors of the Nazi party, for the present war. The Labour Party despised Vansittartism as an extreme right-wing doctrine – not that this prevented them from using 'Now Win the Peace' as one of their own slogans in the 1945 election.

Vansittartism won many supporters in the armed forces. For a serviceman, and particularly for one in Bomber Command, Vansittart's teaching of collective responsibility could hold seductive appeal, for it offered the means of resolving moral doubts raised by area bombing. By now such doubts were beginning to loom large; yet attacks upon German cities and their civilian populations became morally defensible if one began from the Vansittartist premise that the entire German nation was responsible for the war.

Gibson's appearance on the platform that Thursday evening showed, implicitly, his acceptance of Vansittart's position. Seated before the improbable trinity of Vansittart, the mayor and Gibson was an invited audience of civil defence workers, Garfield Weston, Lady Vansittart and Eve. The mayor spoke first, setting out a manifesto for a welfare state. 'We are going to win this war soon,' he said,

and when it is finished we shall be confronted by some tremendously difficult problems. There are many things we should like to see – more and better houses, a finer system of education, security against unemployment, better welfare services, and more adequate old age pensions. But these things will come only through goodwill, less selfishness on the part of us all, and after much wise thinking and careful planning. Then there will be the great international problems – the continued co-operation of the Allied nations . . . the return to their homes of about 20 million refugees, and that very important question, what are we going to do with Germany . . .

Vansittart spoke next and set out to answer at least part of the mayor's question. He began by reminding the audience of his warning, in 1932, that Germany would again go to war. This bid for world domination was being pursued with the same savagery as before. He continued:

When the game is up, the Germans will try to say that it was only a little class in Germany that produced this war. If we accept that thesis we shall be drawn gradually into a frame of mind in which, when that clique has gone, we shall make an easy, makeshift peace, in which case we shall have another war. But if we admit that there is a national German responsibility, we shall take our precautions accordingly and will not have a third war.

Vansittart's policy towards Germany was based upon three considerations. First, he explained, it was clear that the present war was simply a continuation of the last. The Germans had the same motive – world domination. Secondly, Vansittart argued that the present war, and its predecessor, had come about through the 'systematic mis-education' of the German people over the last century. Lastly, he saw the origin of 'national militarism' among the Germans in mis-education – their militarism was the real enemy. He went on:

National Socialism is only a passing phase, and very likely in the course of this year we shall be rid of National Socialism. But national militarism will endure for a long time, and we shall have to curb it for quite a long while. There is no immediate hope of cure.

You can indict a nation, and I do so. What you cannot do is to put a nation in the dock, and I do not propose to do so. Punishment must be reserved for the hands that have actually committed the crimes. But do not assume that the nation is guiltless. On the contrary, the nation has been the accomplice of these mis-leaders.

Our business is to provide security for Europe against Germany. This security will have to be maintained for a good while because real peace cannot come for [sic] a whole generation after the cessation of hostilities. Little can be done with the present generation of Germans. I do not think there is much prospect of re-educating them. We must look to the next generation.

Vansittart concluded by setting out the policy of the Win the Peace movement. First, the Allies must ensure that Germany and the Axis powers were denied any future capacity to wage aggressive war. Second, constitutional and educational reforms must be imposed on the Germans in order that they could begin to take their place within a free and prosperous world.[13]

Gibson's mute appearance on the platform places him, once again, in the role of an exhibit. During his address, Vansittart made occasional references to 'the wing-commander and his colleagues'. We can imagine the gesture. Gibson was cast as a kind of reference point, there to lend sanction to what was being said. But the larger significance of the event is obvious. Whether he had been manoeuvred into it or was there from choice, Gibson's first excursion into an explicitly political forum reflected an implicit alliance with Vansittart. The parliamentary hopeful was happy to be associated with what today might be called an extremist organization. Gibson detested the Germans *en masse*. 'No wonder they stink' is a curious line in his book – sheer, childish abuse – and his opinion that Britain was 'dealing with the mass psychology of a nation – and a bad nation at that' is pure Vansittartism, and written within weeks of meeting him.

Gibson's entry to political life could hardly have been more controversial, and the Macclesfield Labour Party reacted swiftly. *Civil Defence Personnel, and everyone else, should hear the Socialist reply to*

Vansittart ran the announcement of a meeting to be held at the Townley Street Sunday School on 23 March. This meeting was a failure. Denied Vansittart's captive audience, the guest speaker, Rhys Davies MP, found himself addressing an almost empty hall. But politicians usually try to present events in a favourable light and, in a letter to the local Press, the Labour Party's secretary wrote that 'when the Socialists of the town ventured to organize another [meeting] the shallow interest of the attenders at the Vansittart meeting was revealed in the sparse attendance'. This is to jump ahead, but what had become clear to the Labour Party was the nature of Gibson's political position.

Gibson left Macclesfield on Friday 11 February and journeyed to London for another public engagement. Arriving at Broadcasting House around lunch-time, he met Roy Plomley, in preparation for his appearance as the forty-third guest on *Desert Island Discs*. In the early 1940s the programme was constructed differently from today. As a guest, Gibson lunched with Plomley at the Garrick Club, where the two discussed Gibson's choices. A script would then be prepared by Plomley, based on their conversation and, whilst this was with the typist, Gibson and Plomley visited the record library to select the records Gibson wanted. Though somewhat stilted, the script is none the less interesting as a record of Gibson's manner of speech and for glimpses into his open and frankly sentimental personality.

After his customary 'Good evening, everyone' Roy Plomley said: 'Again this week our desert island is privileged to have a serviceman as its castaway.' (Servicemen were then frequent guests.) Plomley continued: 'Sitting opposite me is a fair-haired young RAF officer who, although only twenty-five years old, has already attained the rank of wing-commander.' Plomley went on to sketch Gibson's wartime career, pointing out that he was 'the most highly decorated man in the British Empire'.

Gibson's first comment (perhaps having listened to the previous programme when the guest had included a Debussy nocturne and an extract from a Palestrina mass) was: 'Well, I'm not a highbrow by any means. In fact, I can't claim to know an awful lot about music at all. Somehow I never seem to have had time to do anything about it, except to listen occasionally to something I liked the sound of.' Gibson explained that when he 'came to think this desert island problem over' he knew most of the pieces he wanted, but did not know all their titles.

So he hummed the tunes on the telephone to musical friends, and to
Eve.

Most of the choice, were prompted by associations. The *Warsaw
Concerto* reminded him of life and parties in the mess of 106 Squadron,
where 'we would put it on the radiogram and let it repeat itself again
and again'. 'Where or When' sung by Adelaide Hall recalled his courtship of Eve in the summer of 1940. The overture to *The Flying
Dutchman* was something he had liked 'ever since I was a kid. I don't
believe I should ever get tired of it. It's grand. It's probably because it
reminds me of the sea, and I love the sea.' The fourth record was 'If I
Had My Way'. 'Perhaps, as tunes go, it's a wee bit corny,' said Gibson,
'but then I rather like corny tunes,' adding that he would like to hear
Bing Crosby singing it, because 'I've heard so many imitation Crosbys
giving out over the intercom when we're flying that it would be a treat
to have the real thing.' Next came the US Marines March, 'To the
Shores of Tripoli', which Gibson had first heard at a march-past during
his tour in America. Enthusing about his tour of Canada and the States
and his fortnight in Hollywood, Gibson described this as a souvenir of
'one of the most exciting things ever to have happened in my life'.
Walford Davies's 'Royal Air Force March Past' was selected because
'every time I hear it it never fails to send a shiver down my spine'.

For his last record, Gibson wanted Wagner's 'The Ride of the
Valkyries' from *Die Walküre*. 'Grandiose' was the only word he could
find to characterize it, but he also explained that, 'it reminds me of a
bombing raid, though I don't say it's like one'. Strong emotional
simplicity is willingly revealed. Love, comradeship and memories loom
large.

With a rapidity reminiscent of his American tour, Gibson set off next
day for another round of public engagements. As his train arrived – late
– passengers at Bristol Temple Meads station heard the Tannoy ring
with the name of the celebrity who was suddenly among them. Gibson
was rushed in a car, past gathering crowds, to an engagement at the
factories of the Bristol Aeroplane Company. After speaking to workers
during their lunch-hour, he travelled back into the city where he
inspected an ATC guard of honour before entering the Colston Hall to
give a speech launching Bristol's campaign for blood donors. 'I feel
strongly about this blood business,' he said, explaining that Bristol
'needs 50,000 new donors and although that probably means one in

three of all young people, I don't see why that figure should not be reached'. He went on to stress the need for blood to sustain lives 'when the Second Front opens'.

Then he changed the subject. Quite why he considered the launch of a blood donor campaign to be a suitable occasion for giving, once again, his views on strategic bombing policy is a puzzle. Yet he expressed himself with a new vehemence. He had heard, he said, that there were those who believed that the war could be won by bombing but, he said,

it's time we got rid of that idea. The Germans have taken a terrific whack, but it looks as if they will go on taking it. It would be folly to expect our bombing, devastating though it is, to result in a German collapse.

The strength with which Gibson hammered this point is remarkable, for it placed on public record his flat disagreement with the policy of his former commander-in-chief, Sir Arthur Harris. Harris had predicted that the reduction of cities would so weaken the German economy and undermine the will to resist that no great combined operation to recapture the European mainland would be necessary. Yet here was Guy Gibson, the popular personification of Bomber Command, saying otherwise. Why?

It is faintly possible that he was being used as a mouthpiece for factional interests. The MoI appears to have had a hand in organizing his appearance in Bristol, and his analysis echoed the policy of the air staff. However, it is more likely that he was voicing his own opinion, clarified by his conversations with Churchill and his current preoccupation with *Enemy Coast Ahead*, and that he was speaking off the cuff. His view was widely shared by rank-and-file bomber aircrew, and in itself is unsurprising. What comes as a shock is the timing and frankness of the statement. The Battle of Berlin had reached its peak, and public debate on area bombing was mounting. Gibson never disavowed the principle or practice of area bombing, but he had no illusions about what the destruction of German cities might be expected to achieve.

Whatever prompted his statement, its making shows that he was now fireproof indeed. Very possibly he did not see it as a criticism of Harris, but rather as an opinion about a concept, delivered with his customary insouciance. So he gave blood, had a cup of tea, signed some autographs for the nurses (saying that the women of Hollywood were not the equals of Britain's 'gentle sex') and, with Bristol now familiar with his ideas on winning the war, he went home.

With public engagements still making such demands it is difficult to see how Gibson found much time for his job at the Air Ministry – assuming he really had one beyond the writing of *Enemy Coast Ahead*. During the latter part of February he was increasingly aware that the next landmark in his career as a political candidate was approaching – the meeting of the Macclesfield Conservative Association at which the short list of candidates for Weston's successor would be drawn up. On 4 March, with the memory of Gibson's *Desert Island Discs* programme still fresh in their minds, the committee met. A sub-committee had already reduced the twenty-eight original candidates for the post to eleven, and a final list of five was now drawn up. The competition was exceptionally stiff. Two unsuccessful candidates were fellow RAF officers. Air Vice-Marshal Donald Bennett, the 34-year-old Pathfinder leader, who had no time for 'professional heroes' and had vowed that 'there would be no living VCs in 8 Group' fell at this hurdle. So did Flt Lt Aitken, nephew of Lord Beaverbrook and cousin of Wg-Cdr Max Aitken, of Battle of Britain fame.

Gibson's four competitors on the short list were two soldiers, an airman and a sailor. Capt. Moody had a typical background for a Conservative politician of the time: a Coldstreamer, he had been educated at Eton, travelled in the States and Europe and studied farming prior to service in the Mediterranean. 2 Lt Shepherd was a journalist who had published a book, *Tory Democracy's Better Britain*. Lt Bryant Irvine was a Canadian-born barrister who held an MA from Magdalen College, Oxford, and was a civil engineer. The one truly local candidate was Sqn Ldr Stansfield, an old boy of the King's School, Macclesfield, and a Cambridge graduate who, in his capacity as a barrister, was serving in the office of the judge advocate. He had represented the Conservatives in another division for the 1935 election.

Stansfield, at thirty-eight, was the oldest of the candidates; Gibson, at twenty-five, the youngest. The others were all in their early thirties. Unlike those eliminated in the second round, there were no famous names among them. All had useful experience in civilian life – something which Gibson completely lacked. But whilst all had creditable service careers, none had won high awards or came anywhere near being the most highly decorated airman in the British Empire. Four conventionally strong candidates stood against one another, and against a household name. They would have been justified in feeling some irritation at the way in which the local Press treated the short list announcement. The *Macclesfield Times*, beneath the headline CONSERVATIVES SEEK CANDIDATE, proclaimed, 'Airman VC on short list of five'. Pictures of Gibson filled the local papers, as they had in early February when he visited with Vansittart. Stansfield, Moody, Shepherd and Irvine looked like also-rans from the start.

Anticipating the outcome (they ignored the others), the local Labour Party reacted to Gibson's appearance on the short list. But they were in a difficult position. As a Tory, Gibson was obviously an opponent. Yet he was also a national hero, much loved by the public. Some form of rationale was needed which would allow Labour to deplore Gibson's politics and, at the same time, acknowledge his personal qualities. A fortnight after the short list announcement, the Labour Party held a meeting at Congleton Trades and Labour Hall, at which Councillor C.T. Douthwaite, the Labour PPC, commented on Gibson's selection. Douthwaite considered it 'a tribute to gallantry' that such a 'fine young man' should have entered politics. Nevertheless, he protested, the Conservatives had no monopoly on Gibson's bravery. The Labour Party could not regard Gibson as the property of the Tories, despite the fact that Gibson had freely aligned himself with them. Douthwaite claimed Gibson 'for the people' and not for a political party.

On Saturday 25 March, the Selection Committee met to choose Weston's successor. Having decided not to require a contribution to Party funds, the Committee interviewed each in turn. Garfield Weston addressed the selectors and praised all five candidates. Wing-Commander Gibson, he explained, was the only one known personally to him, and he held a high opinion of his abilities, an opinion shared, as it happened, by the prime minister. After discussion it was decided to eliminate Capt. Moody and to hold a ballot on the remaining four. The local man, Stansfield, gained seven votes. Bryant Irvine won twelve and Shepherd eighteen. Gibson totalled twenty-three. A final vote was taken in which Gibson had seventeen supporters and Shepherd, the runner-up, thirteen. Gibson had won a narrow victory.

W.W. Wood, chairman of the Committee, then summoned Gibson to congratulate him and to convey the resolution that he had been 'unanimously recommended to a General Meeting of the Macclesfield

Division Conservative and Unionist Association for adoption as the prospective National Conservative candidate for the Macclesfield Division'. Gibson thanked the Committee: he would do everything possible to justify the confidence placed in him, but added that winning the war remained his first and most pressing concern.

The Press were outside. By now, Gibson only needed to see a man with a notebook in order to make a speech.

I want to state publicly that I am 100 per cent behind our Prime Minister. If I have the good fortune to reach the House of Commons, he can count on me absolutely as a whole-hearted supporter. I have four simple reasons for entering politics. One, to serve any truly representative body of English men and women who do me the honour of electing me. Two, to support Mr Winston Churchill, both now and after the war, with the utmost loyalty and energy. Three, to champion in the House of Commons the interests of all members of the Forces. When they return to 'civvy street' with their multifarious problems, their welfare will be one of my paramount concerns. Four, to lend a humble hand in shaping the new Britain. Whatever the planners may devise, youth will inherit the legacy. I speak for youth. We have a right, and demand a right, to have some say in moulding the country and the Empire for which youth has fought so hard.

In reply to questions, Gibson was uncertain whether he would live in the constituency if elected. For the moment he had permission from the RAF to be a prospective candidate, which meant 'just that, and very little more'. No, there was no immediate prospect of his resignation from the air force. 'This is my first go at politics,' he added. Few who heard his speech would have doubted that.

The acrimonious debate triggered by Gibson's short-listing was now given new momentum. A week later, Douthwaite was joined by Emanuel Shinwell for a Labour Party meeting. After discussing a recent parliamentary vote of confidence in the government, Shinwell briefly turned to the subject of Gibson. 'He may be good at busting dams, but he will not bust the Labour Party,' he avowed, devoting the rest of his speech to a critique of the Beveridge Report.

Douthwaite then rose to speak. Having told a previous audience that he claimed Gibson 'for the people', not for any political party, he now changed tack, arguing that Wing-Commander Gibson had made a mistake by allying himself with the Tories. Gibson should have joined the Labour Party, Douthwaite felt. But then again, the Conservatives' short list had clearly been drawn up with an eye to the electorate's propensity for hero-worship, and that, said Douthwaite, was why Gibson had been appointed. Douthwaite's confusion reveals the Socialists to have been wrong-footed by Gibson's selection and unable to find persuasive terms in which to counter it.

The following weekend, on Easter Sunday, Gibson had the opportunity to garner wider support by broadcasting in the *Week's Good Cause* series on the BBC Home Service. Having visited the branch establishment of St Mary's Maternity Hospital at Prestbury a few weeks earlier, Gibson now broadcast an appeal for the parent body. In the parts of the script devised by himself, Gibson moderated his usual robust delivery (which might have given us 'this birth business'), but his tone is again rather mawkish:

Perhaps you're wondering why a bomber pilot should be making an appeal on behalf of babies ... Well, as a member of the RAF for the past eight years, and as a married man, I know perhaps better than many of you how much home, wife and children mean in the Services. This thought of home is one of our chief reasons for fighting, and for trying to get the job finished quickly – so that we can get back to our families again. Think of it – many of us are far away just when we are most needed – in sickness, or most of all when a new little life is coming into the world. You know, it means something to a man to know that his wife and baby are to be cared for by experts: especially if the baby is one of those little fellows who has literally to be wrapped in cotton wool, and needs everything that medical science knows to coax him to hold on to life ...

And so on. He explained what St Mary's hospitals were: their history, aims, the medical treatment they provided for women, the 3,000 babies delivered each year, the training of doctors and their costs – £90,000 per year. And then he concluded:

A little while ago the Prime Minister said that science, now perverted to destruction, must raise its shield over the children, the mothers, the family and the home. This is exactly what Saint Mary's are doing – to protect the mothers and to give the babies upon whom the future depends a fair start in life.

And with 'all my heart, and all my reason' he asked his listeners to make the appeal a record.

Aspects of this simple text repay scrutiny. The juxtaposition of children, mothers, family and home was calculated to summon up that sense of snug stability that has appealed to twentieth-century Conservative thinking. A listener might easily have formed the impression that Gibson was himself a father and devoted family man. Yet neither is true. The references to science, as a kind of social panacea, and to the prime minister, in the role of saviour, are particularly forceful. Churchill's view of a secure future protected by scientific rationality is linked through the work of a children's hospital to produce two key messages: 'save the children' and 'vote Conservative'.

The political sub-text and the fact that Gibson was able to speak in support of an establishment within his prospective constituency reveal the episode as, perhaps, not entirely altruistic. Politicians do these things. But that did not detract from the success of the appeal. He received more than 4,000 letters and donations over the next six weeks.

Gentlemen of Letters

Gibson's nomination was trumpeted by the local Press, and a newsreel item in which Gibson announced his selection to the nation was filmed at Garfield Weston's house in Marlow. Political skirmishing continued, in ways which reflected both the continuing public interest in Gibson and the tendencies of individuals and interest groups to claim him for their own.

On 6 April the *Macclesfield Courier* published a letter signed 'Elector in Khaki' from 'Somewhere in England', firmly supporting Gibson's selection. A week later someone signing themselves 'Divisionist' wrote to point out inconsistencies in the Labour Party's arguments. This was conventional, low-key polemic. But there is a particular kind of character who will write letters to the Press on the smallest pretext, on any subject and at considerable length. Arthur Smith, secretary of the Macclesfield Labour Party, was evidently such a man.

Smith's first salvo was launched against 'Divisionist'. The Labour Party's view, as Douthwaite had expressed it, was not inconsistent: as a *national hero*, Gibson belonged to no party, but as a *prospective MP* with an interest in the welfare of servicemen, Smith felt that his natural home was with Labour. 'Divisionist' replied. Did Arthur Smith really suppose that Douthwaite would have made his remarks if Gibson had been standing for any party other than the Conservatives? Things might have ended there, but then news reached Macclesfield on 27 April that Admiral Sir William James, Conservative MP for North Portsmouth, had made a speech to the women members of the British Legion which touched on the Gibson question. James had warned women against prospective leaders who did nothing for their country, and at the same time supported pacifism.

These people are already showing their heads above the dug-outs. I do not say that you should vote for a candidate for Parliament simply because he was a VC, but I should be terribly tempted to do so, because it would show he is a man of character. It is very important to return to Parliament men of real character.

This was too much for Arthur Smith. In a cynical letter published in the *Courier* on 5 May, he took a double swipe at 'Divisionist' and the Admiral. Smith was evidently pleased with this one. As well as posting it to the *Courier*, his field for doing battle with 'Divisionist', he sent an almost identical version to the *Macclesfield Times* where, in the issue of 4 May, it read:

I observe that Macclesfield women are being encouraged to vote for a man because he is a VC. I also note that land formerly thought high priced at £750 to £1,000 is being offered for sale at several thousand pounds an acre. It is more difficult to bust the land profiteers of England than the water dams of Germany. As the Conservative Party has determined that those profiteers shall not be bust it is clear that the women and servicemen of Macclesfield who want better homes and a better town will have to vote for the party that intends to bust the land sharks.

Others joined the fray. The following week one M. Lewis of Alderley Edge wrote to the *Macclesfield Times*:

I observe that the women of Macclesfield are being advised to vote for a man because he is a VC. Moreover, they may feel that it is almost a duty to vote in this way, despite the fact that the latter represents the Conservative Party.

While one recognizes and admires the great service the prospective candidate has rendered his country, we must not let this blind our eyes to the fact that politics control our lives in every way and, in particular, our standard of living. Therefore, I appeal to the women of Macclesfield to vote for their own interests, namely, for a Labour candidate, and think of the future . . . Further, may I say that I am astonished that a working-class town like Macclesfield should return a Conservative Member.

And so the debate rumbled on. It is not clear whether Gibson was aware of it. Certainly, he never sought to defend himself, and there was no official response from the Conservatives. Gibson's activities in the constituency were in any case curtailed, for since mid-March he had been attending a staff course at the RAF Staff College, Bulstrode Park, Gerrard's Cross. He continued to come up for speaking engagements, but these were often to captive, uniformed audiences. Some at least of these speeches were extremely right-wing in emphasis. One, entitled 'This Amazing Empire', was delivered at a meeting whereat questioners critical of the Dominions were ruled out of order. We have Arthur Smith to thank for our knowledge of these events; he, alone, was still writing to the papers, during the last week of August, to complain about them.

Publicly, Gibson confined himself to less controversial issues. On 26 May, in a letter which unites his now-familiar themes of science and the future, expressed in terms combining rhetoric and sentimentality, he wrote to thank those who had responded to his charity broadcast:

Though I have chosen the air as my calling, I still marvel at the miracle of its conquest, both in respect of broadcasting and the navigation of the skies. Science has done much to eliminate distance and bring people together, although they may live at the furthest corners of the earth.

. . . School friends have reminded me of forgotten escapades. Units of the RAF with whom I have served have rallied round, and old family friends have been in touch again. I am deeply moved by letters enclosing gifts in gratitude to the RAF . . .

There were interesting and sympathetic letters from people now retired from service with hospitals . . . from girls who want to be airwomen – a sign of the future – and I must mention gifts from boys and girls still at school – the air service will never lack recruits . . .

Two months earlier one of the first tasks for the forty or so officers attending No. 12 Staff Course had been an exercise in writing letters. It would be uncharacteristic for Gibson to have immersed himself in such study, or to have enjoyed much of the training in administration that followed. But at least the course was rapid, compressing into eleven weeks a syllabus normally spread over a year. Gibson impressed some of the visiting lecturers. Dr R. V. Jones, then head of the Scientific Intelligence Unit at the Air Ministry, was introduced to him. They chatted on matters of operational interest and Jones found Gibson's 'very pleasant and remarkably modest' manner very agreeable.[14]

The pace of the course left little time for relaxation. During the week Gibson lived at the college; there were numerous written exercises, and visits to other establishments to study systems of administration. At weekends he worked on *Enemy Coast Ahead* or journeyed to Maccles-field. One outing was more notable – an All Ranks dance at Woodhall on Friday 18 May where, as Cheshire put it, 'the boys fêted him'.[15] (On the previous Tuesday 617 Squadron celebrated the anniversary of the Dams Raid with a party in the Petwood Hotel at Woodhall Spa. Barnes Wallis and Cochrane were there but, much to his annoyance, Gibson was unable to attend.)

The dance was held in a hangar. Converging lines of tables arranged in a V-shape creaked under the weight of food and airmen eagerly drank their way through 180 gallons of beer. At the base of the V stood another table which bore a special 'Dams cake', adorned with creamy icing. Cheshire and Gibson stood on this table to deliver speeches. Cheshire said how honoured he was to have followed Gibson as commander of 617. Then Gibson moved forward, inadvertently stepping on the area of unsupported tablecloth between the converging tables. He fell backwards on to the cake, spattered those near by with icing and caused a roar of laughter when he stood up and said cheerfully: 'That's the softest thing I've had between my legs lately.'

Gibson was uncomfortable in Cheshire's presence. Cheshire recalled that it was 'difficult for two wing-commanders on an operational squadron'. Cheshire had established a different kind of tradition and for much of the time he withdrew into the background, 'trying to make it easier for the others'. But the two did talk and Cheshire was curious to find that behind Gibson's jovial manner there smouldered an 'unexpressed sense of anger'. For Gibson, Cheshire thought, the war was 'not just a technical business of delivering bombs'.[16]

Back at Gerrard's Cross, the staff course ended a few days later. One of its effects had been to reorientate Gibson's thinking about his future. By the early summer of 1944, even as he started to establish himself as the prospective Member for Macclesfield, he was beginning to wonder whether this was what he really wanted to do. Hitherto his career had been fashioned by others. Remarkable things had happened to him, but that was rather the point: he had been manipulated. He had not asked to go to America; the impetus for the book had come from elsewhere; and he had not chosen to be a politician: a politician had chosen him. Now the staff course, with its emphasis on making decisions, had planted a new seed of doubt in him. What did he really want to do when the war ended? Civilian flying? A permanent career in the RAF? Or should he walk through the door of opportunity which Churchill had opened for him?

Churchill's Young Man

Gibson the politician was 'for' Churchill, Vansittart's ideas on German culpability, the Empire, Science, the interests of servicemen, families, Youth and Conservatism in general. He was against all that threatened these things, and against the Germans most of all. Given his background and career there is nothing surprising here, and his concern with 'youth' and the future echoes widespread contemporary attitudes.

In the summer of 1944 a political career still came second to the war in his priorities. But why did he, a professional airman who only nine months earlier had professed himself shy of publicity, agree to enter politics at all? One answer is that his experiences since the Dams Raid had broadened his horizons. Gibson's circle of acquaintances now included an astonishingly large number of powerful, famous and worldly people. The pace of his life since May 1943 needs a moment's contemplation. He departed for the Möhne dam as a squadron commander in his early twenties. Within a few weeks he had been given the wholly unexpected honour of lunch with the King and Queen, he had been awarded the Victoria Cross and had met Clementine and Winston

Churchill. He had received public adulation. He had been to America with his prime minister, rubbed shoulders with the most senior military men of the day and had met the leaders of most of the Allied nations. He had mixed with film stars. His name had been in newspapers, newsreels and radio broadcasts all over the Allied world. Apart from the comments of the Macclesfield Labour Party, none of this publicity had been remotely critical. In just six months he had become unimaginably famous and had met more or less everyone who mattered.

It is not difficult to see how any individual exposed to such experience might gain an enhanced sense of their own potential. At the same time, Gibson may have been surprised at just how ordinary so many politicians are. Those who enter public life often do so not because they discover deep inner reserves of ability, but because they find out how undistinguished the competition is. Military officers, along with civil servants (like Gibson's father), have traditionally treated the flashy trappings of fame with a reserved scepticism. Though he was now entering ever more public arenas, Gibson retained a sense of proportion. He probably realized that the responsibilities of a back-bench politician (at that date not, in any case, so very great) were quite within his capabilities.

Gibson's entry into politics was not prompted by intellectual or even political motives – at least, not in the wide sense in which we use the term 'political' today. Unlike Donald Bennett, whom he had defeated for the Macclesfield nomination, Gibson was neither a political sophisticate nor any kind of visionary. The comparison is instructive. Bennett was a man riven by frustration and an agitated sense of necessity for social change. His views were in some respects eccentric and in others deeply reactionary; but, like many people who value intellectual independence, his political affiliation eludes conventional definition. Bennett, one suspects, sought office in order to exercise power in his own inspired and individual way. Gibson simply subscribed to a consensus view which assumed that the Conservatives were the natural party of government and Empire. It was not so large a move from commanding a squadron to representing a constituency. In some ways it may even have seemed a regression, dictated by circumstance, a redefinition of duty and the discovery of a new object to which his personal loyalty could be attached.

The real force behind Gibson's entry into politics was his relationship with a politician who, unquestionably, he did regard as special, and who in his turn had flattered him. Churchill's patronage was responsible for the entry of several successful officers into post-war Parliament. He got on well with them; 'one of Churchill's endearing and enduring characteristics was to treat young men as if they were his contemporaries'.[17] Not all were responsive. Captain Evelyn Waugh served throughout the Second World War. On VE Day he wrote in his diary: 'I regard the greatest danger I went through that of becoming one of Churchill's young men, of getting a medal and standing for Parliament; if things had gone as then seemed right in the first two years, that is what I should be now.'[18]

By 1944 Gibson had become one of Churchill's young men. When elected to the Macclesfield nomination his first words to the Press were in support of Churchill. His opinions on strategic bombing were closer to those of Churchill than those of Harris. His Vansittartist streak aside, most of Gibson's domestic manifesto was derived from conversations with the prime minster, to whom he felt a strong bond of loyalty. Gibson's vision of the future was of victory secured and himself lending 'a humble hand in shaping the new Britain', buttressing the Empire, promoting the interests of the young who had fought and survived, serving a re-elected Churchill government and enjoying a newly won peace.

Part Nine

LINES OF CONVERGENCE

May–September 1944

Will his name be Love
And all his talk be crazy?
Or will his name be Death
And his message easy?

Louis MacNeice,
'Prognosis', Spring 1939

Coming Back

Guy Gibson's last months recall the conclusion of a Thomas Hardy novel: as the tale nears its end, old landscapes are revisited, past events acquire unforeseen meaning and half-forgotten characters return in new guise. The intention, of course, was that there was to be no tragedy. Fate had spared him, Harris and Cochrane wished to preserve him. The difficulty was to find something for him to do.

When the staff course finished at the end of May Gibson was given a week's leave. He took Eve back to North Wales, scene of their glorious fortnight in 1942. But the magic had gone. It rained incessantly and Gibson passed most of his days sailing around the estuary in a hired dinghy. Then, on 6 June, came news of Overlord. Gibson became frantic. His first impulse was to cut his leave and demand to be returned to operations. Eve objected, pointing out that his leave was nearly over anyway. He reluctantly agreed and stayed on for two more days. Then he went straight to Harris and pleaded.* Four days later he was posted to the staff of 55 Base at East Kirkby, in the flatness of south-east Lincolnshire. His duties were to understudy the base operations officer – a job which involved operational planning and liaison between the units of a Base – apparently with a view to assuming full responsibility for this role in due course. Gibson disliked desk work, but he was glad to be out of the classroom and back on a bomber station, in the right place to seize any opportunity to reverse his suspension from operational flying.

East Kirkby became the hub of a Base in April 1944, with satellites at Spilsby and Strubby. Several Coastal Command units were currently lodged at Strubby and for practical purposes 55 Base's staff had little to do with it. Spilsby was home to 207 Squadron; 57 and 630 Squadrons were stationed at East Kirkby itself.

There were old acquaintances at East Kirkby. One of them was Ron Williams, victim of Gibson's absolutism during the winter of 1942. Williams was now a flight lieutenant and navigator in the crew of Sqn Ldr Drew Wyness, commander of B Flight in 57 Squadron. Writing to

* This further call upon Harris's patronage recalls the bargain struck between Harris and Gibson in the autumn of 1940, and its fulfilment in March 1942.

his parents, Williams commented with heavy irony: 'I forgot to tell you last letter that my old friend W/Cdr Gibson has been posted to this station (not on flying duties).' Gibson remembered Williams and accosted him for a chat. Finding him to be 'press on' material after all, Gibson went out of his way to be friendly. Williams was unimpressed. 'I still don't think much of him,' he told his parents.[1]

For the next fortnight Gibson did his best to concentrate on his duties. But everything tantalized him. In the Mess, at briefings and in nearby pubs, he watched and remembered the feelings of men who lived by the day. Yet his involvement with real flying seemed scarcely greater than that of the schoolchildren who in the long June evenings gathered beside the road at the end of East Kirkby's runway to wave at the Lancasters as they took to the air.

His addiction to operational flying was now fully reawakened. He was also lonely. It may have been this social isolation, as well as other hopes and feelings, which caused him to renew contact with Margaret. They had not seen each other for the best part of a year, but letters – Gibson's invariably opening with a cheerful 'Maggie Darling' and closing 'Lovesyou' – had been exchanged often enough for Gibson to follow her through several changes of address.

Margaret was now living at her mother's house in Bognor Regis. During the last week in June Gibson made up his mind to see her. He wrote, saying that he would visit. Excited, Margaret replied at once and, sure enough, on the following Monday he appeared on her doorstep early in the morning, a greatcoat draped over his shoulders.

Guy stepped in out of pouring rain. The day was dark and cold, belonging more to November than July. The enclosing mood was reminiscent of Rauceby and helped to put them at ease. Margaret lit the fire. In front of it they sat and talked. For the first time Guy admired and played with his godson, now six months old. Later, Michael slept and there were no distractions.

'How's Honeysuckle Cottage?' inquired Margaret. Guy's reply was wistful. 'I haven't been there recently.'

They talked for hours. 'I had to come and see you,' he kept repeating. At last the guardedness was gone. They rehearsed Margaret's pointless marriage and described what they had actually been feeling and thinking during their winter afternoons and evenings together the year before. Guy was confused about his future, at one moment predicting that the war would soon run to its end and at the next restating his conviction that he was not going to survive it. Nevertheless, with victory in sight, the chance that he might still be alive when it was all over was a possibility that now turned in his mind. 'Afterwards,' he promised, 'I'm coming to find you.' But in other moments he relapsed into a belief that there was to be no afterwards.

The gloom and rain outside increased their sense of seclusion. Nothing disturbed them. Afterwards, not stating but implying the disappointments of their respective marriage partners, Guy observed: 'We owed ourselves this day.' He left in the evening. A day or two later he posted a note. 'The day was perfect. I love you now and for ever.'[2]

Margaret never heard from Guy again. A cynic would admit no surprise, for by now it was quite widely rumoured that Gibson 'spent more time in bed with other chaps' wives than he ever did in the air'. But Gibson's reluctance even to touch Margaret during the winter of 1942–43 places her in a distinctly different category. Her passive loyalty, awaiting a summons that might or might not come, may seem as unselfish as Gibson's behaviour looks outrageously cavalier. Yet there are signs that Gibson drew a good deal of emotional strength from the *thought* that Margaret would be waiting for him. His marriage had been a disappointment; to have some other prospect in the future, a romantic idea, offered the ideal balance of hope without commitment. As for his silence during the next two months, that was par for the course. Eve fared no better.

Back at East Kirkby Gibson's addiction had to be fed. On 5 July tension lifted soon after midday when all operations were cancelled, but Drew Wyness decided to test his Lancaster anyway, and Gibson went with him. 'We flew for half an hour,' wrote Williams afterwards, 'and took W/Cdr Gibson up with us, or at least he did the flying – the first time in a Lancaster for eight months.' Williams was forced to admit – with slight surprise – that 'He coped quite well!'

Gibson's determination to return to war was intensified six days later when Mick Martin arrived in a Mosquito. Martin was now based at Little Staughton with 515 Squadron, a unit which specialized in night intruder operations. Martin took Gibson aloft. Gibson was fired with enthusiasm, asking questions about the machine's manoeuvrability and emergency procedures. Back on the ground, the two caught up with events in each other's lives. Gibson talked of Churchill and politics, but confided doubts about Macclesfield. He remained keen in principle and thought there should be more young MPs in Parliament. But he was also desperate to return to war.[3]

Next day East Kirkby's squadrons took part in a Crossbow operation. The target was a limestone cave system at St Leu-d'Esserent near Criel. A neighbourhood rich in V-weapon sites, Criel was a centre for the storage and forwarding of V1s. A nearby château housed the commander and staff of *Flakregiment* 155 (W) who were responsible for co-ordination of the V1 offensive.

The attack was a failure. The caves were largely proof against ordinary bombs, defences were concentrated and East Kirkby's squadrons suffered accordingly. On the following evening Gibson went into Boston with several men who had flown on the operation. They restored their shaken spirits by drinking until closing time and then returned to the Mess to continue the party. Outwardly convivial, Gibson's frustration was now scarcely containable. Quite apart from his envy of the fliers, his tendency to treat war as a personal vendetta had been increased by first-hand reports of the flying bombs. Heavy civilian casualties were being caused and there was rising public clamour for preventive action. Gibson detested the weapon and would have been only too glad to oblige.

Eight days later he did. By means that are unclear he joined the crew of a Lancaster (probably PB 244)* of 630 Squadron, normally captained by Flt Sgt E. Bowers, in an attack on the same V1 site that had been unsuccessfully raided the week before. On this evening the results were no better, but Gibson was cock-a-hoop. After fourteen months he had brought back a photograph of the aiming-point which demonstrated to colleagues – and perhaps to himself – that his skills were undiminished. 'Successful' wrote Gibson, echoing the laconic triumphalism after the Dams Raid, his last operation, and proudly pasted a print of the aiming-point photograph in his logbook. The controller for this raid was Sqn Ldr Charles Owen, who had been appointed to master bomber duties only a week previously. This was Owen's first sortie in a Mosquito and he decided that 'a Mossie is definitely a safe way of going to war'.[4]

---

* This aircraft, a Lancaster I of 630 Squadron, flew to Criel on 19 July. Gibson was not listed as a member of its crew in the unit's ORB (PRO AIR 27/2152), but his logbook tells us that he was flying with a second pilot, Sqn Ldr Miller. A Sqn Ldr Miller is named in the ORB as PB244's navigator on this evening, and the aeroplane's squadron letters (LE-N) correspond with details on the aiming-point photograph.

54 Base

Two weeks later Gibson was posted from East Kirkby to No. 54 Base Headquarters as Base air staff officer. This was a significant transfer. Centred on Coningsby, 54 Base provided target marking and illumination for 5 Group attacks. 54 Base was a place of tactical innovation and the residence of 5 Group's controllers, like Charles Owen, who operated through the élite 54 Base Flight. Gibson reported for duty on 4 August, his arrival coinciding with a visit by Cochrane and Satterly.

Coningsby and its surroundings were tinged with memories. Gibson was back at the scene of his first command. Digby was near to hand. So was Rauceby. 83 Squadron, his first unit, was stationed at Coningsby itself. Both of the squadrons he had commanded were members of 54 Base's family. 106 was at Metheringham, about ten miles across the fens. 617 was closer still, at Woodhall Spa, an airfield it shared with 627 Squadron.

627 specialized in low-level marking. The only Mosquito unit in 5 Group, like 617, it was a squadron which had been formed for special purposes. Like 617 too its members were drawn from all parts of the Commonwealth and had a strong sense of community. Teamwork was valued, and all the pilots were experienced enthusiasts for low-level visual marking. Several were star performers.

Although 617 and 627 shared the same airfield, there were some who felt that 627 Squadron was unjustly cast in the role of a poor relation. Whereas the officers of 617 messed in the ample surroundings of the Petwood Hotel, 627 had to make do with a humble concrete-sided hut in a wood beyond the aerodrome. One evening Gibson drove over to this building to introduce himself. The aircrew had been stood down and a number were standing about chatting, drinking beer, or playing cards, chess or shove-halfpenny. Into this community atmosphere walked Gibson. Everyone recognized him as he strolled up to the bar. VC and DSO ribbons were unusual, Gibson was famous and his arrival had already been heralded by a friendly paragraph in 54 Base's magazine.

But Gibson's entry had seemed a little ostentatious. The 627 men were accordingly wary and reacted to his arrival with contrived indifference. After a time Gibson called out, in some annoyance and to no one in particular: 'Don't you know who I am? I'm Wing-Commander Gibson.' Whereupon an Australian voice called back: 'So bloody what?' Gibson was momentarily nonplussed. Before he had time to say anything someone else started chanting, 'De-bag! De-bag! De-bag!' The chant took hold. Gibson was seized, his trousers removed, and he was put outside half-dressed. Having attempted to puncture what had seemed to be a balloon of conceit, the 627 aircrew then invited Gibson back in and offered him a beer. But he did not see the joke. He snapped at one man – a Glaswegian who had risen from a background of deprivation to become an officer – who duly snapped back. Disciplinary proceedings were later brought against this man, who was sent to the detested 'Refresher Course' at Sheffield.* After this, Gibson was unwelcome in the 627 Mess.[5]

In early August Gibson secured lodgings for Eve in Skegness, intending that they should spend some time together. In the event, Gibson's posting to Coningsby and the need to get to grips with his new job took precedence – or that is what Eve tells us. Although she stayed in Skegness for a fortnight, their time together was short. It is a question who was avoiding whom, but on 12 August, Guy's birthday, they dined at a local restaurant. An austerity supper for two in Skegness was in sharp contrast to the adulatory Press conference which had marked his birthday in Quebec the year before. The mood was bleak. This was their last meeting.

One matter they probably discussed was Gibson's commitment to the Macclesfield Conservative Association. A few days before Gibson had written to Garfield Weston, explaining that he no longer felt able to sustain his prospective candidature. Weston wrote to the chairman of the Association on 14 August to alert him to Gibson's change of heart. Gibson's letter of resignation arrived a week and a half later:

It is with profound regret, and only after the most careful consideration, that I have decided to ask your committee to release me from my adoption as the prospective National Conservative candidate for the Macclesfield Division.

---

* RAF slang for a short, sharp shock programme for wayward aircrew. There were a number of such centres; that at Sheffield was also known as the Sheffield Glasshouse. Gibson's victim was there for three weeks.

In recent months it has been brought home to me that the demands of my Service career are so exacting that I could not combine them successfully with a political career and do full justice to both. The European war claims all my present time and energies and when it has been won I shall not be satisfied until I have played what part I can in bringing the Japanese war to a victorious conclusion.

May I add – to allay any rumours which might arise – that I have definitely no intention of seeking adoption elsewhere.

My decision has been a most difficult one to make, and I cannot close without expressing a genuine feeling of regret that I am obliged to forgo the great opportunity which your committee was kind enough to offer me.[6]

As we have seen, Gibson had harboured doubts about Macclesfield for several months. His immediate reasons for backing out through the door which had been so graciously opened for him by Churchill are found in the newly invigorating surroundings which 54 Base provided. However, perhaps for the first time, he was also beginning to think about his longer future, and to make choices on his own behalf. Not only was he determined to return to operational flying, but he also had his eyes on a service career.

From his position as BASO Gibson kept a close eye on Intelligence reports about the progress of the war. During late August the Allied armies made sudden gains, sweeping up through northern France and into Belgium. By the beginning of September German resistance in the Low Countries was collapsing. On the 4th British troops were in Brussels. Churchill's private secretary wrote in his diary: 'People are expecting the armistice any day now,' adding, 'though the Huns show no signs of offering to sue.' On that evening the Allies reached Antwerp, and Holland erupted with jubilation at the prospect of imminent liberation.

In Britain there was open speculation that Germany would soon capitulate. Even before the end of August 54 Base's senior officers had begun to give serious thought to what activities might have to be organized to keep hundreds of boisterous, unemployed airmen occupied in the event of a sudden end to hostilities. This was in contrast to their anxious discussions only a month before, when Woodhall Spa's medical officer pointed out that most other ranks had had no leave for six months, and that this was becoming a source of open unrest. Not the least of his concerns was the growing and 'ill-tolerated' harassment of young WAAF personnel.

Now, a month later, everything had changed, and the social problem had a different complexion. Gibson listened with mounting alarm to contingency plans for extra sports, entertainment and educational programmes following an armistice. At the same time there were fears that the Germans might hit out in desperation. Coningsby's personnel were warned of the risks of sudden gas attack and everyone was urged to be 'gas-minded'.

Seized with panic that the war might end before he could properly rejoin it, Gibson increased his agitation for consent to fly on more operations. It appears that Cochrane had already given consent for him to fly occasionally, provided that his role was non-participatory and that the targets were in areas which would minimize the risk of him falling into German hands if he were to be shot down. Bomber Command's reluctance to return Gibson to operations possibly stemmed as much, or more, from his security status and value as a public figure, as from concern for his personal safety.

Gibson was therefore at least able to watch some daylight operations, although on each occasion he was accompanied by a highly experienced colleague. On 15 August he flew with Sqn Ldr 'Count' Ciano (so called because of the eponymous Italian foreign minister) in one of 54 Base's two Lockheed Lightnings* to observe 5 Group's daylight attack on the Luftwaffe base at Deelen in Holland. A few days later Gibson flew in the Lightning again, this time following the bomber stream to Fécamp. Then on 10 September Gibson was accompanied by the veteran controller Woodroffe, this time in a Mosquito, in order to take cine film of a large attack on Le Havre.

Watching, however, was much less fulfilling than leading. These experiences simply tantalized him. The more he was offered, the greater

---

* During August 1944 it is believed that there were two P38s at Coningsby undergoing evaluation for use by controllers. It appears that one was a single-seat aircraft, subsequently exchanged for a two-seat 'droop snoot' aircraft with a glazed nose. (Gibson flew to the Lockheed maintenance base at Langford Lodge in Northern Ireland on 16 September to collect this aeroplane.) Correspondence between Harris and Cochrane shows that if trials were successful there was an intention that four Lightnings should be added to the strength of 627 Squadron, for the use of the controller and his deputy.[7]

was his desire. Surrounded by controllers and mindful that his destiny, like that of his immediate predecessor as BASO, lay in permanent retirement, Gibson pleaded to take a more active part. 54 Base's CO, Air Comm. Bobby Sharp, may well have been sympathetic, for of him it was said at the time that he flew 'on every raid that higher authority would allow'. Cochrane visited Coningsby on three occasions during August, and with him too Gibson pressed his case. However, Cochrane made it clear that if Gibson was to take any serious part in future sorties, he should undergo proper training.

At the start of the last week in August a new officer joined the staff of 54 Base Headquarters. He was Flt Lt James Warwick, posted to Coningsby as the station navigation officer and promoted to acting squadron leader in accordance with the status of the post. 'Paddy' to his friends, Warwick was a man of gentle personality who had completed two tours. His second, with 49 Squadron, had included difficult targets such as Peenemünde, and four trips to Berlin. Several sorties had been dogged by mechanical failure and during two they had been attacked by fighters. Warwick's skill as a navigator earned mention in the squadron's records and, following a commission at the end of September 1943, a Distinguished Flying Cross. At Coningsby Warwick was screened from operations. In theory, he was safe.

Gibson's semi-suspension from operational flying meant that he had no regular navigator. On 2 September he borrowed 627 Squadron's Mosquito R (KB213), which was then on extended loan at Coningsby for the use of 54 Base controllers. His purpose was a flight to Wick in north-east Scotland and Scatsta in the Shetlands. This was the longest trip in a Mosquito that Gibson had yet made, and his lack of type experience became evident when he reached Scatsta and attempted to land. Scatsta was a small airfield which served as support base for the nearby flying-boat station at Sullom Voe. The RAF shared it with a flock of sheep. Wedged between hills to the south and a marine inlet to the north, the shorter of its two runways started at the foot of a hill, ascended a rise and then sloped down to the sea. Landing at such a place required even finer judgement than the skills he had acquired using the small field at Wellingore. His first approach was abortive, the second equally unsatisfactory and it was only at the third try that he managed to put the aircraft down.

Meanwhile, in off-duty hours Gibson was again working on *Enemy*

Coast Ahead. (Propagandists had already begun to quarry from it. A month or two before, a rather silly journalistic sketch of Gibson which drew from the book had appeared in a book entitled *Air Aces*, a compilation of portrait photographs of RAF celebrities by Gordon Anthony, promoted by the Air Ministry's Public Relations Department.) Around the end of August the full typescript was returned to him. It had been full of frank, opinionated comments, quintessentially Gibson, which were now struck out with blue pencil.

The censors had excised his political views, such as:

It wasn't purely the fault of the rotten government, the Yes men and the appeasers who had been in power too long. It was the fault of everyone for voting for them, for that man Baldwin when he said that he would have lost the election if he hadn't planned for disarmament.[8]

They softened his social opinions by eliminating the adjectives he used to describe the socializers in the Oxford pub he visited with Freddy Bilbey on the eve of the outbreak of war:

. . . but what a *rotten* crowd to be seen in that place – *drunken*, long-haired, *pansy-looking* youths, mixed [sic] with foppish women. They so disgusted me that I asked Freddy if they were undergraduates. His reply was perhaps best of all. 'Good Lord, no!' he said. 'They are the types who try to look like undergraduates.'[9]

The deletion of comments about the men alone says as much about the censors as about Gibson. The publishers cut the whole passage.

His cheerfully intolerant views of Britain's lower classes were systematically purged. Thus in the original text Gibson described Lincoln as a city of 'dull unimaginative people', which was first modified to 'dull but homely' and later simply to 'homely'. Farmers in the manuscript were regularly called 'yokels' and Gibson's actual view of Pulford, his flight engineer on the Dams Raid, was not that he was 'a sincere and plodding type' but that he 'was a bit of a dummy'. The 'Little dark-haired maids with the same black stockings with holes in the heels' found in Brighton in the published book were originally 'Dirty, evil-smelling maids with the usual black stockings'. Other changes in this passage illustrate the MoI's concern to project a more subtle and wholesome picture of British society than the fiercely intoler-ant class-based view in Gibson's mind. Even the 'little packed restaurants' which annoyed Gibson in Brighton re-emerge as 'cosy but small'.

Gibson had been as unsparing of the wealthy and of ineffectual senior officers as he was of farmers and the lower classes. An old man who 'looked of foreign extraction' in the book looked 'like a rich Jew' in the manuscript. Out came the blue pencil in defence of Gp Capt. Emmett, Scampton's station commander at the outbreak of war and one of those censured by Ludlow-Hewitt following the submarine episode, of whom Gibson wrote: 'He did not have a lot of brain and found the going pretty tough.' And of another: 'Looking back, I do not think he had much idea of what was going on.' King Leopold of Belgium, a 'bad type' in the book, was 'a bastard' in the original. And so on.

The author seems to have accepted these changes without complaint, but he reacted more vigorously to queries and proposed excisions concerning operational matters. 'All this is out of date,' Gibson wrote in response to the sidelining of a passage on Pathfinder methods. Against a query of his description of a bomber stream he wrote, 'Well known to Jerries', and beside a criticism of his account of target indicators he commented, 'The Germans even imitate them.' His exasperation over pedantic cuts in the interests of security is often evident. 'Press reports have covered this,' he wrote in reaction to the editing out of terminology to do with AI, adding as an afterthought at the top of the page, 'and German nightfighters are ahead anyway.'

Gibson wrote most of his reactions on slips of paper pinned to the pages concerned. Here and there he found that he had trodden on more sensitive toes than those of bureaucrats. His approval of the policy of using the bomber to choke oil supplies attracted someone's attention. The Oil Plan was then being implemented against Harris's will. At this point in his typescript Gibson found vigorous sidelining in red crayon – the first and last indication that his book had been read by someone other than the wielders of the blue and lead pencils.

Gibson completed work on the manuscript in the same week as the Allies reached Antwerp. Rumours circulated that the German retreat had become a headlong rout. Gibson's conversations with senior officers and official visitors such as Sir Archibald Sinclair all convinced him that the war was about to end.

On Sunday 17 September the prospect – in Gibson's frustrated eyes

virtually the threat – of an armistice seemed closer than ever. Within a
week or two, maybe within days, the war could be over. That morning
services and prayers of thanksgiving were held at parish churches to
commemorate the Battle of Britain. Their hymns and prayers were
drowned by the clamour of thousands of engines as the first waves of
1,399 aircraft carrying paratroops and towing gliders set forth for
Arnhem. This was the opening of Operation Market-Garden, the attempt to seize a crossing of the Lower Rhine and force a corridor to it
from the Dutch borders.

Next day there were no operations, but Gibson received a visit from
an old colleague. Since July John Searby had been working at High
Wycombe as Bomber Command's navigation officer, a job which periodically took him out to airfields in Lincolnshire and Yorkshire, and on
this showery morning brought him into Coningsby. Searby found
Gibson in reasonable spirits, but discontented. They walked to a hangar
in which was parked a Mosquito equipped for low-level marking.
Gibson enthused about new tactical possibilities for its use. The problem
was to find an opportunity to put them into practice before the war
ended.[10]

Part Ten

JACK

19/20 September 1944

jack . . . pike, esp. young or small one

*Shorter Oxford
English Dictionary*

Never to bid good-bye,
Or lip me the softest call,
Or utter a wish for a word, while I
Saw morning harden upon the wall,
Unmoved, unknowing
That your great going
Had place that moment, and altered all.

Thomas Hardy, 'The Going',
December 1912

Targets

Towards 9.00 a.m. next morning, Tuesday 19 September, a group of staff officers gathered in Bomber Command's underground operations room near High Wycombe, awaiting the arrival of their commander-in-chief. Air Chief Marshal Sir Arthur Harris's 'morning prayers' followed a routine. If this meeting ran true we can imagine Harris entering at the stroke of nine, removing his hat, and lighting a Camel cigarette. We may also suppose that he asked his usual question, 'How did we get on last night?' and that he received a short report of 5 Group's highly successful attack on Bremerhaven.

Harris would then have turned to the programme for the day, which came at a turning-point in the governance of Bomber Command. Since April the force had been under the direction of the supreme Allied commander for Overlord. SHAEF had insisted that the overriding commitment of Bomber Command should be to tactical support of the invasion. Harris considered this an unwelcome diversion from his aim of bludgeoning Germany to her knees by the bombing of her cities. Nevertheless, he had co-operated, and with highly effective results. In August SHAEF had authorized a series of area attacks on German cities, and only the previous week the combined chiefs of staff had agreed to resume direct control of Strategic Bomber Forces. The directive which followed ordered Harris to concentrate on Germany's oil industry – a priority he found irksome – but on Tuesday 19 September this had yet to arrive, and that week found him looking forward to renewed all-out assault on German cities. It was a question of how many weeks remained in which to attack them. The mood throughout the Allied forces was expectant and impatient.

This was the context in which an Intelligence officer handed Harris a list of priority targets. SHAEF's immediate concerns included the need to gain control of the approaches to Antwerp and the capture of Channel ports which remained in German hands. Support might also be needed for Operation Market-Garden which was in its third day and running into serious trouble.

Dr Spence, the chief meteorological officer, would then have given a weather briefing. Conditions were dominated by an anticyclone centred north-east of the British Isles. This was moving away eastwards. A trough of low pressure approaching from the Atlantic would spread cloud and rain into north-west Scotland, but was not expected to interfere with any operations Harris hoped for. More troublesome were fog and low cloud over Bomber Command's airfields in eastern England. The fog was expected to disperse, but cloud would linger. Visibility over the Continent was variable: reports collated from Allied units in northern France and Belgium mentioned low cloud and dense haze in some areas and clear areas in others. The anticyclone was being challenged at its margins by other weather systems. Apart from the trough approaching from the west, another area of low pressure was moving up from Spain. That would need to be watched, for it was expected to spread thundery conditions. It was predicted that fog would return after dark.

Conditions over Germany looked operable, but there was concern about the fog and cloud. Harris needed to be sure that his crews could regain their bases. If fog came late in the night then a target well inside Germany could be selected, but if it was going to form sooner he would have to settle for a target which was closer to hand.

Even as this discussion was in progress, a Mosquito of 1409 Meteorological Flight was taking off from Wyton near Huntingdon for a Pampa sortie to investigate weather conditions over the Low Countries and the western edge of the Ruhr. Flown by Flt Lt J.M. Briggs with Fg Off. J.C. Baker as his navigator, the Mosquito departed at 09.15 on a route which would take it to Arnhem, south-eastward past Cologne, south to Wiltz in Luxembourg and then back to England across Belgium. Briggs and Baker would be airborne for three hours.

At High Wycombe provisional target choices were made. Late that afternoon a force of 770 Lancasters and Halifaxes would bomb German troops in support of Operation Undergo, the reduction of the Calais pocket. Smaller forces would deliver daylight attacks against tactical targets, including a flying-bomb site. Later, a contingent of 8 Group's Light Night Striking Force Mosquitoes would visit Whitebait (Berlin). Finally, ever eager to maintain pressure against German cities, Harris chose a further target for attack that night by 5 Group alone. Salmon in the whimsical fish code of Bomber Command, this was the city of Bremen.

The conference ended at about 09.20. Harris departed for his office, leaving his deputy, Robert Saundby, to supervise the planning of routes, times and diversionary attacks. Within minutes the targets were notified to the Groups by scrambler telephone, followed at 10.25 by a Preliminary Warning Order Signal which was teletyped to 1, 3, 4, 6 and 8 Groups, alerting them to prepare aircraft for the attack against Calais. 5 Group was ordered to ready 200 Lancasters, with ten Airborne Cigar (ABC) Lancasters from 1 Group, for the attack on Salmon.

Thirty-five minutes later a fresh signal was sent to the Groups in which plans for the day had been curtailed. The projected daylight attack by Lancasters and Halifaxes was cancelled. The reason is unclear, but may have had to do with the mist and cloud which had delayed the departure of the 1st Polish Parachute Brigade and American 878th Airborne Aviation Engineer Battalion to reinforce the assault on the bridges at Arnhem and Nijmegen. Both units were due to depart from airfields in 5 Group's area. The Poles had been due to take off at 10.00, with transport and artillery to be lifted separately in gliders from airfields in the Cotswolds. Poor weather caused the parachute drop to be postponed to 15.00. Even then conditions were not suitable and the drop was rescheduled for the next day. At mid-morning, however, this further delay was not anticipated, and the risks of manoeuvring two large air fleets over the Channel during the afternoon may have been considered too great.

At 11.25 Bomber Command's Action Sheet Signal was teletyped to the Groups, ordering varying contingents of Lancasters, Halifaxes and Mosquitoes to attack tactical targets between 16.00 and 17.00 that afternoon. Whitebait was now deleted from the day's plans. 8 Group's Mosquitoes were directed instead to raid Skate – Brunswick – one of a diminishing number of proscribed German cities which hitherto had escaped serious damage. Plans to raid Bremen in the evening remained unchanged. The timing, marking and routing for this attack were left to the discretion of the AOC 5 Group, Sir Ralph Cochrane.

HQ 5 Group's planning staff at Morton Hall in Lincolnshire embarked upon the usual preliminary consideration of the zone map and photographs of their evening target. So sophisticated were Bomber Command's aiming methods by this stage in the war that the Target Signal detailed four particular districts of the city for destruction and condemned them in order of priority. The marking plan accordingly required careful consideration, and the raid would have to be co-ordinated by a controller. These matters were discussed towards midday at the Flight Planning Conference which linked the Group and station operations rooms by a loudspeaker-telephone. Out on Lincolnshire's airfields petrol loads were calculated and some 650 tons of bombs were drawn from storage and trundled on trailers, to be hoisted up into the long bellics of waiting Lancasters. Autumn ground mist had dispersed and some training flights began.

Shortly after noon Flt Lt Briggs and Fg Off. Baker touched down at Wyton. They had completed their meteorological reconnaissance without incident, although near Cologne they had seen 'a very suspicious-looking contrail' which was 'almost vertical with its base at about 30,000 ft', apparently the trace of a V2 rocket. Briggs reported stratus and altocumulus with 1/10 cumulus over Holland and large clear areas over the rest of the route.

Immediately after lunch it seems that a further planning meeting was held at High Wycombe. Contrary to expectation, reports of weather over the Channel and the Low Countries indicated that visibility was deteriorating. Nevertheless, some 164 resupply aircraft and 43 gliders were finally taking to the air for the delayed third airlift to Arnhem. The combination of uncertain weather and the imminent passage of more Allied aircraft across the Channel to Holland introduced complications unforeseen even a few hours previously. It was decided that one of the raids scheduled for late afternoon should be abandoned.

Meanwhile, Stirlings and C47s followed by tug aircraft towing serials of gliders were crossing the Channel. Nine Stirlings and four C47s were shot down. Several gliders released prematurely and came down in the sea. Others force landed in England or Belgium. The remainder continued, to be savaged by flak on the approach to Arnhem.

Market-Garden was running into trouble. Although the northern end of the bridge at Arnhem had been seized two days previously, the force which held it was now much depleted, and the drop-zones for its resupply had been overrun. The bridge at Nijmegen still eluded capture. The armour of XXX Corps which should have driven north-ward through Eindhoven and Nijmegen up to Arnhem was two days behind schedule. Slippage in Market-Garden's timetable had allowed reinforcements of men, artillery and armour to be rushed into Holland from Germany.

The desperate position of the airborne troops was known to Harris and his group commanders, to whom daily Intelligence summaries were circulated. AVM Bennett, the individualistic commander of Bomber Command's Pathfinder Force, was so moved by these reports that he telephoned Saundby to propose that his crews should drop supplies. As the day passed, fresh reports confirmed that Market-Garden was on the verge of failure. Bennett again telephoned Saundby, pleading that 8 Group should be allowed to put down supplies. Bennett's offer was rejected, but the problem of Arnhem was evidently in Saundby's mind.

So too was the weather. Revised forecasts now suggested that fog might return sooner than had been anticipated and that the cloud base over 5 Group's airfields would descend in the evening. Would deteriorating visibility and low cloud threaten the safety of returning crews? Possible precautions would be to bring forward the time of the attack on Salmon, or divert the 5 Group force to a closer target. Worries over the weather had existed all along, and a reserve target had been selected at the morning conference. By mid-afternoon the decision to change targets was taken. 5 Group's Lancasters would now go to Jack, the twin towns of Rheydt and Mönchengladbach which lay only a few miles inside Germany. Jack was a target where Harris had unfinished business. The towns had been raided ten nights earlier, but destruction had been incomplete.

Mönchengladbach was closer to Lincolnshire than Bremen, but not substantially so. In any case, Bomber Command seldom flew direct to an objective. Diversionary legs were introduced to deceive German defences and when these are included the round trip to Mönchengladbach might be no more than twenty minutes to half an hour shorter than to Bremen. Nevertheless, as events turned out, the difference of an hour between weather conditions for returning aircraft was to be large.

It is not clear if Harris or Saundby chose Jack on his own initiative, or whether the change was at the prompting of SHAEF. Rheydt and Mönchengladbach formed an important centre of railway communications between the cities of Cologne and Aachen, Eindhoven and the Ruhr. Harris may have perceived that the safety of his crews, SHAEF's desire to choke the reinforcement of German forces that opposed Market-Garden, and his own strategic aims could all be answered by transferring the force intended for Salmon to a place which merited area attack and was also an important communications nexus. Whatever the reasoning, at 15.50 yet another signal was sent to 5 Group. The raid on Salmon was cancelled.

Notification of the new target followed fifty-five minutes later. This was a confirmatory signal. HQ 5 Group had already been advised by telephone that the force being readied for Salmon would be used with bomb-loads unchanged to attack Jack. The first of 5 Group's own Task Signals giving details of the attack on Jack was sent only ten minutes after its formal notification from Bomber Command at a quarter to five. 5 Group's Task Signal to its own bases and stations went out half an hour later. The stated aim was to 'complete destruction of enemy industrial centres'.

Late changes of target were common, but this alteration left little time to revise the evening's plans. Although the Lancasters were bombed-up and fuelled, less than two hours remained in which to hold a fresh Flight Planning Conference, settle the marking plan and brief crews. Moreover, the new marking plan was unexpectedly complicated.

As Main Force crews congregated at Messes for their pre-operational meal, the marker leaders and squadron commanders assembled for the second Flight Planning Conference that day. 5 Group attacks at this stage in the war followed a practised routine. Targets were illuminated and marked ahead of the Main Force by what was in effect 5 Group's own Pathfinder Force. Lancasters of 83 and 97 Squadrons provided illumination and flare support, while 627 Squadron's Mosquitoes undertook low-level precision marking. On this evening, however, there was a departure from normal practice. Group announced that there were to be three areas of simultaneous attack, designated Red, Green and Yellow. The Main Force was to be similarly subdivided. Nine Mosquitoes of 627 Squadron would mark the targets, in three groups of three.

The Red sector focused on the town centre of Rheydt. This was the primary target and was to be 'fully controlled', meaning that an experienced controller like Owen or Woodroffe would monitor the marking and co-ordinate the bombing of the Main Force. The seat of the Green Force's attack was about two and a half miles away in an industrial area towards the north-western edge of Mönchengladbach. The marking-point here was the centre of a large factory. Yellow sector's focus lay in the north-eastern region of the town, not far from the railway station, roughly one and a half miles from the Green marking-point. In the event of difficulty in attacking Mönchengladbach, the controller was to divert aircraft to Rheydt. H-hour was to be at 21.45. Counting back from H-hour (21.45) it was decided that the First Flares should fall at 21.35. This would allow about eight minutes for marking.

A little after 17.45 the Main Force crews received their briefings. Their outward route went first to Clacton, thence south-eastwards on a track which took them across the continental coast between Dunkirk and Ostend and then ran roughly parallel to the Franco-Belgian border. Thus far their journey would be over Allied-held territory and, until the next turning-point, the Lancasters were instructed to fly with their navigation lights on, to minimize risks of collision. At a point a little beyond Givet in the Ardennes the Lancasters would turn north-east, heading now towards Cologne. Near Aachen the Force would turn again, flying north for the few remaining miles to the target.

The changes of direction were designed to outwit the German defences. In a further effort to baffle them a subsidiary force from 100 Group, consisting of ten Stirling IIIs of 199 and 171 Squadrons and two Fortress IIIs of 214 Squadron, would continue to fly eastwards from turning-point B, dropping Window to give the impression of an attack aimed at Mainz or Frankfurt. The diversionary force was to be accompanied by three Fortresses equipped with Jostle – a device for the jamming of enemy nightfighter R/T transmissions.

100 Group was instructed to contribute seventeen Intruder Mosquitoes, long-range nightfighters whose task was to harass Luftwaffe aircraft in the vicinity of their home airfields. German nightfighters would themselves be hunted by Serrate Mosquitoes carrying equipment that enabled them to home in on radar transmissions of German defenders. The Main Force included ten ABC Lancasters from 1 Group. In addition to a normal bomb-load, an ABC aircraft carried an extra wireless transmitter and a German-speaking wireless operator to jam directions given by German nightfighter controllers.

The route home ran more or less directly across Holland and the North Sea, with a landfall at Yarmouth. Directions on heights were emphasized at the briefings: no aircraft was to fly below 10,000 feet on the return journey until the continental coast had been crossed. The return route passed over the Allies' thrust from the Dutch border towards Arnhem, to either side of which lay substantial German forces and concentrations of flak.

5 Group's Task Signal had directed that the controller and marker leaders were to be appointed by the commander of 54 Base, Air Comm. Sharpe. The marking plan was unorthodox and called for special expertise. Logically this would be a job for one of 5 Group's regular controllers, or for any of the well-qualified senior pilots of 627

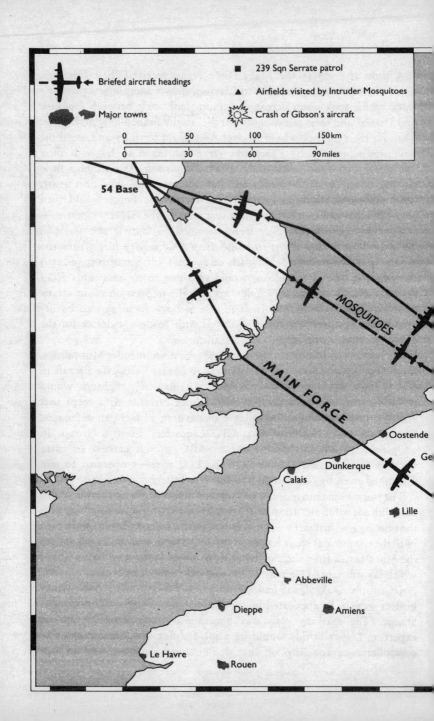

Briefed aircraft headings

Major towns

■ 239 Sqn Serrate patrol

▲ Airfields visited by Intruder Mosquitoes

☀ Crash of Gibson's aircraft

| 0 | 50 | 100 | 150 km |
| 0 | 30 | 60 | 90 miles |

54 Base

MOSQUITOES

MAIN FORCE

Oostende

Ge

Dunkerque

Calais

Lille

Abbeville

Dieppe

Amiens

Le Havre

Rouen

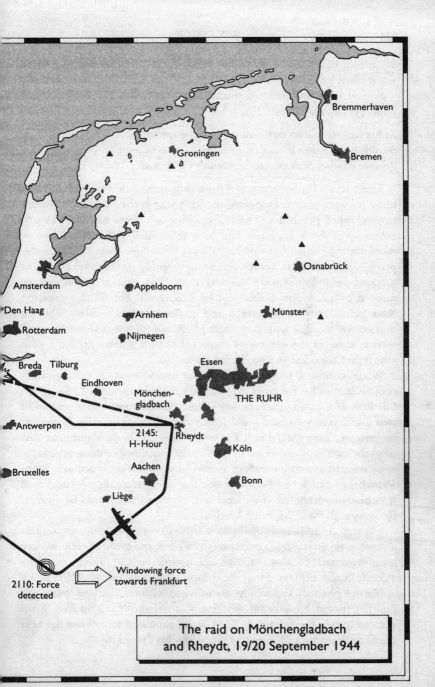

Bremmerhaven

Bremen

Groningen

Osnabrück

Amsterdam

Appeldoorn

Munster

Arnhem

Den Haag

Rotterdam

Nijmegen

Breda   Tilburg

Essen

Eindhoven

Mönchen-
gladbach

THE RUHR

Antwerpen

2145:
H-Hour

Rheydt

Köln

Bruxelles

Aachen

Bonn

Liège

Windowing force
towards Frankfurt

2110: Force
detected

The raid on Mönchengladbach
and Rheydt, 19/20 September 1944

Squadron. But none of them was selected. Instead, the task was to be undertaken by Gibson.

Several 627 crews reacted to this news with incredulity. One of the pilots present recalls:

At briefing, we had an extraordinary surprise sprung on us. The Controller for the night was not to be one of the normal 54 Base Controllers but none other than the Base Air Staff Officer, the Gallant Guy himself.[1]

There was a further stir when it was announced that there were to be three marking-points. Dispersed marking was untried and ran contrary to established principles. True, in recent weeks there had been experiments when the Main Force had been subdivided and bombed two or more aiming-points, but this had always been done from one marking-point. Sometimes, as on the previous evening at Bremerhaven, the marking-point lay outside the target area, so that it would not be masked by smoke or snuffed out by explosions. But on this occasion three points were to be marked and bombed simultaneously. Believing that no one familiar with their methods would suggest such unrehearsed tactics, some of the 627 crews suspected Gibson's hand behind a plan which they regarded as a recipe for confusion.

While Gibson's lack of relevant experience was a talking-point, responsibilities for the marking had been placed in practised hands. Sqn Ldr Ronald Churcher, one of 627's flight commanders and a veteran of two tours, was appointed both deputy controller and marker leader for the primary target. Flt Lts R.L. Bartley and L.C.E. de Vigne – at that time the two most accurate of 627's pilots in dive-bombing practice – were selected as marker leaders for the Green and Yellow sectors. When Mönchengladbach had been bombed ten days before, crews had found it virtually undefended. If all went well perhaps there would be no need for Gibson to involve himself much at all.

5 Group controllers normally flew from Coningsby. However, on this afternoon no serviceable aircraft was available, and towards early evening a call was made to Woodhall Spa, requesting the loan of 627's stand-by aircraft. It was explained that the controller would come to collect it.

Eve telephoned, apparently on impulse. Gibson sounded busy and faintly irritated. He asked if anything was wrong. 'No,' said Eve. 'I just wanted to talk to you, that's all.' Gibson promised to call her the next morning, hung up and went to change into his flying kit.

Flight Out

Around 18.45 the Flare Force Lancasters at Coningsby embarked upon their start-up routines, then edged forward to join a noisy procession which filed along the perimeter track. Lancaster F of 83 Squadron was the first away at two minutes past seven. Twenty-five more followed at intervals of around a minute, the last leaving at 19.27. As usual, their going was watched by a knot of waving spectators who included ground crew, aircrew who were not 'on' that night and WAAF friends and sweethearts. As the well-wishers dispersed, a few went to the station cinema. The film that evening was *Crash Dive*, starring Tyrone Power and Dana Andrews.

The faster Mosquitoes departed later than the Flare Force. This left the best part of an hour in hand, but Gibson still had to go over to Woodhall Spa to collect his aircraft. His navigator for the evening was to have been a recently tour-expired officer from 627, but at the last minute he reported sick. Gibson turned to Coningsby's new station navigation officer, James Warwick.

Charles Owen briefed them. His advice was of special relevance, for it was he who had controlled the raid on Mönchengladbach nine days before. 'Nice little trip to the Ruhr' Owen noted in his diary afterwards. 'Target was only ten minutes flying past the front line and was almost entirely undefended. Few searchlights, but no light flak and I got a good view from 4,000 ft of what was going on. Good prang and some nice fires burning when we left.'[2]

Owen reminded Gibson that he could be out of enemy airspace within ten minutes, advising that he should return south-west from the target into France at medium height, and then set course for England. Gibson began to argue, saying that he would fly direct to England, and at low-level. Owen warned him that all aircraft had been instructed to remain above 10,000 feet until the Dutch coast was crossed. Again Gibson cavilled. He was going to fly home low.

Around 18.30 a car arrived to take them for the three-mile drive to Woodhall Spa. At Woodhall they were told that Mosquito R KB213 had been prepared for them and now stood loaded with four TIs – presumably one each of the three different colours, plus one for cancellation – and flares. Inexplicably, Gibson rejected this aircraft and demanded another. After an argument it was agreed that he should take Mosquito E KB267. This had been assigned to Flt Lt Peter Mallender and Flt Lt Wallace Gaunt, who were now given KB213.

The change, recalls Gaunt, was resented. While armourers exchanged the bomb-loads, Gibson went to the flight office to sign out the Mosquito. By an eerie symmetry, the NCO who handed him the Form 700* was none other than the man who had seen him off on his first operation four years before.

Outside at dispersals the 627 crews walked round their Mosquitoes completing external checks. The evening was warm, a little humid, scented by grass and damp earth, the dusk made darker by the heavy overcast. The windsock drooped, scarcely stirred by the faint breeze. Last cigarettes were trodden out on the hard-standings, nervous men unbuttoned for a final pee. Then, soon after half past seven, the pilots and navigators were secured in their aircraft, alert for the signal to start engines. Gibson and Warwick climbed the short ladder into KB267's nose and settled themselves in the cockpit. Warwick put the floor-panel down, one of the ground staff slid the ladder up into the nose and secured the hatch, and Gibson gestured that all was well.

Now the calm was broken by hesitant crackling splutters as propellers began to turn, followed by a growing roar as ten pairs of engines were run up. Gibson's Mosquito taxied forward slowly, the others moving out to follow him to the threshold of Woodhall Spa's main runway. Gibson drew abreast of the control caravan and for a few moments the queue paused. At 19.51 Gibson released his brakes and roared off into the gloom.† Churcher followed a minute later. The remaining eight 627

---

* An aircraft serviceability sheet, presented by the ground crew, signed by a captain when he formally receives an aircraft and takes over responsibility for it.

† Confusion has surrounded the precise circumstances of Gibson's departure, and several sources maintain that he took off from Coningsby. Such details would normally be recorded in the ORB of the unit to which the aircraft and crew belonged. However, Gibson was not within the membership of 627 Squadron and no details of his last sortie appear in that squadron's records. Operations by Coningsby controllers appear to have been made under the auspices of a '54 Base Flight', but no operational records for such a unit have so far been discovered. Eyewitnesses from 627 Squadron's ground crew recall his departure from Woodhall Spa. Their memory is corroborated by KB267's loss card, which gives the time of his departure and leaves no doubt that Gibson and Warwick led the Mosquitoes off from Woodhall.

Mosquitoes left at short intervals, the last taking to the air at five past eight. Within a few minutes their lights had been swallowed up in the dark and it was quiet.

At Yarmouth the markers set course at their prescribed times, using Gee as they headed out across the North Sea to check the accuracy of forecast winds. For all but one the outward trip was uneventful. The exception was Churcher, the deputy controller, who found that an exhaust stub was working loose on his port engine. The propeller was feathered, causing him to fall behind schedule. Unable to make time, he restarted the engine.[3]

Meanwhile, the outward-bound Lancasters of the Flare Force had formed up over East Anglia where they found much cloud below 10,000 feet and occasional light rain. The Main Force was below 6,000 feet as it crossed the coast, now encountering stratus and stratocumulus. The Lancasters maintained this height across Belgium until turning-point B near Givet. From here on, all were supposed to douse their navigation lights, but a few forgot and continued to the target with their lights burning.

The bombers climbed towards their assigned bombing heights between 10,000 and 15,000 feet. As they ascended they ran into cloud at 9,000 feet. The trough of low pressure noted that morning over Spain had moved north and was attended by convection cloud. For most of the rest of the journey the Lancaster crews experienced difficult conditions, with icing in the cloud and electrical disturbances. Sqn Ldr F.W. Twiggs, captain of an 83 Squadron Lancaster, reported 'considerable static and some icing which blocked out Pitot head putting ASI temp[orarily] u/s'. Twiggs elected to fly just below the freezing level of 9,300 feet. The cloud broke up shortly before the target, and Twiggs put his Lancaster into a fast climb to reach the height band of 13,500–15,000 feet assigned to the Flare Force.

None of the outward-bound Main Force aircraft seems to have encountered any significant opposition, and it was not until 21.10 that the Main Force was being plotted by the domestic German defences. By now the bombers were some fifty miles south-west of Liège, and only 100 miles from their target.

The feint offered by 100 Group's Window Force seems to have succeeded. At 21.50 a *Gruppe* of nightfighters was ordered to land, 150 miles south-east of the target. They may have been airborne against the

spurious threat posed by the Stirlings, which had turned for home half
an hour earlier. As the Main Force changed direction for the last time,
sirens began to wail in Mönchengladbach and Rheydt.

At 21.33 (H minus 12) the first wave of Flare Force Lancasters began
to release sticks of seven-inch cluster flares over the target. Photoflashes
and pairs of red flares were interspersed with the clusters and added to the
ominous incandescence that now began to descend over the two towns.

Mosquito markers liked to arrive early and loiter a few miles out to
ensure a prompt appearance over the target. They now had eight
minutes or less in which to identify their marking-points, deliver their
TIs and escape from the immediate area before the Main Force began
to bomb. As the first flares went down the Mosquito crews were
already circling and scanning the ground for their aiming-points.

The Green markers found that the illumination was not ideal. Most
flares were descending over the south and east of the towns, making it
difficult to identify their target. Nevertheless, Bartley, the Green marker
leader, found the factory and attacked it at 21.37 (H minus 8), diving
from 2,000 feet to 700 feet in order to do so. Bartley placed his TIs so
well that they fell through a factory roof. This caused a problem,
because the TIs were not fully visible.

While Bartley positioned his Mosquito to attack, the crew of Green
Marker 2, Flt Lt Peter Mallender and his navigator Flt Lt Wallace
Gaunt, were poised to do likewise. But for Bartley's warning 'Tally ho'
over the R/T their attacks would have coincided. Mallender held off for
several minutes. Both he and Green Marker 3 were aware that Bartley's
TIs were concealed, and neatly bracketed the building, dropping their
TIs to the south-west and south-east of the factory respectively.

The Mosquitoes of Yellow Force proceeded with similar textbook efficiency. The TIs of the Yellow marker leader were placed accurately.
Within four minutes these were augmented by the second and third
markers, although one of Marker 3's TIs did not release. The Yellow
marker leader considered that they had achieved a good concentration.

It was now two minutes before H-hour. Yet at Rheydt, the primary
target, things had gone badly wrong. While the Green and Yellow
marking-points were set aglow, all efforts to establish the Red marking-
point had been thwarted by a series of mischances. Churcher had
arrived and by 21.40 he had identified the target and begun his marking
run. But the loose exhaust stub of his engine blew off and the sudden glare

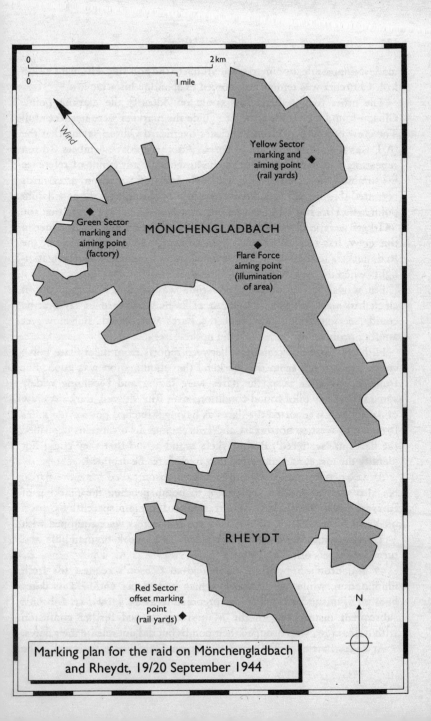

0   2 km
0   1 mile

Wind

Yellow Sector
marking and
aiming point
(rail yards)

Green Sector
marking and
aiming point
(factory)

MÖNCHENGLADBACH

Flare Force
aiming point
(illumination
of area)

RHEYDT

Red Sector
offset marking
point
(rail yards)

N

Marking plan for the raid on Mönchengladbach
and Rheydt, 19/20 September 1944

made it impossible for him to see anything to the port side. His night vision lost, Churcher was temporarily forced to abandon his attack.

The other two Red markers could not identify the marking-point. Gibson found it, but his efforts to guide the markers were unsuccessful. The crew of a 97 Squadron Lancaster overheard Gibson saying that the 'A/P was towards south end of flares'. Another pilot remembers Gibson repeating 'I'm over here', but in the absence of any point of reference his summons was meaningless. Flt Lt K. Anes (97 Squadron) afterwards regretted that he had been unable to assist by dropping a TI as a datum point. His H2S run had been excellent, and it appeared to him that the 'markers were in difficulties'. Fg Off. J. Humphreys, the bomb-aimer in this crew, has recently recalled how he heard Gibson order one of the Red markers to 'Follow me in', saying that he would flash his navigation lights when the Red marking-point was reached.[4]

But it was all to no avail, and time was running out. So Gibson elected to mark Rheydt himself. At 21.42 he was heard to say that he could 'see everything' and that the flares were good. But now yet another problem arose: his TIs did not release.

Hitherto there is a consensus between reports from most Flare Force crews (though not from the markers) that illumination was good. But from shortly after 21.42 the flares were fading and becoming widely spread. One 627 pilot found conditions over Rheydt 'very dark'. A crew of 83 Squadron reported the flares as having stretched out for ten miles from south-west to north-east and two 97 Squadron captains described the flares as 'scattered'. Red markers 2 and 3 said that they could not identify the target and suggested that fresh flares be dropped.

At 21.43, two minutes before H-hour, Gibson called for more flares. He also warned the Red Force not to bomb pending the marking of Rheydt. These instructions were transmitted in plain speech by Gibson on VHF and passed on by W/T. All the Lancasters were equipped with VHF, but some found Gibson's transmissions weak or inaudible and turned their sets off.

97 Squadron's Supporters responded to Gibson's request for fresh illumination, while one Lancaster which had earlier withheld its flares because of misunderstanding also prepared to assist. However, Gibson's subsequent instructions to the Main Force caused further confusion within this crew, who dropped their bombs but did not release their flares.

At 21.43 Bartley called upon the Green Main Force to attack. The

Green aiming-point was almost immediately surrounded by 'large fires' and explosions and as early as 21.45 Main Force crews were being advised that bombing was spreading to the north.

Gibson's primary responsibility, for Rheydt, had still not been discharged. Thus at 21.45 the Red Force received Gibson's order to 'stop bombing' and 'stand by' to await the marking of their aiming-point. Obedient Red Force crews now began to turn away in a left-handed orbit. Such delays were dangerous and feared. Main Force Lancasters were approaching at three miles a minute and, apart from increasing the chances of collision, the order to loiter put them at extra risk from flak and fighters. And the defences were now coming awake. Flak began to intensify as the Main Force arrived. Worse, fighter flares sketching the route of the bomber stream were starting to appear and nightfighters had begun to congregate. Just as H-hour passed a Lancaster perished to a nightfighter. Six minutes later another was attacked and at 21.53 a third was shot down.

Small wonder, then, that an appreciable number of Red Force crews, whether out of confusion or nervous unwillingness to linger, disobeyed Gibson's order and started to bomb the Green sector instead. As Fg Off. R.E. Amery (50 Squadron: Red Force) afterwards reported: 'Scattered bombing. Poor attack. One force were bombing against controller's orders.' By 21.49 Gibson was forced to accept that the Red Force could not be restrained and authorized its remaining crews to attack the Green aiming-point. Gibson's first signal to this effect was transmitted by VHF. His order – 'Attack Green TI direct' – was repeated at 21.52 and again at 21.54 by W/T from the link aircraft. Many Red Force crews obliged. 'Orbited target awaiting Red TIs which, however, did not appear. Bombed Green target indicators as instructed by controller,' reported one. One captain circled for ten minutes before bombing the Green sector and another loitered for seven. By this time the attack was well advanced. The Green markers had been obscured by smoke. Gibson directed crews to concentrate on the fires.

Gibson was now under extreme pressure. His TIs had hung up, and Rheydt was the principal target for which he had special responsibility. His brief had been that if the Green or Yellow targets could not be successfully attacked, he was to order the aircraft to bomb Rheydt. Yet here he was giving orders which reversed this plan. In spite of the stress, however, the evidence is that Gibson remained calm and lucid. One 49

Squadron pilot afterwards reported that 'Controller directed bombing very well.'

It was thus doubly ironic that by the time the Red Force had been diverted to the Green sector, the Red aiming-point had at last been marked. In the midst of trying to steady the nerves of jittery Red Force crews, Gibson had asked the remaining Flare Force for a third phase of illumination. A skymarker went down at 21.48 and by its light Churcher, who had persevered through all the confusion, was at last able to position his Red TIs. They fell accurately, at 21.50 (H plus 5). Flt Lt F.H. Steele (50 Squadron) reported: '. . . bombing on town seemed scattered, but Red TI at 21.51 accurate'. Fg Off. A.O. Wells (50 Squadron) agreed. One of the first to bomb Rheydt, at 21.52, he noted that the Green and Yellow targets had been going 'extremely well . . . Rather a good show. Marking later than usual but good. No trouble from defences but quite a few fighters sighted.'

Following this belated success Gibson now countermanded his earlier instruction and called upon the remaining Red Force Lancasters to revert to their intended target. But by now the attack was not far from its end and, since Gibson had changed his orders twice, his efforts to redirect what remained of the Red Force caused further perplexity. His new instructions were also undermined by the rebroadcasting by the link aircraft of his previous directions. At least one Red Force Lancaster was bombing the Green aiming-point as late as 21.58. Most of the Red Force had in any case been committed to the Green sector, and it was afterwards considered that 'very few' of its members had attacked Rheydt. Nevertheless, between 21.52 and 21.58 a number of Red Force aircraft did attack the Red sector. Fg Off. K.A. Watson (106 Squadron) had been circling the target for fourteen minutes before he 'Bombed a single Red target indicator . . . at 21.58 hrs . . . only a few scattered fires were visible'. Fg Off. C.R. Fairbairn (50 Squadron) 'Bombed and overshot Red TI as directed' at 21.54. He observed: 'Scattered bombing owing to there being two sets of marking . . . Not very satisfactory owing to late TIs causing us to mill around for 15 minutes waiting.' Fg Off. F.W. Firmin (50 Squadron) observed that 'A good attack appeared to develop after a rather difficult bit of marking.'

While the bombing of Rheydt proceeded, 627's Red marker 3 was flying beneath the attack in order to back up on Churcher's TIs. Duty done, Gibson now instructed the markers and illuminators to go home.

This order was given at about 21.57, and was accompanied by a 'Congratulatory message sent . . . to the Flare Force.' Sgt Ron Winton, a wireless operator with 207 Squadron, recalls hearing Gibson 'quite clearly' on the VHF telling the lads to 'beat it for home'.[5]

Journey's End

Gibson's time of departure from the target is not known. The recorded conclusion of the raid was at 21.58, but aircraft were still in the vicinity five minutes later than this. It is unlikely that Gibson left before 22.00; most controllers were in the habit of standing off in a wide orbit around the target, and it was later stated that Gibson 'was last heard of circling the target at 2,000 feet in order to assess results'. The condition of his Mosquito when he left the target is unknown. Nor do we know whether Gibson and Warwick managed to jettison their hung-up TIs. Normal procedure following a hang-up was to climb and release the entire carrier. Whether they did so or not, Gibson stuck to his decision to fly home low, on a direct course across Holland.

Shortly after 22.30 the Mosquito crashed on to the Graaf Hendrikpolder, close to a sugar factory and a farm on the outskirts of the Dutch town of Steenbergen. Several residents later described what they heard or saw.

Mr S.C. Bastiaanse was sitting with his wife in their living-room at about half past ten when they heard an aeroplane. The engines sounded rough. Donning dark coats, they went out behind their house in Blauwstraat. Blauwstraat runs approximately north–south through the centre of Steenbergen, and from their back garden the aircraft was soon in sight, approaching from the east, its cockpit lit by an intense light. Bastiaanse estimated its height at about 3,500 feet. As he turned to comment to his wife, there was a violent explosion and the aircraft dived to the ground.

Anton de Bruyn was night watchman at the sugar factory. A little before ten thirty he caught the sound of a solitary aeroplane. Going outside, de Bruyn saw an aeroplane which seemed to be circling over the town. It was also a source of light, sufficient to silhouette two people in the cockpit.

The engines spluttered. A trail of flame and sparks curved steeply to the ground, followed by an explosion on impact close to the factory.

The brothers Frans and Jan van der Riet, fourteen and sixteen years old respectively, lived at the family farm at Westgraaf Hendrikpolder. The boys heard an aeroplane flying low over the house. The engine noise was odd, making a whistling whine. Moments later they heard an explosion. Running outside, they saw a fire blazing.

Jan van Oers, a blacksmith, lived on the van der Riet farm, close to the site of the crash. From his attic window he saw the aircraft flying low over his house from south to north. The aircraft was burning, and emitting a strange whistling sound. Herr van Oers hurried outside. Climbing on to the Havendijk he met Albert van der Werf who lived near by on a houseboat. Together they walked a short distance along the dyke towards a large fire burning with a bluish flame.

5 Group's bombers, meanwhile, were proceeding homeward. As predicted, conditions over eastern England had deteriorated. By 23.00 the cloud base was down to 1,500 feet, and before midnight the ceiling had descended to 900 feet and fog had formed. Nevertheless, all but one of the surviving Lancasters landed safely. The unlucky exception emerged from the low cloud, swerved to avoid another bomber which was preparing to land and hit the ground.

The first Flare Force aircraft landed at Coningsby at 23.04. Eight minutes earlier Mallender and Gaunt, flying the Mosquito which Gibson had rejected, touched down at Woodhall Spa. All the other marker crews came home without mishap. Mosquitoes were swift: when the last of them reached Woodhall at 23.23, Gibson and Warwick had been dead for less than fifty minutes.

Missing

627 Squadron's pilots and navigators assembled in the crewroom for debriefing. There were the usual anxious glances to see if anyone was missing. Almost everyone was back. Gibson and Warwick were not there, but it was assumed that they had landed at Coningsby. Debriefing

finished around midnight and the men filed out into the warm, damp darkness to board transport back to the domestic site. But as they left, a telephone call came from Coningsby's operations room. Wing-Commander Gibson had not returned; was he at Woodhall Spa?

Fog had settled, and there was speculation that they might have landed elsewhere, but when 627's aircrew met over breakfast the rumours of Gibson's disappearance were confirmed. The news caused a stir, but little surprise. Boyle, de Vigne's navigator on the raid, recalls: 'I thought he would probably kill himself for a rather petty reason, considering that he was not an experienced Mosquito pilot.'[6]

At Coningsby efforts were made to ascertain what had happened. While it was agreed that the raid had been characterized by a 'lack of cohesion and a certain amount of confusion over the target' and its results 'were not all that could be desired', nothing gave any clue to the cause of Gibson's loss. With no evidence for their deaths, 54 Base's staff took refuge in the hope that Gibson and Warwick might have survived: 'Thus, for the moment, the loss is mourned of a very gallant officer, but news of his safety is still eagerly awaited.'*[7] Although efforts were made to prevent it, gossip about Gibson's loss spread rapidly through 5 Group.

In Steenbergen, meanwhile, a number of citizens had made their way on foot and bicycle towards the site of the crash. From a distance there was little to see. The place had been sealed off by German troops soon after the crash. KB267 was unrecognizable. Her heavier components were embedded many feet deep in the polder. The aeroplane had disintegrated on impact, its fragments scattered over a wide area. Fire had consumed much of the splintered airframe. Attempts were made to keep visitors at a distance, but various bits of the aeroplane were later scavenged by bystanders and taken away for recycling.

A Dutch official worked through the scattered debris looking for remains of the crew. He found little. Gibson and Warwick had been blown to pieces and much of what was left of them had been cremated by the intense fire. Warwick's limbless trunk, a piece of skull, two hands and a pair of feet scorched in their shoes were collected in a basket. At

---

* Coastal Command records disclose no evidence that any special aerial searches were mounted in response to Gibson's loss. Air/Sea Rescue units at Lowestoft and Gorleston dispatched boats on 20 September (at 08.30 and 10.00 respectively), but these were routine patrols in relation to Operation Market.

first it was not even clear how many people should be looked for. It was realized that a Mosquito carried a crew of two, but the human remains did not amount to much and there was speculation that one crew member had baled out. The finding of a third hand, however, confirmed that two men had died.

Mr van der Riet is said to have found a wallet that he successfully concealed from the Germans. Other items salvaged included part of an escape kit and Warwick's identity disc, an envelope addressed to 'S/Ldr J.B. Warwick, DFC, RAF Coningsby' and a ring with the initials *JBW* engraved upon it.* The basket holding the pitiful gathering of remains was placed on a barrow and pushed to the mortuary in Blauwstraat. Here the fragments were transferred to a single small coffin and Warwick's name was engraved on its copper breastplate.

Steenbergen was within a few weeks of freedom. The arrival of the Allies at Antwerp in the evening of 4 September had caused panic among the occupying forces and joyous celebration among the Dutch, who for several days remained convinced that the Allies would arrive at any moment. Rumours of imminent liberation were reinforced by the spectacle of remnants of the German 15th Army, 5th Panzer Army and 7th Army fleeing through Holland, discarding their weapons and seizing any means of transport to the German border. On 5 September – *Dolle Dinsdag*, 'Mad Tuesday' – towns and villages throughout Holland had erupted with enthusiasm. Emboldened by the sight of beaten men trekking towards Germany and the collapse of German discipline, jubilant citizens celebrated in streets and squares. At Bergen op Zoom, not far from Steenbergen, exhausted German troops gathered at the railway station under the eyes of jeering onlookers, awaiting trains to evacuate them to Germany.

But the liberators did not come. Over-extended, tired and suddenly cautious, the Allies paused. The delay may have prolonged the war, for while Allied generals argued how best to proceed, a large part of the trapped 15th Army escaped across the Scheldt estuary into Beveland

---

* Gibson's identity disc seems not to have been recovered. It is possible that he was not wearing it and flying incognito. The letter addressed to 'Sqn Ldr Warwick and bearing the name of his station was a flagrant breach of security: aircrew were obliged to hand over such personal items as a matter of strict routine before operations. If this report is correct, could it reflect the hasty circumstances and late hour at which Warwick had been recruited?

and von Rundstedt was brought out of retirement to restore discipline.* Horrocks† later reflected that if he had given orders to bypass Antwerp, the Albert canal could have been crossed and an advance of only fifteen miles north-west towards Woensdrecht would have sealed the Beveland isthmus. The seizure of this area a fortnight beforehand would have denied retreat to thousands of German troops, intensified the panic and might well have precipitated a German collapse in the Netherlands.

Instead, two weeks later, the area was full of German soldiers. In Steenbergen military control had been restored and Market-Garden was on the verge of failure. Nevertheless, the atmosphere of *Dolle Dinsdag* still lingered. The NSB burgomaster had fled, and Dutch administrators and police now exercised greater independence. It was clear to the occupying forces that their eviction was only a matter of time.

Thus it was that the funeral of Warwick became a point of dispute. Chris Herbers, the deputy burgomaster, considered that his remains deserved a ceremonial funeral, with a procession and escort by uniformed members of the Dutch Civil Defence force. The Wehrmacht commander was nervous that the occasion would become a focus for anti-German sentiment. Fearing disturbance, he vetoed Herbers' plan and ordered the coffin to be buried forthwith.

While this argument was in progress news came of a further discovery near the site of the crash. A spectator had been watching children who were foraging among the debris. They appeared to be playing with something. It was a charred sock, bearing a white laundry-tag that read *Gibson*. This meant nothing to anyone present, but the information was passed to the mortuary, where the coffin plate was unscrewed, turned over, and the names of both Gibson and Warwick inscribed.

At three o'clock the German authorities sent word that the funeral should proceed.[8] Herbers, meanwhile, had persuaded the Germans to concede that he and one or two other civic officials should be allowed to take part. A Netherlands flag was draped over the coffin which was placed on a horse-drawn cart. The party then set forth for the Roman Catholic cemetery on the outskirts of the town. The coffin was escorted

* Until 2 July 1944 (when he resigned in anticipation of dismissal) Field Marshal Gerd von Rundstedt was commander-in-chief.

† Lieutenant-General Brian Horrocks was commander of XXX Corps from 4 August 1944, and in the vanguard of the sweep to the Dutch border in early September.

by Herbers, the municipal secretary, the Lutheran pastor, the Reverend van den Brink, and a Roman Catholic chaplain, Father Verhoeven. The procession was swelled by a small spontaneous gathering of townspeople. At the cemetery the coffin was lowered into a single grave. Father Verhoeven prayed the psalm *De profundis*. Reverend van den Brink said the Lord's Prayer in English. The group then withdrew, the cemetery gates were closed and the grave was refilled.

While bits of her husband were being collected in Holland, Eve was at her flat in Aberdeen Place awaiting the telephone call which Guy had promised during their hasty conversation the previous evening. Soon after lunch a messenger boy arrived bearing a telegram, marked PRIOR-ITY. Eve opened the envelope and although the ominous possibilities of such telegrams were well known to her, she afterwards confessed to disbelief at the message which it contained. 'Regret to inform you Wing-Commander G.P. Gibson (39438) reported missing on operational flight on the night of 19/20th September.' Eve subsided into a numb trance from which she was roused by the ringing of her telephone. The caller was Doreen Douglas, who had been with her on the evening that she and Guy had met.

Margaret had been feeling ill when she woke up. Her mother sent her back to bed, where she lay in low spirits. There was no obvious ex-planation for her symptoms. During the morning her thoughts wandered to the possibility that some extraneous event was casting its shadow. Around the middle of the afternoon she decided that Guy was dead.

No one else was so certain. The Germans had no idea that the Gibson who had been buried under their noses was one of the Allies' best-known heroes. In England nobody knew if Gibson was alive or dead and news of his disappearance was withheld from the Press for weeks. The fate that might befall him if he should be taken alive was a subject of conversation at Coningsby. Ron Williams wrote home for the last time about his old tormentor: 'It's not been announced at all yet, but Guy Gibson went for a burton in Mosquito over the Ruhr a week ago – the Germans will have a good time if they get hold of him!'[9]

The Allies reached Steenbergen on 4 November 1944. Witnesses of the crash were interviewed by a Canadian officer, to whom a few personal belongings were handed over. Gibson was publicly listed as missing on 29 November.

Part Eleven

ANALYSIS

1918–1937

The most important thing of all is this cockpit drill business
... All it means is getting to know the position of every tap so
that you can fly the aircraft without having to look down for
the controls. All movements have to be made automatically ...
When flying a big bomber on a misty night, that split second
when the pilot might turn his head away from the instruments
might mean the difference between life and death.

Guy Gibson, *Enemy Coast Ahead*, 1946

Theories

Guy Gibson's crash has prompted almost as much speculation as the fate of Glen Miller or the mission of Rudolf Hess. Plausible theories include pilot error, that he was shot down by light flak, or even that KB267 broke up accidentally. Much later Harris said: 'I believe I know the truth ... I'm afraid his Mosquito broke up. Wood was a funny material to use in a fast aircraft. It had many advantages ... but did not always stand up to the strain.'[1] Cases of structural failure are known; occasionally a wing snapped outboard of one of the engines, and a few Mosquitoes are said to have disintegrated.

Other theories remain to be mentioned, but it is necessary to admit that we do not understand why Gibson and Warwick crashed, and it is unlikely that we ever will. We can list possibilities and identify probabilities. But that is all. The only explanation which can be ruled out is the fatuous allegation that KB267 was sabotaged by disgruntled ground crew.*

Such evidence as we have for Gibson's last operation suggests that the crash was as likely to have been caused by a bundle of factors as by a single stroke of misfortune. Analysts of accidents are well accustomed to a phenomenon whereby a chain of adverse circumstances which individually seem unrelated, even inconsequential, may combine with lethal results. Gibson's last flight looks particularly susceptible to such a line of analysis. In the eyes of many this was an accident waiting to happen. The sortie had been organized in haste. Gibson was ill prepared. He was flying an unfamiliar aircraft. His navigator had not operated

* This ludicrous theory appears in B. Barrymore Halpenny's book *Ghost Stations IV*: 'The story goes that the fuel pipe union nuts leading to the carburation system had been slackened!'[2] In support of this Halpenny cites rumours which he claims (without references) were in circulation 'towards the end of the Second World War'; 'letters which support these rumours'; and two hearsay accounts from former members of the RAF. Leaving aside the historically flimsy basis of these reports, the late hour of Gibson's involvement and last-minute switch of aircraft would have left no time for interference with the fuel system of KB267, even had anyone been minded to do so. Indeed, while Gibson's unpopularity was known, it is difficult to see how he could have provoked someone on another station to attempt to murder him – and the gentle, well-liked Warwick.

for months. Both of them were undertaking complicated duties for which they had not rehearsed. A re-examination of the circumstances which surrounded the raid on Rheydt is thus a useful way to approach an analysis of its end.

Gibson's life at 54 Base followed a year of deepening frustration. For sixteen months the war had passed him by, he had been shunted from job to job and exhibited as a celebrity, and there were few, if any, reserves of consolation left to be drawn from his marriage. After the staff course his logical place would have been as commander of a station or an OTU, where his unusual fund of experience could have been put to good use. But Gibson was temperamentally unsuited to such work. Socially too he had become an outsider. Barred from taking part in operations except as an occasional spectator, he was unable to recapture the special intimacy of operational fliers. Starved of attention, there was no consolation to be found in an inner circle of pilots.*

Gibson's discontent duly declared itself through the resurrection of his least appealing traits. One colleague remembers Gibson as a figure who had 'returned from the USA with a very inflated ego and was not popular in our Mess'.⁴ Others recall him for his pomposity and resistance to advice. A 627 marker pilot who flew on the Mönchengladbach raid began his account by warning: 'Let me tell you, I did not *like* Guy Gibson.'

These impressions must be seen in context: frustration and fear of marginalization, rather than simple self-regard, provide the key to Gibson's temperament in his last weeks of life. Nevertheless, his unpopularity recalls his early days in 83 Squadron, and it is probably significant that his main phases of unpopularity seem to fall to either side of his operational career. Until 1939 he had yet to find a role. After 1943 he had played it.

Even Gibson's prowess as a warrior may have been called into question. Grounded VCs were sometimes looked upon with cynicism and in some eyes Gibson's celebrity had been shaded out by the achievements of Cheshire. Cheshire was certainly the more generally popular figure, a man who went out of his way to acknowledge and

---

* To Frank Boyle, an Australian navigator with 627 Squadron, Gibson at this time 'seemed like a lost soul'.³

respect everybody's role as valued and important. Gibson's feelings towards him were uneasy and he was infuriated by the news of Cheshire's VC. News of the award had been published only ten days before the raid on Rheydt and Gibson's violent reaction to it may have been a factor in spurring him back to operations. About a month before Gibson arrived at 54 Base, Cheshire had taken off in a Mustang III, with no previous experience of the type, in order to mark a target for 617 Squadron. If Cheshire could do that, why should Gibson not seek to fly as a controller in the course of his first night flight in a Mosquito? Ironically, Cheshire looked upon Gibson with a sense of awe and felt himself to be in Gibson's shadow: 'Gibson was a really charismatic figure. He had skill, courage, experience.'[5] Gibson, however, was unaware of the regard in which Cheshire held him, and at Coningsby courage and charisma were not of much relevance to staff work, where his operational experience was out of date and he had no one to lead.

Gibson's last operation recalls earlier moments and remembered voices. Exactly how, for instance, was Warwick recruited? Gibson needed a navigator in a hurry. A sudden demand, cheerful, peremptory and irresistible, has its echoes: 'Come on, Banham – let's get airborne and find sunshine.' We do not know how Warwick reacted to the invitation – nor indeed if it was an invitation. Gibson had no proper authority over individual aircrew at Coningsby or Woodhall Spa, but as BASO he was Warwick's immediate superior. The distinction between a senior officer's wish and a direct order can be slender. Characteristic too is the report that Gibson was enthusiastic about just those unusual aspects of the attack which others regarded as perverse. Then there is the story of the dispute about the route home: 'Guy did not listen. Guy did what he wanted.' And when did he leave Rheydt? Gibson had a record of loitering over targets.

Other memories are jogged by Gibson's lifelong tendency towards monomania. He had always focused on particular things – hobbies, ideas, aims, ambitions, people – to the exclusion of others. Single-mindedness had carried him into the RAF, to Eve and to the dams. 'He was one of the most thorough and determined boys I have ever known,' wrote the warden of St Edward's, Oxford, in February 1945, 'both at school and afterwards, and nothing could move him from his purpose of flying . . .' In 1946 a knowledgeable reviewer of his book shrewdly observed that, 'To it, as to his other jobs, he bent his furious energy, single-heartedly and without self-consciousness racing along at high speed.' One reason why Gibson overrode sense on 19 September was his fear that hostilities were about to end. In 1939 he had been convinced that he would be killed within days. Still alive four years later he fretted that the war would be over before he could once again offer himself to its jaws.

It is not clear when the decision to permit Gibson to make what was subsequently explained as 'one more trip' was taken – if, indeed, such a decision was made at all in the terms in which it was later described. In his essay on Gibson in the *Dictionary of National Biography* Cochrane wrote:

For some weeks Gibson strove hard for permission to fly on operations but met with a firm refusal. However, on the night of 19–20 September 1944, when the main Lancaster force of No. 5 Group was attacking a target involving only slight penetration into enemy-held territory, it was agreed that he should fly in a Mosquito and act as 'master bomber'.

Ralph Barker in his book *Strike Hard, Strike Sure* tells us that Gibson went to Harris and pleaded for permission to return to operational flying.

Harris, quite wrongly according to his own admission, gave in ... Harris agreed that Gibson should fly on just one more raid. But he instructed Cochrane that the target selected must be close to Allied lines, not deep in enemy territory. The raid eventually chosen was a medium-sized attack on München Gladbach and the adjacent town of Rheydt . . .[6]

These accounts invite discussion of three unresolved questions. First, what are we to make of Cochrane's statement that for some weeks Gibson strove hard for permission to return to operations but always met with refusal? Gibson had flown on four operations since June. If Cochrane's words are taken literally, then either he was unaware of Gibson's activities or else he had turned a blind eye to them. Yet Cochrane was both well informed and ruthless in matters of discipline. It seems much more likely that he had assented to the trips flown from Coninsgby, but did so on the grounds that they were non-participatory and went only to the fringes of Occupied Europe.

Second, it is difficult to accept that Rheydt was specifically selected for Gibson's come-back. As we have seen, Bremen was the intended target that night; Rheydt was a last-minute switch and the teletypes show that appointment of the controller was devolved to Sharpe. To be fair to Cochrane, all he tells us is that *it was agreed that Gibson should fly*. Cochrane did not say from whom agreement came. It is possible that Gibson was to have controlled the raid on Bremen, which could be approached from the sea and is not deep inside Germany. This is possible. One of the 627 markers recalls Gibson saying that he would control *four* targets that night,[7] and there were to have been four aiming-points at Bremen. But if that was the case, the statement that Gibson was only to fly to a target close to Allied lines must have been a rationalization after the event.

Third, there is the suggestion that this was to have been 'one last trip'. Cochrane did not say this. Neither did Harris. Harris confirmed Gibson's lobbying and added the interesting detail that Cochrane supported it. But Harris wrote nothing to suggest that Gibson was to be confined to one operation. He confessed only that following pressure from Gibson and Cochrane,[8] 'I quite wrongly allowed him to return to operations.' Far from limiting Gibson to one sortie, Harris may have acquiesced to a number. Very probably he did so at the end of july, legitimizing the Lightning sorties as part of Gibson's preparation for a return to operational flying. All this accords with Gibson's change of outlook in the late summer of 1944 when he began to shed extraneous commitments as a prelude to what he hoped would be a resumption of his operational career. His resignation as PPC for Macclesfield coincided with his posting to 54 Base. Evidently, he was expecting to rejoin the war, at least on an occasional basis.

But there was a catch. Gibson's return to operations was made conditional upon restrictions. The suggestion that a target was to be found for him which required only slight intrusion into enemy airspace was in all probability a *general* condition, calculated to allow him to regain experience of operational conditions, but more particularly to minimize the risk of his capture. Quite apart from the propaganda opportunities which that would have offered, his potential value to German Intelligence was immense. Knowledge of Upkeep was the least of it. His association with Churchill and Harris, his familiarity with 617 and bomber operations generally, and his contact (albeit probably unrealized by him) with figures involved in Tube Alloys, all argued that he should not fall into German hands. His successful campaign for the relaxation of this ban was on condition that any targets to which he

flew should be close to Allied ground. The four previous operations had
followed this pattern. But this only increased his frustration. He balked
at being cast in a role which resembled that of a 'fringe merchant'.

The raid on Rheydt differed from Gibson's four previous operations in
several important respects: it was at night; it was an attack on a defended
German city and Gibson was to be its co-ordinator, not a spectator. On the
earlier sorties Gibson had been accompanied by seasoned colleagues, like
Ciano and Woodroffe, who were fully conversant with current operational
conditions. Warwick, by contrast, had no operational Mosquito experience. Even allowing for the strength of Gibson's desperation, it is
extraordinary that he did so little to ready himself for the leading part that
he craved. Warden Kendall recalled his boy as 'determined' and 'thorough'.
The determination is obvious, but where was the thoroughness?

As BASO Gibson was aware of the need for incessant practice. The
54 Base Operations Reports file contains papers which reiterate the need
for more training of controllers. The schooling of controllers covered
many aspects: radio procedures, codes, enemy countermeasures, low-
level marking – and, of course, the need for mastery of the Mosquito.
According to the memoirs of Hamish Mahaddie, Cochrane's approval
for Gibson's return to operations had been contingent upon Gibson
undergoing a short conversion course at the PFF Mosquito Unit at
Warboys. Mahaddie maintains that Gibson ignored this requirement
and that if Cochrane had been aware of this he would not have
permitted him to fly.[9] It is inconceivable that so uncompromising a
commander as Cochrane would have tolerated any argument from
Gibson that training was unnecessary. In the face of such insistence it
can only be supposed either that Cochrane was misinformed about
Gibson's training status, or that the operation took place in circumstances which caused the issue to be overlooked – or both.

The only relevant tuition which Gibson appears to have received was
a flight he made with Wg-Cdr Woodroffe on 31 August in Mosquito
R KB213 – the machine he rejected on 19 September. The exercise
lasted one and a half hours and involved dive-bombing practice, suggesting that he was being introduced to marking technique. It was customary
for pupil markers to receive demonstrations from their peers and, while
it was feasible for the crew of a Mosquito to change places during
flight, the manoeuvre was chancy. It is just possible that the exercise
began over the airfield, with a landing part-way through to change

places. But it is more likely that the flight was as Gibson described it, with himself at the controls and Woodroffe giving advice. Here again, the tendency for a little knowledge to be dangerous may have fuelled Gibson's over-confidence and impatience.

Gibson's logbook entries break off on 16 September. His logbook was written up at irregular intervals, so it is possible that he made one or two further flights on the Sunday or Monday before the raid. But the fact remains that his logged Mosquito time was nine hours and thirty-five minutes, that very little of this had been devoted to relevant practice and that all of it had been in daylight.

Such unpreparedness is astonishing when it is considered that 627's crews rehearsed daily and that even short breaks would be followed by refresher flying before operations were resumed. A marking attack involved a dive, sometimes a glide, from 2,000–3,000 feet down to around 600 feet, followed by a climb-out of such vigour that the navigator could lose consciousness. The wing-loading of the Mosquito was very high and upon pulling out from a dive the aircraft could continue to sink through hundreds of feet before she would resume level flight or begin to climb again. Conscientious pilots practised diving, dive-bombing and low flying until they were completely accustomed to such tendencies and could allow for them. Gibson did none of these things.

Lack of type experience exposed Gibson and Warwick to other risks. The Mosquito was not an aeroplane which could be abandoned in a hurry. Even on the ground a practice escape through the bottom hatch could take an experienced crew a full half minute. No one knows what occurred in the cockpit of KB267 in the minutes before its crash, but without practice in emergency procedures the chances of either man negotiating a crisis would have been correspondingly reduced.

It was not only flying for which controllers needed constant rehearsal. Raid analyses noted problems with the audibility of the controller's VHF and confusion arising from the mixture of code and plain language. For controllers and markers there were associated disciplines of R/T procedure, which included a speech training course taught by the former Temple Church choirboy Ernest Lough, the memorizing of codes and rehearsal on the Jordan Trainer – an early form of flight simulator which consisted of a rotating table in one of the Coningsby hangars. There is no evidence that Gibson submitted himself to any of these programmes of instruction. At most he had acquired some anecdotal guidance.

In summary, a 5 Group controller normally possessed extensive and regular Mosquito experience, was thoroughly familiar with current operational conditions and had undergone continuing training on the ground and in the air. On 19 September Guy Gibson fulfilled none of these requirements.

By whom, then, was his participation authorized? Remembering the unusual tactics, this was not a raid for a beginner. Unless Gibson had been selected to control the attack on Bremen, two possibilities fit what we know. The first is that in those hectic few minutes after the change of target had been notified, Gibson implored Sharpe to permit him to go and Sharpe assented.

The second possibility is that Sharp was absent when the change of target was notified and that as his deputy at 54 Base Gibson simply appointed himself. This is rather what Harris later implied. In his foreword to *Enemy Coast Ahead* Harris wrote that Gibson 'appointed himself "Master Bomber" the most dangerous and most vital task of all – on his last operation'. Opportunism is further suggested by the entry in 54 Base's ORB: 'It was typical of him to *insist* on undertaking the operation in question, although this was not strictly part of his duties as a Staff Officer.'

The indications that Gibson snatched a chance to fly help to explain the insufficiency of his training. They also accommodate the otherwise baffling problem of why the supervision of untried and potentially awkward tactics should have been entrusted to a novice. Above all, if Gibson was killed *before* he had been properly cleared for operations as a controller this would account for the difference between his own perception of his operational future and the later legend that this was to have been 'one last trip'.

This interpretation might carry the uncomfortable implication that when the full facts of Gibson's inexperience became known, Cochrane and Harris were sufficiently embarrassed by them to be selective in their comments. With the war's end near it was a matter of policy that figures like Cheshire and Gibson should be preserved. Later, Cochrane was reticent about the circumstances of Gibson's disappearance and disinclined to say much about a tragedy for which he seems to have felt some measure of responsibility. Nevertheless, no one sought to contradict the legend of 'one last trip' which circulated after the war. To have done so might have been to concede that the death of one of Britain's greatest warriors had occurred against a background of careless discipline and administrative confusion.

Mosquitoes

The attack on Rheydt was Gibson's first real chance to prove himself since the Dams Raid. Yet, in contrast to that occasion, he was almost wholly unversed in what he had to do. Gibson's position late on this September afternoon was akin to an actor's bad dream, when a large part has to be played, yet no lines have been learned, no movements blocked and no cues rehearsed. But this dream was real and its anxieties were superimposed on normal pre-operational tension which manifested itself in snappy assertiveness. Gibson contested advice, ignored queries about the wisdom of the triple marking and quarrelled.

The change of aircraft is a puzzle. It is not clear whether Gibson demanded the use of KB267 or whether he simply declined to take KB213. He had flown KB213 before and it may be that it possessed some idiosyncrasy which he disliked. Yet such a speculation is difficult to reconcile with the fact that other controllers had used it regularly. Flt Lt Peter Mallender had been due to fly KB267 that evening and was not pleased to be deprived of it:

He took our best aircraft. Our squadron was not blessed with many new aircraft. Most of ours had seen much hard service with various 8 Group Mosquito Squadrons.[10]

Mallender's navigator, Wallace Gaunt, confirms their annoyance: 'I do remember that Guy Gibson was given "our" aircraft, and that this was resented by all concerned . . .'[11]

In fact there was not much to choose between the history of this aeroplane and the one Gibson rejected. Both were Canadian-built B.XXs with Packard Merlins of about the same age. There are no reports of previous battle damage to either machine and their service histories give no hint of mechanical problems beyond the norm. KB267 had suffered a failure of its starboard engine on its first sortie, on 26 July, but this was not unusual for a new Packard Merlin. Fractionally more suggestive is that KB267 did have the makings of a history of hang-ups. A TI hung up on 15 August, and a load of incendiaries had failed to release seven days previously during an attack on Stuttgart. But such incidents were not unusual and in any case it is extremely unlikely that Gibson knew anything about them. If he did, he would have found that KB213 – the aeroplane he rejected – had suffered fewer technical failures than KB267. Indeed, if Gibson refused to take KB213 because he doubted its serviceability, there is a supreme irony in the fact that it was still flying when 627 Squadron was disbanded in 1945.

What else could explain Gibson's demand? If no rational explanation presents itself, what of the irrational? Since KB213 was 627's reserve, did he suspect that he was being provided with an inferior aeroplane? Or did he reject KB213 because of its serial? There is nothing to indicate that he concealed any reverence for fate. He often said that his survival had been due to luck. He flew with a St Christopher in his pocket and often wore two wristwatches; but what does that show? Thousands of aircrew flew with keepsakes, lucky charms or mascots. Some, including Gibson, performed minor propitiatory rituals before they went aloft. But that too was normal. By comparison with the irrationality of the war to which tens of thousands of fit young men had mortgaged their lives, gestures like touching the shoulder of a parachute packer or urinating on a tailwheel seem rooted in sanity.

When all is said, we do not know why Gibson flew in KB267. His agitation may indicate a premonition, a suggestion urged by David Shannon, who remembered Hopgood's resigned certainty before the Dams Raid and had encountered other cases like it. But it may simply be that Gibson's capricious behaviour at Woodhall stemmed from a subconscious admission that he was unqualified for what he was about to do, and that this was concealed by gestures of self-will.

In any case, the ultimate irrationality lies in Gibson's determination to waive his right to safety. The end of the war was in sight. Margaret would be waiting for him at its finish. His fame and connections offered post-war opportunities and no effort had been spared to persuade him to take advantage of them. His survival was assured, if he would allow it to be so. Hitherto his refusal to accept this gift has been explored only with reference to his own psychological needs. Perhaps this underestimates the depth of his humanity. At school he had been noted for his sense of fair play. Churchill had given him unpublished information about the behaviour of the Nazis and the industrialized murder of the Jews. His contact with Vansittart had reinforced an existing hatred of German militarism and the enslavement of European peoples. If any of this contributed to his continuing desire to fight, then that Tuesday

was as good a day as any on which to return to war. The rising in
Warsaw was in its last desperate spasms. Earlier in the day an unusually
modest contingent of 100 men and sixty-five children from the Kovno
ghetto had been gassed at Auschwitz. And 19 September was the Jewish
New Year.

Over the Target

Previous descriptions of the raid have exaggerated Gibson's role. Harris
described the raid as being 'of course, a complete success'. Reports on
the following day spoke otherwise. 'Poor attack' said a pilot from 50
Squadron. 'Attack not concentrated' concluded another. 'Not very
satisfactory' and 'A very poor show on the whole' were further verdicts.
Others took a more buoyant view, but while there were many who
viewed the night's work as a modest success, many who took part
deemed it a partial failure.

Gibson was not responsible for the raid's failings. On the contrary, it
was he who steadied the proceedings when they threatened to slide into
confusion and rallied the attack during its closing minutes. The influence
of a controller's voice, even his personality, could have a marked effect
on the behaviour of the Main Force. Cheshire's persuasive manner once
held them waiting for forty minutes until he was satisfied with the
marking. A controller's ability to quell outbreaks of disorder was a
special gift. During a similar delay on a raid controlled by Woodroffe,
the captain of an orbiting Lancaster had been heard to complain, 'If
we hang around much longer we'll run out of fuel,' to which
Woodroffe instantly retorted, 'Shut up. *I'll* tell you when you run
out of fuel.' After the confusion over Mönchengladbach, at least one
Main Force pilot referred to Gibson's calm and lucid handling of an
awkward situation.

If Gibson emerges with professional credit, it is none the less
important to clarify what he was actually doing. According to a later
account Gibson supervised all the marking and the Main Force attack.
It has also been suggested that the marking of the three points was to

proceed consecutively. The evidence is entirely to the contrary and may in some indirect way have a bearing on the fate which befell him.

627 primary markers routinely worked independently of the controller, identifying their marking-points and validating their accuracy. Several of the Green and Yellow markers who took part confirm that Gibson did not direct them, and add that it would have been unusual if he had done so. The recorded times of marking corroborate this and show that the Yellow and Green marking-points were dealt with concurrently. At this stage Gibson's involvement was restricted to the primary target at Rheydt.

Here we must examine the report that Gibson attempted to mark Rheydt himself and that he experienced a hang-up. The clearest source for this is the Form 541 report for Lancaster C of 97 Squadron, captained by Sqn Ldr S.M. Smith. The report is given in its entirety:

Weather clear. Identified target on H2S. First flares down at 21.35 hrs and at 21.40 heard Marker 1 saying he was going in; he made dummy run. At 21.42 Controller said he could see everything and that the flares were good. Controller made a run but his TIs hung up. Markers said they could not identify and suggested more flares should be dropped. It seemed that markers were not in position as Controller said he could see the whole thing. At 21.43 more flares called for. At 21.45 Red force told to stand by. At 21.49 still no Red markers down, so main force ordered to bomb Greens. At that moment Marker 1 dropped Red on A/P, then main force ordered to bomb Reds with overshoot as at flight plan. All aircraft then told to return to base after bombing. Congratulatory message sent by Controller to Flare Force.[12]

Smith's report clearly differentiates between Marker 1 (Sqn Ldr Churcher) and the controller. Other reports were less explicit. Plt Off. R.H. Lopez stated:

Weather clear, hazy. Visual identification on Marshalling Yards. Arrived shortly after first flares and heard Controller say that A/P was to South end of flares and we headed towards south end of flash [sic] when the B/A saw the railway lines and as H2S was u/s bombs were dropped visually. No markers seen to drop while we were in the target area, although one Mosquito heard to say Tally Ho, but that bombs were hanging up. At 21.49 message 'Attack Green A/P direct['] repeated 21.52 hrs and 21.54 by W/T by Link I. Severe icing conditions encountered on outward trip.[13]

And Fg Off.W.P. Ryan (97 Squadron) reported:

Weather clear, visibility good. Target confirmed on H2S. Flares dropped on time and were sufficient illumination but marker unable to release TIs. First flares died out and Controller called for more flares at 21.44 hrs which we dropped. Later Red TIs were dropped but we were on our way home.[14]

Ryan's statement about 'marker unable to release' might refer either to Churcher or Gibson. Lopez's report that 'one Mosquito heard to say Tally Ho, but that bombs were hanging up' appears to concern a Mosquito other than Gibson's, because his report earlier specifies a message from the controller. Presumably the 'Tally Ho' came from Churcher, and Lopez assumed that Churcher's message about being unable to release his TIs meant that his bombs had hung up.

So the record of Gibson's hang-up really rests upon a single statement. If this statement is accurate – and it looks unequivocal – then the ambiguities in the others are unimportant. However, the fact that there *are* ambiguities leaves room for doubt over whether Gibson did attempt to mark, and whether the report of his hang-up might not have been confused with that experienced by Churcher.*

Uncertainties are multiplied by at least one of the marker leaders, as well as Gibson, having issued directions to the Main Force during the opening stages of the raid. Flt Lt Bartley called upon the Green Main Force to bomb at 21.43 and it may well have been Bartley, rather than Gibson, who at 21.45 cautioned the main Green Force that their bombing was spreading to the north. That Bartley did so seems likely not only because the Green Force attack had opened at his instigation, but also because Gibson was at that time entirely preoccupied with the problem of Rheydt. Multiple control is further suggested by the fact that the various Forces were listening on different frequencies.

From all of this emerges a strong possibility that earlier accounts of the raid itself failed to recognize several strands of disorder which on the following day became perpetuated in official records. The essential points are these: first, contrary to the impression given in some later writings, Gibson was not responsible for co-ordinating the marking or initiating the bombing of all three targets. The attack on the Green

---

* Or Fg Off. J.E. Whitehead and Plt Off. J. Watts, Marker No. 3 (Yellow Force), who attacked at 21.40 and afterwards reported '1 x Y[ellow] TI . . . hung up over target'.[15]

target, at least, was begun under devolved control. Second, Rheydt was not marked on time. Third, Gibson almost certainly tried to mark Rheydt himself, but the contemporary evidence for this seems to pivot on a single source from which all subsequent statements appear to have been derived. When read alone this source is unequivocal, but when considered in conjunction with others there is room for speculation: the account of Gibson's hung-up TIs may have derived from a misinterpretation of messages occasioned by Churcher's difficulty.

54 Base's Operations Record Book stated that Gibson was 'last heard of circling the target at 2,000 feet in order to assess results'. Neither the original source of this information nor the time to which it refers is known, but the reference to Gibson orbiting the target is the last glimpse we have of him until a minute or two before the crash.

In 1963 Ralph Barker asserted that by the end of the attack 'Gibson's Mosquito had been hit'.[16] In 1974 a Dutch newspaper repeated the story that Gibson's Mosquito had been hit by German anti-aircraft fire during the raid and that by the time the machine approached Steenbergen its starboard engine was subsequently 'overheated and useless'. Writing in 1977, Charles Owen considered that Gibson's aeroplane had been hit by light flak after leaving the target.

While it is entirely possible that Gibson's Mosquito sustained battle damage during the closing minutes of the raid, no primary source corroborates the suggestion. All we know is that light flak on this evening was described as 'moderate', that it consisted chiefly of 20-mm green tracer, and that Gibson would have been within its range for the best part of half an hour. When his final message reported from the target was transmitted at 21.57 it contained no suggestion that his Mosquito had been damaged.

The time most often quoted for the crash is 22.38. If Gibson left the target at, say, 22.05, and the wind velocities of the evening are added to the equation, the normal cruising speed of a B.XX Mosquito at low-level would have taken the aeroplane at least seventy miles beyond Steenbergen at the time of the crash. This would suggest either that KB267 had been disabled for all of the journey, or that she had been losing speed progressively, or else that Gibson had set forth at normal speed but was forced to a much slower pace by some mishap *en route*.

If KB267 had been disabled, for example, by damage to the glycol system or the radiator of an engine, then Gibson may well have been flying on reduced power. But if the Mosquito was damaged it seems likely that the full consequences of the problem did not immediately declare themselves, or that Warwick and Gibson assessed it to be less serious than it actually was. If necessary they could have flown south-west and made an emergency landing behind Allied lines in fifteen minutes. Instead, they set course direct for England.

Bomber Command's Interception Tactics Report, issued six days later, stated:

The enemy was . . . able to put some fighters up over the target from the time the bombers arrived and it seems . . . certain that the four Lancasters and one Mosquito which failed to return were shot down by fighters at Mönchengladbach and on the return.

The fighters were hunting at the altitude of the Main Force, above 10,000 feet. It is unlikely that KB267, flying low, was caught by a nightfighter. Mosquitoes were seldom lost in this way. In any case, the phrase 'it seems certain' indicates that the author was speculating. Elsewhere in the same report the cause of loss is given as '4 a/c to fighters, one [Gibson's Mosquito] unknown'.

Last Minutes

If fighter attack can virtually be discounted, it is entirely possible that KB267 was caught by light flak somewhere along the route between the target and the coast. Gibson may even have been shot down by the Allies. During preceding days Allied ground forces had been fighting their way towards the beleaguered airborne troops at Arnhem. On 19 September the Allies' grasp of this narrow corridor was still precarious: it was flanked by German forces and heavily fortified against air and ground attack. This is one reason why the bomber force had been briefed to fly at a respectful altitude. Gibson flew at low-level through a heavily defended area manned by German, American and British troops, all alert to the risk of aerial attack.

Five witnesses agree that the aeroplane approached Steenbergen at low altitude. All likewise concur that the Mosquito was in some way illuminated before the crash. Two reports depict the Mosquito burning while it was still in the air; two others mention a bright light, sufficient to illuminate Gibson and Warwick in the cockpit. One witness states that the aeroplane exploded before it hit the ground; two mention that the engines sounded abnormal and two others reported a jet-like noise emitted by the aircraft during its final seconds.

When these accounts are conflated, all suggest that KB267 was burning before she crashed. References to a bright light, sufficient to silhouette the crew, cannot be explained by the weak cockpit lighting of a Mosquito. The reports of rough-sounding engines could equally suggest battle damage, or some mechanical malfunction such as a faulty fuel pump or contaminated fuel. Either might explain the faltering engine, but not the fire. A damaged fuel line leaking on to a hot engine could cause fire, but an exhaust manifold which had burned out or broken away (not an uncommon problem with Mosquitoes) could also give this impression and account for the references to flames or a trail of sparks. Yet none of these theories is entirely congruent with the statement of one witness that the engines died out before the crash – unless the fact that light travels faster than sound deceived him. Simultaneous engine seizure is difficult to countenance and although it seems certain that KB267 was emitting flame in the air, the weight of evidence is that she did not explode until she hit the ground.

The report from two witnesses that the aeroplane was emitting a whistling whine is curious. This was possibly the distinctive sound of a damaged propeller, or a puncturing of the fuselage or skin of a wing. Either could imply battle damage, or else a collision (for example, with a high tension cable). It seems unlikely that even Gibson would have been flying so low as to collide with a power line, but his inexperience with the Mosquito could very easily have caused him to misjudge the behaviour of the aeroplane during sudden evasive action. Likewise, if the Mosquito was in difficulties because of an engine malfunction, Gibson's inexperience of the type on asymmetric power could have caught him unawares.

The sudden downward plunge of the aeroplane invites several questions. Was this because the Mosquito had become uncontrollable; or could it be that Gibson himself had been injured, and that his ability to

fly the aeroplane had been lost? Engine failure alone would in theory
have offered some prospect for a forced landing, yet most accounts
agree that the Mosquito entered a steep dive in its last seconds. Fire in
one engine, perhaps coupled with loss of aileron control, might have
rendered the aircraft unflyable – a condition exacerbated by Gibson's
inexperience. But the abrupt plunge would also be explained by an
injury to Gibson which caused him to lose consciousness, or by the
result of a stall. Here Gibson's inexperience could have been critical.
Loss of flying speed might have caused him to put the nose down, or
turn towards the dead engine. The handling characteristics of
Mosquitoes flying on one engine varied considerably according to their
age and load, and it was exactly this sort of specialized experience
which Gibson lacked.

Another aspect of the case may be traced back to events over Rheydt.
If, as reported, there was a hang-up, did Gibson remember to climb
after the attack and release the carrier? If not, could it be that a
barometrically fused TI was still in the bomb-bay and became live?
Such TIs would not function until release pulled out the safety wire.
However, occasionally this safety measure could be jeopardized by a
malfunction. If a partly released bomb fell from its carrier into a *closed*
bomb-bay in a way which detached the arming wire, then the TI could
ignite when the aircraft descended below the relevant height. An awareness that the Mosquito was still carrying live TIs may also have
inhibited Gibson from attempting a forced landing. One witness saw
the Mosquito circling and wondered if the crew were attempting to bale
out, a drill which Gibson seems not to have practised. However this
may be, KB267's load of TIs and flares would account for the fierce
intensity of the fire after the crash. TIs of any colour appeared brilliant
white when they burned at close quarters, and the description of the
Mosquito burning with a bluish tinge could be accounted for by the
magnesium alloy in the engine or undercarriage being heated to an
extreme temperature.

Findings

From all that has been said it will be clear that five or six theories answer some of the facts, and that aspects of all or none of them might have played a part. However, there is one remaining possibility, suggested and strongly favoured by several surviving 627 members,[17] which accommodates most – but still not quite all – of what we know. During long flights it was necessary to change fuel tanks, a task often undertaken by the navigator who, upon a signal from the pilot, would operate the fuel transfer cocks which were positioned between and behind their seats. Gibson should have known about this procedure from his flights to Wick and Le Havre. On those occasions he had been assisted by experienced companions. But did Warwick know about it? Even if he did, was he able to judge the settings of the cocks by touch? And in any ensuing hiatus what would have been the effect of their lack of experience working as a team? There had been no time for Gibson and Warwick to build up that essential repertoire of gesture and body language which Mosquito crews required for mutual understanding.

Starved of fuel, one or both engines would have given signs of imminent failure. Under these conditions an attempt to restore power could cause a Merlin to backfire and trail flame and sparks. Loss of an engine could affect other functions, including flaps, electrical and hydraulic systems. All the previously discussed difficulties arising from handling characteristics would now apply. Confusion – even argument? – over diagnosis of the problem, and lack of height within which to resolve it, could have done the rest. But this, like all the others, is only a theory.

Whatever the immediate cause, there is every sign that its consequences were magnified by a chain of miscellaneous mishaps. Nothing that happened after 22.00 on that evening could have been assisted by Gibson's over-confidence, inexperience, or neglect of the training that had been urged upon him.

In 1985 plans for a new industrial park at Steenbergen reawakened memories of the crash, and the possible presence of explosives. On 11 December the Recovery Unit of the Royal Dutch Air Force worked for two days to sterilize the site. They concluded that the Mosquito had 'disintegrated on impact' and that there had been a very fierce fire. They encountered some cockpit instruments, one of the landing wheels, fragments of wood covered with painted fabric, pieces of aircraft skin, rubber from the self-sealing fuel tanks and part of the tail fin and rear fuselage bearing the serial letters KB. Remains of an engine were encountered at a depth of three metres, and a flare. No trace of the crew or their clothing was found. Following excavation of the crash on 11–12 December 1985 an inconclusive report was made to the British Embassy.[18] The *disjecta membra* were taken to the Gilze–Rijen airbase for inspection. Some pieces were then removed to the RNAF Museum at Soesterberg. Others went to the town hall at Steenbergen. Further items disappeared into private hands.

Gibson died not because he was sent back to battle, but because he refused to be left out of it. Wallis made a perceptive comment after he visited Coningsby five months later. He had passed the evening with Air Comm. Satterly, Sharp's successor as commander of 54 Base and they talked of a recent tragedy. Gp Capt. Evans Evans, Coningsby's station commander, had recently been killed in circumstances not dissimilar to those which had claimed Gibson. Screened from operations, Evans had nevertheless arranged to take part in one. He returned safely. Tempted to a second, he strayed into an area held by the Allies and was shot down by American fire. An experienced crew died with him. After his visit Wallis wrote to thank Satterly for his hospitality. The episode still turned in Wallis's mind. 'As in the case of Gibson,' he reflected, 'men of a certain type will only become miserable if they are condemned to inaction, and their fate really lies in their own hands.'[19]

Part Twelve

VALHALLA

Do these, who help the quickened pulse run slowly,
    Whose stern remembered image cools the brow –
Till the far dawn of Victory know only
    Night's darkness, and Valhalla's silence now?

               John Magee, 'Per Ardua', 1941

Silent Minds

It was Harris who thought of it: 'If there is a Valhalla, Guy Gibson and his band of brothers will be found at all the parties, seated far above the salt.' There were a lot of brothers from Bomber Command. Over 55,000 of them. No one is so sure about the parties, least of all John Magee, who wrote his desolate poem at Wellingore a few months after Gibson had left.

A death is a good moment at which to lay foundations for a legend, and not a time when sceptics will raise their voices. Hence when news of Gibson's disappearance was made public, readers of the *Daily Telegraph* were assured that he 'had a natural easy manner which made him greatly loved by the crews under his command', that he 'knew all his aircrew by their Christian names' and that he was a 'fine organizer'. Some of these qualities can be recognized; more derived from the Air Ministry's Public Relations Department.

News of the death was formally announced on 8 January 1945, but many knew sooner. Churchill wrote to Eve in December:

Dear Mrs Gibson

I have been awaiting an opportunity to write to you about the loss of your husband. I can assure you that I write in no formal sense.

I had great admiration for him – the glorious Dam-buster. I had hoped that he would come into Parliament and make his way there after the stress of the war was over, but he never spared himself nor would allow others to spare him. We have lost in this officer one of the most splendid of all our fighting men. His name will not be forgotten; it will for ever be enshrined in the most wonderful records of our country.

May I express to you my profound sympathy in the loss you have incurred, and my earnest hope that you will find in yourself those resilient and earnest qualities of which your husband was the proud possessor.

Yours sincerely

Winston S. Churchill[1]

Gibson's death was mourned by others who had known him and had seen beyond his failings a personification of Britain's heart: courage, service, determination, sacrifice. Ismay, who had met him on the way to

Quadrant, recorded: 'I only know that when I heard that he had "failed to return", I felt a sense of national, as well as personal, loss.' Others, including many who only knew him by reputation, reacted in a similar way. They recall a sense of sickening depression that someone who had achieved and survived so much should have been lost when the end was in view. Comrades of his inner circle – men like Shannon, who knew his weaknesses as well as his strengths – saw his death for the personal, as well as public, tragedy it was.

The main valedictions came early in 1945. On 1 February an obituary appeared in the London *Times*, which printed a memoir from Warden Kendall two days later. News of the death sparked a brief correspondence in *The Times*, in which it was claimed – from lack of knowledge – that the RAF had been wrong to send him back into action. Other tributes appeared far and wide, including many in the United States. On 3 February it was announced that Wg-Cdr G.P. Gibson VC, DSO, DFC, of Aberdeen Place, St John's Wood had left £2,295 and no will. A.J. later assigned his share of the estate to Eve.

Kendall wrote a letter of condolence to Eve, who replied:

Thank you for your letter. By now no doubt you have read in the newspapers that Guy is definitely dead. His death must have been instantaneous for which I am grateful.

I do feel that Guy went the way he wished and that he fulfilled his mission in life . . .[2]

Did he? Had he? And, if so, what was it?

Like all popular saints, Gibson lives on through his legend. Dissemination of the *vita* was already well advanced. Starting on 3 December 1944, the *Sunday Express* had serialized large extracts from *Enemy Coast Ahead*. Under rousing titles like HOW WE SMASHED HITLER'S INVASION, THE SECRET OF THE PATHFINDERS and HOW WE SMASHED THE DAMS, each episode accompanied by a different smiling photograph, the public was introduced to Gibson's exhilarating narrative.

In parallel, the full text was being prepared for publication. The typescript was sent to Michael Joseph at the end of December and went to the Ministry of Information for final approval in February. Given the book's underlying aim as redemptive propaganda, this was timely: the MoI received it five days after the destruction of Dresden. Michael Joseph's editors made a few more changes, carrying out minor surgery for reasons of tact towards others and to improve appearances of Gibson's tolerance.

Deft editing turned some of Gibson's clumsier passages into strong writing. The Churchillian sonority of a phrase such as 'unexampled campaign of cruelty' replacing Gibson's original 'cruelty hitherto unknown' illustrates the subtlety of the editor's method: Gibson's meaning is intact, but now more lofty and mature in expression. Such changes were all the more effective for being sparse: the combination of Gibson's simplicity with occasional editorial intervention to supply` exactly the right word is partly what makes the book so effective.

The icon gilded, *Enemy Coast Ahead* went to press. It was published early in 1946 and immediately became a best seller, reaching its fifth impression by September the following year. Elizabeth Bowen called it a 'work of genius', a 'book to keep for one's sons' sons'. *Punch* considered it an 'extraordinarily adult work for such a young man'. Val Gielgud wrote in the *Sunday Times* that the 'best books dealing with the Second World War certainly remain to be written', but added: 'No book that I have read gives a picture of the Royal Air Force so vivid, so vital, and so moving.' And so began the endless parade.

Endless Parade

The intactness of the Gibson legend is almost entirely due to *Enemy Coast Ahead* which provided source material for other popular books and is recycled in articles to this day. Paul Brickhill quarried from it for the *The Dam Busters* (1951). So did R.C. Sheriff in his script for the film which was premièred four years later. Ralph Barker's portrait of Gibson in *Strike Hard, Strike Sure* (1963) introduced new material, but also drew from Gibson's account. Many other writings about Gibson exhibit uncritical dependency on his book and a shameless willingness to paraphrase it. A few studies have dug deeper, but for the most part it is the self-dramatized personality who lives on.

Just as Gibson described his colourful colleague John Wooldridge in *Enemy Coast Ahead*, so Wooldridge portrayed Gibson. The hero of the film *Appointment in London* is Wing-Commander Tim Mason DFC and bar DSO and bar, the young but operationally stressed commander of a Lancaster squadron who has accomplished eighty-seven trips, acquires a girl-friend called Eve and discourages wives from living near bomber stations. Mason is disciplinarian but human, guards his feelings, rates the contribution of fliers higher than that of ground crew and socializes intensively with his pilots when off duty.

There are many echoes of episodes at 106 Squadron in the film. The chain-smoking Mason sits up all night in the ops room awaiting the return of his crews, just as Gibson had kept vigil for Gray Healey and many others. The loss of Greenho and the arrival of his wife seeking consolation recalls scenes in Gibson's book. There is even a snatch of Wagner's 'Ride of the Valkyries', heard on the film during the raid that is its climax, and on Gibson's choice of *Desert Island Discs* when he said that it reminded him of an air raid.

Dirk Bogarde's performance as Tim Mason often recalls Gibson, although Bogarde warns that a lot of wing-commanders were cast in this sort of mould, being forced to make the most agonizing decisions at a very early age. Although Wooldridge did not mention Gibson during the making of the film, Bogarde recalls that 'practically everything in the script was first-hand'. Mason was probably a conflation of several characters, including Gibson. By an odd coincidence Bogarde's brother-in-law had served with Gibson; he was 'quite startled by the film and its similarities to his own experiences'.[3]

For most, the Gibson legend subsists in the firm benevolence of Richard Todd's portrayal in Michael Anderson's film *The Dam Busters*. Todd's performance was carefully researched, capturing Gibson's body language and, apparently, some of his speech patterns. But close friends missed his 'wicked' humour and unrefined vitality. When asked to name an actor who would have captured the coarser side of Gibson, Ann Shannon replied – without hesitation – 'Mickey Rooney'.[4]

The film, like the books upon which it was based, achieved huge popularity in the 1950s. Audiences thrilled to the flying sequences, hummed Eric Coates's tunes and marvelled at the first clear indication of how Wallis's weapon had actually worked. *The Dam Busters* also answered a need. As the cold war deepened, the bonds of Empire slackened and Britain's marginalization in international affairs loomed, a public exhausted by the recent war could nevertheless return to it and draw comfort from the memory of their victory. *The Dam Busters* celebrated people – mainly British people, or their cousins from the Dominions – who solved technical problems, thought laterally, conquered bureaucracy, trained and played hard, pressed on and eventually triumphed. Wallis's endearingly gentle abstraction contrasted with the institutionalized warmongering of the National Socialism against which it was pitched. Published in the same year as the end of post-war rationing, Brickhill's book had likewise extolled a golden age of British individualism, witnessed in brilliant improvisation, casually laconic dialogue and the cool bravado of confident men. Today much of that seems risible, but golden ages are ultimately created not by authors but by the audiences who need them. The interest of *The Dam Busters* lies not only in the tale but also in the manner of its telling, which reinforced the nostalgic optimism of Britain in the 1950s before Suez: Churchill back in Downing Street, Everest conquered, a new sovereign – years which 'do in retrospect seem like a golden summer'.[5]

Yet behind it all lay a deep unease. Atomic weapons and the cold war undermined all those traits of ingenuity, humour, courage and community which had brought Britain through the war. Within Britain the bomber crew had been a symbol of human potentiality and interdependence. But what did a rocket symbolize? The nuclear age threatened to dehumanize the cherished traditions and community of the services at a time when both were still integral to British society. As Harris had observed to Churchill in 1945, 'The bomber is a passing phase and, like the battleship, it has nearly passed.'[6] Even before the RAF took four Lancasters out of storage for the making of the film, the first V-bombers had taken to the air.

Enemy Coast Ahead remains in print. Time has moderated its impact, historians have exposed its errors (not to mention those of Brickhill), and other pilots have since bettered Gibson as writers. Less smoothly written and urbane than Johnson's *Wing Leader*, Gibson's autobiography also lacks something of the explorative intimacy of books written by his own colleagues. Gibson wrote simply and vividly about action, but produced nothing so awesome as Pierre Clostermann's memories of battles fought in the early spring of 1945, depicted in *The Big Show*. Yet all of these were composed after the war, when hindsight lent perspective, the authors had grown up, style had matured and facts could be checked. To compare like with like we should look at other wartime writings, books like Cheshire's *Bomber Pilot*, or Richard Hillary's *The Last Enemy*.

Cheshire's book is the better written, if at times more self-absorbed. Like *Enemy Coast Ahead* it contains – on Cheshire's own admission – episodes which border on the fictional.[7] Curiously, Cheshire had no opinion of *Enemy Coast Ahead*, because he never read it. When asked why, Cheshire found that he could not answer. Subsequently he wrote to say that the question had been turning in his mind.

I think the reason ... was that I was living and working with aircrew and we were constantly exchanging ideas on tactics, techniques etc. A book written for the public in general didn't, therefore, have a particular appeal to me.[8]

There is irony here, for *Bomber Pilot* found an eager public from the moment it appeared in 1942, and Cheshire preceded Gibson as a household name because of it.

Parts of Hillary's quest for spiritual meaning border the unreadable; but he was so young, and the wonder is not that some pages of *The Last Enemy* are not very good, but that many of them are. Neither Gibson nor Cheshire wrote anything so piercing as did Hillary in his account of the farewell signalled by children in a remote Scottish valley as his squadron's Spitfires departed south.

Hillary, Johnson and Clostermann were fighter pilots, and some have thought it odd that the bomber war produced so little contemporary writing. As Verrier put it in 1968:

The survivors of the strategic air offensive seem more remote from their experience than most men who have pitted courage and skill against death or mutilation. The few personal narratives which were written have a curiously unconvincing air, even when modestly, sometimes artlessly, describing operations calling for a rare combination of qualities. *Enemy Coast Ahead* ... is a case in point, with its schoolboy jokes and suggestions that the whole thing is a kind of party.[9]

But that is precisely the point: the chances of anyone surviving to write a complete book were minimal, and many members of bomber crews *were* little older than schoolboys. Immature as writers, their personal relationships brief and undeveloped, they spoke simply as they knew. Understated nonchalance or fierce frivolity were mechanisms of defence, a means of minimizing confrontation with grief and terror, a tin mirror in which infernal reality could be stared in the eye. Far from trivializing the war, Gibson's book shows how many of his comrades managed to get through it.

What happened to its characters, or those kept off its stage? One day several years after the war Eve Gibson met Anthony Bridgman, Gibson's flight commander of a decade before – the 'Oscar' in *Enemy Coast Ahead* who 'never came back'. Bridgman had kept in touch with Eve socially, and through an acquaintance introduced her to a South African businessman called Jack Hyman. In November 1950 Eve married Hyman and accompanied him to South Africa. In her absence a collection of papers, letters and other materials (including the first volume of Gibson's logbook) were left with a relative who after a time grew tired of the clutter and destroyed them. The marriage did not endure. Eve returned to Britain, Hyman died and she retook her former married name. She kept in touch with Alick and Ruth, but there seems to have been no special intimacy. In later years Eve involved herself in events and ceremonies connected with Gibson's memory and the communities of 617 and 83 Squadrons, remaining in close touch with several survivors of the Dams Raid until her death. She died in 1988, a few days before Mick Martin.

A.J. remained aloof from his family. So little had he seen of his daughter-in-law that when she was introduced to him at the première of *The Dam Busters* he was not sure who she was. In 1966 he met Alick in a London street. They talked for a few minutes and he learned that his eldest son was now executive director of AEI International and that their homes were only a few blocks apart. But A.J. kept his distance, saying that it was better that they should not meet again. He died in 1968, at the age of ninety-two. Alick followed him in 1987. Joan, Gibson's sister, died a few days before the fiftieth anniversary of the Dams Raid.

When Margaret read newspaper reports which confirmed that Gibson was dead, her husband commented acidly that perhaps her talk of him would now cease. But Margaret never forgot him. Her marriage broke up. She married again. For years she kept Gibson's letters and a signed photograph, until one day her second husband found them and flung them in the fire. This marriage too ended in divorce. Margaret returned to Lincolnshire, where she lives today, not far from her beloved Rauceby.

Meanwhile, tokens of the legend have proliferated at home and abroad. His status as a cult figure was early recognized, when Madame Tussaud's contemplated a waxwork, and is maintained today through statuettes, postcards and photographs. The photograph was always a good medium for Gibson, projecting his winning smile and boyish good looks without invoking his opinions.

Gibson and the Lancaster are twin symbols of Bomber Command's offensive against Germany. To an extent public interest in both has swayed with the motion of the debate about that campaign. Former aircrew who were glad enough to put the war behind them when raising families in the 1950s are now in retirement and find themselves looking back. Some do so with pride, others with curiosity, even incredulity, but seldom with self-reproach. Indeed, in recent years the bomber veterans have become more outspoken on behalf of the campaign they fought and have rallied behind the name of the man who led it. An obvious sign of this autumnal flourish is the statue of Sir Arthur Harris which now stands in the Strand beside the RAF church St Clement Danes. The chorus of protest which greeted its raising has been followed by other disputations about the wrecking of German cities: Cologne, Hamburg . . . Dresden. When they have subsided, another generation will inquire into the deeds of its great-grandparents, and new journalists and academics will join the moral and military controversy which has become one of the main historical antagonisms of the late twentieth century. Throughout, Gibson's name will be invoked.

Gibson has already been remembered in a scholarship, in stained glass, in the names of pubs, flowers, aircraft and streets across the UK and Commonwealth. He is commemorated at Porthleven, but the main centre of his cult is in Steenbergen. The RAF has an honoured place in Dutch memory. For four years, night after night, citizens of towns like Steenbergen watched and listened as Bomber Command fought its way into and out of the Third Reich. They helped airmen, some burned and maimed, who floated down out of the darkness from doomed bombers. Dutch people gave refuge to those who lived and buried those who died, watching over their graves until the day that wives and sweethearts would be free to come to them. For the greater part of that time those aeroplanes, and the young victims spewed forth from explosions in the sky, were the only tangible sign of hope that one day the tyranny would be lifted. When that day arrived, so too once more did the RAF, to feed a population close to starvation in April 1945.

Enemy Coast Ahead was translated into Dutch (*In zoeklicht en afweervuur*); so too was Brickhill's book. (Curiously, if the name Brickhill is translated into Dutch, something very like Steenbergen is the word which results.) Appropriately enough, Steenbergen today is a place of pilgrimage. There is a Mosquitostraat in Steenbergen and a Gibsonstraat and a Warwickstraat. It was not always so. In 1967 a citizen of Rotterdam, Mr Jan van den Driesschen, visited Gibson's grave. He found the plot neglected and decided to care for it. News of Mr van den Driesschen's efforts spread to England, whence contributions towards the upkeep of the grave began to arrive. After a time Mr van den Driesschen resolved to establish a more substantial memorial to Gibson and Warwick and with the help of the Royal Air Forces Association this was duly done. In September 1974 Eve Gibson and Warwick's sister travelled to Steenbergen with Mick Martin. Martin unveiled a bronze plaque beside the entrance to the cemetery. Today ex-aircrew go there, some in groups, others alone with their thoughts. Specialized tours which follow the trail of the Dams Raid pause at the cemetery, leaving wreaths, poppies or messages at the graveside.

At the site of the crash, now surrounded by new buildings, is an oak plinth, while in a park near the town centre stands a memorial column of red granite, erected on the initiative of a former member of 106 Squadrom, and others. The monument was dedicated on 7 May 1990 in the presence of former members of 106 and 617 Squadrons, relatives of Gibson and Warwick, members of the Royal Netherlands Air Force, the Dutch Resistance and many others.

Leonard Cheshire was there too. It was fitting that Gibson's successor and the object of his frustration should come to honour him. Cheshire gave an address. He spoke of Gibson's achievement, of the need to face war at different times in history and of the imperative for all to combine in work for peace:

Building peace means removing the root causes of war, injustice, oppression, poverty, division, all the things that disable our one human family. That is the calling to which we need to respond, to go out into the world and remove the causes of division, help uphold the dignity of each human being. That is the message that Guy Gibson and all those in whose name he stands gives us today.[10]

Epilogue

So, who was he, really?

The essence of him was simplicity and an irrepressible spirit. His beliefs were few, clear and uncomplicated. He approached issues, tasks and relationships with uncommon directness. He seldom dissembled. Although utterly practical he was also emotional, a sentimentalist. He was moved by the love of animals. In his dealings with people little deterred him, although the articulation of deeper feelings did not come easily.

He was very much a product of his background. He divided people into classes, often prejudging them accordingly, and was mostly content to accept assumptions with which he had been brought up. He was intelligent, quick-witted, but – being so well furnished with ready-made ideas – not particularly analytical.

In his personal life he was a victim, thrown upon his own resources from an early age, lonely, his real emotions guarded by a carapace of stubbornness or *bonhomie*. His personality was reflexive, its contradictions – veering between modesty and egotism, sensitivity and boorishness – often taking their cue from those he was with. In the company of seniors he could be unpretentious, even diffident. Equals saw his openhearted lively candour; those beneath him might catch his offhandedness, and sometimes a careless cruelty. Boundless energy ran through everything he did.

He was an accomplished rather than a great pilot. Among those with whom he flew there were many with better skills of airmanship, but few approached his single-minded determination to complete whatever task he had been given. As a commander too his doggedness to achieve, and to drive everyone around him to do likewise, was his hallmark.

As for his military influence, he was an executor rather than an instigator. This marks him apart from Cheshire, who was both. Whether in his personal life, the direction of his career, or in his fighting, Gibson was less an innovator (although he loved innovation) than someone who could be relied upon to do what he was told. His versatility, aided by a keen eye and ear for ambience, enabled him to engage fully with whatever task was in hand – flying, writing a book, making a speech. And because of that, he was manipulated.

Those who liked or loved him did so intensely. More looked upon him with a wary respect. Many thought him unpleasantly rebarbative. A few found him insufferable.

Loneliness shadowed him all along. Eve did not assuage his inner isolation and his perpetual search for companions ran in counterpoint with his disappointed passion for her. With Margaret he fantasized about a simple existence – a garden, a cottage, a log fire, and permanent affection.

Harris described him as 'as great a warrior as these Islands ever bred'. He was right, and Gibson served Harris well. Harris and Cochrane failed him. Gibson selected himself to fly to Rheydt, but it was Cochrane and Harris who conceded the opportunity. Harris admitted, 'I quite wrongly allowed him to return to operations.' As Mick Martin put it in a letter to me a few days before he joined his comrade in Valhalla, 'There was no target of sufficient importance for them to endanger his young life again.'[11]

ACKNOWLEDGEMENTS

Many people have helped me to write this book. Dr Noble Frankland provided invaluable guidance and introductions at the start. One of those introductions was to Air Commodore Henry Probert, then head of the Air Historical Branch of the Ministry of Defence, who in the space of a single meeting gave advice and access to sources which have been valued ever since. Another was to Air Marshal Sir Harold Martin, with whom I corresponded for several months before his death in 1988. During those months Mrs Eve Gibson, Guy Gibson's widow, was in her last illness. We never met, but she knew of this book and signalled her interest in it.

Mrs Ruth Gibson talked about her brother-in-law in the course of several interviews. I am grateful for her kindness on those occasions, and the loan of documents and family photographs.

The late David and Ann Shannon sustained the work in ways for which ordinary thanks would be insufficient. Both knew Gibson well, and their strong encouragement, loan of documents, long hours of discussion, sharing of memories and generous hospitality all influenced progress more than they knew. In many ways this book was written for them, as the only proper recompense for their help and trust. I am sorry they did not live to read what they did so much to help me to write.

Another for whom the book itself can be my only proper thanks is Margaret North. I hope it does justice to the memories she confided.

Fay Gillon's recollections of Gibson and of events at Scampton around the time of the Dams Raid were unusually valuable, and I am indebted to her for permission to reproduce her vivid memoir 'Dress Rehearsal'.

To the relatives, to the men and women who flew with Guy Gibson, to those who maintained the aeroplanes of his squadrons, to his schoolfriends, colleagues, contemporaries, commanders and other acquaintances who assisted at interview – often with the greatest kindness – or responded with advice or information to written inquiries,

I extend my best thanks: The Hon. Mrs Nicholas Assheton, Clive Banham, R. L.Bartley, George Beldam, the late Air Marshal Sir Dermot Boyle, F.W.Boyle, Anthony Bridgman, the late Air Vice-Marshal S.O. Bufton, George Chalmers, the late Lord Cheshire VC, Group Captain Ronald Churcher, Diana Collins, Joe Corrigan, Maurice Crawley, Richard Dougan, the late Marshal of the Royal Air Force Lord Elworthy, Douglas Garton, Wallace Gaunt, Michael Gibson, Stan Harpham, Sir Anthony Harris, Jim Heveron, Canon G. Hollis, Harry Humphries, Michael Inskip, Air Vice-Marshal J.E. Johnson, Professor R.V. Jones, Jack Kynoch, Peter Mallender, Lady Wendy Martin, Dr G. McCall, Group Captain J.B. Tait, Dr Alan Upton, Dr Bill Whamond, Air Commodore S.C. Widdows and Mrs Nickie Widdows.

One of many privileges to have flowed from this project has been the opportunity to meet former RAF servicemen who are writing books of their own, or are working to garner original materials while time still allows. Historians will bless them for this work, which touches evanescent material, often from memory or private sources, that would never otherwise find its way into the public domain. Ron Low, Des Richards, Tony Iveson and Alan Webb, sometime secretaries of the 83, 106, 617 and 627 Squadron Associations, respectively, were particularly generous. They provided information and advice which often went beyond the affairs of the units with which they are concerned, and whose fraternity they continue to foster.

There were other helpers. Theo Holleman aided research in Holland. Professor Charles Thomas assisted in matters of Cornish family history. Dr Martin Gilbert provided guidance on Gibson's first meeting with Sir Winston Churchill. Lady Mary Soames gave advice about the context of Gibson's relations with her father. John Matossian kindly allowed me to examine Harlo Taerum's logbook. Derrick Riley and John Morris contributed technical advice on the Mosquito.

Authors often finish books with a sense of frustration. The more work done, the greater seems to be its insufficiency. That this is only partly true here is due to the contribution of Colin Dobinson who in the autumn of 1991 joined me as research assistant, and gave a depth to the investigation of archive sources which otherwise would have taken years to attain. So central did his role become that for several aspects of the story it seemed sensible for him to draft the sections concerned, and to compile the appendices. Hence in its final form this book is the work not of one author, but two, and its remaining acknowledgements are on our joint behalf.

Research on a number of issues was assisted by those who responded to our inquiries. Mr Dennissov dealt with our questions at the Russian Embassy. Dr Sarah Street, archivist to the Conservative Party, Mrs Elizabeth Gilliland and Garry H. Weston gave most useful assistance in connection with Gibson's political career. Mary Burns assisted photographic and newspaper research in the United States. Sir Dirk Bogarde made valuable comment on the making of the film *Appointment in London*. At the Royal Air Force Museum, Hendon, Richard Simpson, Senior Deputy Keeper Aircraft and Exhibits was an instructive guide to the interiors of the Bristol Beaufighter and Avro Lancaster. Francis Prichard enabled the publication of a request for information in the St Edward's School *Chronicle*, and Malcolm Oxley facilitated further inquiries and a visit to the school. Others who helped in various ways included John Bateman, Tony Dale, Frances Griffith, Max Hastings, John Magee, Edward Morris, Lisa Pickering, Julie Rodgers and Roger Whiteley. To all, our thanks.

We record our gratitude to the staff of many archives, libraries, institutions and museums: Sebastian Cox, Air Historical Branch, Ministry of Defence; Barnes Wallis Archive, National Science Museum; Sally Hine, BBC Librarian, Archives and Effects; BBC Script Library; British Film Institute; British Newspaper Library; University Library, Cambridge; Brotherton Library, University of Leeds; Brad King, Imperial War Museum; India Office Archive; Linnaean Society; Mick Wood, National Meteorological Library and Archive; National Monuments Record; Gwynneth M. Stratten, Senior Library Assistant, Rauceby Hospital; Ben Travers and Peter Elliot, Department of Aviation History, RAF Museum, Hendon; Royal Cornish Institute, Truro; Public Record Office, Kew and Chancery Lane; the General Register Office, St Catherine's House and Somerset House.

Our largest debt has been to Robert Owen, the official historian of the 617 Squadron Association, whose scholarship and own immense archive were placed at our disposal with a generosity to which it is difficult to make proper salute. As a source of ideas, guidance, encouragement and informed criticism, Robert's help has been unparalleled. His careful reading of the manuscript has saved us from errors and added new insights. In many ways this book should have been written by him, and so large has been his role in its making that parts of it are as much his work as ours, and some of them more so.

APPENDIX I:
AWARDS AND CITATIONS

8 JULY 1940

Distinguished Flying Cross
Fg Off. G.P. Gibson, 83 Sqn

10 SEPTEMBER 1941

Bar to the Distinguished Flying Cross
Acting Sqn Ldr G.P. Gibson, 29 Sqn

This officer continues to show the utmost courage and devotion to duty. Since joining his present unit, Squadron Leader Gibson has destroyed three and damaged a fourth enemy aircraft. His skill was notably demonstrated when, one night in July 1941, he intercepted and destroyed a Heinkel III.

17 NOVEMBER 1942

Distinguished Service Order
Acting Wg-Cdr G.P. Gibson, 106 Sqn

Since being awarded a bar to the Distinguished Flying Cross, this officer has completed many sorties, including a daylight raid on Danzig and an attack at Gdynia. In the recent attack at Le Creusot, Wing-Commander Gibson bombed and machine-gunned the transformer station near by from 500 feet. On 22nd October 1942, he participated in the attack on Genoa and, two days later, he led his squadron in a daylight sortie against Milan. On both occasions, Wing-Commander Gibson flew with great distinction. He is a most skilful and courageous leader whose keenness has set a most inspiring example.

30 MARCH 1943

Bar to the Distinguished Service Order
Acting Wg-Cdr G.P. Gibson, 106 Sqn

This officer has an outstanding operational record, having completed 172 sorties. He has always displayed the greatest keenness and, within the past two months, has taken part in 6 attacks against well-defended targets, including Berlin. In March 1943, he captained an aircraft detailed to attack Stuttgart. On the outward flight engine trouble developed but he flew on to his objective and bombed it from a low level. This is typical of his outstanding determination to make every sortie a success. By his skilful leadership and contempt for danger he has set an example which has inspired the squadron he commands.

28 MAY 1943

Victoria Cross
Acting Wg-Cdr G.P. Gibson, 617 Sqn

This officer served as a night bomber pilot at the beginning of the war and quickly established a reputation as an outstanding operational pilot. In addition to taking the fullest possible share in all normal operations, he made single-handed attacks during his 'rest' nights on such highly defended targets as the battleship *Tirpitz*, then completing in Wilhelmshaven.

When his tour of operational duties was concluded he asked for a further operational posting and went to a nightfighter unit instead of being posted for instructional duties. In the course of his second operational tour, he destroyed at least three enemy bombers and contributed much to the raising and development of new nightfighter formations.

After a short period in a training unit he again volunteered for operational duties and returned to night bombers. Both as an operational pilot and as a leader of his squadron, he achieved outstandingly successful results and his personal courage knew no bounds. Berlin, Danzig, Gdynia, Genoa, Le Creusot, Milan, Nuremberg and Stuttgart were among the targets he attacked by day and night.

On conclusion of his third operational tour, Wing-Commander Gibson pressed strongly to be allowed to remain on operations and he was selected to command a squadron then forming for special tasks. Under his inspiring leadership, this squadron has now executed one of the most devastating attacks of the war – the breaching of the Möhne and Eder dams.

The task was fraught with danger and difficulty. Wing-Commander Gibson personally made the first attack on the Möhne dam. Descending to within a few feet of the water and taking the full brunt of the anti-aircraft defences he delivered his attack with great accuracy. Afterwards he circled very low for 30 minutes, drawing the enemy fire on himself in order to leave as free a run as possible to the following aircraft which were attacking the dam in turn.

Wing-Commander Gibson then led the remainder of his force to the Eder dam where, with complete disregard for his own safety, he repeated his tactics, and once more drew upon himself the enemy fire (sic) so that the attack could be successfully developed.

Wing-Commander Gibson has completed 170 sorties, involving more than 600 hours' operational flying. Throughout his operational career, prolonged exceptionally at his own request, he has shown leadership, determination and valour of the highest order.

Source: Air Ministry Bulletin 10401, RAF Museum File DC76/74/1324

APPENDIX II:
NORTH AMERICAN TOUR, 1943

Reconstructing Gibson's North American tour involves reliance upon three different types of source. The first is the itinerary given by Gibson himself in his flying logbook. The second is contemporary newspaper accounts from Canada and America, and the third is those few diaries of the units he visited which are preserved in the Public Record Office.

Gibson's own account is so much at variance with the other two that it may as well be dismissed except (i) as a guide to the rough sequence of events and (ii) as an indicator of where he *may* have been during the periods not adequately covered by other sources. It is clear from Gibson's logbook that the entries for the American tour were not made until towards the middle of the following year. These may have been based upon rough notes he made at the time but, if so, those notes themselves must have been in error. It is in any case difficult to see how the schedule itself, given below, would have allowed much time for note-taking.

Detailed references for the sources on which the following itinerary is based will be found in *Sources*. The itinerary is incomplete in some details and further research could certainly be undertaken by anyone thinking it worth the trouble to establish minutiae. The majority of newspaper sources consulted can be found in the British Library (Newspapers) at Colindale, though some additional material was furnished by research in the United States. Principal areas where refinement would be possible are Gibson's time in Kansas and Pittsburgh. No press sources for these areas were available to us.

THE ITINERARY

Date	Place	Activity
8 Aug.	At sea	Gibson addresses Quadrant party
9 Aug.	Halifax	Arrives aboard *Queen Mary*
10 Aug.	Quebec	Arrival with Churchill's party
11 Aug.	Quebec	Visits RCAF recruiting centre accompanied by Wg-Cdr J. Sharpe, secretary to the Hon. C.G. Power and Mr Wellie Begin, Power's local secretary
12 Aug.	Quebec	Holds first formal Press conference at newspaper headquarters. Introduced by the Hon. C.G. Power, Secretary for Air
13 Aug.	Quebec	
14 Aug.	Quebec	Visits No. 1 AGGTS at Quebec Airport, and makes a speech in praise of the BCATP
15–18 Aug.	Quebec	
19 Aug.	Quebec	Attends graduation ceremony for air observers of No. 8 AOS, based at Quebec Airport. Gibson makes a brief speech

Date	Place	Activity
20–31 Aug.	Movements uncertain. According to Gibson's logbook he travelled from Quebec on 20 Aug. to Montreal, Ottawa, Toronto, London, Jarvis and New York, before travelling to Winnipeg via Toronto on 26 Aug. No independent evidence has been found for this part of the tour	
1 Sept.	Brantford	Given civic reception. Visits the base of 5 SFTS
2 Sept.	Centralia	Attends graduation ceremony at 9 SFTS
	Malton	Departs from Malton for New York
3–5 Sept.	New York	Records radio broadcast for station W JZ New York – an episode of their serial, *The Fifth Year*, broadcast at 6.30 p.m. on 5 Sept.
6 Sept.	Winnipeg	Arrives by Trans-Canada Airlines, to be met by representatives of 2 Training Command and officials of the WWI Wartime Pilots and Observers Association. At 5.30 p.m. given a reception by members of the Association at the Manitoba Club

Date	Place	Activity
7 Sept.	Winnipeg	Addresses students of 5 AOS at Stevenson Field. Meets Mr and Mrs E. S. Glinz, parents of Fg Off. Harvey S. Glinz, at their home at 485 Rathgar Avenue
	Carberry	Visits 33 SFTS, makes speech to base personnel
	Rivers	Visits base
8 Sept.	Dafoe	Visits base
9 Sept.	Moose Jaw	Visits 32 SFTS, makes speech to base personnel
10 Sept.	Moose Jaw	Addresses station personnel (again)
	Mossbank	Arrives from Moose Jaw
11 Sept.	Calgary	Arrives 6.00 p.m. at 3 SFTS, Currie Airfield. Welcomed by AVM G.R. Howsam and mayor of Calgary. Meets Mrs H. Taerum, and gives a radio interview. Drives through Calgary to the Palliser Hotel, where he is to be accommodated, and gives another radio interview. Meets LAC Robert Young, brother of Sqn Ldr Young
12 Sept.	Banff	Spends the day here, perhaps sightseeing
	Calgary	Returns to see Mrs Taerum at home at 344, 15th Avenue West, Calgary

Date	Place	Activity
14 Sept.	Vancouver	Arrives at noon by Canadian Pacific. Drive in open car to Hotel Vancouver, together with the mayor and Air Comm. A.H. Hull, Acting AOC Western Air Command. The procession is led up Granville by RCAF drum and bugle band. In the evening, Gibson speaks to 300 air cadets from New Westminster and City schools at Stanley Park Armories
15 Sept.	Victoria	Arrives from Vancouver
16–19 Sept.	Victoria	(For at least the early part of this period)
20 Sept.	Montreal	Visits 1 Wireless School. Attends party in the evening, hosted by Air Force Veterans Association
21 Sept.	Bapotville	Visits
	Mont Joli	Due to visit base of 9 BGS
22 Sept.	Pennfield Ridge	Due to visit
23 Sept.	Debert	Due to visit
24 Sept.	Dartmouth	Due to visit
	Halifax	Arrives during the day, and in the evening spends some time with local airmen. Stays at Nova Scotian Hotel
25 Sept.	Halifax	Press conference, Nova Scotian Hotel
	Greenwood	Due to visit in the afternoon
26 Sept.	?	

Date	Place	Activity
27 Sept.	Moncton	Passes through 31 RAF Depot in transit
	Ottawa	Due to arrive during the late afternoon
28 Sept.–3 Oct.	Ottawa	Rests at the Seignory Club
4–7 Oct.	Uncertain, but the logbook suggests Washington during this period. No independent evidence is available	
8 Oct.	New York	Gives Press conference at the office of the British Information Services, 30 Rockefeller Plaza
9–18 Oct.	Uncertain, but logbook suggests Pittsburgh, Kansas, Orlando, Morrison and Miami over this period	
19 Oct.	Washington	Presented with the Legion of Merit by General Arnold at Bolling Field. Air Marshal Sir William Welsh in attendance
20–22 Oct.	Uncertain, but may be in Pittsburgh according to logbook	
23 Oct.	Chicago	Due to attend a cocktail party hosted by the British consul general, Wilfred H. Gallienne
24 Oct.	Chicago	
25 Oct.	Chicago	
26 Oct.	Chicago	Due to address the Chicago Association of Commerce at La Salle Hotel at noon, and personnel of the Glenview Naval Air Base in the evening

Date	Place	Activity
27 Oct.	Minneapolis	Speaks at Navy Day rally and meets British consul, L.H. Lamb
28 Oct.	Minneapolis	Addresses Minneapolis Traffic Association
29–31 Oct.	?	
1 Nov.	Los Angeles	Press conference
2–9 Nov.	Hollywood	Stays with Howard Hawks
10 Nov.	Los Angeles	Addresses inaugural meeting of the Los Angeles War Chest at the Biltmore Bowl
11 Nov.	Uncertain	
12 Nov.	San Francisco	Press conference. Stays at Palace Hotel
13–30 Nov.	Uncertain, but logbook gives travel from San Francisco to New York, Ottawa and then Montreal	
1 Dec.	Prestwick	Arrives aboard ferry Liberator from Montreal

APPENDIX III:
OPERATIONAL RECORD

This appendix provides a list of all operational flights made by Gibson which qualified for an entry in the Operations Record Books (ORBs) of the units with which he served. Four 'unofficial' operations flown after the Dams Raid are included, the details for these being provided by Gibson's own logbook. The period covered runs from the first bombing operation of the war, on 3 September 1939, to Gibson's last completed sortie, a trip to Le Havre on 10 September 1944.

The format of the table broadly follows that used in a contemporary ORB. The first column records the date of the sortie. Where an operation ran across two dates (as was often the case with bombing missions) the date specified is that of departure. The aircraft serial number (not the squadron code) is recorded in the second column, the aircraft type being given as an overall heading. Names of crew members are given in the third column. These are consistent with those given in the ORB. However, no systematic abbreviations for ranks were used in ORBs of the 1940s, so ranks are given in the modern abbreviated forms used by the RAF. Duties of crew members were not recorded in the ORBs of 83 and 29 Squadrons, or in the early entries for 106 Squadron. However, the ORB entries for 83 Squadron Hampden sorties usually record, in addition to the pilot, the navigator/bomb-aimer, wireless operator/gunner and gunner, in that order. The introduction of NCO aircrew ranks is reflected in the sudden promotion of Gibson's aircraftman gunner to sergeant in June 1940. For the 29 Squadron Beaufighter sorties the second crew member is the AI operator. When the 106 ORB begins to record crew duties the following abbreviations have been used: C = captain; 2 = second pilot (the position occupied by David Shannon in Gibson's early 106 Lancaster sorties, before the introduction of the specialist flight engineer); E = flight engineer; N = navigator; B = bomb-aimer; W = wireless operator; M = mid-upper gunner; R = rear gunner. Some ORB entries also recorded Gibson's DFC.

The column headed 'Duty' is in each case a *direct* quotation from the

ORB or, where ditto marks were used in the original, an echo of an earlier but related entry. 'Time up' and 'Down' are likewise given verbatim. Similarly, the 'Remarks' column contains direct quotation from squadron records, though in both 'Duty' and 'Remarks' obvious errors (for example, of spelling, but not of content) have been corrected. Explanatory matter is given in square brackets.

For comparison, Gibson's logbook entries are given on the right-hand side of the table. Since Volume One of Gibson's log is not available, these begin in November 1940. No attempt has been made to reconcile information in the log and ORBs on the numerous occasions where the two do not correspond. Thus some operations recorded in squadron records do not appear in the log, and vice versa. Note that Gibson's errors (e.g. of spelling, aircraft codes, places, names and ranks of crew members, bomb loads) have been reproduced verbatim.

How many operations did Gibson fly? The final columns contain running counts of operations for each tour, to the left as recorded in the ORBs, and to the right in the log. The final figures in these columns are therefore the *recorded* (not necessarily the actual) totals. To ascertain the actual totals of operations flown it is necessary to consider the evidence of both columns together, and other sources.

It seems that Gibson completed thirty-eight or thirty-nine bombing missions on his first tour. However, it is not clear what Gibson counted as 'an operation' during the early months of the war, and some flights recorded as maritime training sorties in squadron records may have been entered as operations in his log. It is not certain that the operation on 11 September 1940 was actually flown.

In September 1942 Gibson considered that he had flown ninety-nine defensive and offensive fighter operations. 29 Squadron's ORB and Gibson's log yield totals of seventy-nine and ninety respectively. Neither is likely to be accurate, but in this case Gibson's record may be closer to the truth.

Gibson appears to have flown twenty-nine operations with 106 Squadron, although the ORB does not yield this figure. Nor are the statements for 26 February 1943 that this was his seventieth bombing raid (ORB), or 'My 169th war flight' (log) confirmed. When both sources are conflated, the maximum recorded figures by that date appear to have been sixty-eight bomber operations and 158 'war flights'. However, if

Gibson's calculation of ninety-nine fighter sorties is accepted, the second total rises to 167.

The Dams Raid was thus probably Gibson's sixty-ninth bomber operation. Miscellaneous sorties in the later summer of 1944 take the likely overall total to seventy-three completed bombing (or bombing-related) operations, and argue that he was lost on his seventy-fourth.

83 SQUADRON Handley Page Hampden aircraft throughout

(i) RAF Scampton

			ORB						LOG			Recorded number of ops flown (ORB)	Recorded number of ops flown (log)
Date	No	Crew	Duty	Time up	Down	Remarks	No	Crew	Time	Duty			
3.9.39	L4070	Plt Off Gibson Plt Off Warner Sgt Houghton AC Hewitt	Op. B1	1815	2230	Formation of six aircraft ordered to locate and attack enemy fleet. Owing to bad weather and darkness aircraft returned to base having jettisoned their bombs.						1	

(ii) RAF Lossiemouth

27.2.40	L4070	Fg Off Gibson Plt Off Withers Sgt Houghton AC McCormack	Sweep	1130	1440	[North Sea area.]						2	
29.2.40	L4070	Fg Off Gibson Plt Off Withers Sgt Houghton AC McCormack	Sweep	1115	1215	[North Sea area.]						3	

(iii) RAF Scampton

11.4.40	L4070	Fg Off Gibson Plt Off Withers Plt Off Watson LAC McCormack	Reco.	2305	0655	Crews carried out reconnaissance of the area – Frederick [sic] – Middlefart [sic] – Little Belt – Kattegat – and returned to base.						4	
14.4.40	L4055	Fg Off Gibson Plt Off Withers Plt Off Watson AC McCormack	Gardening	1845	0200	[Gardening ops in the Carrot areas Middlefart [sic], Fredericia and Little Belt.] The only successfully planted Carrot was Gibson's.						5	
20.4.40	L4049	Fg Off Gibson Plt Off Withers Plt Off Watson AC McCormack	Ploughing	2355	0755	Failed to locate target before daybreak. [Routed to return from ops. to Lossiemouth. Returned to base 21.4.40.]						6	
23.4.40	L4070	Fg Off Gibson Plt Off Withers Plt Off Watson AC McCormack	Gardening	1850	0315	Successful. Landed at Marham.						7	
13.5.40	L4070	Fg Off Gibson Plt Off Withers Plt Off Watson AC McCormack	Gardening	2050	0305	Attempted to plant a Lettuce, but could not locate target owing to bad weather.						8	

14.5.40	L4070	Fg Off Gibson Plt Off Withers AC McCormack	Gardening	2040	0220	Lettuce successfully planted.	9
17.5.40	L4070	Fg Off Gibson Plt Off Withers Plt Off Watson AC McCormack	Ploughing	2215	0525	Target A.8 at HAMBURG attacked successfully. During the dive a balloon cable hit the stbd wing, causing damage to a slat. Landed at ABINGDON owing to fog at base.	10
22.5.40	L4070	Fg Off Gibson Plt Off Withers Plt Off Watson AC McCormack	Ploughing	2130	0330	Railway bridge over SCHELDE-MAAS canal bombed and destroyed. Landed at Mildenhall.	11
26.5.40	L4070	Fg Off Gibson Plt Off Withers Plt Off Watson AC McCormack	Ploughing	2130	0235	Bombs dropped in entrance to tunnel on railway line. Returned to base.	12
30.5.40	L4070	Fg Off Gibson Plt Off Withers Plt Off Watson LAC McCormack		2110	0315	[Oil tanks at A.7] Bombs brought back to base.	13
9.6.40	L4070	Fg Off Gibson Plt Off Watson Sgt McCormack Sgt Howard	Gardening	2155	0500	Wallflower successfully planted.	14
11.6.40	I4070	Fg Off Gibson Plt Off Watson Sgt McCormack Sgt Howard	Bombing	2155	0310	GIVET target not located. FLUSHING aerodrome bombed.	15
13.6.40	L4106	Fg Off Gibson Plt Off Watson Sgt McCormack Sgt Howard	Bombing	2200	0515	HIRSON not located. Road junction 30 miles EAST of target attacked.	16
17.6.40	L4070	Fg Off Gibson Plt Off Watson Sgt McCormack Sgt Howard	Bombing	2120	0410	A.3 successfully bombed.	17
19.6.40	L4070	Fg Off Gibson Plt Off Watson Sgt McCormack Sgt Howard	Bombing	2155	0315	Railway junction M.405 successfully bombed.	18

21.6.40	L4070	Fg Off Gibson Plt Off Watson Sgt McCormack Sgt Howard	Bombing	2140	0350	F.19 successfully bombed.	19
23.6.40	L4070	Fg Off Gibson Plt Off Watson Sgt McCormack Sgt Howard	Bombing	2110	0410	F.74 successfully bombed, despite very adverse weather conditions.	20
25.6.40	L4066	Fg Off Gibson Plt Off Watson Sgt McCormack Sgt Howard	Gardening	2140	0400	A.2 successfully bombed.	21
27.6.40	L4070	Fg Off Gibson Plt Off Watson Sgt McCormack Sgt Howard	Bombing	2110	0410	F.74 successfully bombed.	22
29.6.40	L4057	Fg Off Gibson Plt Off Watson Sgt McCormack Sgt Howard	Gardening	2150	0350	M.116 successfully bombed. Aircraft damaged by AA shell.	23
1.7.40	L4070	Fg Off Gibson Plt Off Watson Sgt McCormack Sgt Howard	Bombing; *Scharnhorst*	2200	0400	Bomb not seen to burst, though accurate dive reported.	24
4.7.40	L4070	Fg Off Gibson Plt Off Watson Sgt McCormack Sgt Howard	Bombing; *Scharnhorst*	2110	0430	Bomb overshot and burst among buildings in KIEL.	25
9.7.40	L4070	Fg Off Gibson Plt Off Watson Sgt McCormack Sgt Howard	Bombing; *von Tirpitz*	2215	0350	An accurate run was made over the basin at WILHELMSHAVEN but results were not observed.	26
15.7.40	L4070	Fg Off Gibson Plt Off Watson Sgt McCormack Sgt Turner	Bombing	2125	0440	SIMOR, 4 miles N.E. of DORTMUND attacked. Landed ABINGDON.	27
26.7.40	L4402	Fg Off Gibson Sgt Houghton Sgt McCormack Sgt Turner	Bombing; Z.160	?	?	Hits observed on railway line in target area.	28

Date	Aircraft	Crew	Duty	Time Up	Time Down	Remarks				No.
29.7.40	L4070	Fg Off Gibson, Fg Off Barker, Sgt McCormack, Sgt Houghton	Bombing: A.161	2153	0434	Target bombed, but results not observed.				29
24.8.40	L4070	Fg Off Gibson, Sgt Houghton, Sgt McCormack, LAC Middleton	Gardening at St Nazaire and bombing Z.159	2306	0503	Successful.				30
27.8.40	L4070	Fg Off Gibson, Sgt Houghton, Sgt McCormack, LAC Middleton	Gardening and bombing	2300	0525	Gardening successful: E boat attacked, bomb seen to burst within 25 yards; one E boat machine-gunned and extinguished.				31
28.8.40	[illeg.]	Fg Off Gibson, Sgt Houghton, Sgt McCormack, LAC Hedges	Special [?] B.4	2300	0745	Unsuccessful - bomb brought back.				32
1.9.40	L4057	Fg Off Gibson, Sgt Houghton, Sgt McCormack, LAC Stocks	Bombing: M.482	2006	0206	The target was identified and attacked. Bombs seen to burst on marshalling yards. One fire started.				33
5.9.40	P4402	Fg Off Gibson, Plt Off Warner, Sgt McCormack, LAC Hedges	Bombing: D.197 Special	0045	0700	Target not identified. High dive attack made on ship in Elbe, near Brunsbüttel.				34
8.9.40	X2097	Fg Off Gibson, Sgt Houghton, Sgt McCormack, LAC Ingram	Bombing: D.2	2000	0130	Target identified and attacked. Three bombs seen to burst in dockyard area. One small fire seen.				35
11.9.40	L4070	Fg Off Gibson, Sgt Houghton, Sgt McCormack, LAC Bale	?	?	?					36
15.9.40	L4070	Fg Off Gibson, Sgt Houghton, Sgt McCormack, Sgt Bale	Bombing: Z.11	2135	0130	Target attacked and identified from 800' causing two terrific explosions and several smaller ones. One bomb dropped on barge up river.				37
20.9.40	P4402	Fg Off Gibson, Sgt Houghton, Sgt McCormack, AC Bale	Bombing: M.25c	2320	0525	On first attack, a heavy shell passed through cockpit by rudder bar, and rendered intercom u/s. Bombs dropped by pilot.				38

Date	Serial	Crew	Duty	Up	Down	Remarks	Serial	Crew	Time	Operation	No.	No.
23.9.40	X2901	Fg Off Gibson Sgt Houghton Sgt McCormack AC Bale	Bombing: B.58	1930	0400	Potsdamer Station attacked.						39

29 SQUADRON

(i) RAF Digby/Wellingore Bristol Blenheim aircraft

Date	Serial	Crew	Duty	Up	Down	Remarks	Serial	Crew	Time	Operation	No.	No.
19.11.40							L1327	Plt Off Watson	2.06N	X RAID PATROL		1

Bristol Beaufighter aircraft

Date	Serial	Crew	Duty	Up	Down	Remarks	Serial	Crew	Time	Operation	No.	No.
10.12.40	R2350	Flt Lt Gibson Sgt Taylor	Patrol	2140	2245	Chased 'blip' on AI for about 15 minutes, aircraft then identified as friendly by controller.	R2150	Sgt Taylor	1.05N	X RAID PATROL	1	2
11.12.40	R2350	Flt Lt Gibson Sgt Taylor	X Raid Patrol	0750	0855	Bandit chased out over the sea, eventually shot at, 2 short bursts at 800 yards range about 60 miles east of Mablethorpe. Enemy aircraft identified Ju. 88. No return fire from enemy aircraft and no damage observed as result of F/Lt. Gibson's fire. Enemy aircraft lost in cloud. Height of combat about 1,500 feet.	R2150	Sgt Tylor [sic]	2.15N	X RAID PATROL	2	3
12.12.40	R2144	Flt Lt Gibson Plt Off Watson	X Raid Patrol	1900	2115	No enemy aircraft sighted.	R2144	Plt Off Watson	2.25N	X RAID PATROL	3	4
12.12.40	R2144	Flt Lt Gibson Plt Off Watson	X Raid Patrol	2255	0125	No enemy aircraft sighted.	R2144	Plt Off Watson	2.25N	X RAID PATROL	4	5
20.12.40	R2150	Flt Lt Gibson Plt Off Francombe	X Raid Patrol	1845	2135	One enemy aircraft seen by pilot, but lost sight of before any action could be taken.	R[2]150	Plt Off Francombe	2.50N	X RAID PATROL, HE111 SEEN.	5	6
20.12.40							R2150	Plt Off Francombe	0.20N	X RAID PATROL		7
21.12.40	R2150	Flt Lt Gibson Plt Off Francombe	X Raid Patrol	0810	0830	Pilot saw a Ju. 88 shot down by Manby light AA guns at about 0815 hours. Height of enemy aircraft about 150-200 feet.					6	
21.12.40	R2150	Flt Lt Gibson Plt Off Francombe	Patrol: Horncastle/ Waddington	1955	2210	One enemy aircraft seen illuminated in searchlights at about 2150 hours but for too short a period for any action to be taken.					7	
23.12.40							2140	AC Taylor	3.10N	X Raid Patrol, R/T PACKED		8
22.1.41	R2196	Flt Lt Gibson Sgt Parr	X Raid Patrol	1140	1330	No enemy aircraft sighted.	2096	Sgt Parr	2.00D	X RAID PATROL	8	9

Date	Aircraft	Crew	Operation	Up	Down	Remarks	No.	Crew	Time	Operation		
31.1.41	R2144	Flt Lt Gibson Sgt Ashworth	X Raid Patrol	1128	1309	No enemy aircraft sighted.	2140	Sgt Ashworth	1.45D	X RAID PATROL	9	10
31.1.41	R2196	Flt Lt Gibson Sgt Isherwood	Patrol	1510	1535	[Recalled with R/T trouble.]	2196	Sgt Ashworth	??	X RAID PATROL	10	11
1.2.41							2144	Sgt James	0.50D	DAY OPS, A BLENHEIM NEARLY BOUGHT IT		12
4.2.41	R2150	Flt Lt Gibson Sgt James	X Raid Patrol	1835	2125	[See F 541 report for this date.]	2150	Sgt James	2.50N	X RAID, E. AIRCRAFT ATTACKED	11	13
5.2.41	R2150	Flt Lt Gibson Sgt James	Dawn patrol	0725	0845	No enemy aircraft sighted.	2196	Sgt James	1.10N	X RAID, 3 BLIPS!	12	14
5.2.41	R2196	Flt Lt Gibson Sgt James	Patrol	1730	1840	No enemy aircraft sighted.					13	
9.2.41	R2144	Flt Lt Gibson Sgt James	X Raid Patrol	1840	2030	No enemy aircraft sighted.	2144	Sgt James	1.50N	X RAID, AI U/S	14	15
10.2.41	R2144	Flt Lt Gibson Sgt James	Dawn patrol	0700	0930	No enemy aircraft sighted.	2144	Sgt James	2.30N	DAWN PATROL - FLU[S]H-IN[G] DEN HELDER.	15	16
14.2.41	R2150	Flt Lt Gibson Sgt Austin	X Raid Patrol	1810	2040	No enemy aircraft sighted.	2180	Sgt Austin	2.35N	X RAID	16	17
15.2.41	R2150	Flt Lt Gibson Sgt Austin	Patrol	1141	1241	At 1233 aircraft sighted but identified as friendly, viz, a long-nosed Blenheim.					17	
16.2.41							2182	Sgt Strachan	1.40D	DAY PATROL - FRIENDLY		18
28.2.41							2183	Sgt James	0.15D	PATROL OVER WADDINGTON		19
2.3.41	R2094	Flt Lt Gibson Sgt James	Dusk patrol	1850	2235	No enemy aircraft in vicinity so patrolled [sic] developed into AI practice interceptions between Beaufighters R2144 and R2094.	2094	Sgt James	3.40N	DUSK PATROL	18	20
6.3.41	R2250	Flt Lt Gibson Plt Off Watson	Patrol	1115	1245	No enemy aircraft sighted.	2250	Plt Off Watson	1.30D	X RAID PATROL		21
7.3.41	R2250	Flt Lt Gibson Plt Off Watson	Patrol	1030	1340	No enemy aircraft sighted.	2250	Plt Off Watson	0.10D	X RAID PATROL	19	22
8.3.41		Flt Lt Gibson Sgt Pearce									20	
12.3.41							1146	Sgt James	1.50N	X RAID - ONE HUN DESTROYED		23
13.3.41	R2250	Flt Lt Gibson Sgt Pearce	Patrol: Skegness	0007	0200	No enemy aircraft sighted.	2144	Sgt James	0.10D	X RAID	21	24

Date	A/C	Crew	Duty	Up	Down	Combat report	A/C	Operator	Time	Personal remark	No.	No.
13.3.41	R2250	Flt Lt Gibson / Sgt James	Patrol	2300	0105	No enemy aircraft sighted, but one 'blip' obtained about 4 miles S.W. Sutton Bridge, height about 12,000 ft then lost.	2250	Sgt James	2.35N	X RAID, HEINKEL III	22	25
14.3.41			Patrol: Wells	2052	2215	No e/a seen.	2250	Sgt Ryall	1.357N	X RAID, NOTHING ABOUT	23	26
4.4.41	R2250	Flt Lt Gibson / Sgt James	Patrol	21[?]?	2348						24	
8.4.41	R [sic]	Flt Lt Gibson / Sgt Bell	Patrol	2110	2125	No e/a sighted. When landing at WCI a bandit opened fire on the Beaufighter and injured Sgt Bell in the leg.	2250	Sgt Bell	2.00N	X RAID, SHOT UP WHEN LANDING BY JU.88, WENT THROUGH HEDGE, NO DAMAGE, BELL WOUNDED, SELF OK.	25	27
10.4.41	R2250	Flt Lt Gibson / Sgt Taylor	Patrol			Electrical system u/s Aircraft recalled.	2094	Sgt Taylor	0.10N	X RAID, WIRELESS U/S	26	28
16.4.41							2250	Sgt James	2.00N	X RAID - SAW NOUGHT	27	29
16.4.41							2250	Sgt James	1.50N	X RAID, G.C.I. PRACTICE TOO.	28	30
17.4.41	R2250	Flt Lt Gibson / Sgt James	Patrol	0210	0355	'Blip' obtained at AI and held for 15 minutes at 0225 hours at [76/8] 000 ft, 5 miles S.E. of Digby.					29	
23.4.41	R2250	Flt Lt Gibson / Sgt James	Patrol	2050	0130	Several 'blips' obtained . An e/a sighted (Do.17) East of Boston at 0106 hours. Pilot gave two short bursts then broke off engagement as e/a's return fire was very accurate; e/a believed damaged.	2250	Sgt James	4.40N	A GREAT NIGHT, 10 BLIPS, 2 VISUALS, HIT THE SECOND AND DAMAGED IT, RETURN FIRE - QUITE FRIGHTENING -	30	31
(ii) RAF West Malling												
2.5.41	R2250	Flt Lt Gibson / Sgt James	Patrol				2250	Sgt James	2.00D	SECTOR RECCO. A.I.		32
3.5.41	R2250	Flt Lt Gibson / Sgt James	Patrol	2140	2350		2250	Sgt James	2.10D	X RAID PATROL, NOTHING		33
7.5.41	R2250	Flt Lt Gibson / Sgt James	Patrol	2335	0240	1 unidentified aircraft destroyed by visual contact and Observer Corps plot control from Biggin Hill.	2250	Sgt James	3.05N	X RAID - ONE DESTROYED BY LUCKY BURST, IT BLEW UP, ANOTHER DID THE SAME BEFORE I COULD OPEN FIRE!		34
9.5.41	R2250	Flt Lt Gibson / Sgt James	Patrol	2225	0110		2250	Sgt James	2.45N	X RAID PATROL, STOOGEING		35

Date	Aircraft	Crew	Duty	Up	Down	Remarks	Base	Observer	Time	Operation	No.	No.
10.5.41	R2250	Flt Lt Gibson / Sgt James	Patrol	2350	0015		2250	Sgt James	8.35N	X RAID PATROL. A BLITZ ON LONDON. SAW TWO HE III - BUT CANNONS WOULD NOT FIRE. DAMAGED ONE WITH BROWNINGS - NO CLAIM	31	36
10.5.41	R2250	Flt Lt Gibson / Sgt James	Patrol	0110	0420		2250				32	
23.5.41							2250	Plt Off Willis	1.05N	X RAID, RETURNED		37
1.6.41	R2250	Flt Lt Gibson / Sgt James	Patrol	2225	2245		2250	Sgt James	0.20N	N/F TEST	33	38
1.6.41	R2250	Flt Lt Gibson / Sgt James	Patrol	0020	0150		2250	Sgt James	1.30N	X RAID	34	39
11.6.41	R2250	Flt Lt Gibson / Sgt James	Patrol	0110	0415		2250	Plt Off Willis	3.05N	X RAID, 3 BLIPS	35	40
13.6.41	R2250	Flt Lt Gibson / Sgt James	Patrol	2300	0220		2250	Plt Off Willis	3.20N	X RAID	36	41
17.6.41	R2250	Flt Lt Gibson / Sgt James	Patrol	2315	0125	No contacts.	2250	Sgt James	2.10N	X RAID	37	42
23.6.41	R2250	Flt Lt Gibson / Sgt James	Patrol	2320	0150	No contacts.	2250	Sgt James	2.30N	X RAID AI/U/S	38	43
25.6.41	R2250	Flt Lt Gibson / Sgt James	Patrol	2340	0210	No contacts.	2250	Sgt James	2.30N	X RAID, NOTHING	39	44
29.6.41	R2250	Sqn Ldr Gibson / Sgt James	Patrol	2320	0245		2250	Sgt James	3.25N	X RAID, PRACTICE G.C.I. TWO VISUALS OF TARGET - GOOD!	40	45
2.7.41	R2250	Sqn Ldr Gibson / Sgt James	Patrol	2315	0200	No contacts.	2250	Sgt James	2.45N	X RAID PATROL	41	46
4.7.41	R2250	Sqn Ldr Gibson / Sgt James	Patrol	2340	0305	No contacts.	2250	Sgt James	3.25N	X RAID PATROL	42	47
5.7.41	R2250	Sqn Ldr Gibson / Sgt James	Patrol	2340	0250	No contacts.	2250	Sgt James	3.10N	X RAID PATROL	43	48
6.7.41	R2250	Sqn Ldr Gibson / Sgt James	Patrol	2330	0240	No contacts.	2250	Sgt James	3.10N	X RAID PATROL - ONE HEINKEL III DESTROYED OFF SHEERNESS - BLEW UP!	44	49
10.7.41	R2250	Sqn Ldr Gibson / Sgt James	Patrol	0130	0310	No contacts.	2250	Sgt James	1.40N	X RAID PATROL	45	50
12.7.41	R2250	Sqn Ldr Gibson / Sgt James	Patrol	0025	0140	No contacts.	2250	Sgt James	1.15N	X RAID - G.C.I. 3 VISUAL -	46	51

Date	Aircraft	Crew	Duty	Up	Down	Remarks				Pilot	Time	Operation	No.	No.
17.7.41	R2250	Sqn Ldr Gibson / Sgt James	Patrol	2345	0215	No contacts.			2250	Sgt James	2.30N	X RAID PATROL	47	52
22.7.41	R2250	Sqn Ldr Gibson / Sgt James	Patrol	2305	0145	No contacts.			2250	Sgt James	2.40N	PATROL	48	53
27.7.41	R2250	Sqn Ldr Gibson / Sgt James	Patrol	2345	0015	S/L.			2250	Sgt James	0.30N	X RAID, R/T F.	49	54
27.7.41	R2250	Sqn Ldr Gibson / Sgt James	Patrol	0310	0435	No contacts.			2250	Sgt James	1.25N	X RAID	50	55
29.7.41	R2250	Sqn Ldr Gibson / Sgt James	Patrol	2305	0045	No contacts.			2250	Sgt James	1.05N	X RAID PATROL	51	56
10.8.41									2250	Sgt James	1.20D	A.I. PATROL LE TOUQUET		57
25.8.41	R2250	Sqn Ldr Gibson / Sgt James	Patrol	2055	2250	G.C.I.			2250	Sgt James	1.55N	PATROL	52	58
26.8.41	R2250	Sqn Ldr Gibson / Sgt James	Patrol	2240	0125	Searchlight co-operation.			2250	Sgt James	2.45N	PATROL AND SEARCHLIGHT CO-OP	53	59
28.8.41	R2250	Sqn Ldr Gibson / Sgt James		2205	0035	G.C.I.			2250	Sgt James	2.30N	PATROL	54	60
29.8.41	R2250	Sqn Ldr Gibson / Sgt James		2050	2330	G.C.I.			2250	Sgt James	2.40N	PATROL	55	61
29.8.41	R2250	Sqn Ldr Gibson / Sgt James		0020	0200	G.C.I.			2250	Sgt James	1.40N	PATROL	56	62
1.9.41	R2250	Sqn Ldr Gibson / Sgt James	Patrol	2045	2135				2250	Sgt James	0.50N	X RAID	57	63
2.9.41	R2250	Sqn Ldr Gibson / Sgt James	Patrol	2030	2230				2250	Sgt James	1.50N	STOOGE PATROL	58	64
11.9.41	R2250	Sqn Ldr Gibson / Sgt James	Patrol	2330	0125				2250	Sgt James	1.55N	STOOGE PATROL	59	65
12.9.41	R2250	Sqn Ldr Gibson / Sgt James	Patrol	2035	0005				2250	Sgt James	3.05N	OPERATION GIBSON AND X RAID	60	66
13.9.41	R2250	Sqn Ldr Gibson / Sgt James	Patrol	2210	0035				2250	Sgt James	2.25N	OPERATION GIBSON - X RAID	61	67
15.9.41	R2250	Sqn Ldr Gibson / Sgt James	Patrol	2000	2255				2250	Sgt James	2.55N	X RAID TWO BLIPS	62	68
16.9.41	R2250	Sqn Ldr Gibson / Sgt James	Patrol	1950	0001				2250	Sgt James	3.10N	X RAID PATROL, ONE BLIP	63	69
18.9.41		Sqn Ldr Gibson / Sgt James							2250	Sgt James	0.20D	A.I. PATROL.		70

Date	Aircraft	Crew	Duty	Up	Down	Duty	Aircraft	Observer	Time	Remarks	Ref	Ref
29.9.41	R7573	Sqn Ldr Gibson / Sgt James	Patrol	1905	2230		7673	Sgt James	3.25N	PATROL, SAW A HEINKEL	64	71
1.10.41	R7627	Sqn Ldr Gibson / Sgt James	Patrol	1955	2005		7627	Sgt James	0.10N	PATROL	65	72
3.10.41	R7646	Sqn Ldr Gibson / Sgt James	Patrol	1850	2210		7641	Sgt James	3.20N	PATROL. NO HUNS -	66	73
21.10.41	R2250	Sqn Ldr Gibson / Sgt James	Patrol	1800	2130		2250	Sgt James	3.30N	X RAID, SAW AND DAMAGED TWO JU 87'S B. OFF DOVER.	67	74
25.10.41	R2250	Sqn Ldr Gibson / Sgt Ellis	Patrol	2010	2305		2250	Sgt James	2.55N	PATROL, NOTHING.	68	75
26.10.41	R2250	Sqn Ldr Gibson / Sgt James	Patrol	1740	2035		2250	Sgt James	2.55N	PATROL, NOTHING.	69	76
31.10.41	R2250	Sqn Ldr Gibson / Sgt James	Patrol	1800	2020		2250	Sgt James	2.20N	PATROL, NOTHING.	70	77
2.11.41	R2250	Sqn Ldr Gibson / Sgt James	Patrol	1815	2000		2250	Sgt James	1.45N	PATROL, G.C.I.	71	78
3.11.41	R2250	Sqn Ldr Gibson / Sgt James	Patrol	1735	1745	Patrol	2250	Sgt James	0.10N	N. Patrol.	72	79
6.11.41	R2250	Sqn Ldr Gibson / Sgt James	Patrol	1800	2000	Patrol	2250	Sgt James	2.00N	X RAID PATROL.	73	80
10.11.41							2250	Sgt James	1.20D	PATROL IN ESTUARY		81
12.11.41							2250	Sgt James	2.15N	PATROL, TWO INTERCEPTS		82
17.11.41	R2250	Sqn Ldr Gibson / Sgt Miller	Patrol	1730	2100	Patrol	2250	Sgt Miller	3.30N	X RAID, TWO BLIPS FILTHY W.	74	83
20.11.41							2250	Fg Off Willis	0.35N	PATROL.		84
21.11.41	R2250	Sqn Ldr Gibson / Fg Off Willis	Patrol	1900	2150	Patrol	2250	Fg Off Willis	2.50N	PATROL, TWO VISUALS BEAU.	75	85
27.11.41	R2250	Sqn Ldr Gibson / Fg Off Willis	Patrol	1700	2100	Patrol	2250	Fg Off Willis	4.00N	PATROL. Queer control.	76	86
8.12.41							2250	Sgt James	3.05N	PATROL. NOTHING ABOUT.		87
11.12.41	R2250	Sqn Ldr Gibson / Sgt James	Patrol	1815	2005		2250	Sgt James	1.50N	X RAID PATROL.	77	88
15.12.41	R2250	Sqn Ldr Gibson / Sgt James	Patrol	1655	1925		2250	Sgt James	2.30N	X RAID PATROL, NOTHING ABOUT.	78	89

15.12.41	R2250	Sqn Ldr Gibson / Sgt James		Patrol	2210	2345	S/L. Co-op.	1.35N	Sgt James	2250	79	90	X RAID PATROL, NOTHING ABOUT.
106 SQUADRON Avro Manchester aircraft													
(i) RAF Coningsby													
22.4.42	7418	Wg Cdr Gibson / WO Boyce / Sgt Greenwood / Plt Off Wickens / Sgt Carter / Sgt Jordan / Sgt Youngs		Gardening: Radishes	2020	0330	Clear. Good visibility. Garden was located by means of pin-point on island [of] Fehmarn and four mines were successfully dropped in required position.	6.50N	7 crew	L7418	1	1	Minelaying in the Baltic.
25.4.42	R5770	Wg Cdr Gibson / Sgt McNair / Sgt Hosler / Plt Off Wickens / Plt Off Churcher / Sgt Jordan / Sgt Garbett		Bombing; Rostock	2215	0505	No cloud. Very good visibility. Attacked by level run at 4,800 ft at 220 IAS. Bombs certainly fell on target but result not seen owing to smoke.	7.20N	7 crew	R5770	2	2	Bombing Rostock, 3500'. Good Results.
4.5.42	L7378	Wg Cdr Gibson / Flt Sgt Vivian / Sgt Herbert / Sgt Smith / Plt Off Grain / Sgt Morgan / Fg Off Combie		Gardening: Rosemary	2115	0225	7/10th cloud. Visibility 6 miles. Four mines in required position, dropped at 5 seconds intervals. Slight opposition from SYLT.	5.10N	7 crew	L7378	3	3	Minelaying off Sylt.
8.5.42	R5770	Wg Cdr Gibson / Plt Off Vivian / Plt Off Hutchison / Sgt Cartwright / Plt Off Grain / Plt Off Wickens		Heinkel works: Warnemunde	2200	0520	Very clear but dark. Target located and bombed on straight and level run from 3,500 ft. Bombs believed to have fallen on target. Fierce opposition.	7.10N		R5570	4	4	A hot trip. BOMBING WARNEMUNDE. 3500 ft. LOAD 6 x 1000.
Avro Lancaster aircraft													
8.7.42	R5681	Wg Cdr G P Gibson (C) / Plt Off D J Shannon (2) / Fg Off I Vivian (N) / Plt Off F Ruskell (B) / Sgt D A Jordan (W) / Flt Lt Combie (M) / Plt Off J F Wickens (R)		Bombing; Wilhelms-haven	0015	0415	Very good but dark. Bombed from 12,000 ft. Bombs fell in dock area but not sure whether submarine yards were hit. Opposition fairly accurate.	4.00N	Usual crew	5681	5	5	OPERATIONS. BOMBING WILHELMSHAVEN. 10,000ft. load 5 x 2000 H.C. GOOD PRANG.

Date	Aircraft No.	Crew	Duty	Time Up	Time Down	Remarks	No.	Crew	Time	Remarks	No.	No.
11.7.42	R5861	Wg Cdr G P Gibson (C) / Plt Off D J Shannon (2) / Fg Off F Ruskell (B) / Sgt G Flowerday (W) / Sgt J Gaffney (B) / Flt Lt F Combie (M) / Plt Off J F Wickens (R)	Bombing: Submarine works, Danzig	1700	0315	Bomb Load: 4 x 1,000 lb RDX. Very low cloud and heavy rain storms. Arrived over target too late and did not attack. Bombed a ship about 800 tons Gdynia but nearest bomb was 20 yards away. Machine-gunned flak ship. Returned same route as outward journey. Weather was exceptionally bad throughout.	5681	Crew	10.15ND	DAYLIGHT RAID ON DANZIG. LOAD 5 x 1,000, MISSED A SHIP IN HARBOUR BY 20 yrds FROM 1000 ft.	6	6
18.7.42	R5670	Wg Cdr G P Gibson (C) / Plt Off D J Shannon (2) / Plt Off A Maxwell (N) / Sgt J Gaffney (B) / Plt Off R E Hutchison (W) / Flt Lt Combie (M) / Plt Off J F Wickens (R)	Bombing: Essen	1325	1605	Reached Flushing when the order to return was received. Bombs jettisoned safely into the sea.	5678	Usual crew	2.40	DAYLIGHT RAID ON ESSEN.	7	7
26.7.42	R5750	Wg Cdr G P Gibson (C) / Plt Off D J Shannon (2) / Plt Off F Ruskell (B) / Sgt J Gaffney (B) / Plt Off R E Hutchison (W) / Flt Lt Combie (M) / Plt Off J F Wickens (R)	Bombing: Hamburg	2320	0530	Little or no cloud, excellent visibility, moonlight. Target easily located and bombed visually from 14,000 ft. Bombs fell in burning area S.W. of aiming-point causing more fires in the shipyards. Flak was very heavy and accurate. A very successful trip. Bomb Load: 1 x 4,000 lb / 6 x 500 lb, GP / 6 x 250 lb, GP	5681	Usual crew	6.10N	OPERATIONS. 700 AIRCRAFT ON HAMBURG. LARGE FIRES BURNING ALL OVER TOWN. FLAK VERY INTENSE AND WE NEARLY BOUGHT IT COMING OUT AT BRUNSBUTTEL.	8	8
31.7.42	R7579	Wg Cdr G P Gibson (C) / Plt Off D J Shannon (2) / Plt Off F. Ruskell (N) / Sgt J J Sleo (B) / Plt Off R E Hutchison (W) / Flt Lt Combie (M) / Plt Off J F Wickens (R)	Bombing: Düsseldorf	0035	0425	No cloud, visibility good. Target found to be well alight on arrival and bombs were dropped into centre of town from 12,000 ft. Opposition not heavy. Average speed over enemy territory was 230 m.p.h. Bomb Load: 1 x 4,000 lb, HC / 6 x 500 lb, GP / 6 x 250 lb, GP	5681	Usual crew	3.50N	OPERATIONS. THIS TIME DUSSELDORF. COLLECTED A PACKET FROM 500 AIRCRAFT. LOAD 1 x 4000 + 12 SBC. HEIGHT 12000.	9	9

Date	Aircraft No.	Crew	Duty	Up	Down		Remarks	Time	Operations	Details		
8.8.42	L7434	Wg Cdr G P Gibson (E) Sgt J Russell (N) Plt Off F E Drew (B) Sgt R D McPherson (W) Sgt G G Chalmers (M) Sgt A P Jamieson (R)	Gardening: Baltic	2300	0605	5637	Usual crew	7.05N	OPERATIONS MINING SKAW.	10/10th cloud at 500 feet with very poor visibility. After long search pin-pointed on SKAW and made timed run from there. Five mines were dropped in the SILVERTHORN Garden at intervals of 20 seconds. Operations successfully completed.	10	10
10.8.42	R5901	Wg Cdr G P Gibson (E) Sgt A F Adamson (E) Plt Off F Ruskell (N) Sgt B R McNair (B) Sgt J J Wakerley (W) Sgt G.N. Feltham (M) Sgt D Garbett (R)	Gardening: Asparagus	2115	0445	5801	Usual crew	7.30N	OPERATIONS MINING BALTIC. BOTH THESE RAIDS WERE CARRIED OUT IN THE WORST WEATHER IMAGINABLE.	Visibility fair but some seamist. Identified Helskov Point, made DR run from there and dropped five mines in the required position. There was no opposition.	11	11
12.8.42	R5899	Wg Cdr G P Gibson (E) Sgt F E B Burton-Burgess (E) Plt Off F Ruskell (N) Sgt D Crozier (B) Sgt R S Thompson (W) Flt Sgt E R Clarke (M) Flt Sgt E M Banks (R)	Bombing: Mainz	2300	0445	5899	Usual crew	5.05	OPERATIONS. 150 a/c BOMBED MAINZ. We bombed from 5000' under cloud. Load. 5 x 2000 lb. This raid was an outstanding success. 135 acres of the centre of the town was [sic] destroyed!	10/10ths cloud with Base at 6,000 feet. Pin-point on island in Rhine and made attack at 6,000 feet, below cloud. Target was definitely in sight at moment of release of bombs but results were not seen owing to evasive action. Considerable opposition from light flak but this was avoided by diving to ground level; no interference on homeward journey. Bomb Load: 4 x 2,000lb, HC	12	12
27.8.42	W4118	Wg Cdr G P Gibson (E) Sgt R F Crossley (E) Plt Off F Ruskell (N) Sqn Ldr R Richardson (B) Plt Off R E Hutchison (W) Flt Lt W B Oliver (M) Plt Off J F Wickens (R)	Bombing: Warships at Gdynia	2000	0550	Y	S/Ldr Richardson + Crew	9.50N	OPERATIONS. SPECIAL raid on GDYNIA WHERE 3 GERMAN WARSHIPS WERE LYING. ATTACKED FROM ALL HEIGHTS 6-12000 ft but haze made it hard to make a good run up with the SABS (bomb sight). After the 12th run, we bombed Gneizeneau [sic] but missed it with our 6 x 1000 lb bombs by 100°. Bad luck.	9/10th cloud over target with some haze. Impossible to locate any warships despite making twelve separate runs over the area. Managed to locate docks and finally bombed these from 8,000 feet in the estimated position of the Gneisenau. Bursts were seen across the docks. Disappointing trip. Bomb Load: 6 x 1,000lb, RDX	13	13

Date	Aircraft	Crew	Duty	Time	Time	Code	Details	Crew	Duration	Remarks	No.	No.
1.9.42	R5551	Wg Cdr G P Gibson / Sgt R P Howard (E) / Plt Off F Ruskell (N) / Plt Off D S Margach (B) / Plt Off R E Hutchison (W) / Flt Lt W B Oliver (M) / Plt Off J F Wickens (R)	Bombing: Saarbrucken	0010	0620	V	Weather fine. No cloud, good visibility. Located target area but misled by Pathfinders' flares and bombed town afterwards plotted as Saarlouis. Eight-thousand-pound bomb was seen to burst in centre of town causing terrific explosion and starting large fire. No opposition. Bomb Load: 1 x 8,000 lb.	Crew	5.10N	OPERATIONS. BOMBING. SAARLUTEN. (which the Pathfinders mistook for SAARBRUCKEN. LOAD. 1 x 8000 LB. TARGET DESTROYED.	14	14
13.9.42	W4127	Wg Cdr G P Gibson / Sgt R P Howard (E) / Plt Off F Ruskell (N) / Plt Off D S Margach (B) / Plt Off R E Hutchison (W) / Flt Lt W B Oliver (M) / Plt Off J F Wickens (R)	Bombing: Bremen	2340	0355	C11	Little cloud, thick ground haze. Target located by river and part of town. Bombed from 11,000 feet and although bursts were seen, not certain where they fell - believed in town. Opposition heavy. Photograph revealed semi built-up area. Bomb Load: 1 x 4,000 lb. 12 SBC (30 lb.)	Usual crew	4.15N	BOMBING BREMEN. A VERY HOT TARGET. LOST 10% ATTAKING [sic] FORCE.	15	15
23.9.42	W4102	Wg Cdr G P Gibson / Sgt H J Lowe (E) / Plt Off F Ruskell (N) / Plt Off A L Dickinson (B) / Flt Sgt T H Anderson (W) / Flt Lt W B Oliver (M) / Plt Off J F Wickens (R)	Bombing: Dornier factory, Wismar	2230	0605	E	7/10th cloud, visibility good. Aiming-point seen and target in bomb-sight when bombs were dropped from 2,000 feet. Bombs not seen to burst. Opposition very intense and it was necessary to come down to 300 feet to get away from town. Bomb Load: 14 SBC (30 lb.)	Usual crew	7.35N	BOMBING DORNIER FACTORY AT WISMAR FROM 2,000 FT. LOTS OF GUNS. RAINING AND DARK. HIT IT OK WITH OUR INCENDIARIES.	16	16
(ii) RAF Syerston												
15.10.42	W4118	Wg Cdr G P Gibson / Sgt D A Jordon (E) / Plt Off F Ruskell (N) / Plt Off F W Walley (B) / Plt Off R E Hutchison (W) / Flt Lt W B Oliver (M) / Plt Off J F Wickens (R)	Bombing: Cologne	1905	2330	Y	Cloud over the target at 6,000 feet, visibility was good. Identified bridges over the river and dropped bombs from 10,000 feet - they were believed to have burst on the east side of the river. Flak was very heavy and the aircraft was hit. Bomb Load: 1 x 4,000 lb. 12 SBC (4 lb.)	Crew	4.25N	OPERATIONS. COLOGNE. VERY SCATTERED DUE TO HIGH WIND.	17	17

17.10.42	W4118	Wg Cdr G P Gibson Sgt A L McDonald (E) Plt Off F Ruskell (N) Sgt R N Lindsay (B) Plt Off R E Hutchison (W) Flt Lt W B Oliver (M) Plt Off J F Wickens (R)	Bombing: Le Creusot	1200	2225	No cloud, visibility good. Flew out in formation but broke away near Le Creusot to make a special attack, the objective being Montchanin powerhouse. Bombed from 500 feet and scored direct hits. Afterwards machine-gunned transformer plants. Very little opposition. Successful raid.	Y	Crew	10.25ND	DAYLIGHT LOW LEVEL ATTACK ON THE TRANSFORMER STATION AT LE CREUSOT. BOMBED AT 500 FT AND RECEIVED A FEW BULLET HOLES. LATER INFORMATION SAID THAT THIS TARGET WAS DESTROYED. [Gibson has subsequently added:] This transformer was later reported to be destroyed and would take two years to repair!	18	18
22.10.42	W4118	Wg Cdr G P Gibson Sgt A L McDonald (E) Plt Off F Ruskell (N) Sgt R N Lindsay (B) Plt Off R E Hutchison (W) Flt Lt W B Oliver (M) Plt Off J F Wickens (R)	Bombing: Genoa	1730	0300	Bright moonlight, some smoke haze. Target located visually and bombed from 10,000 feet. Target was in bomb-sight and the bombs were seen to burst in a built-up area about ½ mile north of aiming-point. Photograph showed area 1½ miles distant. Opposition slight. Successful trip. Bomb Load: 2 x 1,000 lb. 2 SBC (4 lb.)	Y	Crew	9.30N	OPERATIONS GENOA. A GOOD PRANG. PHOTO 1¼ m from AIMING POINT. LANDED BRANSTON [sic]	19	19
24.10.42	R5492	Wg Cdr G P Gibson Sgt G. Peglar (E) Plt Off F Ruskell (N) Plt Off B R McNair (B) Plt Off R E Hutchison (W) Flt Lt W B Oliver (M) Plt Off J F Wickens (R)	Bombing: Milan	1220	2245	Cloud unexpectedly high over France, had to fly at 6,000 feet. Flew on and reached target, only to find it covered by 10/10ths cloud. Came down to 4,000 feet. Saw railway station in Milan, finally bombing through break in cloud at 6,000 feet. Bombs seen to burst in built-up area. Saw a CR42 but no attack developed. Took photographs of town. Bomb Load: 4 x 1,000 lb. RDX 3 SBC (4lb.)	Y	Crew Sgt Peglar Plt Off Ruskell Flt Sgt Lewis Plt Off Hutchinson Plt Off Wickens Flt Lt Oliver	7.25D	DAYLIGHT RAID ON MILAN, ITALY. WENT DOWN TO 4000 ft. OVER MILAN. BOMBED FROM 5,000 FT, JUST IN CLOUD. A MARVELLOUS TRIP WITH MOST MAGNIFICENT SCENERY OVER THE ALPS.	20	20
6.11.42							Y	Crew	9.30N	OPERATIONS - GENOA. THE MOST CONCENTRATED RAID I HAVE EVER SEEN. LANDED W. MALLING.	21	21

No.	Date	Aircraft	Crew	Duty	Up	Down	Remarks	Code	Crew	Time	Ops Remarks	No.
21	7.11.42	W4118	Wg Cdr G P Gibson / Sgt J L Irvine (E) / Plt Off F Ruskell (N) / Flt Sgt T W Lewis (B) / Plt Off R E Hutchison (W) / Flt Lt W B Oliver (M) / Plt Off J F Wickens (R)	Bombing: Genoa	1730	0145	No cloud, visibility good. Town and harbour clearly seen and bombs were aimed, from 9,500 feet, slightly east of aiming-point and own bomb bursts were seen. Attack appeared to be concentrated and devastating. Bomb Load: 2 x 1,000 lb. 6 SBC (4 lb.)					
	18.11.42							Y	Crew	7.25N	OPS. TURIN. FIAT WORKS. 6000 ft. Good trip. Landed Middle Wallop.	22
22	28.11.42	R5551	Wg Cdr G P Gibson / Sgt P J Page (E) / Plt Off F Ruskell (N) / Flt Sgt T W Lewis (B) / Plt Off R E G Hutchison (W) / Sgt T H Cartwright (M) / Plt Off J F Wickens (R) / Major J B Mulloch (No 5 Gp. FLO)	Bombing: Turin	1900	0300	Bombing conditions very good. Target in bomb-sight when bombing from 8,000 feet and bombs seen to burst in centre of town. Flew around over target for 30 minutes taking a movie-film of the bombing - this turned out to be very successful. Passenger taken on this trip - Major Mulloch, the 5 Group flak liaison officer. Bomb Load: 1 x 8,000 lb.	Y	Crew + Major Mullock + Sgt Cartwright	8.00N	OPS. Turin. A Grand Prang. 7000 ft. Took Cine-Camera photos. 1 x 8000 bomb on the lilies.	23
23	11.1.43	LM303	Wg Cdr G P Gibson (C) / Flt Sgt L W Cronk (2) / Plt Off F Ruskell (N) / Sub Lt G Muttrie (B) / Plt Off R E G Hutchison (W) / Flt Lt W B Oliver (M) / Fg Off J F Wickens (R)	Bombing: Essen	1630	2210	10/10ths cloud. Target located by skymarker technique. Bombed at 1935 hrs from 2,000 feet when the red and green warning flares were seen, the bombing being carried out the white flare [sic]. Trip did not seem to be too successful. Flak heavy. Bomb Load: 1 x 4,000 lb. 12 SBC (4 lb.)	M	USUAL CREW S/LT MUTTRIE	5.40N	OPS. ESSEN. P.F.F. Technique. Came back the wrong way, left R/T on transmit. Result very embarrassing.	24
24	16.1.43	R5611	Wg Cdr G P Gibson (C) / Sgt G O McGregor (2) / Fg Off F Ruskell (N) / Sub Lt G Muttrie (B) / Plt Off R E G Hutchison (W) / Flt Lt W B Oliver (M) / Fg Off J F Wickens (R) / Major R Dimbleby (BBC War Correspondent)	Bombing: Berlin	1635	0150	Thick haze made pin-pointing difficult. Three runs made over target before dropping 8,000-lb. bomb from 18,000 feet near the red marker flare. Results not seen. Believed that bombs fell in Berlin but trip was disappointing due to weather. Bomb Load: 1 x 8,000 lb. HC	W				

Date	Aircraft	Crew	Duty	Time Up	Time Down	Remarks	Code	Crew	Time	Remarks	No.	No.
17.1.43							W	RICHARD DIMBLEBY Fg Off Ruskell Sub Lt Muttrie Flt Lt Oliver Plt Off Hutchison Fg Off Wickens Sgt McGregor	9.15N	OPS. BERLIN, 1 x 8000 LB. A good trip and fairly successful. The residential quarters got it! Dimbleby broadcasted next day. This is my 67th Bombing trip.	25	25
14.2.43	W4842	Wg Cdr G P Gibson (C) Flt Lt T Morrison (2) Flt Lt W M Burnside (N) Sgt J Cunningham (B) Plt Off R E G Hutchison (W) Sgt H Rigby (M) Fg Off J F Wickens (R) Sgt Cartwright, Movie Operator	Bombing: Milan	1820	0300	No cloud, very little haze. Target easily identified in the moonlight and a straight run was made across the target at 11,000 feet, bombs being released at 2241 hours and seen to burst near the aiming-point. Took excellent photograph 1 1/2 miles from aiming-point. Flew around for 20 minutes taking movies. Enjoyable and successful trip. Bomb Load: 1 x 4,000 lb. 4 SCB (4 lb.)	O	Crew + Flt Lt Morrison	8.40N	OPERATIONS - MILAN SQUADRON GOT SIX AIMING POINTS. A GOOD TRIP!	26	25
25.2.43	ED649	Wg Cdr G P Gibson (C) Sgt D N Britton (2) Flt Lt W M Burnside (N) Sgt K Newby (N) Flt Lt R Lodge (B) Plt Off R E G Hutchison (W) Flt Lt W B Oliver (M) Fg Off J F Wickens (R)	Bombing: Nuremberg	1920	0230	Conditions very good for bombing; no cloud, excellent visibility. Target located visually and bombed from 12,000 feet. A very concentrated attack which caused huge fires and explosions. A good but frightening trip - aircraft circling around waiting for the PFF. Rather dangerous. Bomb Load: 1 x 4,000 lb. 12 SBC (30 lb.)	X	Flt Lt Burnside Flt Lt Oliver II Fg Off Wickens Sgt Britton Flt Lt Lodge Plt Off Hutchison	7.10N	OPERATIONS:- NUREMBERG. QUITE A GOOD TRIP. HAD TO WAIT FOR P.F.F. LOAD 1 x 4000 LB + 5000 INCEND	27	26

Date	Aircraft	Crew	Duty	Time	Remarks	Code	Crew	Hrs	Remarks		
26.2.43	ED649	Wg Cdr G P Gibson (C) Sgt D N Britton (2) Flt Lt W M Burnside (N) Plt Off R E G Hutchison (W) Flt Lt W B Oliver (M) Fg Off J F Wickens (R)	Bombing: Cologne	1835	Weather good, slight ground haze but river and ground detail seen, these were in sights, bombing in a straight, fast (220 IAS.) run from 16,000 feet at 2121 hours. Bombs seen to burst near aiming-point. Concentration was achieved and it seemed that the target had been accurately bombed. Heavy flak encountered in barrage form. This was pilot's 70th bombing raid. Bomb Load: 11 x 4,000 lb. 12 SBC (30 lb.)	X	Same crew	5.25N	OPERATIONS:- COLOGNE. A WIZARD PRANG. HUGE FIRES. FLAK MODERATE. SAME LOAD. MY 169TH WAR FLIGHT.	27	28
11.3.43	ED649	Wg Cdr G P Gibson (C) Plt Off W R Thompson (E) Flt Lt N H Scrivener (N) Sub Lt G Muttrie (B) Flt Sgt D H Marshall (W) Flt Lt J Oliver (M) Sgt J R Stone (R)	Bombing: Stuttgart	2020	Patches of stratus cloud at 15,000 ft., hazy. Most of trip was made on 3 engines at 4,000 feet, climbing to 12,000 feet to make bombing run. Bombs dropped at 2320 hours and seen to burst near a concentration of fires. Photograph plotted 4 miles from aiming-point. Bomb Load: 1 x 4,000 lb. 12 SBC (4 lb.)	X	Plt Off Thompson Sub Lt Muttrie Flt Lt Scrivener Flt Lt Oliver Sgt Hargreaves Sgt Hayhurst	6.30N	MY LAST TRIP. 71st BOMBERS. OPERATIONS. STUTTGART. FLEW THERE/BACK ON THREE ENGINES + ¼. GOOD TRIP. FLAK LIGHT. PHOTO. MAIN ATTACK FELL SW OF MAIN TOWN.	28	29

617 SQUADRON Avro Lancaster (Type 464 Provisioning)

RAF Scampton

Date	Aircraft	Crew	Duty	Time	Remarks	Code	Crew	Hrs	Remarks		
16.5.43	ED952	Wg Cdr G P Gibson (C) Sgt J Pulford (E) Plt Off H T Taerum (N) Plt Off F M Spafford (B) Flt Lt R E G Hutchison (W) Flt Sgt G A Deering (FG) Flt Lt R O Trevor-Roper (R)		2139	Identified target and carried out first attack on the Möhne Dam. Came under light flak but dropped his mine accurately and then directed the remainder of the attack by R/T. He also flew alongside one aircraft as it attacked, machine-gunning the defences to allow it to attack undisturbed. He then carried on to the Eder Dam and indicated the target to searching aircraft and stayed to ? the result. Bomb Load: 1 mine	G	Sgt Pulford Plt Off Deering Fl Lt Trevor-Roper Flt Lt Hutchison Plt Off Spafford Plt Off Taerum	6.40N	LED ATTACK ON MÖHNE AN [sic] EDER DAMS. SUCCESSFUL.	1	1

RAF East Kirkby	Avro Lancaster aircraft							
19.7.44				N	Sqn Ldr Miller Crew		DAYLIGHT OPERATIONS THIVERNY NR CREIL. 25m NW. PARIS. SUCCESSFUL. AIMING POINT. MOD. FLAK.	2
54 BASE								
RAF Coningsby	Lockheed Lightning aircraft							
15.8.44*				LOB26	Sqn Ldr Ciano	2.50D	OPS. 74th DEELEN AIRFIELD	3
18[?].8.44				LOB26	Sqn Ldr Howard	2.40D	OPS - FOLLOWED STREAM TO FECAMP	4
de Havilland	Mosquito aircraft							
10.9.44				D	Wg Cdr Woodroffe	3.05D	OPS. LE HARVRE [sic] CINE.	5

* The raid on Deelen is incorrectly dated to 18 August in Gibson's logbook. Gibson's logbook for August 1944 contains many errors both of date and sequence. On the 16th, for instance, he has himself visiting Swinderby with a member of 5 Group's Operational Research Section. On that day Gibson was advising crews at Coningsby on a difficult mission to drop mines in the Swinemünde canal. The meeting attended by Gibson was actually held on 19 August. Its outcome, a decision to form a Daylight Tactical Committee, led to a second meeting for 5 Group BASOs, including Gibson, held at Waddington on 21 August. However, Gibson recorded his visit to Waddington on 23 August, and places himself and the Lightning in Northern Ireland on the 21st. This is unlikely, as Gibson's reason for delivering the Lightning to Lockheed's maintenance base at Langford Lodge was for the fitting of Gee – an episode which correspondence between the USAAF and Sharpe tells us began on 26 August. In the interim, Gibson had flown himself to London, possibly to lobby for his reinstatement to operations.

BIBLIOGRAPHY

Allen, C., (ed.), *Raj: A Scrapbook of British India 1877–1947*, Penguin, Harmondsworth, 1977.

Anonymous, 'Preservation Profile no. 52: G.A.L. Cygnet', *Aeroplane Monthly*, August 1977, p. 430.

Anthony, G., *Air Aces*, Home & van Thal, London, 1944.

Barker, R., *Strike Hard, Strike Sure*, Pan, London, 1965.

Bennett, D.C.T., *Pathfinder: A War Autobiography*, Goodall, London, 1988.

Birtles, P., *Mosquito: A Pictorial History of the DH98*, Jane's, London, 1980.

Blake, R., Hodgson, M. and Taylor, B.M., *The Airfields of Lincolnshire since 1918*, Midland Counties Publications, Leicester, 1984.

Bowyer, C., (ed.), *Beaufighter at War*, Ian Allan, Shepperton, 1976.
  (ed.), *Bomber Group at War*, Ian Allan, London, 1981.
  For Valour: The Air VCs, Grub Street, London, 1992.

Braham, J.R.D., *Scramble!*, William Kimber, London (first edn, Frederick Muller, 1961), 1985.

Brickhill, P., *The Dam Busters*, Evans Bros, London, 1952.

Chant, C., *The Encyclopaedia of Code Names of World War Two*, Routledge & Kegan Paul, London, 1986.

Cheshire, L., *Bomber Pilot*, Hutchinson, London 1943.

Cochrane, R.A., 'Guy Gibson', in L.G. Wickham Legg and E.T. Williams (eds), *Dictionary of National Biography*, Oxford University Press, 1959, pp. 297–8.

Colville, J., *The Fringes of Power: Downing Street Diaries. Volume Two: October 1941–April 1955*, Sceptre, London, 1987.

Cooper, A., *Born Leader*, Independent Books, Bromley, 1993.

de Seversky, A.P., *Victory through Air Power*, Garden City, New York, 1943.

Desmond, R., (ed.), *Dictionary of British and Irish Botanists and Horticulturalists*, Taylor & Francis, London, 1977.

Dimbleby, J., *Richard Dimbleby*, Hodder & Stoughton, London, 1977.

Frankland, N., 'The Dams Raid', *Royal United Services Inst. J.*, May 1964.

Gibson, A.J., *A Forest Products Laboratory for Australia*, Pamphlet no. 9, Council for Scientific and Industrial Research, 1928.

Gibson, G.P., 'Cracking the German Dams', *Atlantic Monthly*, Vol. 172, no. 6, pp. 45–50, 1943.

Enemy Coast Ahead, Michael Joseph, London, 1946.

Gilbert, M., *Road to Victory: Winston S. Churchill 1941–1945*, Heinemann Minerva, London, 1989.

Auschwitz and the Allies, Mandarin, London, 1991.

Hagerty, J.M., *Leeds at War*, EP Publishing, Wakefield, 1981.

Halpenny, B.B., (ed.), *Action Stations 2: Military Airfields of Lincolnshire and the East Midlands*, Patrick Stephens, Wellingborough, 1981.

Hancock, T.N., *Bomber County: A History of the Royal Air Force in Lincolnshire*, Lincolnshire Library Service, Lincoln, 1978.

Bomber County 2, Lincolnshire County Council, Recreational Services Department: Libraries, 1985.

Harris, A., *Bomber Offensive*, Collins, London, 1947.

Hastings, M., *Bomber Command*, Michael Joseph, London, 1979.

Henshall, P., *Hitler's Rocket Sites*, Robert Hale, London, 1985.

Hill, R.D., *A History of St Edward's School 1863–1963*, St Edward's School Soc., Oxford, 1962.

Hillary, R., *The Last Enemy*, Macmillan, London, 1942.

Ismay, *The Memoirs of General the Lord Ismay*, Heinemann, London, 1960.

Jones, H.A., *The War in the Air*, Oxford, 1937.

Keegan, J., *The Mask of Command*, Penguin, London, 1989.

The Face of Battle, Pimlico, London (first edn, J. Cape, 1976), 1991.

Kershaw, R.J., *It Never Snows in September: The German View of Market-Garden and The Battle of Arnhem, September 1944*, Crowood Press, Ramsbury, 1990.

Lawrence, W.J., *No. 5 Bomber Group RAF (1939–1945)*, Faber & Faber, London, 1951.

Loewenstein, F.J., Langley, H.D., and Jonas, M., *Roosevelt and Churchill: Their Secret Wartime Correspondence*, Berrie & Jackson, London, 1975.

Lucas, P.B. (ed.), *Wings of War: Airmen of all Nations Tell Their Stories*, Hutchinson, London, 1983.

Macbean, J.A. and Hogben, A.S., *Bombs Gone*, Patrick Stephens, London, 1990.

McLaine, I., *Ministry of Morale: Home Front Morale and the Ministry of Information in World War II*, George Allen & Unwin, London, 1979.

Mahaddie, Hamish G., *Hamish: The Story of a Pathfinder*, Ian Allan, Shepperton, 1989.

Martin, J., *Downing Street: The War Years*, Bloomsbury, London, 1991.

Marshal, S.L.A., *Men against Fire*, William Morrow, New York, 1947.

Mason, F.K., *The Avro Lancaster*, Aston Publications, Bourne End, Buckinghamshire, 1989.

Matossian, J., 'Gibson – The Missing Months', *Flypast Dambusters Supplement*, 1993, pp. xii–xiv.

Meijer, A., *Vijf en vijftig namen op heidehof*, Gemeente Archief Apeldoorn, 1985.

Middlebrook, M., *The Nuremberg Raid*, Allen Lane, London, 1973.
   The Battle of Hamburg: Allied Bomber Forces against a German City in 1943, Penguin, London, 1984.
   and Everitt, C., *The Bomber Command War Diaries: An Operational Reference Book, 1939–45*, Viking, Harmondsworth, 1985.

Ministry of Information, *Aerial Bombing – The Facts*, 1944.

Morpurgo, J.E., *Barnes Wallis*, Longman, London, 1972.

Moyle, H., *The Hampden File*, Air-Britain, Tonbridge, 1989.

Pawle, G., *The War and Colonel Warden*, George Harrap & Co., London, 1963.

Plomley, R., and Drescher, D., *Desert Island Lists*, Hutchinson, London, 1984.

Price, A., *Instruments of Darkness: The History of Electronic Warfare*, Macdonald & Jane's, London, 1977.
   Luftwaffe Handbook 1939–45 (second edn), Ian Allan, London, 1986.

Ramsey, W.G. (ed.), *The Blitz Then and Now. Volume 2: September 1940– May 1941*, After the Battle, Battle of Britain Prints International, London 1988.

Report of the Committee of the Privy Council for Scientific and Industrial Research for the Year 1930–31, HMSO, 1931.

Revie, A., *The Lost Command*, Corgi, London, 1972.

Robertson, B., 'Bombing Task', *Flypast*, March 1982, pp. 59–62.

Roddis, H., 'The Original Ground Crew', *Dambuster Fiftieth Anniversary Commemoration*, Severn/Trent Water, Matlock, 1993, pp. 14–15.

Rolfe M., 'Dambusters Remembered': supplement to *Grantham Journal*, 1993.

Ryan, C., *A Bridge Too Far*, Coronet, London, 1975.

Saward, D., *'Bomber' Harris*, Cassell and Buchan & Enright, London, 1984.

Searby, J., (ed.), *The Everlasting Arms*, Martin Middlebrook, William Kimber, London, 1988.

Shannon, D., 'Guy Gibson: The Legend Who Lit the Way', in L. Lucas (ed.), *Thanks for the Memory*, S. Paul, London, 1989.

Simpson, D., 'Affair of the Hart', *Aeroplane Monthly*, November 1988, pp. 668–70.

Smith, Malcolm, 'Sir Edgar Ludlow-Hewitt and the Expansion of Bomber Command, 1939–40', *Royal United Services Inst. J.*, March 1981.

Smith, Maurice, 'Guy Gibson's Log Book', *Aeroplane Monthly*, May 1977, pp. 262–3.

Stebbing, E.P., *The Forests of India*, John Lane The Bodley Head, London, 3 vols, 1922–26.

Sweetman, J., *The Dams Raid: Epic or Myth*, Jane's, London, 1982. Second revised edn: *The Dambusters Raid*, Arms & Armour Press, London, 1990.

Sykes, C., *Orde Wingate*, Collins, London, 1959.

Terraine, J., *The Right of the Line: The Royal Air Force in the European War, 1939–1945*, Sceptre, London (original edn, Hodder & Stoughton, 1985), 1988.

Thompson, W.R., *Lancaster to Berlin*, Goodall, London and St Albans, 1985.

US Department of State, *The Conferences at Washington and Quebec 1943*, 1970.

van den Driesschen, Jan, *De dammen brekkers*, Van Holkema & Warendorf, Bussum, 1979.

Verrier, A., *The Bomber Offensive*, Batsford, London, 1968.

Webb, A. (ed.), *At First Sight: The History of 627 Squadron, Royal Air Force*, Mosquito Aircraft Museum, London Colney, St Albans, 1991.

Webster, C., and Frankland, N., *The Strategic Air Offensive against Germany, 1939–45*, 4 vols, HMSO, 1961.

Whitaker, W.D., and Whitaker, S., *The Battle of the Scheldt*, Souvenir Press, London, 1985.

SOURCES

1. GENERAL

Public Record Office, Kew
AIR 4/37   Pilot's flying logbook, Wg-Cdr G.P. Gibson
AIR 14/1213   Code-names

Royal Air Force Museum, Hendon
DC76/74/1324   Miscellaneous Gibson papers

Air Historical Branch, Ministry of Defence
Brief service record of G.P. Gibson

Miscellaneous
Memoir by Mrs Evelyn Gibson, 'He Shall Not Grow Old: The Story of Five Years with Guy Gibson' (typescript)

The Air Force List 1937–44

2. FAMILY AND CHILDHOOD

Public Record Office, Chancery Lane
RG 33/146   Register of baptisms, marriages and burials, British and American Church, Alexandroffsky, St Petersburg, 1858–85

Public Record Office, Kew
FO 518/3   Register of births, British Consulate, Moscow

India Office Archive

General Register Office, St Catherine's House
Certified copy of an Entry of Birth BXBZ 185114 (L.M. Strike)
Certified copy of an Entry of Marriage MX 504484 (A.J. Gibson = L.M. Strike)

General Register Office, Somerset House
Wills and Letters of Administration

Archive of St Edward's School, Oxford
Miscellaneous records and correspondence file, G.P. Gibson

St Edward's School *Chronicle*

Press Sources
Cornishman, 25.12.13 (marriage of A.J. Gibson and L.M. Strike)
Oxford Mail, 16.6.33 (SES Gaudy)
Times of India, 20.8.18 (birth of G.P. Gibson)

Miscellaneous
Photograph albums of Mrs L.M. Gibson (courtesy of Mrs Ruth Gibson)
India List, various dates covering A.J. Gibson's career
Memoir by George Beldam (letter)
Memoir by Maurice Crawley (typescript)

3. EARLY SERVICE CAREER

Public Record Office, Kew
AIR 29/558   ORB RAF Netheravon
AIR 29/618   ORB RAF Yatesbury

Press Sources
Lincolnshire Echo, 8.36 (crash at Sutton Bridge)
Salisbury and Winchester Journal, 6.8.36 (SES OTC at Tidworth)

4. 83 SQUADRON

Public Record Office, Kew
AIR 14/853   Attack on submarines
AIR 28/861   ORB RAF Turnhouse
AIR 28/681   ORB RAF Scampton
AIR 27/686   ORB 83 Sqn
AIR 29/652   ORB 14 OTU RAF Cottesmore
AIR 29/655   ORB 16 OTU RAF Upper Heyford
AIR 14/1213 Bomber Command target codes

Air Historical Branch, Ministry of Defence
RAF Intelligence Summary, Aug. 1939
Papers of Tactical Committee, Oct. 1939–Aug. 1940
AHB5/83 Sqn   Notes on 83 Sqn

Miscellaneous
Memoir by Douglas Garton (MS)
Memoir by Ron Low (typescript)

Clive Banham, logbook
Stan Harpham, pilot's flying logbook

5. DEATH OF MRS LEONORA GIBSON

General Register Office, St Catherine's House
Certified copy of an Entry of Death DXZ 048082

General Register Office, Somerset House
Probate records

Press Sources
Kensington Post, Middlesex Independent and *West London Star*, 6.1.40
West London and Hammersmith Gazette, 5.1.40
West London Observer, 5.1.40

6. BIOGRAPHY AND CAREER OF EVELYN MOORE

General Register Office, St Catherine's House
Certified copy of an Entry of Birth 003188

Press Sources
Brighton and Hove Gazette, 1.6.40; 8.6.40
Brighton and Hove Herald, 8.6.40
Brighton Standard, 4.6.40
Glasgow Evening News, 12.2.40; 13.2.40; 16.2.40; 19.2.40; 20.2.40
Glasgow Observer and *Scottish Catholic Herald*, 2.2.40; 9.2.40; 16.2.40
Midland Daily Telegraph (Coventry), 9.12.39; 13.12.39
Sheffield Telegraph and Independent, 6.2.40
Star (Sheffield), 3.2.40; 5.2.40; 6.2.40
Sussex Daily News, 4.6.40

7. MARRIAGE OF FG OFF. G.P. GIBSON AND MISS EVELYN MOORE

General Register Office, St Catherine's House
Certified copy of an Entry of Marriage WMXZ 002458

Press Sources
South Wales Echo and *Express*, 23.11.40; 25.11.40
Weekly Mail and *Cardiff Times*, 30.11.40
Western Mail and *South Wales News*, 8.10.40; 26.11.40

8. 29 SQUADRON

Public Record Office, Kew
AIR 27/341   ORB 29 Sqn
AIR 27/343   ORB 29 Sqn (Appendices)
AIR 28/201   ORB RAF Digby
AIR 28/202   ORB RAF Digby
AIR 28/907   ORB West Malling

Air Historical Branch, Ministry of Defence
AHB5/29   Notes on 29 Sqn

Royal Air Force Museum, Hendon
Sgt Richard James's logbook

Miscellaneous
Biographical summary of Air Commodore S.C. Widdows (MS)

9. 51 OTU CRANFIELD

Public Record Office, Kew
AIR 29/680   ORB No. 51 OTU

10. 106 SQUADRON

Public Record Office, Kew
AIR 14/2434   Operations room log, RAF Coningsby, 2.42–6.42
AIR 27/832   ORB 106 Sqn, 1.41–12.42
AIR 27/833   ORB 106 Sqn, 1.43–12.43
AIR 27/834   ORB 106 Sqn
AIR 27/836   ORB 106 Sqn
AIR 27/838A   ORB 106 Sqn (Appendices), 2.41–12.42
AIR 27/838B   ORB 106 Sqn (Appendices), 9.41–5.45
AIR 27/839   ORB 106 Sqn 10.42
AIR 27/840   ORB 106 Sqn 1.43
AIR 28/171   ORB RAF Coningsby
AIR 28/172   ORB RAF Coningsby (Appendices)
AIR 28/798   ORB RAF Syerston
AIR 28/800   ORB RAF Syerston (Appendices)
AIR 28/1177   ORB RAF Syerston (manuscript notes for Appendices)
AIR 29/764   Unit diary, RAF Hospital, Rauceby

Imperial War Museum Archive
86/15/1   Letters of Flt Lt R.H. Williams

Air Historical Branch, Ministry of Defence
Armament. Volume 1: Bombs and Bombing Equipment, Air Ministry, AHB, 1952
David Shannon
Pilot's flying logbook

Press Sources
Illustrated, 12.12.42
Sunday Express, 7.3.43

Miscellaneous
Gwyneth M. Stratten, 'RAF Hospital, Rauceby, 1940–47' (MS)

11. 617 SQUADRON

Public Record Office, Kew
AIR 4/48   Pilot's flying logbook, Sqn Ldr G. Holden
AIR 27/2128   ORB 617 Sqn
AIR 28/682   ORB RAF Scampton

Owen Collection

Shannon Collection
Pilot's flying logbook

Matossian Collection
Navigator's flying logbook, Fg Off. H.T. Taerum

12. OPERATION CHASTISE

Public Record Office, Kew
AIR 8/1234   Operations [*sic*] Upkeep and Highball
AIR 14/229   [Dams]
AIR 14/840   Operation Chastise, 2.43–6.43
AIR 14/841   Upkeep: disposal for storage
AIR 14/842   Upkeep: progress reports, 5.43
AIR 14/844   Operation Chastise, 5.43
AIR 14/595   617 Sqn: operations against dams, 4.43–10.43
AIR 14/1636   [Dams]
AIR 14/2036   [Chastise]
AIR 14/2060   [Upkeep]
AIR 14/2061   [Upkeep]
AIR 14/2087   [Chastise]

AIR 14/2088   [Chastise]
AIR 14/5832   [Chastise and Tallboy]
AIR 20/994   [Upkeep]
AIR 20/995   [Upkeep]
AIR 20/996   [Upkeep]
AIR 20/2617   [Upkeep]
AIR 20/4797   [Upkeep]
AIR 20/4820   [Upkeep]
AIR 20/4821   [Upkeep]
AIR 20/5776   [Upkeep]
AIR 27/2017   ORB 542 Sqn

Imperial War Museum Film Archive
Film of training with Upkeep, 13/14.5.43

Miscellaneous
Memoir by Fay Gillon, 'Dress Rehearsal' (MS)
Memoir by J. Heveron (MS)

13. POST-CHASTISE PERIOD

Public Record Office, Kew
AIR 14/717
AIR 14/2215   Visit of Their Majesties the King and Queen to RAF Scampton
617 Sqn A Flight authorization book
AIR 14/2161   617 ORB

Press Sources
Gloucester Citizen, 2.6.43 (VC ribbon)
Sheffield Telegraph, 28.5.43; 29.5.43; 31.5.43 (visit of Gibson to Sheffield)

Royal Air Force Museum, Hendon
A1248   Collection of Press reports dealing with Operation Chastise

Shannon Collection
'The Dam Busters, 16/17 May 1943' (miscellaneous sources and papers of David Shannon)

Science Museum, South Kensington
D2/10/97H   Barnes Wallis papers: correspondence between Gibson and Wallis

14. NORTH AMERICAN TOUR

Public Record Office, Kew
AIR 2/5365   Correspondence files, Department of National Air Service/CAS

AIR 2/9599   US awards to RAF personnel
AIR 19/304   1941–43, Publicity in USA. Sinclair: private office papers
AIR 20/1370   Empire Air Training Scheme: Training Schools, 1941–42
AIR 20/1379   Empire Air Training Scheme, Committee minutes 1940–45
AIR 20/1382   British Commonwealth Air Training Plan
AIR 20/4108   Empire Air Training Scheme: Committee papers, 12.43–12.44
AIR 29/473   ORB Transatlantic Air Terminal, Prestwick
AIR 29/572   Unit diary, 32 SFTS, Moose Jaw
AIR 29/572   Unit diary, 33 SFTS, Carberry
AIR 29/697   Unit diary, 31 RAF Depot, Moncton
AIR 45/3   Monthly reports, RAF Delegation, Washington
CAB 66   War Cabinet memoranda
CAB 122/587   Quadrant Conference: organization
INF 1/566   Overseas Planning Committee, MoI: propaganda plan for
   Canada, 1944–5
INF 1/858   Propaganda policy and issue of news, MoI, 1941–45
INF 1/966   Morale and the war against Japan
INF 2/16   MoI: VC booklet for circulation to Canada, 1943
PREM 10/1   PM Washington diary

Press Sources
Calgary Herald, 10.9.43; 11.9.43; 13.9.43
Chicago Daily News, 20.10.43
Chicago Daily Tribune, 20.10.43; 26.10.43
Chicago Sun, 25.10.43
Evening Citizen (Ottawa), 13.8.43; 27.9.43
Halifax Herald, 25.9.43
Los Angeles Times, 2.11.43; 9.11.43
Minneapolis Sun Journal, 28.10.43
Montreal Daily Star, 18.9.43
Montreal Standard, 14.8.43
New York Herald Tribune, 5.9.43; 9.10.43
New York Times, 13.8.43; 9.10.43
Quebec Chronicle–Telegraph, 10.8.43; 12.8.43; 13.8.43; 16.8.43; 20.8.43
San Francisco Chronicle, 12.11.43; 13.12.43
Toronto Daily Star, 2.9.43; 3.9.43
Vancouver Sun, 14.9.43; 15.9.43
Winnipeg Free Press, 16.8.43; 1.9.43; 3.9.43; 7.9.43

British Film Institute National Film Archive
'The Dams', Movietone News, 1943

'America Honours a VC' (newsreel item), 1943

Miscellaneous
The Diary of W.L. Mackenzie King, University of Toronto microfiche
World War Two Through the American Newsreels, US Library of Congress
Summaries

15. POLITICAL CAREER AND CONTEMPORARY PUBLIC ACTIVITIES

Press Sources
Bristol Evening World, 10.2.44
Macclesfield Advertiser, 11.2.44; 31.3.44; 7.4.44; 14.4.44; 1.12.44
Macclesfield Courier, 10.3.44
Macclesfield Times, 10.2.44; 17.2.44; 9.3.44; 23.3.44; 30.3.44; 6.4.44; 13.4.44;
27.4.44; 4.5.44; 11.5.44; 25.5.44; 31.8.44; 7.9.44

Miscellaneous
Records of the Macclesfield Conservative Association Minute Book, 1944

BBC Script Library
Script, *Desert Island Discs*, 19.2.44
Script, *The Week's Good Cause*, 9.4.44

16. WRITING, EXTRACTS AND REVIEWS, *ENEMY COAST AHEAD*

Royal Air Force Museum, Hendon
DC71/8/118–23   Typescript (1944) of *Enemy Coast Ahead*

Pre-publication Press Extracts
Atlantic Monthly, Vol. 172, No. 6, December 1943
Evening Citizen (Ottawa), 29.11.43
Sunday Express, 3.12.43; 3.12.44; 10.12.44; 17.12.44; 24.12.44; 31.12.44; 7.1.45;
14.1.45; 21.1.45

Reviews
Times Literary Supplement, 9.3.46

Miscellaneous
Memoir by J. Heveron (MS)
Letter from Air Marshall Sir Harold Martin, 1988

17. SERVICE CAREER, 1944

Public Record Office, Kew
AIR 28/172   ORB Coningsby
AIR 28/191   ORB Coningsby (Appendices)
AIR 28/956   ORB Woodhall Spa, App. 114 (medical officer's report)
AIR 29/854   ORB 54 Base Headquarters
              ORB East Kirkby
AIR 27/2152   ORB 630 Sqn

Air Historical Branch, Ministry of Defence
Air Staff Operational Summary and Summary of Reports of Enemy Action against the United Kingdom, August–September 1944 (Nos. 1,349–1,409), Vol. 27

Imperial War Museum Archive
86/15/1   Letters from Flt Lt (Fg Off.) R.H. Williams (57 Sqn, East Kirkby) to his parents
109489   Operational diary of Sqn Ldr Charles Owen

18. SERVICE CAREER OF SQUADRON LEADER J.B. WARWICK

Public Record Office, Kew
AIR 27/482   ORB 49 Sqn
AIR 27/483   ORB 49 Sqn
AIR 29/613   ORB 1661 HCU
AIR 29/871   ORB 1485 BG Flt
AIR 29/854   ORB 54 Base Headquarters
AIR 30/181/23   Submissions for awards

19. THE RAID ON RHEYDT AND MÖNCHENGLADBACH, 19.9.44

Public Record Office, Kew
AIR 14/868   5 Gp target-marking procedures
AIR 14/1213   Bomber Command target codes
AIR 14/2145   Intelligence watch diary, 5 Gp, vol. vii
AIR 14/3125   Command signals, 9.44
AIR 14/3323   100 Gp: reports on Serrate operations
AIR 14/3412   Night Raid Report, 19/20.9.44
AIR 24/292   ORB Bomber Command (Appendices)
AIR 24/293   ORB Bomber Command (Appendices)
AIR 24/294   ORB Bomber Command (Appendices)
AIR 24/296   54 Base Operations Reports

AIR 25/110   ORB 5 Gp Headquarters
AIR 27/288   ORB 29 Sqn
AIR 27/290   ORB 29 Sqn
AIR 27/482   ORB 49 Sqn
AIR 27/487   ORB 50 Sqn
AIR 27/539   ORB 57 Sqn
AIR 27/688   ORB 83 Sqn
AIR 27/691   ORB 83 Sqn (Appendices)
AIR 27/706   ORB 85 Sqn
AIR 27/707   ORB 85 Sqn
AIR 27/768   ORB 97 Sqn
AIR 27/803   ORB 101 Sqn
AIR 27/834   ORB 106 Sqn
AIR 27/840   ORB 106 Sqn (Appendices)
AIR 27/1046   ORB 157 Sqn
AIR 27/1047   ORB 157 Sqn
AIR 27/1094   ORB 169 Sqn
AIR 27/1095   ORB 169 Sqn
AIR 27/1456   ORB 239 Sqn
AIR 27/1606   ORB 278 Air/Sea Rescue Search Sqn
AIR 27/1610   ORB 279 Air/Sea Rescue Search Sqn
AIR 27/1612   ORB 280 Air/Sea Rescue Search Sqn
AIR 27/1981   ORB 515 Sqn
AIR 27/2152   ORB 630 Sqn
AIR 27/2148   ORB 627 Sqn
AIR 28/172   ORB RAF Coningsby (Appendices)
AIR 28/191   ORB RAF Coningsby
AIR 29/443   ORB 24 Air/Sea Rescue (Marine Craft) Unit
AIR 29/854   ORB 54 Base Headquarters
AIR 29/867   ORB 1409 (Meteorological) Flt

Air Historical Branch, Ministry of Defence
Air Ministry Weekly Intelligence Summary, 265
ASO Summary No. 1395
ASO Summary No. 1400

Imperial War Museum Archive
109489   Papers of Gp Capt. Charles Owen
Operational Film 231: *Mönchengladbach and Rheydt*

National Meteorological Archive, Bracknell
Daily weather reports log (UK), 9.44
Daily weather reports log (Germany), 9.44
Coningsby weather log
Woodhall Spa weather log

Miscellaneous
Memoir by Peter Mallender (letters and MS)

20. POST MORTEM

General Register Office, Somerset House
Letter of Administration: the Estate of G.P. Gibson

Air Historical Branch, Ministry of Defence
CAS File No. P423401/44   Excavation of Mosquito KB267

Press Sources
Flight, 21.9.44

Obituaries
Times, 1.2.45
St Edward's School *Chronicle*, 3.45

Miscellaneous
Text of speech at Steenbergen by Lord Cheshire V.C (MS)

NOTES

ABBREVIATIONS

AHB   Air Historical Branch, Ministry of Defence
AM   Air Ministry
DR   'Dambusters Remembered', by Mel Rolfe, a collection of reminiscences published as a supplement to the *Grantham Journal*, May 1993
ECA   *Enemy Coast Ahead* (extracts quoted are from the first edition, published by Michael Joseph, 1946)
ECA draft MS (1944) of *Enemy Coast Ahead*, RAF Museum, Hendon, DC 71/8/118–23.
EG   Eve Gibson, MS narrative of her life with Guy Gibson
IWM   Imperial War Museum
ORB   Operations Record Book
PRO   Public Record Office
SAO   Webster and Frankland 1961, *The Strategic Air Offensive Against Germany 1939–45* (official history)
SES   St Edward's School
WP   War Cabinet Memo

PROLOGUE

1. Shannon, 1989, p. 359.
2. 'Psychological Disorders in Flying Personnel', August 1942 (PRO AIR 2/8038).

PART I: BOYHOOD

1. Allen, 1977, p. 15.
2. Saward, 1984, p. 2.

3. Elsie Balme's book *Seagull Morning* (Tabb House, 1990) contains a vivid evocation of a Porthleven childhood in the 1930s.
4. Letter from A.J. Gibson to Warden Kendall, 13.9.46, in SES archive.
5. Hill, 1962, p. 211.
6. *ECA* draft, *passim*.

PART 2: LONG WEEKEND

1. *ECA*, p. 44.
2. Douglas Garton, letter to author, 15.5.91. For accounts of life and personalities in 83 Squadron I am particularly indebted to Anthony Bridgman, Richard Dougan, Stan Harpham, Clive Banham and Ron Low, and to correspondence with Douglas Garton and the late Air Marshal Sir Dermot Boyle. See also Ken Cook's evocative memoir in Bowyer (ed.), 1981, pp. 15–22.
3. Terraine, 1988, pp. 84–5, with further references.
4. Clive Banham, letter to author, 10.10.90.
5. *SAO*, Vol. i, p. 113, n. 1.
6. *ECA* draft, 118/B, p. 22.
7. Anthony Bridgman, conversation with author, 5.8.91.
8. *ECA*, p. 37.
9. Ibid., pp. 36–40.
10. Ibid., p. 43.
11. D. Garton, letters to author, 3.5.91 and 15.5.91; conversation with author, 2.12.90.

PART 3: RITES OF PASSAGE

1. EG, p. 1.
2. *ECA*, p. 52.
3. *ECA* draft, 118/B, pp. 54–5.
4. Ibid., p. 57.
5. Ibid., pp. 48–9.
6. Ron Low, conversation with author, 29.9.90, and MS memoir.
7. *ECA* draft, 118/B, p. 62.
8. Contemporary records state that two submarines crash-dived, and that both were British.
9. Gp Capt. E.C. Emmett to HQ 18 Group, Coastal Command, 2.3.40 (PRO AIR 14/853).
10. *ECA*, p. 58.
11. Ludlow-Hewitt to AOC 5 Group, 12.3.40 (PRO AIR 14/853).
12. Harris, 1947, p. 34.

13. *ECA*, p. 35.
14. *ECA* draft, 118/B, p. 89.
15. D. Garton, letter to author, 26.5.92.
16. *ECA*, p. 119.
17. *ECA* draft, 71/8/120, p. 20.
18. Harris archive, RAF Museum, Hendon, File H 59, letter 22.3.42.
19. *ECA*, p. 97.
20. R. Low, MS memoir.
21. Churchill to Beaverbrook, 8.7.40, quoted in Hastings, 1979.
22. *ECA*, p. 117.
23. Letter from Harris to AVM J.C. Slessor, 22.3.42, Harris archive, File H 59.
24. Ibid.

PART 4: STARLIGHT

1. Air Commodore Charles Widdows CB, DFC, interview with author, 27.5.92.
2. Braham, 1985, pp. 24–5.
3. 29 Sqn ORB, appendices, 19.12.40 (PRO AIR 27/343).
4. Ibid., 22.12.40 (PRO AIR 27/341).
5. Ibid., 31.12.40.
6. *ECA*, p. 139.
7. Fred Pedgeon in Bowyer (ed.), 1976, pp. 29–33.
8. Intelligence Combat Report (PRO AIR 27/343).
9. *ECA*, p. 140; Ramsey (ed.), 1988, p. 481.
10. *ECA*., p. 156.

PART 5: NEMESIS

1. Keegan, 1991, p. 296.
2. Paper circulated by Chiefs of Staff, 30.10.42; *SAO*, Vol. i, p. 366.
3. Keegan, 1991, p. 297.
4. Lawrence, 1951, p. 17.
5. Keegan, 1988, p. 329.
6. For the development, problems and operational use of the Avro Manchester consult Mason, 1989, pp. 36–54.
7. Gp Capt. R. Churcher, interview with author, 17.5.91.
8. Harris, 1947, pp. 108–112.
9. Middlebrook and Everitt, 1985, p. 269.
10. David Shannon, interviews with author, 2–3.7.89, and conversations February and June 1990, and July 1991.

11. DR, p. 45.
12. Ibid.
13. 'Bombs and bombing equipment', *Armament*, Vol. i, AHB, 1952, pp. 131–7.
14. *ECA*, p. 204.
15. Comment on *ECA* draft 71/8/122, p. 16, comparing with AM communiqué No. 7952, 2.9.42.
16. Margaret North, conversation with author, 27.9.91.
17. 106 Sqn ORB, 1.10.42 (PRO AIR 27/836).
18. Searby, 1988, p. 26.
19. Ibid., p. 42.
20. *SAO*, Vol. i, pp. 446–7.
21. Searby, 1988, pp. 58–60.
22. Williams letters dated 12.11.43, 23.11.43 and 11.12.43 (IWM, 86/15/1).
23. Searby 1988, pp. 57–8; *ECA*, pp. 217–18; Syerston ORB, 8.12.42 (PRO AIR 28/798).
24. Meijer, 1985, pp. 31–5.
25. Searby, 1988, p. 86.
26. Dimbleby, 1977, pp. 159–60.
27. Ibid., p. 160.
28. Ibid.
29. 106 Sqn ORB, 14.2.43 (PRO AIR 27/836).
30. *Sunday Express*, 7.3.43.
31. Thompson, 1985, pp. 53–6.

PART 6: JAVELIN

1. Jim Heveron, letters to author, 9.9.90, 15.9.90, 25.9.90 and MS memoir.
2. Fay Gillon, interview with author, 10.3.90.
3. *ECA*, p. 241.
4. Sweetman, 1982, pp. 60–1.
5. David Shannon, interview with author, 3.8.89.
6. Letter dated 2.4.43, cited in Sweetman, 1982, p. 79.
7. *ECA* draft, 71/8/118/B, p. 3.
8. Transcript in Owen Collection.
9. DR, p. 15.
10. Ann Shannon, interview with author, 3.8.89.
11. Fay Gillon, see note 2 above.
12. 2.5.43 and 3.5.43 (PRO AIR 14/2061 Upkeep, documents 22B and 22A).
13. Dr Alan Upton, conversation with author, April 1993.
14. DR, p. 15.
15. Margaret North, conversation with author, 27.9.91.

16. *ECA*, pp. 278–9.
17. MS from Fay Gillon.
18. Air Marshal Sir Harold Martin, letter to author, 30.8.88.
19. Sweetman, 1982, p. 101.
20. David Shannon, conversation with author, 1992.   •
21. J. Chalmers, conversation with author, January 1990.
22. Sweetman, 1982, pp. 157–60.
23. *ECA*, p. 278; Ann Shannon, conversations with author, 2–3.7.89 and February and June 1990.
24. Sweetman, 1982, p. 168.
25. Fay Gillon, see note 2 above.
26. J. Heveron, see note 1 above.
27. Harris, 1947, p. 159.
28. DR, p. 15.
29. Letter from Gibson to Warden Kendall, 25.5.43, SES archive.
30. *Gloucester Citizen*, 2.6.43, p. 4.
31. The timetable, itinerary and other details of the royal tour are given in PRO AIR 14/2215.
32. George Beldam, letters to author, 5.6.89, 14.7.89.
33. 'Guy Gibson', *Aeroplane Monthly*, September 1992, p. 41.
34. Letter 22 June, 22.6.43, Harris Archive, RAF Museum, Hendon, File 594.
35. J. Heveron, note 1 above; D. Shannon, conversations with author, June and July 1989; February and June 1990; July 1991.
36. Terraine, 1988, p. 538; *SAO*, Vol. ii, p. 179.
37. Air Vice-Marshal D. Bennett, *Pathfinder*, 1988, p. 185.
38. Matossian, 1993, pp. xii–xiv.
39. Prime Minister's Personal Minute D. 141/3, 24 July 1943: Churchill papers, 20/104; cited in Gilbert, 1989, p. 451.
40. Harris to Churchill, 22.4.43, cited in Saward, 1985, p. 264.
41. *ECA*, pp. 5–6.
42. Middlebrook, 1984.
43. Cooper, 1993, p. 143.

PART 7: AMERICA

1. Sykes, 1959, p. 451.
2. The Lady Soames, letter to author, 3.5.91.
3. Martin, 1991, p. 107.
4. References to newspaper reports and unpublished material relating to Gibson's tour of Canada and the USA are grouped under Sources, pp. 369–70.

5. Harris archive, RAF Museum, Hendon, File H 51.
6. *Atlantic Monthly*, Vol. 172, No. 6, December 1943, pp. 45–50.
7. DR, p. 36.
8. 'Anglo-Canadian Relations', 14.8.43 (PRO WP [43] 368); 'RAF/RCAF Relations' (PRO WP [43] 380).
9. 'Morale and the War against Japan', 5.6.43 (PRO WP [43] 232).
10. Wallis Papers, Science Museum, Kensington (D2/10/97H).
11. Ibid.
12. Quoted in H.A. Jones, 1937, Appendix.
13. A.P. de Seversky, 1943, p. 145.
14. Terraine, 1988, p. 544.
15. *SAO*, Vol. i, p. 366.

PART 8: 'CHURCHILL'S YOUNG MEN'

1. The MS was given to the RAF Museum, Hendon, by Gibson's widow.
2. Gerald Pollinger, letter to author, 16.6.92.
3. Wallis Papers, Science Museum, Kensington.
4. Lady Wendy Martin, letter to author, 29.9.88.
5. Ibid.
6. Searby, 1988, p. 186.
7. *ECA*, p. 9.
8. J. Heveron, MS memoir, p. 2.
9. *ECA*, p. 224.
10. Air Vice-Marshal S.O. Bufton, letter to author, 4.9.92.
11. *The Gen*, August 1944 (copy in 54 Base ORB, PRO AIR 29/854).
12. *ECA*, p. 236. Cf. 'Cracking the German Dams', *Atlantic Monthly*, Vol. 172, no. 6, p. 46.
13. References to sources for speeches, letters and broadcasts between February and April 1944 are collected in Sources, pp. 370–71.
14. Professor R.V. Jones, letter to author, 10.4.91.
15. Lord Cheshire VC, interview with author, 9.7.91.
16. Ibid.
17. Colville, 1987, pp. 284–5.
18. Sykes, 1977, p. 278

PART 9: LINES OF CONVERGENCE

1. Letters from Flt Lt R.H. Williams to his parents, 21.6.44 and 6.7.44 (IWM, 86/15/1).
2. Margaret North, interviews with author, July 1991, 27.9.91, May 1992.

3. Air Marshal Sir Harold Martin, letter to author, 23.8.88.

4. Charles Owen, operational diary, 19.7.44. Papers held by IWM.

5. Peter Mallender, letter to author, 27.3.91; interview with author, 29.4.91; cf. Wallace Gaunt in Webb (ed.), 1991, p. 102.

6. Macclesfield Conservative Association minute book, 1944.

7. Letter from Cochrane to Harris, 22.7.44, Harris archive, File H 59.

8. ECA draft, 71/8/118/B, p. 20.

9. Ibid., p. 22.

10. Searby, 1988, pp. 185–6.

PART 10: JACK

1. Peter Mallender, letter to author, 15.3.91.

2. Charles Owen, letter to *Aeroplane Monthly*, May 1977, Vol. 5, No. 5, pp. 262–3; operational diary, papers held by IWM.

3. 627 Sqn ORB (F541), 19.9.44 (PRO AIR 27/2148).

4. DR, p. 38.

5. Ron Winton in Bowyer (ed.), 1981, p. 89.

6. F.W. Boyle, letter to author, 3.8.91.

7. 54 Base Headquarters ORB, (F540), general summary for September, para. 8 (PRO AIR 29/854).

8. Herr J.D. Mulder of Arnhem, Holland, made inquiries about Gibson's funeral in the early 1970s. He thought that the ceremony took place 'a few days' after the crash: letter of 25.12.73, SES archive.

9. Letter from Flt Lt R.H. Williams to his parents, 26.9.44 (IWM accession 86/15/1).

PART 11: ANALYSIS

1. Harris, in Revie, 1972, p. 238.

2. Barrymore Halpenny, 1991, pp. 51–5.

3. Boyle, in Webb (ed.), 1991, p. 61.

4. Wallace Gaunt, letter to author, 31.7.91; cf., F.W. Boyle in Webb (ed.), 1991, p. 61.

5. Lord Cheshire VC, interview with author, 9.7.91.

6. Barker, 1965, p. 115.

7. F.W. Boyle, letter to author, 3.8.91.

8. Harris, foreword to *ECA*, p. 6.

9. Mahaddie, 1989, p. 60.

10. Peter Mallender, letter to author, 27.3.91; interview with author, 29.4.91.

11. Wallace Gaunt, letter to author, 31.7.91; cf. Gaunt in Webb (ed.), 1991, p. 102.

12. 97 Sqn ORB (F541), 19.9.44, p. 107 (PRO AIR 27/768).
13. Ibid.
14. Ibid.
15. 627 Sqn ORB (F541), 19.9.44, p. 64.
16. Barker, 1965, p. 119.
17. Webb (ed.), 1991, p. 85; interview with author, November 1990; Douglas Garton, conversation with author, 2.12.90; letters to author.
18. AHB, CAS File No. P423401/44.
19. Wallis Papers, Science Museum, Kensington (D2/10/97H).

PART 12: VALHALLA

1. Dated December 1944. Transcript from Eve Gibson via David Shannon.
2. Letter from Eve Gibson to Warden Kendall, 4.2.45, SES archive.
3. Sir Dirk Bogarde, letter to author, 4.4.92.
4. Ann Shannon, conversation with author, 3.7.89.
5. Colville, 1987, pp. 286–7.
6. Ibid., p. 204.
7. Lord Cheshire VC, interview with author, 9.7.91.
8. Cheshire, letter to author, 31.7.91.
9. Verrier, 1968, p. 198.
10. MS kindly provided by Lord Cheshire.
11. Air Marshal Sir Harold Martin ('Mick'), letter to author, 23.8.88.

INDEX